CRITICAL CONDITIONS: FIELD DAY ESSAYS AND MONOGRAPHS

Edited by Seamus Deane

Critical Conditions: Field Day Essays

Ireland's Others

Ethnicity and Gender in
Irish Literature and Popular Culture

Elizabeth Butler Cullingford

UNIVERSITY OF NOTRE DAME PRESS
in association with
FIELD DAY

Published in the United States in 2001 by
University of Notre Dame Press
Notre Dame, IN 46556

And in Ireland by
Cork University Press
University College Cork, Ireland

A record of the Library of Congress Cataloging-in-Publication Data is available upon request.

ISBN 0-268-03167-3

Dedication

For my 'little platoon':
My mother Margie, whose energy, curiosity, and sense of humour
continue to amaze me; My husband Alan, who shares with me the
satisfactions and the tribulations of research and teaching, and who
always knows where to find my keys; My son Daniel, who has
watched a lot of Irish films and old westerns, and knows more than I
do about *Babylon 5*.
And for Arcadia.

CONTENTS

List of Illustrations

ACKNOWLEDGEMENTS

This book has relatively few footnotes but many intellectual debts. My most important inspiration has been Luke Gibbons, whose lecture on Irish ruins at Sligo in the late eighties first opened my eyes to the pleasures of cultural criticism and showed me that there was life after Yeats. I didn't begin that life right away, but it was another of Luke's lectures (this time on *Hush-a-Bye Baby*) that definitively shaped the course of my research in the nineties. Luke's fingerprints are all over this book, especially in the sections that deal with Irish cinema. I no longer know exactly what I have borrowed from him: a method, a way of seeing, a different sense of what it means to do Irish studies. I do know that his reckless generosity with his own ideas, his enthusiasm for the work of others, and his ability to cross disciplinary boundaries have inspired a whole new generation of scholars in literature and media. I hope I may claim to belong to that generation despite my relatively advanced years.

The literary criticism of the prolific Declan Kiberd has continued to stimulate and instruct me, as it has done from the beginning of my career. In writing this book I have tried to copy his lucid and genuinely popular style, to free myself from academicism without falling into oversimplification, and to widen the scope of my interests. Declan's magisterial breadth of knowledge I could never equal. The rigorously critical politics of David Lloyd have inspired me in a different way. I run almost all of my writing past the question: What would David think of this? Often the answer is uncomplimentary, but the internalized theoretical debate helps me to clarify my own unapologetically moderate positions. My series editor Seamus Deane, doyen of the critical nationalist school of Irish studies, plays a somewhat similar role in my intellectual phantasmagoria. His criticism has long been an indispensable reference point for those of us who place politics at the centre of our literary and cultural enterprise. From the start of the book process he has been unfailingly supportive and helpful.

One of the delights of writing on a living artist is that you can occasionally bypass laborious research and get direct answers to your impertinent questions. Frank McGuinness and Margo Harkin have been exceptionally generous in this respect: both have given me information and assistance that I could not have obtained in any other way. McGuinness's plays are as central to the argument of my book as they are to contemporary Irish drama, while Harkin's film *Hush-a-Bye Baby* has provided me with a model of feminist film-making. For those of us in the area of Irish cultural studies, the journalism of Fintan O'Toole is indispensable. His observations, struck off in the heat of the moment, are nevertheless informed by an encyclopaedic knowledge of Irish culture and a keen eye for significant new trends. He has taught me a great deal. Among those whose work has also influenced me profoundly are Margaret McCurtain, to whom all feminist scholars of Irish history are indebted, and Angela Bourke, whose research on the burning of Bridget Cleary has brought feminist folklore to the centre of the Irish critical stage. The incisive and clear-minded Carol Coulter has always been a source of shrewd political insight as well as wonderful food and wine: to Angela, Carol, and Harry I owe thanks for years of friendship and for great hospitality in Dublin. I am also lucky enough to count Roy Foster, Marjorie Howes, Marilynn Richtarik, Paul Muldoon, Clair Wills, Adrian Frazier, Lyn Innes, James Pethica, Terry Eagleton, George Bornstein and Meg Mills Harper as friends as well as highly respected colleagues in my field. Their work, like that of the other scholars mentioned in these necessarily perfunctory lists, has helped me in ways that footnotes cannot adequately document. In a different way, I am grateful to Nancy Curtain, Maureen Murphy and Mary Helen Thuente for helping me to survive my first and last foray into the snake-pit of professional academic politics. I salute their sustained commitment to the greater good even as I resolve never to emulate it.

On a practical note, I am deeply indebted to Kevin Whelan, George Bornstein, Marilynn Richtarik, Richard Haslam, Bill Rolston, Ed Madden, Stan Walker, Andy McGowan, Juli White and the indefatigable Ray Ryan for providing me with ideas, articles and information during the writing of this book. My present and former graduate students in Irish Studies have been an unfailing source of inspiration: I have learned as much from them as they have from me. Margot Backus, Ed Madden, Laura Lyons, Joe Kelly, Karen Steele, Susan Harris, Mary Trotter and Ellen Crowell have already made significant contributions to the field of Irish Studies, and will go on to make many more.

Without a grant or two it is hard to write a book. My distinguished senior colleagues Jim Garrison, Jane Marcus, Terry Eagleton, Declan Kiberd, Luke Gibbons and George Bornstein have not only contributed to my knowledge, critiqued my methodology and kept up with my publications, but they have undertaken the thankless task of writing numerous letters of recommendation for me. Without those invaluable letters and the grants they elicited from the ever-generous University of Texas Research Institute I would still be struggling to finish the manuscript. Letter writers are the unsung heroes of our profession: I thank mine for their constant readiness to stamp my academic passport. I am especially grateful to my Chair, Jim Garrison, for fostering an atmosphere of collegiality in our English department, and for supporting me in numerous material and intellectual ways.

I have presented extracts from my material at several conferences, where I have enjoyed the intellectual companionship of Richard Haslam, Bob Quinn, Katie Conrad, Diane Negra, Vincent Cheng, Kieran Kennedy, Jahan Ramazani, Mary McGlynn, Rob Savage, Kevin O'Neill, Kevin Rockett, Dudley Andrew and Margaret Kelleher. I have also been invited to try out some of these ideas as a guest lecturer at Williams College, University College Galway,

University College Cork, the University of Hawaii, the University of Michigan, Georgia State University, the University of Notre Dame, the Yeats Society of New York, and the Sorbonne Nouvelle (University of Paris 3). My heartfelt thanks are due to everyone who helped to organize these enjoyable visits and who have hosted me so graciously over the years. As I sat on the beach in Hawaii early one morning, looking through my notes on Westerns for that afternoon's lecture, I realized that academic life can indeed provide some exquisite pleasures.

Although they have been expanded, re-organized, and in one case completely dismembered, some parts of this book have already appeared in the following publications:

'The Stage Englishman of Boucicault's Irish Drama: National Identities in Performance.' *Theatre Journal* 49 (October 1997): 289–303.

'Gender, Sexuality, and Englishness in Modern Irish Drama and Film.' *ACIS Journal* 1.1 (Fall 1997): 159–86.

'British Romans and Irish Carthaginians: Anti-colonial Metaphor in Heaney, Friel, and McGuinness.' *PMLA* 111.2 (1996): 222–39.

The publishers would like to thank Amelia Stein for permission to reproduce a photograph of Druid Theatre's production of *Carthaginians*, Bill Rolston for 'Ira/PLO One Struggle' and 'ANC/Cumann na mBan', Little Bird Ltd., Dublin for stills from *Into the West* and Besom Productions Ltd., Derry for stills from *Hush-a-Bye Baby*. Every effort has been made to trace copyright holders of material reproduced herein. If there are any ommissions Cork University Press will correct them in reprints or future editions of this book.

INTRODUCTION

Richard Kearney considers it 'unwise for anyone today to speak *about* the 'national question' without also stating where he/she is speaking *from*' (*Postnationalist* 1). I can only say: from the outside. One Irish grandparent called Butler does not make an ethnic heritage. Raised a Catholic in the former colonies (the West Indies) in the last days of Empire, educated in the 'mother' country and presently domiciled in Texas, I find it hard to assign myself a precise location from which to speak. This geographical indeterminacy means that, while I am deeply interested in Irish history and politics, and disposed towards a reading of Irish culture as determined by its status as a postcolonial country, I am inevitably more detached from the immediate issues than local commentators. Although politics and history inform all my readings, this book is intended as a cultural rather than a political intervention.

Nor do I rehearse at length the historiographical debate between nationalist, postcolonial and revisionist scholars,[1] although it inevitably colours many of my arguments. While a critical version of Irish nationalism has most of my instinctive and intellectual allegiance, and like many others I am deeply indebted to the work of Declan Kiberd, Luke Gibbons, Seamus Deane and David Lloyd, numerous revisionist historians have also been my sources and guides. My status as an outsider permits (or perhaps mandates) the kind of balancing act that would be difficult for inhabitants of, say, West Belfast, or that fictive universe called Dublin 4.[2] Of course, this position carries its own ideological risks: Texas wisdom has it that the only thing you find in the middle of the road is a liberal or a dead skunk. Liberal is a word that smells as bad to the radical academy as it does to the average Texan, so it is with some trepidation that I admit to a weakness for seeing both sides of the national question.

To summarize that complex question is necessarily to oversimplify and polarize a debate that has more than two sides; but to locate myself within this debate, however obliquely, I need to set out some of its terms. Revisionists deride nationalist versions of Irish history as propagandist fictions, but are sometimes less aware of the interests served by their own ostensibly factual narratives. They are generally unsympathetic to postcolonial theorists, who view the Irish past and many aspects of its present as negatively determined by British imperialism, and look to 'Third World' thinkers like Fanon and Said for their interpretative paradigms. While postcolonial theorists are fully aware that bourgeois nationalism tends to replicate the imperial structures that it was developed to resist, they contend that nationalist ideals have provided indispensable imaginative and practical fuel for anti-colonial struggles.[3]

1

They argue that, despite its many failings, nationalism is a necessary stage on the road to ultimate liberation. In Ireland, this analysis permits approval of most varieties of revolutionary nationalism before 1921, in tandem with a rejection of the conservative and religious nationalism that subsequently constructed the Irish Free State. The execution of James Connolly in 1916, and the defeat of the anti-Treaty Republicans in the Civil War, meant the extinction of the socialist, feminist and non-sectarian possibilities inherent in the Proclamation of the Republic.

Revisionists contest the postcolonial analysis for numerous reasons: they claim that the Republic of Ireland, while it was once a colony (opinions differ as to when), definitively ceased to be one in 1921 and should have recovered by now from the cultural hangover caused by English rule. Partition was not the fault of the British: the North remains a part of the United Kingdom because the Irish Unionists insisted that it must. The violence since 1969 is therefore an Irish tribal quarrel, not an anti-colonial struggle. Revisionists dismiss what they see as the misleading equation of Ireland with more distant colonies of the British Empire, preferring to emphasize its status as a white, European and relatively prosperous member of the North Atlantic community. Proponents of this analysis celebrate Ireland's membership of the European Union, and point to the current surge in economic prosperity that has produced that tedious cliché, the Celtic Tiger, as evidence that the country is finally discarding its obsessive attachment to tradition and becoming a modern, almost secular state, ready to reap the benefits of the information revolution and global capitalism.

I will nevertheless continue to use the words 'colonial' and 'postcolonial' in the full awareness that they are open to semantic challenge. While the analogy they posit between Ireland and, say, India or Africa is not exact in all particulars, nor relevant at all times, it has considerable explanatory power. The case for Ireland as a postcolonial country has both its 'strong' and its 'weak' forms. I do not know enough about colonialism in other countries to argue for, or even to assume, the 'strong' form, which suggests that the colonial model accounts for all of Ireland's social and political ills. But the dictionary definition of colonialism, 'now frequently used in the derogatory sense of an alleged policy of exploitation of backward or weak peoples by a large power' (OED), is more than adequate to support a 'weak' postcolonial thesis. It is a central part of my project to examine the use of analogy in the creation of imaginative culture, and to show how pervasive is the intellectual habit of speaking of one thing in terms of another. The dictionary tells us that the further the term 'analogy' departs from its origin in mathematics the 'weaker' and more inexact it becomes: it is the 'resemblance of things with regard to some circumstances or effects' or, 'more vaguely, agreement between things, similarity' (OED). The position of Ireland in postcolonial theory depends on the use of analogy as a comparative historical tool. Is Ireland more 'like' or more 'different from' other former colonies? To insist too much on the 'like' (the strong

form of the argument) is to fall into some historical absurdities and some contemporary misconceptions (that the British Empire is still alive and well and
eager to hang on to the North, for example). To insist too much on the 'different' is often a way of airbrushing historical wrongs by giving them another
title. If Ireland in the nineteenth century was not officially a colony because
after the Act of Union it was constitutionally integrated with the United Kingdom, does this excuse or explain the incompetence with which British
authorities responded to the Famine, the systematic discrimination experienced by the Catholic population, or the brutality of the coercion applied
against nationalist dissidents? It is hard to imagine these things happening in
Sussex. Colonialism by any other name would smell as bad; and because I am
a literary–cultural commentator and not a political scientist or an Irish historian, the debate over terminology is not my primary concern.

Similarly, this book makes use of theory but it is not a book of theory. My
subjects are texts (plays, novels, poems, films, television) within their historical and cultural contexts. I begin from and remain grounded in the experience of imaginative literature and visual media. The trajectory of some
leading scholars in Irish studies, most notably Seamus Deane and David
Lloyd, is towards philosophical reflections upon topics such as national
identity and state formation.[4] I admire this work, I have benefited from it
enormously and it has enabled many of my conclusions, but it is not my
work. My relation to theory is a difficult one. I was a literary historian long
before I gave my practice a name: for an Oxford-educated student of Richard
Ellmann in the seventies, writing on Yeats's politics was doing what came
naturally. When I moved to America, and to the left, and became a feminist,
my work on Yeats's love poetry was still full of what my colleague and mentor Jane Marcus called, approvingly, 'stuff' (since then I have learned to call
it 'thick description', which sounds more impressive). I did not, as the
phrase goes, 'do theory', even feminist theory, though I read a lot of it, with
varying degrees of comprehension and not a great deal of pleasure. I wish I
could say that during the ascendancy of deconstruction I skulked in the
archives plotting revolution and muttering 'our day will come', but I did not.
I felt more like a beached whale.

As the eighties wore on, however, I was surprised to feel the tide of the
latest American paradigm shift lifting me off the shoals, and to be told that
some people thought I was a New Historicist. I hastened to find out what
that was, and was disappointed to discover that I was probably just an Old
Historian in drag. I suspected that the same was true of many self-pro-
claimed New Historicists; but the advertisement of novelty is an indispensable weapon in the displacement of academic power from one hermeneutic
to another. A decade of undecidability had left many of us hungry for information, but that hunger needed to be couched in terms of revolution rather
than retreat. My Old Historicism, in any case, proved perfectly compatible
with my new feminism.

In the Irish, as distinct from the American, academy, the pressure of events in the North has never permitted literary critics the luxury of disregarding history. Much of the energy (as well as the acrimony) of Irish studies has been generated by that conflict (now possibly edging toward resolution), which reminds us of the close connections between representation and violence, and the role of the past in the perpetuation of current struggles. Perhaps for this reason, in the nineties Irish studies became increasingly visible in the United States. As the American critical emphasis shifted from language to cultural politics, from Derrida and de Man to Bakhtin, Fanon and Said, from Yeats and Joyce as international modernists to Yeats and Joyce as Irish writers, I began to feel increasingly at home. Deconstruction did not disappear: via the work of Homi Bhabha it migrated towards the high-theory end of postcolonialism, becoming in the process more practically relevant, if no less arcane. Gayatri Spivak reminds us that, for many former colonial subjects (peasants, tribal peoples, the urban proletariat), the triumph of anti-colonial nationalism was an imperfect liberation. My book is informed by Spivak's contention that, if the male subaltern is always silenced, 'the subaltern as female [or gay male] is even more deeply in shadow' (Spivak 287).

Finally, the empirical practice of British cultural studies permitted me to use my traditional close-reading skills not to discover the inevitable *aporia* at the heart of every canonical text, nor its postcolonial successor, the inevitable complicity with imperialism of every supposed act of resistance, but to talk about the social and political issues that concerned me – issues of gender, ethnicity and class – no matter where I found them. Throughout this book I have adhered to the method of strategic and historically informed close reading, but I have extended the range of my texts to include melodrama, film and television, and I have attempted wherever possible to bring high and popular culture into productive juxtaposition. Although my interests lie mostly in the twentieth century, my first chapter is on the melodrama of Dion Boucicault, who provides an important reference point for the whole project. Boucicault was realistic about the aesthetic value of his own output (he called it 'guano'), and he calibrated it carefully to appeal to the taste of his audiences. He nevertheless created a genuinely popular theatre, and his Irish work conveys a nationalist political vision, as well as a plea for eventual reconciliation between Ireland and England. The politics of mainstream culture, Boucicault understood, operate through empathy rather than intellectual analysis: melodrama shares with its successor, the Hollywood movie, and with other manifestations of popular culture (soap opera, for example) the crucial attributes of narrative (over) drive and a blatant appeal to sentiment.

Those who live by the pen or the box office are necessarily closer to their audiences than most academics are. Like Boucicault's work, contemporary popular culture usually fails to incorporate political attitudes that satisfy academic theorists, either because card-carrying radicals in the film and television business are rare, or because their financial backers would not tolerate a genuinely subversive analysis. Perhaps for this reason, Marxist postcolonial critics like David Lloyd offer few examples of the kind of popular work they would like to validate, probably because there is relatively little available. Lloyd goes back to the past for his examples, but a handful of Dublin street ballads and the activities of agrarian secret societies do not constitute an overwhelming body of evidence. (His choices are governed by the theoretical and semantic distinction between 'mass' and 'popular' culture, the first an inauthentic product of commercialization, the second the spontaneous expression of the people's life.) Similarly, Irish feminist scholars (myself included) return again and again to two works by the Derry Film and Video Collective (the documentary *Mother Ireland* and the television drama *Hush-a-Bye Baby*), and to Orla Walsh's short feature, *The Visit*.

Under the conditions of an increasingly globalized anglophone entertainment economy, to be truly 'popular' is almost by definition to take up a political position alongside the liberals and the dead skunks. Even in the less obviously commodified worlds of theatre, poetry and the novel, most Irish creative artists, whether left-wing or conservative, revisionist or anti-revisionist, are also liberal humanists, and therefore inadequate to the stringent requirements of the Marxist strand of postcolonial theory. Many writers have their own political as well as aesthetic priorities – feminism, gay liberation, pacifism, socialism, nationalism – but very few texts or films provide an analysis of colonialism, or of the situation in the North, that would content David Lloyd (if I may use him as shorthand for a certain set of positions with which I hold a constant and bracing internal dialogue).[5] The divided reception of Neil Jordan's *The Crying Game* and Jim Sheridan's *In the Name of the Father* provides an illustration of what it means to be caught in the headlights. Brian McIlroy claims that all Irish films, including Jordan's, have a Republican bias; yet Lloyd takes Jordan to task for producing yet another negative stereotype of the Irish terrorist (*Ireland* 65–7). Sheridan is attacked by the British press for distorting the truth to 'blacken British justice' (Jenkins), and by Irish sympathizers for distorting the truth to blacken the Irish Republican Army (Backus 67–8).

In attempting to map an honest and politically responsible course through the minefield that is contemporary Irish studies, I am often reminded of the moment when a male Irish academic characterized me as a British imperialist bitch. 'British' I could not disown, 'bitch' is purely a matter of opinion, but 'imperialist' caught me off guard. The problem was that, in a 1991 article on Yeats, Pearse and Heaney,[6] I had criticized the nationalist tendency to use women as icons of the land or of the national struggle. That view, also expressed by the poet Eavan Boland (*Scar*) and the IRA member Mairead Farrell (*Mother Ireland*), is by now utterly commonplace; even then it seemed a somewhat belated intervention of feminist ideas into Irish discourse. But a feminist critique of nationalism risks being interpreted as support for British troops on the streets of Belfast. I was amused when Colm Tóibín rose to the defence of the ladies during the controversy over the lack of female writers and editors in the *Field Day Anthology of Irish Writing*, because his sudden and opportunistic conversion to feminism provided a transparent fig-leaf for an attack on the whole nationalist tradition.[7] Nevertheless, this incident showed me how easily a radical theory could be used to give ideological cover to a revisionist one.

Since Arthur Griffith attacked John Synge for traducing the chastity of Irish womanhood by showing Nora leaving a loveless marriage to follow the tramp, and Eamon de Valera declined to let the women of Cumann na mBan fight alongside him in Boland's Mills, questions of gender and sexual orientation have often (though not inevitably) troubled the discourse of nationalism.[8] Wilde and Casement appear to have established themselves in both the gay and the nationalist canons, but to argue that in 'Little Lad of the Tricks' Padraig Pearse produced a touchingly naive representation of the plight of the closeted schoolmaster, or to debate the question of Michael Collins's bisexuality, still raises the national eyebrow.[9] Maud Gonne, Constance Markievicz and Hannah Sheehy Skeffington combined their Irish nationalism with varying degrees of commitment to feminism, and Bernadette McAliskey thinks that the best feminists in Ireland today are products of the Republican movement (*Mother Ireland*). Yet progressive women sometimes challenge nationalists because their commitment to equality involves a rejection not only of the cultural dominance of Irish men, but of Irish patriarchy as an institutional structure. Since issues of reproductive choice and sexual orientation pit many women and most gay men against the categorical imperatives of the Catholic Church, which is often considered a defining marker of Irish nationality, the hostility of gender theorists to Catholicism can appear to be (and sometimes is) an attack on nationalism. Critical nationalists argue (and I agree) that the identification of Irishness with a repressive version of Roman Catholicism is not an essential aspect of nationalist ideology, but rather a product of the bourgeois nationalist state that betrayed the Republic.[10] Nevertheless, the modernizing secularism of the Irish media and academic establishment (colloquially known as Dublin 4) has long set itself against the conventional pieties of 'priest-ridden' rural Ireland. In *Jiving at the Crossroads* John Waters movingly explains the bewilderment and alienation of country people in Roscommon, who genuinely do not see Ireland as priest-ridden and find consolation in the practices of the Church, in the face of a revisionist discourse that patronizingly writes them off as backward 'culchies' (82–6). But a gay writer like Frank McGuinness, one of the central figures in this book, cannot afford to take the sensibilities of such people into account when he attacks Ireland's dependence on Rome.

The price of insight into one injustice (in this case the injustice of British rule in Ireland) may be blindness to a variety of others. The 'Others' of my title are numerous, and they are both real and fictive. Ireland is accustomed to being stigmatized as the feminized object of English discourse, but in women, gays, abused children, travellers and the working class it has produced its own internal Others. Much critical attention has already been paid to the English view of the Irish character, but in the first section of this book I examine a reversal of the Othering process, the Irish construction of the stage Englishman. 'Acting the Englishman' focuses on questions of gender, class, sexual orientation and national identity in Irish drama and film, moving from the melodrama of Boucicault through plays by Shaw, Behan, Friel and McGuinness, to movies by Jordan and Sheridan. Against the familiar background of the gendered analogy that aligns England with the powerful male, Ireland with the weaker female, and tells the story of the Union through the metaphor either of rape or of heterosexual marriage, I trace an alternative narrative of homosocial or homoerotic bonding between English and Irish males, which constitutes an imaginative attempt to overcome the antipathy between the two countries. In this tradition the stage Englishman is seldom the villain; indeed, he is usually a decent chap, and often he becomes the object of Irish desire. In the politically charged context of Ireland's neutrality during World War II, the Englishman may even become the hero, as he does in Frank McGuinness's *Dolly West's Kitchen*. Because texts have an inconvenient way of disrupting the coherent patterns into which I would like them to fall, I include in the last chapter of this section, 'Brits Behaving Badly', a discussion of those plays and films (most notably Neil Jordan's *Michael Collins*) that constitute a counter-tradition to the one I establish in the three previous chapters.

The second section of the book, 'Carthaginians or Cowboys: Analogy, Identity, Ambiguity', continues my discussion of works that vary the analogy between femininity and Irish nationality. My project in these chapters is to explore and critique the practice of making ethnic analogies between the Irish and other defeated peoples, both ancient and contemporary. The construction of a pseudo-oriental, Black, or Native American identity by a writer from a colonized rather than an imperial nation is a complex process in which a white Other attempts, by invoking analogy (my culture and my colonial predicament resemble yours) or genealogy (my culture originates with yours), to create an alternative and exotic Self. Like gender analogies, however, ethnic analogies can be slippery things. What looks from a postcolonial Irish perspective like a sympathetic and intellectually coherent identification with the descendants of slaves may appear to an American Black as shameless appropriation, or strike a revisionist as spurious ethnic chic.

I begin by considering the myth of Irish descent from the Carthaginians, which is evoked by Seamus Heaney and Brian Friel, then revised and queerly gendered by Frank McGuinness in his play *Carthaginians*. I go on to examine the ideology of an imaginative geography (also derived from the Carthaginian analogy) that allows James Joyce to connect Ireland with the Orient and North Africa rather than with the British archipelago. Against the reclamation and affirmation of the pejorative Irish/African association in Joyce, some of Heaney's bog poems, Brian Friel's *Dancing at Lughnasa*, Alan Parker's film of

Roddy Doyle's *The Commitments* and several Republican murals in Belfast, I set versions of the analogy proposed by the documentary film-maker Bob Quinn and the poet Paul Durcan, both of whom explore the Irish/Black connection but are suspicious of its appropriation by Republicanism.

Even less easy to categorize politically are the numerous cultural re-workings of the American West that I examine in the last chapter of this section. Although the distinction is not absolute, the Western analogy works differently in the North and in the South. Thanks to the films of John Ford and the craze for country-and-western music, the Southern Irish are frequently aligned with the cowboys or the cavalry.[11] In the movie *Into the West*, the traveller children would like to join the cowboys, but the racism of the settled people forces the audience to connect them with the Native Americans instead. On the other hand, Northern Catholics, acutely conscious of their minority status within a hostile and more powerful culture, deliberately choose to identify with Geronimo and Sitting Bull; while, in *Mustn't Forget High Noon*, Jennifer Johnston constructs an elaborate and damning analogy between the Protestants and the white male heroes of the classic Western.

The third section of the book, 'Reviewing Literary and Political Canons', maintains the previous focus on questions of gender, modernity and Irish identity. Its unifying theme is the refraction of three 'canonical' nationalist poets and politicians – W. B. Yeats, Eamon de Valera, and Seamus Heaney – through the lens of contemporary popular culture. Yeats's evocation of 'The Lake Isle of Innisfree' has helped to create the Bord Fáilte mystique of the West of Ireland as a pastoral Eden in which foreign vacationers can return to a simple and unspoiled past. In this rural romanticism Yeats is linked with Eamon de Valera, an equally iconic figure. Even though de Valera's ideal of frugal self-sufficiency was the product of wartime necessity, it resonates ideologically with the image of Yeats raising his beans and gathering honey in a 'small cabin' on an isolated island. Seamus Heaney has also dug into the rich peat of the Irish pastoral, although (like de Valera but unlike Yeats) his roots have real earth on them. Whether they are admired or despised, all three men have come to embody certain popular definitions of 'Irishness'.

The Yeats who resonates in contemporary global mass culture, and in cyberspace, is the Yeats of apocalypse, romantic love and rural nostalgia. Although John Ford's *The Quiet Man*, which takes place in 'Inisfree', can be read as a cultural satire on both Yeats and de Valera, most popular English and American appropriations of Yeats, while they may use him as shorthand for various imaginary Celtic qualities, are unqualifiedly positive, indeed reverent. Not so the Irish representations of Eamon de Valera, who, fairly or unfairly, has become the symbolic representative of an era marked by bitter political divisions, unthinking adherence to the past, religious conformism and repression of women. De Valera is a lightning rod in the debate between tradition and modernity. The agenda of Neil Jordan's *Michael Collins* is no less than the re-invention of Ireland's paternity, the undoing of de Valera's right to be called 'the father of us all'. His film is the culmination of a modernizing social and political critique of de Valera mounted by the poets Paul Durcan and Thomas McCarthy and the novelist Julia O'Faolain.

Feminist film-maker Margot Harkin, equally suspicious of Irish political and religious patriarchy, nevertheless chooses a poem by Seamus Heaney as an emblem of the suffering of Irish women, North and South, rural and urban, in a culture that has until recently made it difficult to obtain contraception, and refuses abortion. 'Limbo', which empathetically recreates the predicament of a woman from the West of Ireland who chooses to drown her illegitimate son, stands at the emotional centre of Harkin's film *Hush-a-Bye Baby*, which deals with teenage pregnancy in Derry against the traumatic background of the Ann Lovett and Kerry Babies cases in the Republic. Sinéad O'Connor, who played a small part in the film and wrote its music, went on to act out its sexual politics when she tore up a picture of the Pope on *Saturday Night Live* (3 October 1992). Her crusade against child abuse (a subject Heaney has treated movingly in 'Bye-Child') was revealed as more than a personal obsession by the series of scandals involving paedophile priests that unfolded during the nineties. O'Connor's subsequent ordination in a breakaway Tridentine order continues her quixotic attempt to rescue God from the orthodox Church. Jordan's casting of O'Connor as the Virgin Mary in his recent film *The Butcher Boy* is emblematic of her iconoclastic spirit, which affirms even as it satirizes the imagery of Catholicism. Both Jordan and O'Connor are using the economic resources offered by a globalized popular culture to question the ascendancy of the Fathers in Irish social, imaginative and political life.

PART ONE

'ACTING THE ENGLISHMAN'

THE STAGE ENGLISHMAN OF THE IRISH DRAMA
Boucicault and the Politics of Empathy

The categories of 'Britishness' and 'Englishness' are currently undergoing rapid change and, as a result, attracting intense scrutiny. Unmoved by the prospect of the break-up of Britain, Tony Blair has not only worked to sustain the precarious new power-sharing assembly in the North of Ireland, but supported the establishment of devolved parliaments for Scotland and Wales. Hardline Irish Unionists cling doggedly to a constitutional arrangement that is dissolving in their embrace. Like Australia and New Zealand before them, they have discovered that the European Union and the process of globalization have compromised the loyalty of the 'Mother Country' to her former 'children'. Popular culture reflects the changing construction of Englishness: films such as *Sammy and Rosie Get Laid* (1987), *Beautiful People* (1999) and *East is East* (2000) demonstrate that in certain big cities Asian, West Indian and eastern European immigration is radically redefining cultural norms and expectations. In *Beautiful People*, for example, a Celtic dissident who shares a hospital room with a warring couple from 'the former Yugoslavia' is not the usual Irish stereotype, but a Welsh nationalist who suffered burns while preparing to fire-bomb English second homes in Wales.

Even the national character is showing cracks: the outpouring of grief on the death of Princess Diana was striking precisely because it contradicted the stereotype of the English as incorrigibly reserved and hostile to public displays of emotion. The Queen's misunderstanding and mishandling of the situation laid bare the clash between the old and the new. When she compelled Diana's sons to demonstrate their stoicism by attending church as usual on the morning of their mother's death, many people were horrified by her unnatural behaviour. 'Englishness' is fracturing emotionally as 'Britishness' has fractured politically and geographically. Both become visible on the critical stage precisely at the moment of their threatened disappearance.[1]

Reversing a critical practice that has been central to Irish studies, I intend to analyse the representation of Englishness upon the Irish stage and screen.[2] I am interested in the Irish use of the stereotype of Englishness to complicate and reconcile rather than to deepen the binary opposition between colonizer and colonized, ruler and subaltern, metropolitan and provincial.[3] Because stereotypes of Englishness have changed over time, I am concerned only with those qualities that were popularly identified as English during the nineteenth and

13

twentieth centuries: independence, industry, common sense, self-control, devotion to duty, simplicity, honesty, magnanimity and concern with fair play. Less attractive English characteristics were taciturnity, emotional reserve, obsession with propriety, insensitivity to the arts, unthinking conservatism, dullness, lack of hospitality, rudeness and contempt for foreigners. These supposedly national qualities were derived primarily from the middle class: the behaviour of aristocrats and members of the lower classes was less easy to codify.

The production of the stage Englishman was a reflex reaction to nineteenth-century representations of Irish characters by English dramatists. These took both positive and negative forms: virginal colleens and violent Paddies; quick-witted servants and loud-mouthed soldiers; warm-hearted but impecunious noblemen and calculating fortune hunters. However mutable the stereotype, the drunken savage and the charming Celt belonged to a long-established theatrical genre that identified all non-English characters as different, dangerous, or ridiculous. As Shaw argues, 'there are not many types of character available; and all the playwrights use them over and over again. Idiosyncrasies are useful on the stage only to give an air of infinite variety to the standard types.'[4] The idiosyncrasies of the stage foreigner have always been useful for novelty and dramatic contrast, good for an easy laugh or a shiver of horror. The Elizabethans, for example, represented Germans and Danes as drunks, Frenchmen as vain fops, and Italians as murderous Machiavels.

This pervasive othering of foreigners had a particular sting in the case of Ireland because of the closeness of the relation and the imbalance of power between the two nations. Although Ireland suffered dislocations of culture, language and identity analogous to those experienced by colonized people in India and Africa,[5] the Irish could not be distinguished from their imperial rulers by the colour of their skin. They were 'proximate' rather than 'absolute' Others, a disturbing mixture of sameness and difference, geographical closeness and cultural distance.[6] English dramatists therefore indicated Irish inferiority and need for governance by emphasizing character traits that signalled political incompetence: from amiable fecklessness to drunkenness, stupidity and violence.[7] The popular Irish dramatist Dion Boucicault (1820–90)[8] tried to redefine the stage Irishman as faithful, clever and supremely lovable, though still very fond of a drink: his 'peasant' characters, Shaun the Post, Myles-na-Coppaleen and Conn the Shaughraun, all of whom he played himself, were intended to overturn what he called the 'libel' on the Irish character that had been perpetrated by English dramatists.[9] Opinions differ about his success: Bernard Shaw charged that, instead of dispelling the libel on Irish character, he perpetuated it. Boucicault's counter-stereotype of the upper-class English colonizer, on the other hand, has largely escaped suspicion or even notice.[10] In pragmatic terms, his stage Englishman demonstrates the pressure of generic conventions, the fear of censorship, and his need to please London audiences. More interestingly, it reveals the complicated and ambivalent attitude to power of the politically powerless, and exemplifies Boucicault's commitment to the ideal of reconciliation between ancient enemies.[11]

The performance of both English and Irish characters was inflected by the gender typing associated with each nation on stage and in print. Irishness was construed, negatively by imperialists and positively by the Irish themselves, as difference from successful English capitalist modernity. The cultural production of Irish Otherness as pre-modern, however, placed it on the feminine end of the representational spectrum, which spelled disadvantage as well as distinctiveness. Following Ernest Renan, Matthew Arnold described the perennially defeated Irish as a 'feminine' people (*Lectures* 347). Although many Irish dramatists concerned to assert their manliness resisted it, the connection between Irishness and femininity was reinforced by the native image of Ireland as a woman. Ancient sovereignty goddesses, eighteenth-century *aisling* poems, in which a beautiful maiden lamented her rape by the colonizer or the loss of her Irish prince, and post-Famine devotion to the Virgin fed into an over-determined tradition that, whether it valorized or despised 'feminine' qualities, regularly attributed them to the Celts.[12]

Conversely, English imperialists saw themselves as masculine, even paternal, in relation to these backward colonial subjects. Both foreigners and the English themselves considered that they enjoyed 'a kind of ethnic virility, a superior masculinity which had to do with the race as a whole' (Langford 71). The feminized Irish were defined and subordinated by the masculine English gaze, as English visitors obsessively chronicled the characteristics of the neighbouring island: in his anthology of English travel writings John Harrington conceptualizes Ireland as a 'spectacle' (*English* 9). There is no comparable anthology of the writings of Irish travellers in England. As if complicit with this imbalance between watchers and watched, many Irish dramatists responded to English constructions of Paddy by re-staging Irish identity, not by returning the gaze of the colonizer. No English roles exist in the plays of Yeats, Synge or Gregory. Shaw argued that a secure national identity must be achieved before it can be forgotten: 'A healthy nation is as unconscious of its nationality as a healthy man of his bones. But if you break a nation's nationality it will think of nothing else but getting it set again' (842). Nineteenth-century British imperial power was so great as to permit the imaginative universalization, and thus paradoxically the disappearance, of Englishness. The theatricality of Englishness, which is no less a performance than masculinity, lies in its apparent refusal to perform, its strategic withdrawal from scrutiny. The Englishman on the nineteenth-century English stage appears less 'English' than human; the Irishman, on the other hand, is always marked as different, as Irish, even by his own countrymen.

While stage types are not peculiar to colonial situations, the political sensitivity of the colonized may render them especially contentious. As we have seen, although Boucicault declared that it was his 'vocation' to abolish the stage Irishman, he was accused of reinstating the caricature: in the twentieth century the same charge was levelled against both J. M. Synge and Sean O'Casey.[13] As the turbulent history of the Abbey Theatre amply demonstrates, any Irish character who takes the stage risks being seen as a stage Irishman. But no questions were raised about the stage Englishman. Indeed, L. P. Curtis notes 'the absence from the Irish scene of a stereotype of English character as rigid and elaborate as Paddy' (*Anglo-Saxons* 110). Nevertheless, in response to the persistent denigration of their own people, Boucicault and his followers did produce several recognizable 'Stage English' types. With the exception of Shaw's Tom Broadbent, who plays against the stereotype, their Englishman is a minor character, an outsider, as the stage Irishman was in English plays. He is represented as a soldier, a businessman, or a bureaucrat, roles the English usually performed in Ireland. Although colonial officials were sometimes accompanied by their wives, few Englishwomen appeared on the Irish stage, where Englishness was synonymous with masculinity.[14]

When imperial encounters are staged by those on the periphery of the Empire, even by someone so relatively free from oppression as the Protestant, rich and successful Boucicault, we might expect the colonizing Englishman to be a wicked character. But melodrama's Manichean dualities, which pit virtuous hero against dastardly villain, absolute good against absolute evil, are not mapped directly onto the colonial relation between Ireland and England. The 'heavy' in the melodramas of Boucicault and his successor Whitbread is invariably Irish: an informer, land agent, lawyer, or process-server. He may be a cog in the imperial machine, a spy or a servant of landlordism, but he is not English.[15] Indeed, through the despicable character of Harvey Duff in *The Shaughraun*, Boucicault may be said to have established the importance of the 'informer' as a central trope in Irish literature and, later, film.

Because Irish informers contributed heavily to the failure of the 1798 rising against the British, the historical setting for many Irish melodramas,[16] Irish traitors ranked higher than English oppressors on the scale of melodramatic evil: men with conflicting loyalties are far more dramatically striking than men who are merely doing their job. The melodramatic villain was a star, and Irish villains played by actors like Frank Breen and Sheil Barry became theatrical legends. Conversely, both political and theatrical problems militated against the creation of large English roles. Although many Irish actors worked in London and Dublin, few English actors worked regularly in Ireland, and their Irish counterparts apparently had difficulty with English accents. Willie Fay told Yeats that the Abbey could not stage *John Bull's Other Island* (1904) because he had no one to play Broadbent, who 'must both look and sound English' (Fay 207). Moreover, a dramatist who planned a London performance knew that unflattering portrayals of the English would not be good box office, and that hostile depictions of landlords were regularly censored.[17] Although the Lord Chamberlain had no jurisdiction in Ireland, Boucicault and Whitbread usually censored themselves. Only a few later historical melodramas, such as P. J. Bourke's *When Wexford Rose* (1910) and *For the Land She*

Loved (1915), written for the nationalist audience of the Queen's Theatre, during the troubled years before the 1916 Easter Rising, and not intended for production in London, feature English villains with financial and sexual designs on the Irish heroine.[18] Responding immediately to this departure from dramatic convention, the British banned *For the Land She Loved*.[19]

A writer from the periphery must frequently copy metropolitan genres in order to find an oppositional voice, but the Irishman Boucicault, the most popular playwright in the English-speaking world between 1840 and 1900, became the model others sought to emulate.[20] The status of Boucicault's Irishness, like his birth, was ambiguous. His mother's family were middle-class Protestants, as were both the candidates for his dubious paternity. He spent the first nine years of his life in Ireland, but thereafter lived in England and America, although he never lost the brogue that authenticated his playing of Irish parts. His relations with English theatre managers and critics were often hostile, but English audiences liked his plays, and he had been a successful dramatist for twenty years before he took up the subject and setting of his native land in *The Colleen Bawn* (1860), *Arrah-na-Pogue* (1864) and *The Shaughraun* (1874).

In his play *Heavenly Bodies* (1986), the Irish dramatist Stewart Parker imagines an already-dead Boucicault demanding a chance to defend his theatre, his personal conduct and his political beliefs, in order to gain a reprieve from the limbo to which he is apparently condemned. Parker interrogates Boucicault through the mouth of his near contemporary Johnny Patterson, the Irish Singing Clown, who wrote 'In the Garden Where the Praties Grow.'[21] Patterson, who came from a rural Catholic background, demands: 'So tell us, Mr. Boucicault, how did you react during the Great Irish Famine?' and then mockingly answers his own question, 'Oh, I kept London well supplied with me comedies of manners' (104). Johnny's potato-patch ballad has greater relevance to the starving people of Ireland than the French melodramas that Boucicault spent the Famine years adapting for the London stage. But Parker's Boucicault, denominating himself 'a born poet of Ireland' (85), defends his position in personal terms, asserting that he 'knew in my bones the meaning of enslavement and dispossession' (121). Proud of his Irish plays, and of his adaptation of the rebel ballad 'The Wearing of the Green', he claims that 'It was me who gave the voice of Ireland a hearing on the stages of the world, which it had never before received, in all its tormented history!' (122). Patterson counters that Boucicault's 'Ireland' was a lucrative commercial commodity, and his public declarations of patriotism were merely publicity stunts. He declares that 'your colonial soul discovered its strength in fraudulence and deceit . . . you conjured up a never-never emerald island, fake heroics and mettlesome beauties and villains made of pasteboard, outwitted through eternity by the bogus grinning peasant rogue as only you could play him' (134).

Parker's play dramatizes the debate about Boucicault's 'colonial soul' without entirely resolving it, although on the strength of the wake scene in *The*

Shaughraun the dramatist is ultimately pardoned and granted a comic semi-apotheosis in his own sensational style. Parker, himself a writer who tried to reach beyond ethnic and religious partisanship, recognizes that, although Boucicault's plays were popular on both sides of the imperial divide and on both sides of the Atlantic, his inclusive appeal does not mean that his stage practice was politically meretricious. When, ten years after the Famine, Boucicault began to write Irish plays, he was addressing distinct but not homogeneous ethnic audiences. Not all American playgoers shared the anglophobia of recent Irish immigrants. In Ireland, Boucicault's audience was drawn from both the nationalist working classes and the Unionist Anglo-Irish gentry. In England, at Drury Lane or the Adelphi, wealthy political conservatives sat next to liberals who felt guilty about coercion in Ireland; while at the Britannia Irish immigrants mingled with English artisans. Richard Cave correctly argues that Boucicault's non-confrontational dramaturgy and appeal to sentiment instructed his mixed English audiences how to view situations from an Irish point of view, and his careful representation of both Anglo-Irishmen and Englishmen avoided giving direct political offence (102–5).

Boucicault was intelligent enough to know that much of his lucrative output was, as he said himself, 'guano' (quoted in Walsh 96), and he never deceived himself about the extent to which he pandered to popular taste. He thought that an audience got the drama it deserved, and what the Victorian audience got was him. Nevertheless, at a time when melodrama was the 'alternative' culture of the people,[22] he exploited its capacity to direct the emotional allegiances of its hearers, even against their will: 'The author looks at the audience as his natural prey, and when he gets it in his power he does not relax his grip', he said (Walsh 30). His work was, as Luke Gibbons has pointed out, the direct precursor of the cinema that displaced him and his illusionist tricks in the hearts of popular audiences. Steven Spielberg, a later master of special effects, similarly uses the financial and affective capital built up by blockbusters like *Jurassic Park* in order to confront serious issues of genocide and slavery in *Schindler's List* and *Amistad*, movies which eschew both high art and radical politics, but nevertheless touch hearts as well as wallets. In Boucicault's Irish plays, character, setting and plot are constructed to produce not rational assent, but warm feelings. Mass culture, he understood, operates not through intellectual analysis, but through the politics of empathy. Boucicault's charismatic portrayal of Irish heroes exploited his popularity as an actor in favour of the Irish underdog; his most sympathetic characters, Myles-na-Coppaleen, Shaun the Post, and Conn the Shaughraun, were all Irish Catholic peasants. He also manipulated his 'sensation scenes' so that technical triumphs of staging were invested with non-verbal political affect. In both *Arrah-na-Pogue* and *The Shaughraun*, complex mechanical scenery produces the spectacle of an Irish prisoner escaping from an English-run jail and compels even an English audience to cheer for the fugitive. In *Robert Emmet* (1884) the walls of Kilmainham prison part and an allegorical figure

of Ireland descends from the sky. The escape from confinement was a standard melodramatic motif: Boucicault consistently politicized it. Even if they
came merely to see Boucicault act or to watch his scenery move, the internal
logic of his drama, which compels us to root for the escapee rather than the
jailer, constructed his audiences as Irish sympathizers.

Seamus Deane does not share Stewart Parker's doubts about Boucicault's
'colonial soul'. Indeed, he opens the 'Fenianism' section of the *Field Day
Anthology of Irish Writing* with two scenes from *Arrah-na-Pogue*, citing Boucicault's nationalist sentiments and his support for Fenian prisoners and their
families (2: 234–8). Boucicault's plays seldom betray the overt hostility to
imperialism of his little-known pamphlet, *The Story of Ireland* (1881), which
describes his country as 'the victim of a systematic oppression and contemp-
tuous neglect, whose story will appear to you unparalleled in the history of
the world'. Yet his attitude towards the English theatre-goer conforms to the
sentiments expressed in his political tract. As befits his status as a purveyor of
popular rather than high culture, Boucicault appeals to the masses against
their rulers: 'I lay the story of Ireland before the English people, as an indictment against the governing class' (*Story* 3, 24). Central to that story, according to Boucicault, was the Famine, in which

> the people became victims of the first failure of the only crop of food on which
> their abjection had been taught to rely. The potato failed. Multitudes died by
> the ditch-side. Rents fell into arrear. Ireland, cleared by eviction and famine,
> was swept across the Atlantic into the United States. Sixty years ago her popu-
> lation numbered over eight millions. It is now short of five. (*Story* 23)

The Irish Republican Brotherhood, popularly known as the Fenians, a secret
society founded in America and Dublin in 1858 and dedicated to the freeing
of Ireland from England by physical force, was the first Irish revolutionary
organization to appeal to the citizens of the Irish diaspora, that other Ireland
that had been 'swept across the Atlantic into the United States', where Boucicault lived from 1853 to 1860. Although we cannot read the indignation and
the passionate patriotism of *The Story of Ireland* back through his entire career,
the New York and Dublin successes of his first Irish play, *The Colleen Bawn*
(1860), refocused Boucicault's attention on his native land just as the Fenian
movement was gaining momentum.

The Colleen Bawn undermines Anglo-Irish snobbery by legitimating the
marriage of the squireen Hardress Cregan to Eily O'Connor, a peasant girl
with a marked Kerry brogue. Boucicault later claimed that his play effected a
'revolution' in 'Irish drama and the representation of Irish character' ('Leaves'
232). No Englishmen appear on stage, but stage Englishness operates as an
externally imposed linguistic discipline that cancels out those local particu-
larities of which Boucicault is so fond. The Anglo-Irish heroine Anne Chute,
who normally speaks the Queen's English, exclaims, 'When I am angry the
brogue comes out, and my Irish heart will burst through manners, and graces,

and twenty stay-laces' (*Plays* 216). While the brogue is associated with pas-sion and Irishness with 'heart', English is figured as a corset that holds in anger and disciplines excess flesh. Social 'manners and graces' impose British middle-class uniformity on eccentric behaviours; the Queen's English main-tains linguistic hegemony throughout the British Empire. By condemning Hardress's rejection of his beloved's brogue and bringing the representatives of different dialects and classes into a sentimental union, Boucicault suggests that the larger political and social conflict embodied in the dissonance between dialects is dissolved or at least neutralized by love and marriage. In accepting Eily O'Connor and her local accent, the representative of English-ness in Ireland embraces Irish Otherness rather than censoring it. For Bouci-cault, if not for postcolonial and feminist critics, matrimony both provides a satisfactory dramatic happy ending and draws an optimistic analogy between sexuality and politics.

When Boucicault took *The Colleen Bawn* to Ireland in April 1861, its enor-mous popularity spurred him to write another Irish play, which premiered in Dublin.[23] *Arrah-na-Pogue* (1864), a patriotic melodrama set four years after the rising of 1798, follows the fortunes of an Irish rebel chieftain, the 'wild goose' Beamish MacCoul, who, after being condemned to hang for his part in the rebellion, has escaped from Wicklow Gaol and taken refuge in France. Four years later he secretly returns to Ireland to organize an insurrection in the Wicklow Mountains, but, convinced that such an insurrection will result in 'a useless waste of life' (*Arrah* 157), he is about to return to France with his sweetheart Fanny Power. Both the subject and the stage setting of *Arrah-na-Pogue* demonstrate an increase in the intensity of Boucicault's concern for the land of his birth. His well-documented theatrical predilection for striking stage pictures is put to patriotic use in the first scene, which takes place beside the Round Tower at Glendalough.[24] In the shadow of this well-known emblem of Ireland, Beamish MacCoul robs the Irish villain, the cowardly rent-collector and process-server Feeney, of the rents accruing to his own estate, which has been confiscated by the British government. So powerful are the conventions of melodrama that Boucicault's contrasting characterization of the bold rebel and the cowardly villain compels the audience, whatever their prior political loyalties, to approve of MacCoul's rough justice. The more thoughtful among them might have been prompted by his symbolic scenery to make a political analogy: the whole of Ireland is confiscated land, and an Irish rebel is no criminal, but a man intent on reclaiming his own property.

MacCoul's flamboyant act leads, via some of Boucicault's most tightly-woven plotting and breathtaking coincidences, to the arrest first of his foster sister, Arrah Meelish, and then of her new husband Shaun the Post, who gal-lantly takes the blame for the robbery in order to save her life. As Shaun, Boucicault gave himself most of the best moments in the play. One of these occurs at his wedding feast, when the guests ask him to sing 'The Wearing of the Green'. At first he objects: 'Is it sing that song and the soldiers widin gunshot? Sure, there's sudden death in every note of it'. Having first established the seditious credentials of his performance, Shaun then proceeds to a full rendition. From the original street ballad of 1798 Boucicault kept only the lines about Napper Tandy; the opening lines of the first stanza and the whole of the second and third were his own, and have subsequently become the authorized version:

> O Paddy dear, and did you hear the news that's going round?
> The shamrock is forbid by law to grow on Irish ground;
> St. Patrick's Day no more we'll keep, his colours can't be seen,
> For there's a bloody law again [sic] the wearing of the green.
> I met with Napper Tandy, and he took me by the hand,
> And he said, 'How's poor old Ireland, and how does she stand?'
> She's the most distressful country that ever yet was seen,
> They are hanging men and women for the wearing of the green.

The second verse suggests that 'since the colour we must wear is England's cruel red, / Sure Ireland's sons will ne'er forget the blood that they have shed', and the third concludes that Irishmen, 'driven by a tyrant's hand', may have to take refuge in America, a country 'Where the cruel cross of England shall nevermore be seen' (Arrah 133–4).[25]

In this context of cruelty, blood and tyranny, we might expect the leader of the English soldiers to be a monster, and he is indeed one of the least pleasant Englishmen to be found on the nineteenth-century Irish stage. Nevertheless, the appropriately named Major Coffin is something of a melodramatic disappointment: he is merely a cold, efficient, duty-bound officer who strives – and fails – to maintain his dignity among uproarious Irish peasants. The plot demands a formal antagonist, a representative of colonial power to challenge the Irish rebel leader. The main antagonist, however, is the Irish process-server Feeney, whose unwanted love for the heroine, the 'colleen' Arrah, marks him as the 'heavy'. In nineteenth-century melodramas the lead villain usually competed with the hero for the heroine's affections: Coffin's lack of libido invalidates his claim to serious wickedness.

When Shaun the Post claims responsibility for the robbery he has not committed, it is Major Coffin's duty to arrest and condemn him: 'the country is agitated, and prompt measures are required to restore order. It is my firm conviction that an example is particularly required at this moment to check a popular disturbance. This man's case admits of no doubt, and his execution will, I hope, prove a salutary public lesson'. Coffin's severe rhetoric marks him as the embodiment of English martial law, which operated brutally after the rebellion of 1798. The O'Grady, a British officer but also head of an Irish sept, comments on the difference between English principle and Irish passion: 'There goes a kind-hearted gentleman, who would cut more throats on principle and firm conviction than another blackguard would sacrifice to the worst passions of his nature' (*Arrah* 140). An anomaly in a play dependent upon bravura performance energy, Coffin appears less a villain than a mechanical adherent to the imperial code.

Peter Brooks has rescued melodrama from the critical doldrums by revaluing precisely those formal elements that have most embarrassed academic commentators: he characterizes it as the theatre of excess, of 'acting out', which 'represents a victory over repression' (*Melodramatic Imagination* 41). The stage Englishman, however, acts at the behest of patriotic duty: repression is his watchword, civilization the ideal for which he sacrifices his emotions and desires. Boucicault figures the opposition between the English and the Irish as that between head and heart, law and justice, restraint and spontaneity. Since the genre as he inherited and transformed it functions through 'excess', it excludes the Englishman from the centre of the action.

Coffin embodies British imperial rule in a period of revolutionary upheaval from Europe to the Americas. In *The Story of Ireland*, Boucicault quotes an unnamed 'statesman' who compares the British government unfavourably with her people:

> Never was there so much charity and humanity towards the poor and distressed. Any act of cruelty and oppression never failed to excite a sentiment of general indignation . . . people in private life . . . are full of generous feelings and noble exertions of benevolence. Yet, amidst this profusion of private virtue, there is almost total want of public spirit, and the most deplorable contempt of public principle. (24)

Boucicault could condemn the British Empire while admiring many of its citizens, and distinguish between official policy and individual generosity. Exploiting the sentimentality characteristic of melodrama, he constructed plots that invariably place his Irish characters in situations of political 'distress', thus evoking in some of his English characters and many of his English audiences those 'generous feelings' he knew them to possess.

In *Arrah-na-Pogue* the sympathetic English sergeant who is Shaun's jailer illustrates the distinction between the 'private virtue' of individual Englishmen and the inhumanity of their public code. He is a stage cockney, Boucicault's answer to 'Teague', the comic Irish servant of English theatre, and his class status reflects that of many of Boucicault's auditors.[26] (His comic counterpart is the stage butler, Winterbottom, who serves the Chief Secretary at Dublin Castle and shares with the sergeant a cockney tendency to misplace his aspirates.) Like all the decent Englishmen in Boucicault's Irish plays, the sergeant knows a villain when he sees one, defending the dejected Shaun against the triumphant Feeney, whom he ejects from the prison with the words, 'Clear out! . . . This is a man in trouble, and not a badger in a hole to be baited by curs like you' (*Arrah* 143). Every interaction between Shaun and his jailer increases our sense of the benevolence of the sergeant, who weeps in sympathy with Arrah on the night before Shaun's execution. Shaun interprets his sympathetic tears as feminine: 'the milk of a good nature is as new in your heart this minute as when you first dhrew woman's kindness from your mother's breast'. Even the best of Englishmen, however, are subject to 'the regulations', and the sergeant distinguishes between his feminine kindness and his masculine duty: 'If I am obliged to refuse your girl admission to see you, don't blame me, Shaun. It is my duty, and the reg'lation, you know'. Shaun replies, 'Av coorse it's your jooty; you can't help it. I would do the same if I was in your place'; yet once the Sergeant is gone he adds, 'That's a lie, but no matter; it will be a comfort to him to think so' (164–5). The Irishman would allow his kindly nature to override his national duty: even the best of Englishmen would not.

On the stage, where idiosyncrasies of human nature create the illusion we call 'character', the Englishman's character is submerged within the requirements of his national role. In the hilarious trial scene, Major Coffin's concern is less for himself than for the dignity of the court and his 'debt of duty' to the Crown he represents: Shaun manages to subvert both through a combination of deliberate obtuseness and verbal play. When Coffin observes that Shaun must be the Irish for John, he reverses the Major's linguistic imperialism, 'No, sir; John is the English for Shaun' (150). The formal and taciturn stage Englishman makes a perfect straight man for the loquacious Celt. Shaun's vivid abuse of Feeney depends on local dialect, accent and metaphor: 'When St. Patrick drove all the crapin' things out of Ireland, he left one sarpint behind, and that was your great grandfather'. The O'Grady argues that the prisoner should be let off on the grounds of 'the eloquence of the defence', but Coffin sees Shaun's verbal facility as nationally marked and legally irrelevant: 'I regret to say that we cannot admit so Irish a consideration' (153). As in *The Colleen Bawn*, Irishness is linked with eloquence and rhetorical excess, the markers of a stage 'character', while Englishness is identified with unadorned and therefore 'normal' (or truthful) speech.

Although he is the rhetorical loser in this confrontation, Coffin has absolute legal and physical control over Shaun. Yet, even when he sentences Shaun to the gallows, Coffin disclaims personal responsibility: 'Prisoner, we deeply regret the sentence which it is incumbent upon us to pass upon you; but the Court knows only its duty and the penalty ascribed to your crime. . . . Heaven have mercy upon you'. Shaun's response, which belongs to the important dramatic and rebel genre 'the speech from the dock', is a masterpiece of ambiguity that must have been received very differently upon London and Dublin stages:

> Well, yer honour, I don't blame ye, for you have done your jooty, I suppose, by the King that made ye what ye are – long life to him! – and that jooty is now to hang me; and I have done my duty by the man that made me and mine what we are, and that's to die for him. I could do no more, and you could do no less. I dare say you would let me off if you could, so God bless ye, all the same. (154)

Boucicault, who played Shaun in both Dublin and London, doubtless inflected the lines differently in each city. Played straight, Shaun's 'speech from the dock' is a generous acknowledgement that Major Coffin acts without malice in condemning him. The stage Englishman as a man of honour is preserved, and the sensibilities of an English audience hostile to the Fenians remain undisturbed.[27] But an ironic accent on the words, 'you have done your duty, I suppose, by the King that made ye what ye are – long life to him!' transforms the Englishman's duty into an excuse for colonial brutality, and Shaun into a potential martyr.

Arrah-na-Pogue was politically in tune with its time. The play opened in Dublin in November 1864, by which time the Fenians claimed roughly 54,000 working-class adherents and were planning a rising for the next year. Boucicault's choice of the 1798 rebellion as the historical setting of his play was therefore apt: the Fenians invoked the republican ideals of Wolfe Tone, one of the heroes of 1798. *Arrah-na-Pogue* ran in London from March to September 1865, in which month the offices of the Fenian newspaper *The Irish People* were raided and the leaders arrested. On stage, Shaun the Post escapes from an English prison; in November 1865 the Fenian leader James Stephens broke out of Richmond jail. After the abortive Fenian rising in early 1867, *Arrah-na-Pogue* played in London again from September to November of that year.[28] In September the Fenian leaders Kelly and Deasey were rescued from a Manchester prison van, and during the rescue a policeman was accidentally killed. In November three Irishmen who became known as the Manchester Martyrs were executed for the murder. Shaun's trial and sensational escape held the stage during the trial and condemnation of the Manchester Martyrs for abetting a real escape.

Arrah-na-Pogue pre-dated these political events: fiction anticipated history. Nevertheless, Boucicault subsequently associated his play with the turbulent occurrences of 1867. Shaun's friend Patsey suggests rescuing the condemned prisoner by blowing up the prison: 'I know where gunpowdher is stored in the vaults below the Castle. Wouldn't it be easy to blow the place to smithereens?' (163). In December 1867 Irish dynamiters, attempting to free yet another Fenian, blew up the wall of Clerkenwell prison, killing twelve people and injuring a hundred more. After this event, Shaun's rebel song, 'The Wearing of the Green', was banned throughout the British Empire.[29] Proud to be associated with the Fenians, and seeking to emphasize the analogical if not the causal connection between explosion and performance, Boucicault later incorrectly claimed that the first night of *Arrah-na-Pogue* was 13 December 1867, the night of the Clerkenwell bombing.[30] In his later play, *The Shaughraun*, which according to its author 'is founded on an episode in the Fenian insurrection of 1866' (Walsh 137), the villain Kinchela counts on the police to shoot the escaping Fenian hero because 'The late attack on the police-van at Manchester, and the explosion at Clerkenwell prison in London will warrant extreme measures' (*Plays* 284).

As if to confirm Stuart Hall's view that popular culture inevitably encodes contradictory impulses towards resistance and containment, Boucicault also provides the audience of *Arrah-na-Pogue* with an attractive stage Englishman, the Chief Secretary at Dublin Castle, who lacks Major Coffin's enthusiasm for hanging rebels and gives the British public a less obnoxious character with whom to identify.[31] Although many English artisans hated the immigrant Irish because they undercut them on the labour market, others responded to Fenian appeals for working-class solidarity, and the Manchester Martyrs attracted considerable English sympathy.[32] Unlike the British court that condemned the three Irishmen, the Chief Secretary, a benevolent *deus ex machina*, exercises clemency. Boucicault's good Englishman/bad Englishman routine became a favourite with Irish dramatists who wanted to condemn colonialism without condemning all its functionaries, and needed to give English audiences a foothold within their plays. When Shaw rewrote *Arrah-na-Pogue* in the context of the American revolution and called it *The Devil's Disciple*, he borrowed not only Dick Dudgeon's willingness to be hanged in Anderson's place, and much of Boucicault's famous trial scene, but also the prototypical stage English duo: the unimaginative proponent of the gallows, Major Swindon, and his attractively urbane superior, Gentlemanly Johnny Bourgoyne.

To save his friend Shaun, Beamish MacCoul comes to Dublin to claim responsibility for the robbery and to surrender himself to the Secretary:

> SECRETARY. And you come here to claim his release and your own execution?
> BEAMISH. If you please, my lord.
> ‚SECRETARY. I presume, then, that you and this fellow are disputing which of the two shall die?
> BEAMISH. And I rely on your lordship's sense of justice to give me the preference.

In response to this elegantly absurd piece of dialogue, the Secretary formulates the standard stage English reaction to Irish impetuosity and generosity of spirit: 'Shall I ever be able to understand this extraordinary people?' (*Arrah* 157). If the Irish are extra-ordinary, different from the norm, the English, Boucicault implies, are ordinary, unmarked by extravagant speech or behaviour. If the stage Irishman in England was an outsider trying to ingratiate himself, the stage Englishman in Ireland was an outsider trying to understand a puzzling subordinate race. Boucicault savours the subversive potential of eccentricity, which renders the Irish indecipherable to the gaze of the colonizer.

Despite his perplexity, however, Boucicault's English Secretary is clever enough to orchestrate the farcical unravelling of the complications of *Arrah-na-Pogue*. MacCoul hands him a paper that explains both Shaun's innocence of the robbery and the labyrinthine complexities of the plot. As the Secretary is reading it, The O'Grady and MacCoul's fiancée Fanny arrive one after the other, also hoping to save Shaun. Concealing MacCoul and The O'Grady behind separate screens, the Secretary performs a metatheatrical masquerade of power and surveillance. He pretends that the knowledge that he has in fact just gathered from

MacCoul's document is derived from his own Castle spies: 'Government sources of information are much more extraordinary than we care to acknowledge'. Although this is, in context, a comic line, its resonance for a Dublin or New York audience would be sinister. In boasting, 'how perfect is our detective system of police', the Secretary is play-acting, but in reality Dublin Castle ran an efficient espionage operation. The only organ that proves impenetrable to English surveillance is Fanny's 'woman's heart' (158–60).

The scene represents both colonial and dramatic power: pardoning the rebel MacCoul and the wrongly condemned Shaun, the Secretary 'directs' the actions of all the characters. 'I seem to have conducted this affair to a successful eruption', he congratulates himself (161). Yet his cool and detached manipulations, which turn his visitors into comic eavesdroppers and thus reduce potential tragedy to farce, are not expressions of 'character'. Rather, they represent the dramatist's power to impose the happy ending that melodrama requires: the pardon of the wronged hero and the triumph of good over evil. Although historical Irish melodramas must acknowledge that for the real rebels, Henry Joy McCracken, Lord Edward FitzGerald and Robert Emmet, no pardon ever came, in Boucicault's Irish comedy MacCoul is forgiven and reunited with Fanny, after which happy event he is no longer disposed to rebel. The facts of history are displaced by theatrical convention as death on the gallows is transformed into the characteristic melodramatic reprieve. The rhetoric of this optimistic scene represents subordinates as regulation-bound, their superiors as generous, if paternalistic. Boucicault's appeal to sentiment both flatters his English audience and suggests to the English government that magnanimity rather than coercion is the way to deal with the Irish Question.

While the Fenians were organizing themselves in Ireland and *Arrah-na-Pogue* was delighting audiences in Dublin and London, Matthew Arnold gave the series of Oxford lectures published in 1867 as *On the Study of Celtic Literature*. It is habitual to deplore Arnold's patronizing reading of the Celt; [33] but his less than flattering description of the 'Saxon' was also an important document in the codification of English national character. In contrast with the lazy, prevaricating, imaginative Irish, the genius of the English is characterized as *'energy with honesty'* (*Lectures* 341), but in their practicality they are also 'prosaic' (296). Arnold is describing the Philistines, the industrious English middle classes whose lack of Celtic soul and passion bears out the old Irish adage: *'For dulness, the creeping Saxons'* (342). If the English are boring, they are nevertheless politically effective, 'disciplinable and steadily obedient within certain limits, but retaining an inalienable part of freedom and self-dependence' (347). Matthew Arnold's phlegmatic and practical Saxon is still alive and well: introducing *Saint Oscar*, his play about Wilde, Terry Eagleton derides the moralism and gravitas of 'the genetically empiricist English' (xi) who, like Arnold's nondescript Philistines, are repressed, joyless and stupid by comparison with the quick-witted Irish. Eagleton is free to use this essentialist caricature because it is ethically acceptable to stereotype the powerful. Gesturing towards 'what is going on in Ireland', by which he means the Fenian troubles, Arnold is clear about his own nation's capacity for dealing with the despotism of fact:

> Strength! alas, it is not strength, strength in the material world, which is wanting to us Saxons; we have plenty of strength for swallowing up and absorbing as much as we choose; there is nothing to hinder us from effacing the last poor material remains of that Celtic power which once was everywhere. (*Lectures* 298)

Partly disguised by that rhetorical 'alas', we hear the voice of imperial authority and the veiled threat of coercion. Arnold affected an interest in the reconciliation between Ireland and England, but that reconciliation was to be on England's terms.

After the failure of the Fenian rising, Boucicault understood that England's strength permitted no practical challenge; he therefore chose to mount a theatrical challenge instead, using his power to move audiences as a political tool. Crucial to this strategy was his most attractive stage Englishman, Captain Molineux, a figure who, while he owes much to the Saxon stereotypes promoted by Arnold, far surpasses them in generosity and humanity. Molineux appears in Boucicault's most subversively Fenian play, *The Shaughraun*, which premiered in America in November 1874 and is set some time after the Clerkenwell explosion.[34] Robert Ffolliet, a young Fenian from an old Irish Catholic family, has been trapped and denounced by the Irish villain Kinchela and the local informer Harvey Duff. His transportation to an Australian penal colony leaves his sister Claire and his betrothed Arte O'Neale at the mercy of the treacherous squireen Kinchela, who holds the mortgage on Robert's estate. Boucicault's choice of dramatic premise was topical, for although an Amnesty movement demanding the release of Fenian prisoners had been launched in 1867, by 1874 a significant number of Fenian prisoners were still imprisoned in English jails. Lyons calls the Amnesty association 'a means of keeping the cause of irreconcilable republicanism vivid in the minds of the people' (*Ireland* 127), and Boucicault strongly supported it.

Appropriately, Boucicault's play enacts an Irish escape: Robert Ffolliet's shrewd and charming boyhood companion Conn the Shaughraun rescues him first from the penal colony and subsequently from an Irish jail. (As in the case of *Arrah-na-Pogue*, Boucicault's imagination ran just ahead of historical events: in 1876, two years after the first performance of *The Shaughraun*, six Fenian prisoners were rescued from Freemantle, Australia, by the Clan na Gael.[35] (This rescue now has its own dramatic memorial in the recent play *Catalpa* by Donal O'Kelly.) At the beginning of the play Robert, who has made his way back from Australia via America, is about to pay a fleeting visit to his sister and his fiancée, and word of his intentions has filtered back to the authorities. Captain Molineux and a detachment of British soldiers have been instructed to re-arrest this 'distinguished Fenian hero' (*Plays* 261), but the

Englishman's devotion to duty is undermined when he falls in love with Robert's sister Claire. On his first entrance, Conn's mother exclaims, 'But, oh, miss! who's this coming up the cliff? It can't be a vision!' (259). Though Captain Molineux must have been dressed in 'England's cruel red', presumably it became him well enough: his appearance constitutes a reverse *aisling*, a masculine 'vision' that both echoes and opposes the beautiful feminine apparition who laments the fate of oppressed Ireland in the bardic poetry of the eighteenth century. Boucicault wrote the part of Molineux for the English actor Henry J. Montague, an extremely handsome man who became a matinée idol in America on the strength of this role.

> Montague's forte was the portrayal of gentlemen; and he was gentlemanly off the stage as well as on. Men idolized him, and Wallack's Theatre used to be crowded on matinée days by women who came to see Montague act and nobody else. There was a story current about a New York girl who turned her closet into a shrine and burned candles around his picture. (Walsh 91)

The casting of Montague ensured that even Irish-American Fenian sympathizers would find it hard to hate such an attractive representative of the Empire.

As a stage Englishman infatuated with an Irish woman, Molineux supplies an influential link in a long representational chain. On eighteenth-century stages the Irishman was often an amorous rogue or a fortune hunter, like Sir Lucius O'Trigger, looking for an English heiress to repair his finances.[36] After the Act of Union (1800), however, British men usually made love to Irish women. Supporters of the Union frequently represented it in terms of heterosexual marriage, thus naturalizing and domesticating the colonial relation between England and a people who could not be visually distinguished from their rulers. The difference between an English man and an Irish woman accurately reflected the unequal relationship that geographical proximity and common Caucasian origin rendered awkwardly intimate. The analogy between sexuality and politics was popularized by Sydney Owenson's widely read novel *The Wild Irish Girl* (1806), in which the callow young Englishman Horatio is educated out of his anti-Irish prejudices by the beautiful Irishwoman Glorvina. Their eventual union signals a new contract between Ireland and England, which is to be guaranteed by mutual affection rather than brute force.[37] Although the proponents of the matrimonial analogy saw it as an ideal paradigm, designed to promote harmony and end strife, they were not accustomed to reflect that the conditions of nineteenth-century matrimony did not favour the female partner. As long as Ireland occupied the feminine role 'she' could be viewed as close but completely subordinate. In legal terms, marriage transformed husband and wife into one person, and that person was the husband: we can therefore see that matrimony was a better (and more damning) analogy for political union than many of its proponents realized. Even those who were not enthusiastic about British rule and sought to ameliorate its harsher effects used the trope with little consciousness of the gender disadvantage to the feminine partner. Owenson saw herself pleading for Ireland at the bar of English public opinion; and in this Boucicault resembled her. His melodramas required a love plot, and a story that involved a colonizing English male and a colonized Irish woman heightened the erotic interest by framing it within a hostile political situation. The resolution of sexual tension between a man and a woman functions as an analogy for the resolution of political conflict between dominant and subordinate nations.

The dramatic formula of love between enemies is as old as *Romeo and Juliet*, but there is no imbalance of power between Montagues and Capulets. In the opening scene of *The Shaughraun*, Boucicault emphasizes the power differential between England and Ireland by translating it into class terms. Although they are well-bred young women, Arte O'Neale and Claire Ffolliet have been rendered almost destitute by the villainous machinations of Kinchela. Claire is reduced to churning her own butter, and Captain Molineux takes her for a dairymaid. Sustaining his misapprehension, Claire mischievously performs the role of a pert 'colleen' with a 'delicious' brogue:

> MOLINEUX. Is this place called Swillabeg?
> CLAIRE. No; it is called Shoolabeg.
> MOLINEUX. Beg pardon; your Irish names are so unpronounceable. You see, I'm an Englishman.
> CLAIRE. I remarked your misfortune. Poor creature, you couldn't help it.
> MOLINEUX. I do not regard it as a misfortune.
> CLAIRE. Got accustomed to it, I suppose. Were you born so?

As usual, the Irish character is witty and the Englishman stiffly impervious to her verbal play. Like Major Coffin, who thinks Shaun is the Irish for John, Molineux assumes that Irish names are 'unpronounceable' rather than that he is ignorant of their pronunciation, yet his linguistic imperialism is undermined by Claire's assertion that speaking English is not natural, but a misfortune to which one must adapt. Disconcerted, Molineux takes refuge in his class and economic superiority: he employs Claire on an errand to her mistress and promises her a crown. Claire asks him to take over the churn, feminizing and equalizing him as she does so: 'You were intended for a dairymaid!' Molineux feels constrained to reassert his masculinity:

> MOLINEUX. I know a dairymaid that was intended for me.
> CLAIRE. That speech only wanted a taste of the brogue to be worthy of an Irishman.
> MOLINEUX. [*kissing her*]. Now I'm perfect.
> CLAIRE. [*starting away*]. What are you doing?
> MOLINEUX. Tasting the brogue. Stop, my dear; you forget the crown I promised you. Here it is. [*He hands her the money.*] Don't hide your blushes, they become you.

Boucicault sets up this transaction in class terms: it appears to be a gentleman's seduction of a working-class girl, in which money is exchanged for sexual favours. Yet, though Claire initially indicts Molineux's sexual forwardness as worthy of an Irishman, his advances take on the resonance of colonial allegory when he offers her a 'crown' in exchange for a taste of the brogue. The 'crown' is a retroactive compensation for what he has already stolen, a kiss nationalized by its metonymic relation to that most Irish of attributes, the brogue. It asserts his physical rights over the feminized Irish colony; perhaps it even suggests that the Act of Union, which brought Ireland directly under the Crown, repaired the violent conquest of earlier centuries. The irony, however, is all at the expense of Molineux, for whom the encounter has been mockingly 'staged' by the nationalist Claire. When he learns that she belongs to his own class, his embarrassment is acute: 'Don't hide your blushes, they become you' needles Claire (*Plays* 260–1).

The exposure of Molineux's sexual imperialism as illegitimate undermines the political imperialism of the army and country he represents. Yet, once his political education at Claire's hands begins, his anti-Irish prejudices are swiftly dispelled. First she demonstrates to him that the unpronounceability of Irish names is simply a matter of linguistic perspective: the Queen's English is not normative in Ireland.

> CLAIRE. What's your name again – Mulligrubs?
> MOLINEUX. No; Molineux.
> CLAIRE. I ax your pardon. You see I'm Irish, and the English names are so unpronounceable. (260)

Molineux has come to request the privilege of hunting over the grounds of Suil-a-more Castle, the ancient seat of Claire's family, whose ruin makes a picturesque backdrop to the opening scene. According to Claire, the ruin has been appropriated not only by Kinchela, but also by the discourses of tourism and aesthetics:

> Do you see that ruin yonder! Oh – 'tis the admiration of the traveller, and the study of painters, who come from far and near to copy it. It was the home of my forefathers when they kept open house for the friend – the poor – or the stranger. The mortgagee has put up a gate now, so visitors pay sixpence a head to admire the place, and their guide points across to this cabin where the remains of the ould family, two lonely girls, live.

The picturesque, however, obscures the political. In the absence of an interpretative centre, Molineux rather crassly assumes that he can read the ruins through the lens of English prejudice: 'You have to suffer bitterly indeed for ages of family imprudence, and the Irish extravagance of your ancestors'. But Claire snaps back: 'Yes, sir, the extravagance of their love for their country, and the imprudence of their fidelity to their faith!' When he learns that the dilapidated state of the family fortunes is the result of their brother's political imprisonment in Australia, Molineux is abjectly apologetic. His distress at his own misreading reveals him as 'a good fellow, although he is an Englishman' (261–2).

With this 'decent chap' version of the colonial official Boucicault established a long-lasting dramatic convention (part observation, part Utopian desire and part conduct lesson from the colonized to the colonizer) that gave English audiences a character who flattered their national pride while disturbing their national prejudices. Molineux's instinctive decency is revealed by his immediate dislike of the Irish villain, which overrides his normal English politeness: when Kinchela asks why the two girls have failed to introduce him, the Captain replies with stylish offensiveness, 'They paid me the compliment of presuming that I had no desire to form your acquaintance' (263). Molineux's contempt for the Irish traitor is matched by his immediate friendliness towards the disguised Fenian, whom he discovers by accident on the cliff top. Robert prevents him from falling over the cliff, whereupon the Captain reveals that he has already fallen in love with Claire. Robert then offers a toast to both Claire and Arte, an act that threatens to betray his identity when Molineux astutely observes that the whiskey is American rather than Irish. Nevertheless, the Englishman deliberately refuses to draw the obvious conclusion that a man on the seashore in 'yachting costume' with bourbon in his pocket might be a felon newly landed from America. He even uses the whiskey to warn his new-found friend not to stay in this hiding place:

> [I]t reminds me of a duty I have to perform. We have orders to capture a dangerous person who will be, or has been, landed on this coast lately, and as these rocks are just the kind of place where he might find refuge . . . I propose to revisit this spot again tonight with a file of men. Here's your health. (269)

In return, Robert prevents Molineux from falling prey to his concealed accomplice Conn, and the scene closes, after the Englishman's obligatory exclamation, 'This is the most extraordinary country I was ever in', with the stage direction '*Exeunt, arm-in-arm*'. Their unspoken complicity (potentially a betrayal of duty on Molineux's part) is thus given emphatic physical expression (270).

Molineux's decency is insufficient to counteract his military obligations once Robert's identity has been plainly established by Harvey Duff, but his reluctance to arrest the Fenian fugitive and his delicacy of feeling are almost comical. 'I am sorry to be obliged to perform so painful a duty', he says awkwardly. Conn mocks this high-minded politeness when, on being told that his mongrel has bitten four English soldiers, he riposte: 'Tatthers was obliged to perform his painful duty' (280). Molineux's stage English reliance on honesty proves more effective than any brutality when he offers to take Father Dolan's word that Robert is not hiding in his house, which prompts Robert to emerge rather than allow a priest to lie for him. Meanwhile Robert's 'rebel sister' Claire (279) is torn between her passionate opposition to England and her unwilling love of Molineux, 'who has the impudence to upset all my principles with his chalky smile and bloodless courtesy' (287). She hates his country and his people, but neither she nor any of the sympathetic Irish characters can bring themselves to hate him: after he leaves with his prisoner they testify effusively to his gentle forbearance and teary-eyed goodness. Molineux assures the audience that his English soldiers are just as kind-hearted as himself: 'my men have such a distaste for this business, that I believe, if left to defend their prisoner against an attempt to rescue him, they would disgrace themselves' (299). Throughout the play all anti-Fenian actions are attributed not to the soldiers but to the local Irish police.[38]

Boucicault's characterization of Molineux dramatizes the fact that English politeness restrains those excesses of behaviour used to create character on the stage. 'Bloodless courtesy' is normative rather than individual. Adherence to a code is antithetical to the development of a 'character', since all the code's representatives behave in the same way. When two codes intersect within the same role, however, the resulting conflict mimics psychic depth. In Molineux, stage English reserve struggles with melodramatic sentimentality: he weeps as he performs his 'painful duty' and, when he asks Claire's 'pity for my position last night, when I found myself obliged to arrest the brother of the woman I love', the curtain falls upon their passionate embrace (289–91). But the union of hearts between England and Ireland, symbolically sealed with a heterosexual kiss, is subversively triangulated when Claire forces Molineux to choose between English honour and her brother's life. To keep him out of the way during Robert's second escape attempt, she lures him to Rathgarron Head, where she is supposed to signal the rescue ship by kindling a tar barrel. After some stage business with Molineux's cigar, she finds herself without a light. Laying the whole situation before him, she explains exactly what his matches mean: 'You can redeem your professional honour; you can repair the past. I have no means here of lighting that beacon. If the signal is not fired, my brother will be recaptured' (306). Boucicault is too tactful to place before his audience the spectacle of a uniformed officer setting fire to a Fenian beacon, but in the following scene we learn that the tar barrel has been ignited, that Duty has bowed before Sentiment, and that an English officer has facilitated a Fenian escape.

The play is concluded, in proper melodramatic fashion, by a general pardon, after which Robert gives his consent to the marriage of Claire and Molineux. Boucicault uses this formulaic happy ending for the purpose of political exhortation: the relation between the English soldier and the Fenian rebel is a homosocial model for the desired relation between England and Ireland; through the transfer of Claire as symbolic property from Robert to Molineux, the two men will become brothers-in-law.[39] Mediated by the Irish woman who loves them both, this bond between two men on opposite sides of the political divide is thus legally sanctioned. The play implies that the relation between colonizer and rebel, honourable enemies and decent fellows, is threatened not by the 'generous' English people, but by the land-grabbing Kinchela and the informer Harvey Duff, lower-class Irishmen complicit with a corrupt colonial system. When *The Shaughraun* went on tour in England, Boucicault insisted that special performances be given to benefit Fenian political prisoners. According to Christopher Fitz-Simon, 'It is an extraordinary tribute to the broadmindedness of the British people that they should have supported a fund for the relief of those who, by British law, were convicted felons' (103). But the powerful can afford broadminded gestures, and the favourable reception of the play seems less remarkable when we consider its optimistic representation of Englishness.

Boucicault's construction of Molineux was strategic. In 1876 he took advantage of *The Shaughraun's* success in England to address a widely reprinted open letter to the Conservative Prime Minister, Disraeli, adducing the enormous popularity of his play as evidence that English audiences supported a pardon for all the Fenians.[40] Whatever an English audience's political prejudices might be, the pre-ordained logic of melodrama encouraged them to cheer the escape of an unjustly condemned hero. Robert's innocence is a complicated matter, since he is indubitably an escaped felon: to 'feel' his theatrical innocence is to reject the categorization of the Fenians as criminals. Although his role might operate differently in America or Ireland, in England Molineux functions as a moral barometer for the audience. Because he is presented throughout as the epitome of the finest kind of stage Englishman – honest, upright, law-abiding and aware of his duty to his country – his willingness to collude in Robert's escape reassures them that such an escape is ethically desirable. He represents the best and most generous self of the English people, separated from the Irish not by any essential difference or repulsion, but by the artificial policy of their rulers. Transforming love of Ireland into theatrical eloquence, Boucicault self-consciously manipulates the politics of sympathy:

> It was surely not the cunning of the dramatist nor the great merit of the actors that lifted the whole audience to their feet, as cheer after cheer shook the old walls of the National Theatre when the fugitive convict escaped from his prison. Surely there is no attempt throughout the play to deceive the spectator as to the nature of the sympathy they extend; they are plainly invited to sympathize with one who is endeavouring to elude the penalty of a great offence. Why do they watch his progress with interest? and when an announcement is made that Her Majesty's pardon has been granted to all the political prisoners, why are these words greeted with hearty applause? May we answer, It is because the English people have begun to forgive the offence, and heartily desire to forget it? So I believed when I wrote this work, with the deliberate intention to ask that question in plain language, and I have done so. (Quoted in Walsh 138–9)

Possibly some of the audience's enthusiasm had to do with the sliding scenery that facilitated Robert's 'sensational' escape, but Boucicault believed that he had seduced not only his stage Englishman but also his English audience into sentimental complicity with Irish rebellion. He reminded Disraeli that the pardon that concludes the play is 'granted (under poetical license) during your ministry. This pardon is the *Deus ex machina* of the drama' (Walsh 137). Suggesting that Life ought to imitate Art, Boucicault invited Disraeli to take his cue from the merciful Secretary in *Arrah-na-Pogue*, and play God. Not usually averse to such a role, Disraeli in this case declined the suggestion.

Captain Molineux was Boucicault's most interesting, effective and influential stage Englishman. His role in his creator's famous and often-revived drama kept him before the public eye long after the first run was over. When Boucicault later attempted to improve his flagging fortunes by turning once again to the matter of Ireland and exaggerating the theme of homosocial attraction between honourable male enemies, the result was less successful. His historical melodrama *Robert Emmet* failed in Chicago in 1884, and he did not attempt to revive it.[41] This rambling play lacks both the coherence and the energy of *The Shaughraun*, yet its subject matter was potentially incendiary. Emmet, whose defeat and execution in 1803 was a postscript to the rebellion of 1798, was a nationalist icon whom Boucicault had long revered. *The Story of Ireland*, published in 1881, ends with an appropriation of Emmet's last words from the dock, 'I have done' (24). With the rise of Parnell, the Land War of 1879–82 and the Phoenix Park murders of 1882, relations between England and Ireland had significantly worsened. Boucicault took up and adapted a previous script after Henry Irving, who had intended to play Emmet, was warned by the British government not to attempt it during such troubled times.[42]

In *Robert Emmet* an Irishwoman, Sarah Curran, once again stands between a nationalist rebel and a British officer; but unlike the trio composed by Claire, Robert and Molineux, this later cross-national triangle involves potential erotic competition. Sarah is engaged to Robert Emmet, but Norman Claverhouse, a Scottish officer in the British army, is in love with her. Claverhouse, who is not technically a stage Englishman but usually behaves like one, thus occupies the structural role of the melodramatic villain, but he steadfastly refuses to perform it. (The villains of *Robert Emmet* are the Irish informers Quigley and Finerty and the legendary Major Sirr, the Irish Chief of Dublin's Police.)[43] Once Claverhouse realizes that Sarah loves Emmet, he facilitates his rival's affair with a generosity and self-control improbable even by Boucicault's elastic standards of plausibility. He tells Sarah: 'Before this night is past you must bear my rival's name . . . I will never quit your side until you are Robert Emmet's wife' (*Plays* 338–39). He escorts Sarah to Emmet's hideout, telling him that 'as her rejected lover I now bring her to the only man who can repair the injury this night's business may do to the name of a lady to whom we are equally devoted' (350). Emmet is stunned by

Claverhouse's punctilious courtesy, for he is 'an outlaw, whom to see and not to betray is a crime; a rebel, whom to serve is a capital offence'. The Captain's behaviour, while exquisite by the standards of sentimental melodrama, is, like Molineux's, treasonous: he too is willing to overlook his duty when it clashes with his love. He formulates his relationship with Emmet in terms that clearly demonstrate the circulation of homosocial desire through the body of the beloved woman: 'I only know that she loves you – that makes me at once your foe and your accomplice' (350). Eve Sedgwick defines desire as the 'glue, even when its manifestation is hostility or hatred . . . that shapes an important relationship' (*Between Men* 2). Boucicault's sentimental portrayal of Claverhouse implies that, if only such honourable foes could embrace one another, their rivalry for the feminized body of Ireland would evaporate; and embrace they do, as Robert declares, 'Let me feel your hand in mine; the other on my shoulder' (*Plays* 350). Claverhouse urges the couple to fly the country, but he also warns Emmet that, should he continue with his doomed plans for an insurrection, 'I'll find myself within three months heir to your widow' (351). This prophecy is based on the historical fact that after Emmet's execution Sarah Curran married a British officer.[44] Through his homosocial relation with the Irish hero, the British soldier will inherit the Irishwoman he desires.

Claverhouse, whose part is sometimes written in the broadest stage Scottish, and sometimes in the stilted phraseology of a Victorian Englishman behaving frightfully well, is one of Boucicault's most peculiar characters. Although he is himself a member of an imperial garrison, he has Molineux's instinctive dislike of Irishmen who betray their country: he insults Major Sirr and challenges him to a duel. His exaggerated sense of fair play in love extends to war: when he is assigned to capture Robert Emmet he tries to warn him by singing loudly. Sirr protests that he is 'betraying our presence to the foe we are in pursuit of', but Claverhouse replies, 'British troops always betray their presence. D'ye want us to skulk?' (374). When Emmet is taken and condemned to death, Claverhouse's generous reliance on the honour of his prisoner prevents Michael Dwyer from making a rescue attempt: 'Captain Claverhouse ordered the irons off him and shared wid him his own quarters in the prison, taking only his word not to escape, and Emmet will kape it. That's why we failed' (391). So Claverhouse and Emmet spend a last night alone together, but the price, ironically, is Emmet's death.

The final scene of the play, Emmet's execution, openly stages the homosocial implications of Claverhouse's conflation of foe and accomplice, hatred and love. Boucicault reverses the usual gendered relations of power, feminizing the colonizer Claverhouse – 'NORMAN *falls in his [Emmet's] arms weeping'* – and Emmet urges him, 'Come, come, do not let your tears unman me'. (If Claverhouse's tearfulness were not shared by Molineux and the Sergeant we might be tempted to put it down to his Celtic genes; as it is, we must assume that Boucicault wanted to complicate the unemotional English stereotype by sentimentalizing it.) The weeping Claverhouse is overtly substituted for the two women who have loved Emmet – 'ROBERT *embraces* NORMAN *tenderly*' – and says, 'This for Sarah, and this for Tiney. (*Kisses him twice farewell*)'. The naming of Sarah and Tiney legitimates the two kisses: the desire between Emmet and Claverhouse is mediated through the invocation of the absent women. The emotion, however, is in excess of the ostensible object, and only the executioners' volley puts an end to what threatens (or promises) to become a homoerotic embrace. But the transgressive overtones of this *Liebestod* kiss between men are swiftly obscured by Boucicault's patriotic and heterosexual 'sensation' scene: the release of the martyr's spirit from the prison of Kilmainham. Claverhouse is sidelined as the heavens open and the figure of Ireland descends, '*clothed in palest green and with a coronet of shamrocks in her hair*' (397). Everyone loves Emmet, it seems, but his real sweetheart is Ireland herself. The play attempts to seduce the whole audience, both men and women, both English and Irish, into a quasi-erotic relation with the dying hero, and by implication with the cause for which he died.

In his letter to Disraeli, Boucicault described himself disarmingly as 'one who loves his country and its people, and feels that affection to be his only eloquence' (Walsh 139). Even more clearly than Molineux, Norman Claverhouse marks out for an English audience the politics of empathy and affection. Modelling for his compatriots the proper attitude towards Ireland, he offers respect, admiration and love instead of coercion. Indeed, the two British officers, who at every turn express their distaste for the disagreeable actions their colonial duty requires them to perform, represent the 'private virtue' of the English, as opposed to the 'deplorable contempt of public principle' shown by their rulers. Boucicault, who understood the role of popular culture in shaping public opinion better than most of the playwrights of his day, was not content with the easy cheers of a patriotic Irish or Irish-American audience. He also undertook the more difficult task of modifying English prejudices without raising English apprehensions. Successful popular culture is seldom radical enough for the tastes of contemporary commentators, and Boucicault was certainly no revolutionary; but the sentimental desire for a relationship with the English Other manifested in his cross-national homosocial pairings – Shaun with his jailer, Robert with Molineux and Emmet with Claverhouse – powerfully influenced subsequent Irish representations of Englishness. The relationships between the Irishman Larry Doyle and the Englishman Tom Broadbent in Shaw's *John Bull's Other Island* (1904), Owen O'Donnell and George Yolland in Friel's *Translations* (1980) and Jody and Fergus in Jordan's *The Crying Game* (1992) continue to affirm that Irishmen are capable of loving Englishmen while abhorring the British state. Rarely has the compliment been returned.

DECENT CHAPS
Gender, Sexuality, and Englishness in Twentieth-Century Irish Drama and Film

Boucicault's Irish-loving Englishmen were the products of particular histori-cal, economic and theatrical exigencies, as well as of their author's concilia-tory temperament. They were also the product of political wish-fulfilment. Nevertheless, his patterns of heterosexual and homosocial bonding between official enemies provided a durable dramatic model which still has currency in the very different circumstances of today. In Brian Friel's *Translations* (1980) Owen suggests that the Irish are capable of distinguishing an individual Englishman from his imperial mission:

> OWEN. Come on man – speak in English.
> MANUS. For the benefit of the colonist?
> OWEN. He's a decent man.
> MANUS. Aren't they all at some level? (46)

While Manus's irony suggests that to find the decent man inside the colonist one has to dig deep, his cynicism is atypical: many twentieth-century Irish plays and films take Owen's line and depict Englishmen as good fellows at heart. To create affection where an audience might expect antipathy is clever dramaturgy, but more than technique is required to explain the presence of the numerous stage Englishmen who fail to operate as villains even when the piece is anti-colonial, and whose significant Other, whether male or female, is Irish. Neil Jordan's description of 'the friendship that develops between two protagonists in a conflict, that grows paradoxically deeper than any of their other allegiances' (*Crying* viii) may suggest why so many colonizers are repre-sented as decent men.

Decent *men*, naturally. In modern Irish drama and film, Englishness remains almost completely identified with maleness, though not always with masculinity. Virginia Woolf's rhetorical claim, 'as a woman, I have no country' (109), was legally accurate: an Englishwoman lost her British citizenship on marriage to a foreigner. Though Woman may represent Nation, a person whose nationality is provisional cannot be a stable repository of particular national characteristics.[1] Her maternal and domestic qualities are universal and transferable. Forster's *A Passage to India* implies that no male imperialist can match the arrogance and insensitivity of the colonial wife, but English-women like Forster's domineering memsahibs are absent from the Irish stage or screen. Indeed, few Englishwomen appear at all.

Hugh O'Neill's 'New English' wife, Mabel Bagenal, who appears in Friel's *Making History* (1989), is the exception who demonstrates how the rule is constructed. Mabel, the Protestant sister of Queen Elizabeth's Lord Marshal, 'Butcher' Bagenal, deserts her people and her religion to marry the Gaelic chieftain O'Neill. Despite the cultural strains caused by her change of allegiance, and despite her sister's horticultural warnings about the dangers of cross-fertilization (21), Mabel assimilates to her husband's way of life and remains loyal to him after the defeat at Kinsale, although she dies in childbirth before O'Neill flees Ireland for Europe. She is a central character both in Friel's play and in O'Neill's life. But *Making History*, which occasionally sounds like a programmatic dramatization of the ideas of Hayden White, uses Mabel to demonstrate the sacrifice of inconvenient truth to politically expedient narrative. Mabel will be reduced to a footnote in the 'official' story of Hugh O'Neill the Gaelic hero because their mutual love and respect, their cross-fertilization, weakens the binary opposition between the English and the Irish. The nationalist historian Peter Lombard argues persuasively that he must construct a strong fiction in order to energize 'a colonized people on the brink of extinction' (67). The time demands the myth that O'Neill unified the Gaelic clans and founded 'the nation state' (64); Mabel's narrative (like that of many women) is 'the stuff of another history for another time' (67). Mabel's obliteration provides a symbolic paradigm for Irish drama as well as Irish historiography. As we have seen in the previous chapter, the colonial allegory either operates through heterosexual analogy, locating the colonizer in the superior male position and representing the colony as the feminized object of desire and control, or is inscribed on an all-male continuum ranging from the homosocial to the homoerotic. Until we reach the era of Margaret Thatcher, an Englishwoman has no place in this gendered constellation.

In the early years of the twentieth century, before Boucicault's drama fell into the neglect from which it only recovered in the 1970s, his presence in the dramatic repertoire and his influence in Ireland were pervasive. Writers either copied him or, like the Abbey directorate, reacted against him. Bernard Shaw responded critically to Boucicault's stage Irishmen, but *John Bull's Other Island* (1904), his attempt to rewrite *The Shaughraun* with all the stereotypes reversed, paradoxically helped to keep the elder dramatist's inheritance alive. In Shaw's play Boucicault's cross-national homosocial pairings of Ffolliet with Molineux and Emmet with Claverhouse are echoed and intensified in the intimate relationship between the Irishman Larry Doyle and the Englishman Tom Broadbent. Larry and Tom, civil engineers who share lodgings in London, pay a visit to Roscullen, the town of Larry's birth. Under the shadow of a round tower 'quoted' from the first scene of *Arrah-na-Pogue*, Tom falls in love with Nora Reilly, Larry's discarded girlfriend, and the next morning decides to stand as Member of Parliament for Roscullen, a project Larry refuses to undertake. Larry has no objection to the match, and it is clear that Broadbent will win the seat: their friendship continues unabated because Larry will not compete with Tom either sexually or polit-ically. Larry's love for Tom is the most important emotion of his life.

Shaw sets out to explode national stereotypes, and he succeeds best with a bogus stage Irishman, Tim Haffigan, who is briskly dismissed after being exposed as a Glaswegian with incipient delirium tremens and a fraudulent brogue picked up in the theatre.[2] Larry, whose own theory of Irish character is founded on climate and nutrition rather than ethnicity, attacks Matthew Arnold's formulations: 'When people talk about the Celtic race, I feel as if I could burn down London. That sort of rot does more harm than ten Coercion Acts' (908). But Broadbent, who surprises the Irish by referring to himself as a 'Saxon', a term they have never heard, accepts Arnold's notion of English character as prosaic, reserved, and commonsensical, even when his own behaviour flatly contradicts it: 'I think you will accept the fact that I'm an Englishman as a guarantee that I am not a man to act hastily or romantically', he says to Nora (943–4). Since he immediately proposes to a woman he has only just met, the audience knows better. When he thinks that Nora is going to reject him he weeps, insisting in the teeth of the evidence that he is 'a plain unemotional Englishman' (2: 1002). Broadbent, in fact, is a hopeless roman-tic. Shaw acknowledges his debts to Boucicault, but fails to mention that, in his tearfulness, his hibernophilia and his success with an Irish girl, Broadbent is the colonizer as decent chap: a Molineux for the twentieth century.

Indeed, despite Shaw's claim to be dismantling fictions about the English, in many respects Broadbent replicates the 'standard' stage English type. His sentimentality reverses Arnold's equation of Irishness with emotion and Eng-lishness with rationality, and he lacks the supposedly English virtues of com-mon sense and self control. Nevertheless, his xenophobia, masculinity, earnestness, lack of humour, energy, efficiency and ultimate victory confirm Arnold's analysis. His attraction to Ireland does not extend to other foreign lands: he is unapologetically anti-Semitic, and laments that England is now monopolized by 'Germans, Jews, Yankees, foreigners, Park Laners, cos-mopolitan riffraff. Dont call them English' (908). Implicitly endorsing Arnold's characterization of the Irish as an essentially feminine race, and the corresponding view that the English are essentially masculine, he insists that England has 'made a man' of his Irish friend Larry (912), and Larry himself agrees. Nora's refusal may prompt Broadbent's tears, but those tears do not feminize him for long, and when he has finally won her he reverts to mascu-line chivalry and 'confident proprietorship' (1004). The English found the play hilarious, but, as Shaw points out in his Preface, they could afford to. Broad-bent's foolishness is the ideological camouflage of a winner: like the caterpil-lar who 'instinctly [sic] makes itself look exactly like a leaf' (916), Broadbent plays the 'plain' Englishman in order to be an effective predator.

Because he is 'a lover of liberty, like every true Englishman' (897), Broad-bent is a Home Ruler who advocates limited independence for Ireland. Yet he substitutes for overt imperialism a neo-colonial capitalist tourist industry that will subjugate Ireland more thoroughly than the British military ever did. His possession of the land is allegorized by his conquest of Nora, Shaw's ironic version of Yeats and Gregory's Cathleen ní Houlihan.[3] The cynical Larry Doyle disparages the nationalist pretence that Ireland is 'a little old woman', and de-romanticizes Nora by attributing her charm to poor nutrition. For Larry, Nora is '*an everyday woman fit only for the eighteenth century, helpless, useless, almost sexless, an invalid without the excuse of disease, an incarnation of everything in Ireland that drove him out of it*'. Through his overbearing stage directions Shaw ruthlessly deprives her, as he also deprives the '*in no way remarkable*' Aunt Judy and Larry's spiritless father Cornelius, of any claim to ethnic distinctiveness or stage Irish charm (910, 927, 934). For Broadbent, however, she is the essence of Ireland, an ethereal being with harps in her voice, encountered at twilight beside a round tower that neither he nor his first American audiences, who thought it was charming, recognized as Shaw's satirical jab at Boucicault.[4] Irishness is in the eye of the English beholder. In the end Broadbent appropriates both his romantic image and her material environment, on which he intends to build a hotel and a golf course. Through Tom's 'proprietorship' of Nora and the Roscullen estate, Shaw satirizes but ultimately affirms the trope that naturalizes the Union between England and Ireland as a marriage: John Bull proposes successfully to Cathleen ní Houlihan, who would prefer an Irish lover but has to make do with a stage Englishman instead. In a heterosexual reconciliation scenario that recalls *The Shaughraun*, gender assumes allegorical significance,[5] but, unlike Boucicault, for whom the trope was genuinely optimistic, Shaw makes it plain that this marriage is an English business take-over.

Shaw's mockery of the marriage trope is subordinated to his representation of a serious relationship between men. Broadbent and Doyle are '*bachelors and bosom friends*' who work and live together in rooms '*no woman would tolerate*', and whose mutual fondness is constantly reiterated. Larry's preference for aggressive women who take the sexual initiative, 'animated beefsteak[s]' who are 'solid and bouncing and rather keen about him' (893, 1003), suggests that he also plays the passive, feminine role in relation to Tom, who is something of an animated beefsteak himself. Their intimate interdependence easily survives the fact that Nora, who still loves Larry, nevertheless agrees to marry his 'bosom friend'. Although Nora was his first romantic interest, Larry has long since abandoned her; only on her engagement to his friend is the triangular circuit of desire re-established and Larry's affection briefly rekindled: 'I'm an Irishman and he's an Englishman. He wants you; and he grabs you. *I* want you; and I quarrel with you and have to go on wanting you' (1008). This is the first we have heard of Larry's wanting Nora, and he does not want her much; but he describes his relationship with Tom in matrimonial terms:

> LARRY. . . . we must be friends, you and I. I dont want his marriage to you to be his divorce from me.

NORA. You care more for him than you ever did for me.

LARRY. (*with curt sincerity*) Yes of course I do: why should I tell you lies about it? Nora Reilly was a person of very little consequence to me or anyone else outside this miserable little hole. But Mrs Tom Broadbent will be a person of very considerable consequence indeed. (1008–9)

Larry's cold-blooded ceding of Nora to Tom, irrespective of her own desires, demonstrates his preference for homosocial over heterosexual bonds. Tom, who refuses to pursue Nora until he is sure that he is not 'interfering with Larry' (943), operates on the same scale of values. Eve Sedgwick argues that, although in contemporary western society homosociality (men promoting the interests of men) is sharply differentiated from homoeroticism (men loving men), this differentiation is designed to repress and deny 'the potential unbrokenness of a continuum between homosocial and homosexual' desire.[6] Larry embodies this continuum when he speaks as though he and Tom were erotic as well as business partners: 'I don't want his marriage to you to be his divorce from me'.

Shaw's political motivation for situating homosocial desire at the heart of his play, and of Larry's character, is clear. A supporter of Irish self-government, he nevertheless respected the English and advocated a close voluntary relationship between the two nations.[7] Larry's father, the nationalist and separatist Cornelius, is feminized by his colonial subject position, but residence in England and Tom's friendship have 'made a man' of his son Larry. Only the love between men can adequately symbolize political equality: heterosexual love signifies asymmetries of power between men and women. (According to Aristotle, men and women cannot even be friends, since friendship depends upon equality.) Gayle Rubin argues that in many societies relationships between male kinship groups are cemented by 'the traffic in women'.[8] Like Claire in *The Shaughraun*, Nora is a national token exchanged between males to guarantee continued mutual support and profit. An internationalist for whom flags and frontiers are a hindrance, Larry chooses the masculine energy of global capitalism represented by his partnership with Tom over the wilted feminine symbol of Irish particularity. Nora's 'consequence' to the Irishman depends on her relationship to the Englishman, through which 'Nora Reilly' will be subsumed in 'Mrs. Tom Broadbent'.[9] She may insist to Larry that she will keep him out of their new home, but we do not believe her. 'The conquering Englishman' (1010) will insist on Larry's inclusion in a *ménage à trois*.

Shaw is no more enamoured of the coming exploitation of Roscullen by the international leisure and heritage industries than he is of nationalist complaints, but the universalist Catholic socialism propounded by the visionary Peter Keegan provides an unconvincingly Utopian alternative. While Tom and Larry stand condemned as capitalists, the play confusingly endorses their homosocial political alliance: even the censorious Keegan plans to vote for Broadbent. In the absence of the socialist millennium a hotel is inevitable, and the play ends with Larry and Tom setting out together to choose a site for the golf course. (Nora, absent from the scene during the conclusion of the play, is forgotten both by the men on stage and by the audience.) Shaw's desire for co-operation between England and Ireland wars with his socialist presentiment about the exploitative form that such co-operation may take, and his approval of the bond between Larry and Tom clashes with his bleak (and historically accurate) analysis of the tourist prospects of Roscullen, where, Keegan prophesies, 'golf links and hotels [will] bring idlers to a country which workers have left in millions because it is a hungry land, a naked land, an ignorant and oppressed land'. Keegan also predicts that Broadbent will commodify the 'heritage' represented by the round tower, which will be equipped with 'refreshments and penny-in-the-slot mutoscopes to make it interesting' (1018).

Through Broadbent's interest in old stones and the idea of charging admission to the restored tower (a detail anticipated in *The Shaughraun,* where the Ffolliets' ancestral castle can be viewed for sixpence), Shaw suggests that the real audience for the Irish-Ireland movement is the English cultural tourist, and another stage English stereotype, the amateur ethnographer, is born. Boucicault had provided an embryonic folklorist in Captain Molineux, who is fascinated by cultural difference and infuriates Claire by his repeated comments on the bizarre customs of 'you Irish' (*Plays* 311). Boucicault's comic staging of Conn's wake is a piece of mock folklore that anticipates Synge's description of a wake on the Aran Islands, Maurya's keen in *Riders to the Sea,* and the reviving corpse in *The Shadow of the Glen.* No Irish practices have attracted more scholarly attention than the wake and its attendant keen: Maria Edgeworth's long antiquarian footnotes in *Castle Rackrent* and Sydney Owenson's shorter ones in *The Wild Irish Girl* attest to their importance in any ethnographic definition of 'Irishness'. The wake's 'festive solemnity', as the puzzled Molineux calls it, mingles 'whiskey, and cakes, and consolation, and fiddlers, and grief, and meat and drink for the poor'. In a Heisenbergian irony, this 'melancholy . . . entertainment' is literally produced by the English observer, the Captain, whose gift of 'five golden pounds' pays for the whole performance, and whose bemused comments underline the 'quaintness' of the primitive rite his money has called into being (*Plays* 311, 317, 310).

Unlike Molineux, whose curiosity and comparative spirit are relatively untutored, his descendant Broadbent has the benefit of the Celtic Revival to guide his observations. He comes to Roscullen with field-glasses and Murray's guidebook in hand, determined to admire such distinctively Irish sights as 'Finian's die-cast' (Shaw 932), a large rock about which the locals themselves are unrepentantly uninformed. He gives a peculiarly ethnic explanation for his antiquarian romanticism: 'as a stranger and an Englishman, I thought it would be interesting to see the Round Tower by moonlight' (940). The local people have no such interest. Round towers competed with wakes as the focus of antiquarian enquiry, and Broadbent is eager to join the debate about their function. Father Dempsey, hastily forestalling discussion of the theory that they were phallic symbols (by no means the most exotic of the many speculations as to their origin), shuts down the argument: they were, he says, 'forefingers of the early Church, pointing us all to God' (933).

Shaw's stage English ethnographer takes an influential detour into the novel in the person of James Joyce's 'ponderous Saxon' Haines, the Oxford-educated Gaelic-speaking collector of folklore who 'thinks we ought to speak Irish in Ireland' and does so himself, much to the amazement of the anglophone natives, who cannot understand a word he says (*Ulysses* 1.51, 431–2). Joyce's portrait of Haines lacks the tone of indulgent amusement with which Boucicault and Shaw depict the primitivist enthusiasms of their English characters. For Stephen, the Englishman as cultural tourist embodies the epistemological (rather than physical) dynamic of the imperial encounter: the colonizer observes and thus subjugates the colonized object of knowledge. The Martello Tower in which Haines visits Stephen and Buck Mulligan in the first chapter of *Ulysses* stands in political opposition to the round towers that dominate the landscape of Roscullen and emblematize 'Romantic Ireland' in Boucicault's patriotic drama of 1798. Built in the 1790s to prevent the French navy from coming to the assistance of Irish rebels, the squat Martello Tower marks not the fantasy of exotic Irish origins, but the failure of the Irish uprising and the foundering of romantic hopes.

In Stephen's imagination, Haines, whose Imperial credentials are established by the fact that his unconscious is populated by panthers and 'His old fellow made his tin selling jalap to Zulus' (1.156), is connected with Matthew Arnold, who advocated the establishment of a Chair of Celtic Studies at Oxford so that the Celt might be produced as an object of investigation and preserved in a museum. Arnold, who was never a don himself, appears in an Oxford quadrangle as a servant. 'A deaf gardener, aproned, masked with Matthew Arnold's face, pushes his mower on the sombre lawn', while the moneyed English upper classes strip off each other's trousers in an outburst of homosocial enthusiasm (1.172–4). Haines has acquired from his Arnoldian studies at Oxford a 'portfolio full of Celtic literature' (14.1013) and a predictable set of stage Irish stereotypes. Malachi Mulligan wants Stephen to embody them; failing that, he is determined to act them out himself. 'Smiling at wild Irish', Haines is the perfect audience, obtuse enough to be taken in by Mulligan's satirical antics, rich enough to be useful. But his lack of intellectual discrimination does not disable his authority, which is based upon the Empire that is one of Stephen's 'two masters'. Although Samuel Chenevix Trench, the model for Haines, was an Anglo-Irish nationalist sympathizer (Ellmann 179), Joyce turns him into a stage imperialist: 'Eyes, pale as the sea the wind had freshened, paler, firm and prudent. The seas' ruler, he gazed southward over the bay' (1.573–4). Though firm, he is 'not all unkind' (1.635), and naturally he is decent enough to acknowledge that 'We feel in England that we have treated you rather unfairly'. Nevertheless, he is unwilling to take personal responsibility, for 'It seems history is to blame' (1.648–9). More repulsively, he shares Broadbent's xenophobia and anti-Semitism: 'Of course I'm a Britisher, Haines voice said, and I feel as one. I don't want to see my country fall into the hands of German jews either. That's our national problem, I'm afraid, just now' (1.666–8).

Haines's role in the opening section of *Ulysses* is not to bond with an Irish man or woman, but to disrupt the homosocial relationship between Stephen, who refuses to flatter his preconceptions by playing 'wild Irish', and Mulligan, the 'gay betrayer' (1.405), who will do anything for English money. Vincent Cheng describes Mulligan as the 'native informant' who panders to the ethnographic curiosity of the colonizer.[10] He also occupies the structural role of the treacherous 'native informer' in Irish melodrama: he would sell the conscience of his race for Saxon guineas. In this uneasy all-male triangle the Englishman Haines is the rival, the stranger in the house, the reason that Stephen, though he has paid the rent, will not return to the tower that night. Stephen reflects that his smile, like the 'smile of a Saxon' in the old proverb, is not to be trusted, and the last word of the opening chapter, 'Usurper', applies to him as well as to Mulligan. Joyce frames Haines's usurpation in the language of erotic betrayal:

> – Tell me, Mulligan, Stephen said quietly.
> – Yes, my love?
> – How long is Haines going to stay in this tower? (1.47–49)

Mulligan's ironic and feminine 'Yes, my love' suggests that Haines's visit threatens to disrupt a quasi-conjugal tie. In 'The Oxen of the Sun' Stephen conflates the national and sexual implications of the territorial struggle between the three young men:

> Bring a stranger within thy tower it will go hard but thou wilt have the secondbest bed. . . . Remember, Erin, thy generations and thy days of old, how thou settedst little by me and by my word and broughtedst in a stranger to my gates to commit fornication in my sight . . . forget me not, O Milesian. Why has thou done this abomination before me that thou didst spurn me for a merchant of jalaps. (14.365–73)

Yeats and Gregory's Cathleen ní Houlihan complained of too many strangers in the house; Haines the 'stranger', son of the 'merchant of jalaps', is a synecdoche for the Empire in Ireland, which relegates the rightful owners to the 'secondbest bed'.

The phrase 'secondbest bed' also evokes Stephen's theory that the plot of *Hamlet* encodes the story of Ann Hathaway's sexual betrayal of Shakespeare with his brother. Haines occupies an analogical position in that narrative too. When he arrives at the lying-in hospital, he is carrying not only his portfolio of Celtic literature but a 'phial marked *Poison*'. This phial identifies him with the 'usurper' Claudius, who combined political with erotic treason by poisoning

Hamlet's father, marrying his mother and taking his place on the throne of Denmark (14.1013–14). Although at first blush Mulligan is a somewhat unlikely stand-in for Ann Hathaway/Gertrude, in this Shakespearean structure of male desire the 'gay betrayer' occupies the role of faithless wife, Haines is the adulterous and murderous brother and Stephen the dispossessed son.

Joyce's English hibernophile, then, is much more overtly imperialist than Shaw's. While Broadbent, despite his economic and sexual conquests at Larry's expense, is viewed with affection and respect by his Irish partner, there is no bond between Stephen and Haines. Indeed, Enda Duffy suggests that Stephen's attitude to Haines is reverse racism (40–52), and Emer Nolan thinks Stephen's attitude is Joyce's own (52). Stephen is not the only voice in the novel, however. Leopold Bloom advocates tolerance towards the English: 'It's a patent absurdity on the face of it to hate people because they live round the corner and speak another vernacular', he says, and he would like to 'try to make the best of both countries even though poles apart' (*Ulysses* 16.1101–3, 1039–40). Nevertheless Bloom's good-hearted middle-of-the-road views remain theoretical and disembodied, while Joyce's concrete representation of Haines prevents the reader from harbouring too many illusions about the 'decency' of the conqueror. Haines is a Broadbent without a heart, and his relation with Mulligan betrays and excludes Stephen.

Haines, the stage Englishman of the Irish novel, provides an important non-theatrical link between Boucicault and Shaw and later Irish dramatists. In Brendan Behan's *The Hostage* (1958) he is reincarnated as Monsewer, a crazy Arnoldian Anglo-Irishman who owns a brothel in Dublin that he fondly imagines to be an IRA safe house. Monsewer was born and raised in England until 'one day he discovered he was an Irishman' (*An Giall* 92). Renouncing his father's English family in favour of his mother's Irish one, he donned a kilt, played Gaelic football on Blackheath, took a correspondence course in Irish and finally came to Ireland to join the rebels in the Easter Rising and the War of Independence, becoming more Hibernian than the Hibernians themselves. Since the defeat of the Republicans in the Civil War he has been living in the past, nurturing political and linguistic aspirations that Behan regards as totally unrealistic:

> MONSEWER. And as we Irish say, 'It's one after another they built the castles. Iss in yeeg a Kale-ah shah togeock nuh cashlawn'.
> PAT. [*To the audience*] Do you hear that? That's Irish. It's a great thing, an Oxford University education! Me, I'm only a poor ignorant Dublin man. I wouldn't understand a word of it. (86)

Pat, Monsewer's cynical sidekick, exposes the futility of a patronizing foreigner's desire to give back to the Irish a language that they have already abandoned. Behan here re-stages Haines's encounter with the old milk woman, who is 'ashamed I don't speak the language myself. I'm told it's a grand language by them that knows' (*Ulysses* 1.433–44). Behan pushes Monsewer's linguistic obsession to farcical lengths: at one time he refused to speak anything but Irish, and therefore needed an interpreter to accompany him on the Dublin buses (*An Giall* 90).

Nevertheless, Pat's account of Monsewer's nation-change suggests that the transplant has not fully taken: 'Monsewer is terrible strict and honest. You see, he's an Englishman' (92). While Haines confines his nationalist fashion statements to the emerald on his cigarette case, Monsewer attempts total sartorial identification with his adopted country. Yet he cannot camouflage his original Englishness: he makes his first appearance '*looking like Baden Powell in an Irish kilt and flowing cloak*' and playing horribly on the bagpipes (85). Pat explains to the other inmates of the brothel that despite the kilt and the bagpipes Monsewer was 'born an Englishman, remained one for years. His father was a bishop'. To dispel the shocking aura of sexual irregularity produced by the connection of bishops with fatherhood (shocking in the fifties, that is; now we know better), Pat informs his audience that Monsewer's father was a *Protestant* bishop. Without missing a beat his 'wife' Meg suggests a different type of sexual deviance, one particularly associated with English public schools and the upper classes who attended them:

> PAT. He went to all the biggest colleges in England and slept in the one room with the King of England's son.
> MEG. Begad, it wouldn't surprise me if he slept in the one bed with him, his father being a bishop.
> PAT. Yes, he had every class of comfort, mixed with dukes, marquises, earls and lords.
> MEG. All sleeping in the one room, I suppose?
> ROPEEN. In the one bed. (92)

Behan runs together the last two items in Joyce's catalogue of English national characteristics: 'Beer, beef, business, bibles, bulldogs, battleships, buggery and bishops' (*Ulysses* 14.1459–60).

The stage direction comparing Monsewer to Baden Powell, founder of the Boy Scout movement, reinforces this homosexual in-joke. Monsewer anticipates the martyrdom of an eighteen-year-old IRA volunteer in terms that echo the sacrificial rhetoric of Padraig Pearse, who had his own Boy Scout troop: 'I would give anything to stand in that young man's place tomorrow morning. For Ireland's sake I would hang crucified in the town square'. Behan's distaste for such rhetoric informs Pat's sardonic response, 'Let's hope it would be a fine day for you' (*An Giall* 113). Monsewer's resemblance to both Pearse and Baden Powell implies that an extreme nationalist is the mirror image of the quintessential imperialist: this stage Irishman is just a stage Englishman in drag. Haines and Monsewer invest in aspects of Irish identity that belong to the real or the invented past, while the Irish people themselves are eager to move on. Taken together, these characters suggest that from an Irish perspective it is better to be despised than to be imitated.

Indeed, the study of the Irish language may represent not simply an over-identification with the victim, as in Monsewer's case, but a counter-terrorist strategy. Arnold recommended cultural vigilance as a political tool: 'what we want is to *know* the Celt and his genius' (*Lectures* 328). In her film *Hush-a-Bye Baby* (1989), Margot Harkin takes an Arnoldian line on the Irish-speaking Englishman: she represents mastery of the local language as a conscious infiltration by the colonizer, a method of surveillance and intimidation. Since the outbreak of the present Troubles in the North of Ireland, the Irish language has become both a marker of nationalist identity and a resource for IRA prisoners who need a method of communication that is not understood by their jailers. In a witty scene that nevertheless offended many nationalists, the IRA sympathizer Ciaran, a student of Irish, tries to impress his girlfriend Goretti by taunting an impassive British soldier with a meaningless recitation of the names of state-supported Southern enterprises: Bord Fáilte, Aer Lingus, Bord na Móna. When he concludes with the Republican slogan *tiocfaidh ár lá* (our day will come), the soldier demands in fluent Irish, 'Tell me what impact the Troubles have had on Irish social, political, and economic life?' and the stunned Ciaran is unable to frame a reply. Like Haines and Monsewer, the Englishman speaks much better Irish than the locals. Placed in an inferior position by this unexpected linguistic competence, Ciaran is reduced to patronizing Goretti: 'You wouldn't understand what we were saying'. Although it is possible that British army intelligence offered crash courses in Irish to selected Belfast-bound soldiers, Harkin's Irish-speaking squaddie probably owes more to literary tradition than to the streets of Derry.

Broadbent, Haines and Monsewer are middle or upper-middle class. The working-class stage Englishman, whose genealogy may be traced to the valet Winterbottom and the kind-hearted sergeant in Boucicault's *Arrah-na-Pogue*, plays a different and increasingly important part in twentieth-century Irish drama. His development reveals the extent to which the most obvious characteristics of stage Englishness properly belong not only to males, but also to the bourgeoisie. The imperturbable, discreet and self-effacing butler, a shadow of the gentleman whom he serves, and thus the 'gentleman's gentleman', has long been a useful prop on the English stage and screen: P. G. Wodehouse made an industry out of Jeeves (In Kazuo Ishiguro's *The Remains of the Day* the butler becomes emblematic of an outmoded Englishness, sacrificing individuality and personal emotion to an absolute ideal of service but failing to judge the morality of the political ends to which that service is dedicated.) Boucicault's Winterbottom, the gentleman's gentleman of the Secretary at Dublin Castle, is a stolidly superior alien in a country full of excitable people. When his master urges him to get some sleep, he replies pompously: 'No Hinglishman hexpects hanny, my lord, in this country. It keeps us hall hup, and continually deprives Hingland of her natural rest . . . (*aside*) I 'ope the gentleman will take the 'int' (*Arrah* 158). (His misplaced aspirates are the English equivalent of the brogue.) He spends the remainder of the scene being summoned from his bed by a sequence of agitated Irish visitors. Broadbent's valet Hodson is similarly condescending about the possibility of getting a decent night's sleep in such an uncivilized place: 'One expects to rough it here, sir' (Shaw 947). Like Claire and Molineux, the English and the Irish are separated by a common language: Winterbottom has to suffer the indignity of being addressed as Summerbottom, and Broadbent gets no porridge because, as Hodson explains, those ignorant Irish don't know how to describe it: 'They call it stirabout, sir . . . They know no better' (948).

The superior Winterbottom is no more than a tiny comic sketch, but Shaw develops Hodson in some depth. To Broadbent's query, 'How do you like the Irish, Hodson?' he replies, 'Well, sir, they're all right anywhere but in their own country. I've known lots of em in England, and generally liked em. But here, sir, I seem simply to hate em' (947). The peasant proprietor Matt Haffigan's laments about injustice and starvation in Ireland cause Hodson's hatred to boil over: he drops his 'gentleman's gentleman' accent and emerges as a stage cockney with a red-hot class agenda:

> [W]hen Oi think of the things we Englishmen as to pat ap with, and eah you Awrish ahlin abaht your silly little grievances, and see the wy you mike it worse for haz by the rotten wiges youll cam over and tike and the rotten plices youll sleep in, I jast feel that I could tike the aowl bloomin British awland and mike you a present of it, jast to let you fawnd aht wot reel awdship's lawk. (975)

This outburst is uncharacteristic of the imperturbable stage butler, who is trained not to share his real opinions. Shaw pulls off Hodson's vocational mask to reveal not only his local accent but also the contradiction between class and national loyalties. He supports Home Rule for xenophobic reasons; he wants parliament to reform the condition of England rather than being continually distracted by her troublesome neighbour: 'I'm just sick of Awrland. Let it gow. Cat the caible' (975). Shaw intends Hodson's argument to attract our sympathy; he saw that, while the British bourgeoisie reaped the economic benefits of imperialism, English workers, the victims of internal class oppression, got little out of it but spurious national pride. We learn that Hodson's wife died of pneumonia when they were evicted from their lodgings for being four weeks behind on the rent. Starving Irish immigrants caused already disastrous conditions in the English slums to deteriorate further: Hodson's analysis of the depressing effect of their competition on the wages of English workers comes straight out of the writings of Friedrich Engels.

Frank McGuinness also explores the connection between Engels, Ireland and the English working classes in his play *Mary and Lizzie* (1989). Winterbottom the butler and Hodson the stage cockney play roles in which class is important but gender has no part. McGuinness combines an awareness of class disparities with the familiar romance between an English male and an Irish female; his variation on the normal pattern is that there are two females instead of only one. He imaginatively re-creates the long-enduring relationship between Engels the wealthy socialist theoretician and the two poor Irishwomen who were his lovers. 'They showed him the poor and they showed him their father and they showed their race and themselves to him', says Lizzie (32). Despite his intimate knowledge of Mary and Lizzie, and genuine indignation about the condition of the poor, Engels, an ethnographer of the slums, was still capable of reproducing the familiar stage Irish caricature. Marx's embittered wife Jenny reads the Burns sisters some of Engels's most racist descriptions of their countrymen:

> 'With such a competitor the English working man has to struggle, with a competitor on the lowest plane possible in a civilized country, who for this reason requires less wages than any other. All such as demand little or no skill are open to the Irish. For work which requires long training or regular, pertinacious application, the dissolute, unsteady, drunken Irishman is on too low a plane'.
>
> (*Mary and Lizzie* 40)

When they hear what he has written, Mary and Lizzie tell Engels that he has failed them. As 'native informants' they showed him the Irish slums of Manchester not so that he could denigrate their 'race' as barbarians, but so that he could defend all the poor, English and Irish alike. McGuinness's Engels, though he is a bourgeois male who lives and works in Manchester, is not a genuine stage Englishman (for one thing he was German by origin), but his stance as a superior observer transforms his female lovers into objects of sociological inquiry, and thus suggests his structural relationship to Joyce's Haines. He has betrayed the destitute Irishwomen who trusted him and, although they forgive him, the audience is prompted to feel that scientific socialism, like the imperialism to which it is ostensibly opposed, has little to offer the Irish 'race'. Paradoxically, the real Friederich Engels welcomed the effect of Irish immigrants on the British working classes: he thought that, by making conditions for both groups absolutely intolerable, the immigrants would hasten the revolution, which their choleric temperaments would also help to foment.[11] In the hope of future social justice, he consigned to oblivion those who were suffering in the present. He was, in any case, wrong: in 1914 European workers rallied to the imagined communities of their different nations, rather than to the economic interests of their class. Despite having *The Condition of the Working Class in England* in his pocket, Shaw's Hodson would probably have been one of the first to join up.

Following in the tradition of Boucicault even as it revised him, *John Bull's Other Island* set a precedent for those later Irish writers who stressed fundamental similarities rather than local differences between the English and the Irish. Often these writers were socialist in sympathies and were attracted to the idea of universal brotherhood and the repudiation of essentialist racial or cultural nationalism. Both O'Casey and Behan, who were sceptical about the ethnic particularity of the Celtic Revival, admired Shaw's play. O'Casey's *The Plough and the Stars* (1926), which is set in 1916 during the Easter Rising and World War I, introduces an affable British Tommy for the specific purpose of demonstrating the dangerous supremacy of national over class loyalties. When an Englishman's patriotic duty calls, his internationalism is forgotten. The doctrinaire Irish socialist The Covey tries to explain to Corporal Stoddart why his presence in Ireland is a betrayal of his own interests and a rejection of his class:

> THE COVEY. . . . D'ye know, comrade, that more die o' consumption than are killed in th' wars? An' it's all because of th' system we're livin' undher?
> CORPORAL STODDART. Ow, I know. I'm a Sowcialist moiself, but I 'as to do my dooty.
> THE COVEY. (ironically) Dooty! Th' only dooty of a Socialist is th' emancipation of th' workers.
> CORPORAL STODDART. Ow, a man's a man, an 'e 'as to foight for 'is country, 'asn't 'e?
> FLUTHER. (aggressively) You're not fightin' for your counthry here, are you?
> . . .
> THE COVEY. Fight for your counthry! Did y'ever read, comrade, Jenersky's *Thesis on the Origin, Development, an' Consolidation of th' Evolutionary Idea of the Proletariat*?
> CORPORAL STODDART. Ow, cheese it, Paddy, cheese it! (*Three Plays* 208–9)

Stoddart conventionally equates English patriotism with virility ('a man's a man, an 'e 'as to foight for 'is country'), and Fluther does not disagree; he simply denies that Stoddart's present task, the putting down of the Easter Rising, amounts to fighting for his country. His challenge, which implies that Stoddart would really be defending his country were he in the trenches with Bessie Burgess's son and the Dublin Fusiliers, is more effective than The Covey's insistence on abstract socialist theory, which has been a running joke throughout the play.

Stoddart is merely a bit part, a briefer version of the sergeant in *Arrah-na-Pogue* who was as kind as his duty and the regulations permitted him to be. Though he calls himself a socialist, his three watchwords, patriotism, manliness and duty, ally him to the English officers he serves, not to the lower-class Irishman whose beliefs he supposedly shares. Despite this failure of solidarity, O'Casey is not unsympathetic to his English Tommy, who treats the locals with friendly condescension rather than outright brutality. As the final attack on the General Post Office begins in the background, Corporal Stoddart and Sergeant Tinley end the play alone on stage with the corpse of Bessie Burgess, whom they have just accidentally shot. They sip a cup of tea made by the mad Nora for the dead Jack and sing the famous World War I song, 'Keep the Home Fires Burning'. Although this overloaded tableau may suggest 'a fiercely satiric image of colonial occupation',[12] Stoddart and Tinley are Tommies, not the drunken and brutal Auxiliaries of *The Shadow of a Gunman*. (The distinction between Tommies, working-class lads who were just doing their job, and Tans or Auxies, who were noted for their gratuitous cruelty, is routinely preserved in Irish writing: it provides another version of Boucicault's good Englishman/bad Englishman routine.)[13] In shooting Bessie the Tommies have scored an own goal, for Bessie was no Shinner but a loyal Unionist.[14] (A contemporary Unionist might find O'Casey's irony prophetic.) The words of their song reinforce Stoddart's association between manliness and patriotism, 'the country found 'em ready / At the stirring call for men', and urges women to keep the domestic hearth warm, 'Til the boys come 'owme' (*Three Plays* 218). We know that Bessie's boy is coming back from the front, but, thanks to these English soldiers on whose side he has been fighting, her home fire will not be burning for him. Since the two Tommies are sitting in Dublin rather than Flanders, moreover, the idea of going home anticipates not the return from the trenches, but the British military withdrawal from Irish soil which was to follow five years later. The English may be winning this particular battle, but they will lose the Irish war.

The Treaty of 1922, which radically changed political relations between the two islands, did not immediately transform Irish representations of English males, although it conditioned their tone and questioned the equation of Englishness with success. Even *British* representations of Englishmen in Ireland borrowed from and replenished existing Irish tradition. After the War and the Troubles, the increased popularity of cinema and the lack of an indigenous film industry meant that Irish audiences, who transferred their allegiance from Boucicauldian melodrama to its cinematic successor, became dependent on American and British representations of Ireland. In *Ryan's Daughter* (1970), set in the South of Ireland just after the Easter Rising, English director David Lean and scriptwriter Robert Bolt re-create the cross-national erotic triangle popularized by Boucicault and Shaw. Posted to a small community on the south-west coast of Ireland after the failure of the Rising, the upper-class British officer Major Doryan replaces the local schoolteacher in the affections of his wife Rosie. While Claire has no previous sexual loyalties to prevent her marrying Molineux, Claverhouse refuses to compete with Emmet for Sarah's love, and Larry willingly cedes his rights in Nora to Tom Broadbent, Rosie's affair with Major Doryan produces an adulterous love triangle that is bound to end badly for someone. The stage Englishman's desire for an Irish girl is no longer a figure for national reconciliation: it means the betrayal of community pride and the humiliation of a kindly and patient Irish husband. The situation recalls the eighteenth-century *aisling*, in which the woman who is Ireland laments her rape by the English military invader, but the spoiled and dissatisfied Rosie, who finds her husband dull and her village provincial, is not complaining.

Although Lean chose the Irish setting simply because it was remote and picturesque, Bolt, who had already written the screenplay for *Lawrence of*

Arabia and would go on to write *Gandhi*, had a liberal anti-imperialist agenda. He uses the script of *Ryan's Daughter* to represent the end of Empire and the decay of the landed gentry. Major Doryan, whose snapshots reveal that his family owns a castle, is a formulaic repressed stage Englishman. If the Irish talk a lot, the handsome Major hardly talks at all, and his most high-affect gesture consists in tapping his cigarette on his talismanic silver cigarette case as a preliminary to lighting up. (In cinema the cigarette frequently serves as a silent mediator between enemy males, but, while Stephen accepts Haines's cigarettes, the IRA man whom Doryan captures refuses them.) The taciturn reserve of the 'crippled bloody hero' results from shellshock, and the stiff upper lip hides a shattered psyche. World War I and the Easter Rising have cracked the façade of English imperturbability: unlike the winner Broadbent, this English outsider in Ireland maintains a fragile equilibrium within a history that is no longer unequivocally on his side. Although his passion for Rosie fails to loosen his tongue, it liberates other parts: unusually for an Englishman he seems to be good in bed – or rather, on the turf, since all the sex, improbably enough in Ireland, takes place out of doors. Despite the overblown poeticism of Lean's thrashing leaves and drifting dandelion seeds, however, sex between political enemies cannot closet itself within an idyllic 'natural' space. Rosie's adultery, inadvertently betrayed by the mute idiot Michael, who adores her, is resented by the villagers as a national as well as a sexual transgression. To them, she is a 'British soldier's whore', and they assume that her erotic treachery has political dimensions, blaming her for the betrayal of IRA weapons and men. (The real traitor is her father, who joins the long and dishonourable line of Irish informers.) Although Lean and Bolt represent the villagers at their best when they join forces to recover German arms floated ashore during a massive storm, the community becomes a lynch mob when they turn on Rosie, stripping off her clothes and cropping her hair. Rosie's humiliation is a version of the tarring and feathering that was to become commonplace during the Northern Troubles, a savage response to a woman who undermines her nation's masculinity by sleeping with the enemy. Seamus Heaney's poem 'Punishment' captures the disturbing conflation of sexuality and politics in this 'exact / and tribal, intimate revenge' (*North* 38). Rosie's punishment reveals the impossibility of transnational romance in such charged historical circumstances. With impeccably English good manners, Major Doryan removes himself from an awkward situation by blowing himself up, and Rosie returns to her long-suffering Irish husband.

Although it is motivated not by politics but by Rosie's ending of their affair, Major Doryan's climactic withdrawal from the plot, like the end of *The Plough and the Stars*, prefigures the British retreat from Ireland.[15] His last moments, like his last cigarettes, are shared with the mute Michael, a character who manages to be in turn cruel, pathetic and threatening. Michael's twisted body and grotesque features (a triumph of stage make-up and physical control by the English actor John Mills, who won an Oscar for his performance) deliberately recall the simian Paddy of post-Fenian, post-Darwinian Victorian cartoons,[16] but his muteness and mental incapacity render him innocent of the harm he commits. Peter Brooks highlights the 'text of muteness' in Victorian melodrama, claiming that 'extreme physical conditions . . . represent extreme moral and emotional conditions', and that mute characters evoke 'the extremism and hyperbole of ethical conflict and manichaeistic struggle' (56). In *Ryan's Daughter* Michael's body can be read as a Wildean 'picture' that silently records Irish suffering at the hands of the English. A silhouette shot in which the jerky, prognathous Caliban walks behind the crippled Major reveals that their limps are identical: both characters are physically and emotionally maimed. Michael's frightening ugliness is the portrait in the attic on which the appropriately named Doryan's accumulated historical transgressions are inscribed. Fittingly, it is Michael whose parodic parade down the street wearing Doryan's medal draws attention to his illicit affair, and Michael who seals his fate. Identified in silhouette with the handsome 'screen' Englishman, his grotesque doppelganger, the mute screen Irishman, shows his gratitude for the cigarettes by leading Major Doryan to a box of dynamite washed ashore during the German arms shipment to the rebels. Misunderstanding the Major's warning demonstration that the fuses are live, however, he runs away, pursued by Doryan's last words, 'I thought we were friends'. A similar appeal from Fielding the Englishman to the Indian Aziz at the end of E. M. Forster's *A Passage to India*, 'Why can't we be friends now?' is definitively answered: 'No, not yet' (362). Waiting until the sun sets (possibly upon the British Empire), Major Doryan kills himself by detonating the dynamite procured for him by the film's most extreme caricature of Irishness. His tentative intimacy with Michael only hastens his destruction.

The timing of *Ryan's Daughter* was fortuitous, but its pessimism about English/Irish relations was instantly proved accurate. It was shot during the civil rights agitation in the North of Ireland, and released in 1970, after the British army had returned to the province in the summer of 1969. Through its treatment of the aftermath of the 1916 Rising it foregrounded contemporary issues of colonial occupation, fraternization and gunrunning. Sophisticated Irish critics disliked the film's Oscar-winning cinematography, which dwarfed political issues by its long-drawn-out attention to spectacular western landscapes; nevertheless *Ryan's Daughter* was a popular success in Ireland, and ran for a year in Dublin (Rockett, 'Irish Film Studio' 113). Whether or not Brian Friel saw it, *Translations* (1980) displays a similar debt to Boucicault and Shaw, and is structured upon an identical erotic triangle – the British officer Yolland displaces the Irish schoolmaster Manus in the heart of the 'colleen' Maire – and the community, personified by the invisible Donnelly twins and the mute Sarah (who plays exactly the same role in Friel's plot as the mute Michael does in Bolt's), exposes and punishes their exogamous love. At the end the Englishman dies, the Irishman is on the run and the colleen will soon emigrate. Although the play is set in 1833, it was written and must be read in the context of the Northern Troubles,[17] which explain both Friel's departures from historical accuracy and his modifications of dramatic tradition. In 1980 Boucicault's optimistic vision of a decent English officer marrying an Irishwoman was no longer viable.

Directly descended from Molineux and Broadbent, Yolland comes to Ireland not as a colonizer but more or less by mistake (he missed the boat for Bombay, enlisted to avoid the wrath of his imperialist father and was sent over to take part in the Ordnance Survey project) and falls in love immediately. He is enchanted by the countryside, by the language and, inevitably, by an Irishwoman. His Irish friend Owen introduces him to the villagers of Baile Beag as a pre-existing dramatic stereotype, 'a committed Hibernophile', something of a joke (*Translations* 32). Despite this, Friel goes to great pains to make him lovable. Using an old trick from *Arrah-na-Pogue*, he contrasts Yolland's naive innocence and good faith with the cold efficiency of the 'ramrod' Lancey, his superior officer and 'the perfect colonial servant' (39). Lancey, uneasy among the 'foreigners' and quite happy to contemplate their extermination, is a dead ringer for Major Coffin, while Yolland is the epitome of English 'decency': polite, apologetic, awkward and initially reluctant to speak. He has none of Haines's patronizing gestures: he is humbled by his inability to communicate, and he understands his presence to be an intrusion that alters the world with which he has fallen in love. Irish nationalist audiences could displace their hostility to colonialism onto Lancey, or George's absent father, while retaining empathy with Yolland; British audiences could flatter themselves that Yolland was the 'real' Englishman.

Friel reverses Arnold's stereotypes in the manner of Bernard Shaw. Like Broadbent, Yolland is a 'bloody romantic' who once saw Wordsworth plain, and an incorrigible sentimentalist: he imagines the West of Ireland as another Eden (*Translations* 38).[18] Although he loves Maire, they cannot understand each other, and his most sustained relationship is with the Irishman Owen, who, in his cleverness, efficiency, cynicism, preference for English employers and lack of heterosexual enthusiasm, resembles Larry Doyle. Their long scene together at the beginning of Act Two, in which Owen briskly goes about the task of anglicizing the Irish names while Yolland tentatively tries on a new Irish personality (he is better at drinking poteen than at pronouncing Bun na hAbhann), is longer and more substantial than his famous love scene with Maire. Richard Pine describes their drunken collaboration on the new map as a 'symbolic . . . embrace' (*Friel* 176), while Kearney calls it 'an exchange of identity' (*Transitions* 137). When Owen reclaims his Irish name ('It was never Roland?') they explode in joyful laughter, overlapping lines and syllables until their names fuse into 'Oland'. So genuine is Yolland's intuitive identification with his friend's birthplace that Friel permits him to voice the suspicion of the colonial enterprise that properly belongs to the Irishman. (An Englishman who argues against colonial proceedings is counter-intuitive, and therefore dramatically effective.) At first Yolland wants to leave the placenames alone simply on the grounds of euphony: 'there's no English equivalent for a sound like that' (*Translations* 35). After his discussion of language with Owen's father Hugh, however, his resistance to the re-mapping increases, and he calls the name changing 'an eviction of sorts', asserting that 'Something is being eroded'. (His insight is, ironically, borne out by Lancey's threat of real evictions at the end of the play.) To resist this erosion, he insists that the Irish tradition of *dinnseanchas* be respected by retaining the name 'Tobair Vree' in order to 'keep piety with a man long dead' (43–4).

Although he is a British soldier, then, Yolland's potential relation to Ireland is far less damaging than Broadbent's, and his hibernophilia is neither appropriative like Haines's, nor manic like Monsewer's. But while he would never have built a hotel or a golf course, Yolland might well have bought a quaint Irish cottage and painted the door a clichéed emerald green, like John Wayne in *The Quiet Man*. The romantic Englishman who falls in love with a mythical Irish past may be relatively attractive, like Broadbent and Yolland, or sinister, like Haines and Monsewer, but he is usually a comic and always a slightly suspect figure. Yolland does not understand Hugh's realistic warnings about the danger of imprisonment in fossilized linguistic contours, of which the name Tobair Vree is an excellent example. (The name means Brian's well: Brian is forgotten and the well is no longer there.) Although he falls in love with the countryside and wants to stay there 'always', he fails to appreciate the narrowness and poverty that drive Maire towards the emigrant ship and the English language. The famous scene in which they communicate their love through the recitation of Irish placenames seems idyllic at first, but it ends in total misunderstanding: Yolland insists that he will never leave, while Maire begs him to 'Take me away' (52). Like Larry Doyle, she sees no romance in the parochial Irish life that to Yolland appears Edenic: to her the names of *English* villages – Winfarthing, Barton Bendish, Saxingham Nethergate – represent the exotic Other. Even after Yolland's death she persists in her desire to speak English, though she will be doing it in Brooklyn rather than Barton Bendish.

Yolland is not represented as sexually culpable in beginning the romance that leads to his death: he has no idea of any pre-existing agreement between Maire and her Irish suitor, the lame schoolmaster Manus. Friel softens Maire's change of allegiance from Manus to Yolland by making her decide to leave Baile Beag for America before she first encounters the Englishman: in her own eyes she is already a free woman. Yet the aura of national betrayal that accompanied Rosie's adultery with Major Doryan also hangs over the relationship between Maire and Yolland. Yolland is handsome, optimistic and physically whole; he seems to have the power of the British Empire behind him and the future on his side. Manus is crippled in body, economically at a disadvantage and fully identified with an Irish way of life whose passing has already been signalled by Daniel O'Connell, the new National School and the activities of the English mapmakers. His one hope for economic survival is a job on the Aran Islands, in what will become the Irish-speaking margins. Friel has said

that Manus's lameness, like Sarah's muteness and Hugh's alcoholism, figures
the deprivation of the doomed community (quoted in Richtarik, *Acting* 49).
Given the apparent imbalance of advantage between Yolland and Manus, the
former's easy appropriation of Maire's affections looks to the local people like
a cynical and demystified enactment of the heterosexual colonial allegory, in
which the alpha imperial male demonstrates his ascendancy over the subordinate and emasculated 'native' by stealing his woman. We cannot know
whether the invisible Donnelly twins are motivated by sexual as well as
national *ressentiment*, but Yolland is kidnapped directly after taking Maire
home from the dance. Like Major Doryan, he fails to survive his attempt at
cross-cultural sexual relations. Lancey, of course, survives. The audience is
privileged to understand that Yolland is not in fact a callous seducer, and
Friel's plot dénouement is constructed to demonstrate the impossible position
of the colonizer who refuses (Memmi's phrase). The more decent the Englishman, the more likely he is to fall victim to the forces of history unleashed by
the imperialism of people like Lancey. In 1904 Tom Broadbent's hibernophilia
amused the inhabitants of Roscullen, but while they were laughing he took
over the village and its local heiress. In 1980 Yolland's passionate love of Ireland is punished as though it were Major Doryan's adulterous affair. Romantic liberalism can no longer justify or protect the stage Englishman in Ireland.

'THERE'S MANY A GOOD HEART BEATS UNDER A KHAKI TUNIC'

Tom Broadbent, Major Doryan and Yolland embody the power disparity between the English male and the Irish female through class as well as gender: Nora, Rosie, and Maire are lower in social status than their English lovers. In both the Irish and English versions of Brendan Behan's *An Giall* (*The Hostage*) (1958), however, class differences are erased. In conformity with the move away from the upper-class hero in twentieth-century English drama, Behan's characterization of Leslie removes the working-class stage Englishman from his stereotypical minor role as valet or non-commissioned officer and gives him the romantic lead. The love of the doomed hostage for the Irish girl Teresa replicates the colonial allegory of the English male and the colleen, but both soldier and servant girl are displaced and impoverished orphans who are symbolically outside history (Kiberd, *Inventing* 526), about which they are refreshingly ignorant. To Teresa's suggestion that England has been 'doing something to Ireland' Leslie replies, 'That was donkey's years ago. Everybody was doing something to someone in those days' (*An Giall* 126). Though he was accused of exploiting stage Irishness when he allowed Joan Littlewood to adapt his play for her Theatre Workshop, Behan is less interested in national peculiarities than in the similarities between ostensible opponents. He compares cockneys with Dubliners, Monsewer with Leslie's old British Colonel, and Leslie with his fellow victim, the IRA 'boy in Belfast Jail' whose hanging will precipitate the hostage's death (109).

Behan's obvious thematic debt to Frank O'Connor's 1930 story 'Guests of the Nation' extends to the characterization of his English hostage. O'Connor's two Englishmen, Belcher and Hawkins, are working-class lads who have no trouble relating to their Irish 'hosts'. They learn Irish dances, charm their old landlady and, like other hibernophile Englishmen, get to know the country better than their captors. The narrator, one of their guards, is struck by their powers of assimilation: 'you could have planted that pair down anywhere from this to Claregalway and they'd have taken root there like a native weed. I never in my short experience saw two men take to the country as they did'. O'Connor's organic metaphor establishes that nationality is not exclusive to the soil in which it was nourished, since it can be so easily transplanted. Hawkins is a communist, and Belcher seems to be a fellow-traveller; their close relationship with their two captors is an example of international brotherhood in action. The narrator gives the hostages the tribute proper to the stage Englishman: they are 'decent chaps' (*Guests* 5–6). So is Behan's Leslie:

VOLUNTEER. He's a decent boy, for all he's a British soldier.
MEG. Ah, there's many a good heart beats under a khaki tunic. (*An Giall* 138).

Although he does not appear to be a socialist, Leslie's realistic assessment of his unimportance to the English upper classes, and his immediate love for his Irish fellow-orphan, align him with the liberal and internationalist world-view expressed in 'Guests of the Nation'.

The prudishness of the IRA and the Gaelic League was a prime target in *An Giall*, but the bisexual Behan nevertheless knew his Irish-speaking audience well enough to keep overtly gay characters out of the Dublin theatre. In the London production of *The Hostage*, he and Littlewood introduced the male prostitute Rio Rita ('a homosexual navvy') and his 'coloured boyfriend' Princess Grace, who at one point parades around the stage carrying a placard inscribed 'KEEP IRELAND BLACK' (80, 141). (The Irish origins of the film star Grace Kelly, who became Princess Grace of Monaco, suggest that 'Princess Grace' is an example of the tendency to equate the ethnic disadvantage of Irishness with the racial disadvantage of blackness, a strategy I will discuss in Chapter Six.) This odd couple, who contribute nothing new to the plot, raise previously closeted issues of race and sexual orientation simply by appearing on an English stage. As they sing

> We're here because we're queer
> Because we're queer because we're here. (159)

Littlewood and Behan present their 'whores and queers' as 'the outcasts of the world', but they nevertheless manage to 'corrupt the morals' of the secret policeman Mulleady, and nearly succeed in seducing Leslie, who admits that he would like to try their kind of life. In leading an abortive attempt to rescue the British soldier, the three queers, Mulleady, Rio Rita and Princess Grace, oppose the patriotism and sexual puritanism of the officer of the IRA, a '*thin-faced fanatic*' who, like Pearse, is a schoolmaster (104). The repressiveness of extreme nationalism contends with the power of homoerotic desire to breach national and racial boundaries, but that power proves insufficient and Leslie is accidentally killed: either suffocated in a cupboard, or, in the Littlewood version, cut down in the crossfire.

A contemporary reviewer of the straight play *An Giall* complained that Behan had exploited the audience's natural attraction to the young lovers in order to blacken Leslie's IRA captors, who cause his death. Behan juxtaposes the cause of Irish freedom with 'the cruellest and most unanswerable of media [*sic*] – love between boy and girl. No ideology or idealism has yet found an answer to such a challenge' (quoted in *An Giall* 8). Behan certainly intends his audience to find his teetotal, God-fearing, Irish-speaking, fanatical IRA men repulsive, but hostage drama frequently uses the clash between erotic attraction and political loyalties as its motivating conflict. In *The Crying Game*

(1992) Neil Jordan, who has acknowledged his debts both to O'Connor and to Behan, turns the Irish girl Teresa into a man without changing the function of her role, which is to bond with the ostensible enemy, the English prisoner. The relation between Jody the working-class British soldier and Fergus the working-class IRA volunteer blackens the rest of Jody's IRA captors by contrasting their fanaticism with the love between boy and boy.[1] The 'Patty Hearst Syndrome', in which the hostage falls in love with her captor and identifies with his cause, is here reversed: after bonding with the hostage Jody, it is Fergus the captor who abandons his cause, who fails to keep the faith.

Both Behan and Jordan increase audience sympathy for their English characters by downplaying their political responsibility for events in Ireland. In *An Giall* Leslie is a regular soldier, but he has joined up early to anticipate the inevitable draft. In *The Hostage* he has even less political agency: he is a National Service conscript. When asked, 'Ah you murdering bastard. Why don't you go home to your own country?' he replies with perfect justification, 'You can take me out of it as soon as you like. I never bloody-well asked to be brought here' (*An Giall* 122). Jordan's Jody does not have the excuse of conscription, but as a working-class black man in a racist society he certainly needs the employment:

> JODY. What the fuck am I doing here.
> FERGUS. What the fuck were you doing here?
> JODY . I got sent.
> FERGUS . You could have said no.
> JODY. Can't. Once I signed up.
> FERGUS . Why did you sign up?
> JODY. It was a job. So I get sent to the only place in the world they call you nigger to your face. (*Crying* 12)

While Fergus's sceptical grunt reveals that Jordan finds this argument politically irresponsible, the audience nevertheless empathizes with Jody. In *Carthaginians* (1986), however, Frank McGuinness had already exposed the 'job' scenario as a stage English cliché. In his play-within-a-play 'The Burning Balaclava', a parody of Troubles literature, McGuinness's gay hero Dido impersonates 'a British soldier, nameless, faceless, in enemy uniform, in deep torment because he is a working-class cockney sent here to oppress the working class'. His camp exaggeration reveals the shallowness of an argument that uses class as an excuse for violence: 'Oh, the agony of being a working-class boy sent here to oppress the working class. Why did I do it? Why do I do it?' The answer, of course, is 'The money' (*Carthaginians* 36, 38).

Jordan complicates the significance of his stage cockney by crossing class with race. Jody, whose family comes from Antigua, is not only a working-class lad sent to oppress the working classes, but also a victim of British colonialism sent to police his fellow victims. In his reading of *Mansfield Park*, Edward Said identifies Sir Thomas Bertram's slave plantation in Antigua as the 'Other' space that guarantees the prosperity of his English estate (*Culture* 100–16). Jordan's choice of Antigua as Jody's place of origin performs a similar 'reading' of post-war British culture. In the fifties, immigrants from the West Indies were encouraged to come to the 'mother' country to take up the low-paying jobs that the English no longer wished to perform. Fergus's final address to the dead Jody's picture, 'You should have stayed at home' (*Crying* 68), suggests both Jordan's critique of the economic argument and his interrogation of geographical and racial identity: would Jody's 'home' be Tottenham or Antigua? And where does Jody's girlfriend Dil, who is also black, come from? Since World War II the homogeneity of Englishness has been altered by immigration, and the texture of society, at least in the metropolis, is no longer monocultural.

The Crying Game begins by gesturing towards the traditional gendered formula as the English soldier Jody crudely attempts to seduce the Irishwoman Jude, girlfriend of the IRA volunteer Fergus. But this dramatic cliché no longer functions outside of quotation marks; it is 'performed' by the IRA in order to capture a gullible Englishman. Like Shaw's Nora, Jude is marginalized by the intense relation that develops between the two men, whom she cannot tell apart erotically:

> JUDE. . . . One of you made me want it . . .
> [*She puts her lips to his neck.*]
> FERGUS. Which one?
> [*She doesn't answer. They embrace.*] (*Crying* 7)

Claiming, 'there's always homoerotic feeling between men in conflict',[2] Jordan develops the relationship between the British hostage and his Irish captor at the expense of Jude, whose brutal attacks on Jody express her frustration at being sexually marginalized. The erotic initiator is Jody, who flatters Fergus ('You're the one about five ten with the killer smile and the baby face') and seduces him into increasingly intimate bodily contact. Three separate 'love' scenes, in which Fergus feeds Jody, tells him his name and takes his penis out of his trousers to help him urinate (the problem is borrowed from Behan, but not the intimate solution), end with the IRA man saying, 'My pleasure', 'My pleasure, Jody', and 'The pleasure was all mine' (8, 13, 14). The direction 'Fergus begins to laugh, without knowing why' indicates his ignorance of his own desires and potential pleasures,[3] although his cryptic allusion to St Paul provides a clue to his feelings towards his intended victim: 'When I was a child . . . I thought as a child. But when I became a man I put away childish things' (20). These gnomic lines about achieving manhood, which are also spoken by the dying IRA man Johnny in Carol Reed's *Odd Man Out*, should be read in their full original context, St Paul's famous celebration of 'charity', now often translated as 'love'. Love, according to the apostle, is more important than the willingness to become a martyr: 'though I give my body to be burned, and have not charity, it profiteth me nothing' (1 Corinthians 13.3). If we substitute the IRA for the early church, the quotation from Corinthians, carrying with it the weight of its previous use in *Odd Man Out*, becomes an intertextual reminder that commitment to the cause of Ireland must be accompanied by love towards one's fellow men.[4] Neither St Paul nor Carol Reed had homoerotic love in mind, but Neil Jordan certainly does.

Through the love between Fergus and Jody, Jordan reclaims and revalues the nineteenth-century racist discourse that linked the Irish with Negroes rather than with 'white' Caucasians.[5] Echoing Princess Grace's hopeful placard 'KEEP IRELAND BLACK', Jordan stresses the resemblance rather than the national or racial differences between his two 'simple' soldiers. Jody's blackness ought to align him politically with Fergus rather than with the British state that has colonized them both, and although Jody does not intellectualize this kinship, he expresses it intuitively. Jordan's intentions are open to misunderstanding: the black feminist critic bell hooks attacks the film's representation of race without acknowledging the Irish experience of imperialism. For her, Fergus is 'the white colonizer', not a freedom fighter (*Outlaw Culture* 59). Nevertheless, Jordan's film attempts to enforce a political analogy between the Irish and the Afro-Caribbeans. As their brief, sexually charged relationship draws to its close, Jody deliberately gives his 'female' lover Dil to his Irish 'brother': his last wish is that Fergus should take her to the Metro for a margarita. The use of the 'woman' to mediate forbidden desire between two men is no longer the subtext (as in *John Bull's Other Island* or *Translations*); it is the main theme of the film. Jordan writes: 'A hostage, a captor, and an absent lover. The lover became the focus for the erotic subtext, loved by both men in a way they couldn't love each other' (*Crying* viii). Because the British transvestite Dil is also black, the pattern of racial, national and erotic boundary crossing is sustained in the second part of the film, when Fergus follows Jody's instructions and seeks out his lover. Jody has set Fergus up for a confrontation with his own ambiguous sexuality, and although he vomits in shock when he sees Dil's penis, denying his homoerotic desires, Dil thinks she knows better: 'even when you were throwing up, I could tell you cared'. Fergus's 'charity' towards Dil contrasts with the crude racism of Jude, who contemptuously gestures towards the golliwog on a pot of Robertson's jam to characterize 'The wee black chick' (45, 49).

By substituting Dil for the violent and dehumanized Jude, Jordan alters the convention in which the woman in the cross-national triangle is Irish, and even the convention that 'she' is a woman; but his manipulations of the formula only underscore its previous hegemony, and emphasize the continuum between homoerotic desire and the homosocial bonds that subtend more conventional erotic triangles. The developing relationship between Fergus and Dil is constantly mediated and even blessed by the dream-apparition of Jody in his cricket gear. Cricket, the film's most complex visual metaphor, is at once the emblem of English fair play ('that's not cricket') and the means by which Caribbean nations have struck back at their former masters. In England cricket still belongs to the 'toffs', but in Antigua it belongs to the people. Like the Irish mastery of the English language, cricket has become a way of beating the colonizer at his own game. Jody the 'shit-hot bowler' (12) has appropriated both the sport and the 'whiteness' of its uniform. When, in a scene of displaced eroticism, Fergus dresses Dil in Jody's 'whites', the circuit of desire between the Irishman and the dead soldier is re-established. Acknowledging the influence of Behan, Jordan claims historical sanction for queering the colonial allegory:

> The attraction of such a theme for Irish writers, the friendship that develops between two protagonists in a conflict, that grows paradoxically deeper than any of their other allegiances, lies in the broader history of Anglo-Irish relationships: two cultures in need of each other, yet at war with each other.

The irrelevance of women in Jordan's formulation of 'an erotic possibility, a sense of mutual need and identification' between Fergus and Jody, is highlighted when he writes that Behan 'dealt with simple friendship between two men' (*Crying* viii). Behan dealt with nothing of the sort: Jordan has forgotten that Teresa is a woman.

Whatever the degree of Jordan's misogyny, as revealed in the vicious characterization of Jude, or of the unconscious racism implied by his exoticization of Dil,[6] his representation of the love between Jody and Fergus as a nexus of nationality and desire is the culmination of one strand of Irish theatre history. Boucicault established the decent military stage Englishman as less villain than love object, but the gradual shift in power between colonizer and colonized since Independence has adversely affected his ultimate theatrical fate. Molineux got Claire, Claverhouse will get Sarah Curran and Corporal Stoddart got his cup of tea; but things have changed. Whether he is upper-class like Major Doryan, middle-class like Lieutenant Yolland or lower-class like Leslie and Jody, the stage Englishman is doomed as well as beloved. Blown up on the beach, 'disappeared' in the borderlands, asphyxiated in a cupboard or squashed by a Saracen, the decent British soldier in Ireland no longer heads for a happy ending.

Irish drama has provided a medium through which the historical relationship between English and Irish males can be imaginatively renegotiated. Although the colonial connection can be seen from the Southern perspective as old history, and revisionists argue that nationalist *ressentiment* should finally be laid to rest, from the Northern perspective the relationship between England and Ireland is continually in crisis. Like *The Crying Game*, Frank McGuinness's hostage drama *Someone Who'll Watch over Me* appeared in 1992. Although McGuinness moves his characters out of Ireland and into a Lebanese prison cell, he took up the topical subject of the Beirut hostages 'because of the nationalities involved. If you put an Englishman and an Irishman in a room together there will be war – ancestral voices predict it'

(McGuinness, 'A Dramatist'). Those 'ancestral voices prophesying war' come from Coleridge's orientalist fantasy 'Kubla Khan', and McGuinness has displaced potential English villainy onto the Arab hostage-takers, who, like Friel's Donnelly twins, are never seen on stage but who are deployed as the necessary external enemy. McGuinness insists that his characterizations are not based on the actual hostages, the Irishman Brian Keenan and the Englishman John McCarthy, and he did not read Keenan's book, *An Evil Cradling*, until after he had written his play. Rather, he sets out to accomplish a Shavian re-organization of national stereotypes. Recognizing that the sun has set on the Empire, both Jordan and McGuinness compromise the 'imperial' masculinity of their English characters by representing them as gay. The emergence of overt representations of gay men coincides historically with the liberalizing of Irish anti-homosexual legislation that was initiated by Senator David Norris's 1988 victory in the European Court of Human Rights, and completed in 1993.[7] Jordan and McGuinness inherit the same matrix of Irish literary, popular and legislative culture.

Jordan's Jody, who plays the protective 'gentleman' in his relationship with the 'feminine' Dil, has no camp mannerisms. He is homosexual without being effeminate. McGuinness, however, turns his stage Englishman Michael into a queer by camping up specific aspects of his Englishness. His Irish fellow hostage Edward stereotypes him instantly (and incorrectly):

> MICHAEL. I'm terribly sorry, but where am I?
> EDWARD. So it's yourself, is it?
> MICHAEL. Pardon?
> EDWARD. Do you not recognize me? We were at school together.
> MICHAEL. I don't think so.
> EDWARD. Eton, wasn't it? Or Harrow?
> MICHAEL. No, I don't – where am I?
> EDWARD. In the officer's mess, Brit Boy. (*Someone* 9)

Edward's references to the public school and the officer's mess locate Michael within the representational tradition of the military stage Englishman, but he is actually a civilian, middle-class lecturer in English literature. The stereotype fits awkwardly. If Michael is a stage Englishman he is devoid of Etonian swagger: he is absurdly polite, he apologizes for everything, agrees for agreement's sake, abhors swearing and suggests that 'We could at least maintain the semblance of civility'. Writing an imaginary letter to his mother, he says, 'I share accommodation with an American and an Irishman and so I am often flooded by a torrent of emotions, which I rise above'. Michael's quintessentially English attempts to rise above his emotions are frequently sabotaged by Edward, who is initially unable to see the man for the stereotypical mannerisms he thinks he ought to have: 'How dreadfully unfair. Not cricket'; 'Come on, give us a dose of the stiff upper lip. Raise our morale, old boy' (31, 24, 10, 16).

Edward also treats the Englishman's ambiguous sexual orientation as an occasion for homophobic jokes. When Michael mentions the pear flan he was making when he was kidnapped, Edward calls him 'sweetheart', suggesting none too subtly that real men don't cook, especially not dessert. The pear flan becomes a running gag, which, combined with Michael's constant worry about his mother in Peterborough, offers Edward plenty of ammunition. Michael comes to anticipate his innuendoes: 'Oh go ahead, Edward. . . . Attack me for writing to my mother. Pansy little Englishman. I don't mind. I've had it before. I can tell you, there were people who were surprised I got married' (10, 24–5). If the Englishman is a 'pansy', the symbolic association of British power with masculinity has vanished. By locating the victim of homophobia within the stereotype of the oppressor, McGuinness defies conventional ideas about nation and sexuality.

The decay of Empire and the loss of international influence are figured in Michael's academic redundancy and economic impotence: 'They're not teaching much Old and Middle English these days. A dying concern'. Deploying a trope from recent Irish cultural criticism, Edward represents the language Michael teaches as a battlefield on which the Irish have triumphed over their oppressors:

> Listen, times have changed, you English mouth, and I mean mouth. One time when you and your breed opened that same mouth, you ruled the roost, you ruled the world, because it was your language. Not any more. We've taken it from you. We've made it our own. And now, we've bettered you at it. . . . We took you and your language on, and we won. (12–13, 30)

Jody might have said the same about cricket. But there is something strained about Edward's triumphalism, which is sexual as well as linguistic. In captivity, he obsesses: 'Have they, or have they not, made me less of a man, by reason of what they've done to me?' His constant aggression against Michael is fuelled not only by Irish grievances (he holds the Englishman 'personally responsible' for the Famine), but also by fear of diminished manliness if he ruptures the barrier between homosocial bonding (his unspoken love for Adam, the black American) and homoerotic experience. After Adam's death, he gives rein to an outburst of overt homophobia: 'There are times the sight and sound of you disgust me. I can feel a smell off you. Sickening'. Michael's rejoinder, 'Did you sleep with Adam?' is only superficially a non sequitur (28, 30, 48–9).

Both Jordan and McGuinness associate repression with the Irish, not the English, character. Jody has no problem with his sexual orientation, but Fergus's homophobia has to be eroded by Dil's persistence. Edward denies his desire for Adam, cancelling the possibility of erotic attraction between men in order to keep intact the sex/gender categories that subtend the patriarchy: 'I need to be a father to my children'. But Michael refuses to endorse the conventional connection between weakness and femininity. When Edward goes on hunger strike to protest Adam's murder, Michael teaches him to accept Adam's death, and to celebrate him: 'Bury him . . . Remember him' (49, 40). Edward's inarticulacy, 'I believe it goes without saying, love, so I never said', is revised by Michael's recitation of George Herbert's poem 'Love', a non-ironic testament to the therapeutic powers of the English poetic canon:

> MICHAEL. . . . You must sit down, sayes Love, and taste my meat:
> So I did sit and eat.
> EDWARD. I'm hungry.
> MICHAEL. Then eat.
> EDWARD. Dear friend.
> (EDWARD *eats*.) He's dead.
> MICHAEL. We are not. (41–2)

In stopping Edward's hunger strike, which resonates with the Irish hunger strikes of 1981, Michael asserts that strength resides not in self-destruction, but in love and endurance.

High camp becomes a medium of political reconciliation in the brilliant scene where Michael re-enacts Virginia Wade's triumph in the 1977 Wimbledon Ladies Final, which was attended by Queen Elizabeth. The national and sexual implications of this performance are complex. To impersonate Virginia Wade is to impersonate a woman who, like Billie Jean King, is more noted for strength than femininity. Nevertheless, her victory for Great Britain interrupted a long history of defeat: no British woman has won Wimbledon subsequently, and Britain's waning dominance in sports reflects her waning influence in the world. Edward, for whom sport is politics by other means, starts off rooting for Virginia's opponent, 'poor wee Betty Stove' (43), but his knee-jerk Irish sympathy for the six-foot, twelve-stone underdog is modified by a discussion of the limits of England's colonial responsibility for Ireland's problems, a topic that the two men raised earlier in connection with the Famine. For the Englishman the Famine happened 'a hundred and fifty fucking years ago', but for the Irishman it was 'yesterday' (30). Neither man is right: Michael's literal-minded reliance on clock time must be tempered by some acknowledgment of the contemporary resonance of historical pain. His insistence that the outcome of Virginia's match is historically predetermined prompts Edward to remark, 'That's unfair'. Michael replies flatly, 'That's history'. But when the conversation moves to the situation in Derry, he asks a serious question: 'Is it really our fault for your troubles at home? Is it the English people's fault?', to which Edward replies: 'Ridiculous'. By the end of the scene, the men's verdicts on the tennis match are closer, more generous and less chauvinistic. Edward now celebrates Virginia Wade, while Michael sympathizes with the loser Betty Stove:

> MICHAEL. And have we faith?
> EDWARD. Do you want proof?

MICHAEL. Yes. Give it to me.
EDWARD. Who won the 1977 Wimbledon Women's Final?
MICHAEL. An Englishwoman won it.
EDWARD. I rest my case that there is a God.
MICHAEL. Well done, Virginia.
EDWARD. Well done, Virginia.
MICHAEL. Poor wee Betty Stove.
EDWARD. There always has to be a loser. In every game, a loser.
MICHAEL. Yes, that's history.
EDWARD. (sings) For she's a jolly good fellow . . . (46–47)

This mutual understanding, generated by two men impersonating powerful women (Edward plays the 'Queen'), ends with the Irishman singing a gender-bending version of a British song in honour of an English lesbian tennis player. Michael offers to the heterosexual Edward the political liberation of camp. As they loosen the bonds of gender identity, the two men also begin to discard antagonistic conceptions of national loyalty.

McGuinness equates the maintenance of straight gender categories and sexual orientations with a politics of national difference and historical grievance. But Michael's straight devotion to his dead wife is as intense as his 'queer' obsession with his living mother and his literary identification with his dead father. Despite his parodic stage Englishness, Michael's capacity for love, his fluid sexual identity and his refusal to identify femaleness with the exaggerated femininity travestied by Dil make him the unexpected sexual hero of McGuinness's play. His defence of the stiff upper lip, the controlling of pain and fear, derives as might be expected from his father, but it is not 'masculine': 'You have been raised by a strong woman. The bravest men sometimes behave like women. Before the Spartans went into battle, they combed each other's hair. The enemy laughed at them for being effeminate. But the Spartans won the battle'.

Spartan stoicism is also the message of the Old English elegy 'The Wanderer', from which Michael derives his paternity and his national identity: 'I heard my father . . . in that ancient poem, speaking with the voice of England, talking to itself, for the first time. Our beginning, our end, England's'. 'The Wanderer', a lament over loss, loneliness and defeat, allows Michael to express a legitimate national pride predicated not upon conquest, but upon courage in the face of adversity and admiration for the creative act: 'I love my country because I love its literature very much'. McGuinness suggests that English patriotism is acceptable once England's imperial power is gone. His use of a gay character to recuperate the father, the English literary canon and the idea of Englishness is an imaginative act of courage and generosity that resembles his dramatic rapprochement with the Ulster unionists in *Observe the Sons of Ulster*. As in the earlier play, political border crossing and sexual border crossing become reciprocal metaphors, in which it is impossible to say which is the vehicle and which the tenor. Edward, whose release leaves

Michael, like the speaker of 'The Wanderer', alone at the end, acknowledges the superior strength of the 'pansy little Englishman' and overcomes his homophobic fear of effeminacy: in an expressively 'Spartan' gesture he combs Michael's hair and allows Michael to comb his. 'I need you', the Irishman says to the Englishman (*Someone* 50–51, 58).

Although they may be Utopian in impulse, encounters between male opponents that modify the exclusionary outlines of national stereotypes are not necessarily progressive. Narratives of homosocial or homoerotic bonding between English and Irish males may function to obliterate women except as objects of exchange between men, or they may appropriate 'feminine' qualities while demonizing real females. Frequently they challenge Republican dogma, which until recently has argued that reconciliation is impossible while the last vestige of England's imperial power still manifests itself in the North of Ireland. Strategies of resistance do not necessarily inhabit the same counter-hegemonic space, and the interests of men who love men do not always coincide with those of women or nationalists. Yet neither is it axiomatic that they should conflict. While acknowledging ethnic differences, the homosocial tradition that leads from Boucicault, Shaw and Friel to *The Crying Game* and *Someone Who'll Watch over Me* attempts to level real or symbolic inequalities of power, and makes a case for peace based on mutual need.

McGuinness's latest play, *Dolly West's Kitchen* (1999), self-consciously combines the homosocial with the more common heterosexual paradigm of union, and takes his queerly gendered model of reconciliation between ancient enemies a step further. The play, which once again sets up a three-way relationship between England, Ireland and America, is set in neutral Southern Ireland during World War II. As the Allies prepare for the D Day landings, the West family of Buncrana (McGuinness's home town in Donegal) plays host to an Englishman and two American GIs who have crossed the border from an army base in Derry. The outspoken and unconventional matriarch Rima West (a funny and loving study of McGuinness's own mother)[8] deliberately brings 'a bit of badness' (30) into the lives of her three children, the unmarried Dolly, the unhappily married Esther and the prudish, repressed and anti-British Justin, an officer in the Irish army. In the 'grotto' (her local pub) she picks up Marco Delavicario, a flaming queen from New York, and his straight cousin Jamie O'Brien. She brings them home to share the dinner her daughter Dolly is cooking for an Englishman, Alec Redding, an old friend from her student days at Trinity College, Dublin. This oddly assorted agape explodes when Justin turns on Alec, who has joined the British army to fight against Hitler: 'Alec, do you know how deeply you are hated? How deservedly you are hated? . . . Germany will win the war. The might of Hitler's army will win the war'. Alec refuses to be silenced by reminders of England's colonial record in Ireland, and responds vigorously that the ordeal of Hitler's victims is 'a damned sight worse than whatever you and your people have suffered' (36–7). England's previous mistreatment of her colony does not justify abstention from the present battle against a greater evil; the enemy of my enemy is not necessarily my friend.

In *Dolly West's Kitchen*, World War II and the Holocaust have radically altered the ethical and historical values attached to Englishness, and to the wearing of a khaki tunic. The former imperial oppressor has become a defender of freedom for the West, including the 'Wests' of neutral Ireland. Apart from Alec, Rima is the only character who fully understands what Hitler is doing to the Jews, and McGuinness is careful to give his condemnation of Ireland's refugee policy to his most powerful Irish character, not to the Englishman:

> RIMA. And the Jews?
> *Silence*
> Is it as bad –
> ALEC. It's worse, I think. We don't know –
> RIMA. We do.
> *Silence*
> If any country should have opened the door to any people facing what they are facing – Ireland –
> ALEC. It might not be as bad –
> RIMA. We did nothing to save them.
> ALEC. Ireland's a neutral country.
> RIMA. Do you believe that?
> ALEC. No. (48–9)

Objectively, Rima is right. Although de Valera himself was friendly towards the small Jewish community that was already in Ireland, the policy of the Department of Justice towards Jewish asylum seekers was consistently 'illiberal and ungenerous' (Keogh 161). The number of Jews admitted into Ireland during the Emergency may have been as low as sixty (192), a fact that painfully updates Mr Deasy's tasteless joke: 'Ireland, they say, has the honour of being the only country which never persecuted the Jews . . . Because she never let them in' (*Ulysses* 2.438–42). Dermot Keogh quotes a post-war document that attempts retroactively to justify Justice Department policy, but in so doing blindly repeats the kind of arguments that led to the Holocaust in the first place:

> Our practice has been to discourage any substantial increase in the Jewish population. They do not assimilate with our own people but remain a sort of colony of a world-wide Jewish community. This makes them a potential irritant in the body politic and has led to disastrous results from time to time in other countries. (Keogh 161)

It is almost impossible to imagine how these words could have been written in 1946.

McGuinness's condemnation of Irish refugee policy echoes Thomas McCarthy's 'The Dying Synagogue at South Terrace' (1989), a poetic testament to the fact that the Jewish population of the Republic has presently dwindled to just over a thousand (Keogh 224). McCarthy's speaker shares Rima's view that 'we did nothing to save them':

> We who did nothing for you, who
> remained aloof with the Catholic world
> and would have cried *Jew!* like the others –
> David forgive us –
> we who didn't believe the newsreels,
> preferring hatred of England to love of you,
> we might shut our hypocrite mouths,
> we want a West Bank but not a Stormont.
> We have no right over your batons,
> having made nothing for you but L. Bloom. (*Seven Winters* 131)

McCarthy posits a politically counter-intuitive analogy between the Palestinians and the Protestants, both of whom claim the right to self-government over the portion of the land in which they now live. If 'we want a West Bank' and condemn the Israelis for repressing the PLO, we should be able to tolerate a Stormont. The Protestants, a majority in the Six Counties, are a minority within the island of Ireland. While McCarthy indicts the practical failure of the Irish to help the Jews in their hour of greatest need, he relates contemporary Zionism to Irish nationalism: neither can tolerate an alien community in their midst. The IRA may see its desire to unite Ireland as analogous to the struggle of the PLO for a Palestinian state (Bill Rolston reproduces a mural that reads 'IRA PLO one struggle [50]), but McCarthy turns that familiar analogue inside out: in their attitude to the Protestants, he suggests, the Republicans resemble the Likud party.

Although Irish political leaders knew about the Holocaust as early as the autumn of 1942, how Rima came by her knowledge not only of Hitler's final solution but also of Ireland's closed-door policy towards Jewish refugees is unclear, since wartime censorship in Ireland was extremely severe. Joseph Lee explains that

> Censorship was . . . a prerequisite for maintaining the necessary sense of righteousness. It was unfortunate that the first war in which the Irish found an opportunity of investing their self-respect was also one in which the scales of bestiality would be so unevenly weighed. By the simple device of excluding all accounts of Nazi atrocities as propaganda, the censorship deprived the populace of much of this knowledge. (266)

McGuinness grants Rima a dispensation from government-endorsed ignorance so that she can give her blessing to Alec's decision to join the British army:

'You're alive, Alec. May you stay so. Hard fight ahead, God protect you' (*Dolly* 26). Dolly similarly endorses his 'life's purpose': 'It's to fight, to save us from Hitler. It's a great purpose. I hope you win. I'm frightened you'll die. I'm frightened you'll lose'. England's difficulty, once Ireland's opportunity, is now her danger: if England loses, Ireland will lose too, although she has not fought. Alec's response, a 'strong curtain' that ends the first act, is 'God save Ireland' (40).

Justin, however, is obsessed by the possibility that the Allies will invade Southern Ireland in order to repossess the Treaty Ports that control the western naval approaches. These ports, whose return to Irish control had been successfully negotiated by Eamon de Valera just before the outbreak of war, were essential to the maintenance of Irish neutrality. One of the most important was Lough Swilly in Donegal, on the shores of which stands the town of Buncrana. 'The ports of Ireland are ours, and ours alone. Look out there. That's what they want. The ports of our free neutral country' (36), says Justin. Churchill, who hated de Valera personally and was furious about the loss of the ports, certainly wanted them back.

McGuinness is not the only Irish writer to have meditated upon the ethical and practical consequences of de Valera's refusal to allow the Allies to use the ports for refuge and refuelling, a refusal that cost lives, ships and supplies.[9] (How many is still a matter for dispute.) Bernard Shaw suggested that Churchill should repossess them by force for the duration of the war. Thinking of all the sailors torpedoed by German U-boats, the Northern Protestant Louis MacNeice gave a hideous twist to Yeats's exuberant vision of Ireland's 'mackerel-crowded seas' (*Poems* 193). In 'Neutrality' he excoriated Ireland as

> The neutral island facing the Atlantic,
> The neutral island in the heart of man,
> . . .
> While to the west off your own shores the mackerel
> Are fat – on the flesh of your kin. (MacNeice, *Poems* 202)

On the evening of Rima's death, Dolly comes home pushing a wheelbarrow full of mackerel for dinner. Rima expresses her dislike for the fish, warns that they will soon 'turn' and dies before she has to eat them. While those intertextual mackerel suggest that McGuinness agrees with MacNeice's condemnation of de Valera's neutrality policy, he is careful to qualify his disapproval. Although it has led him towards a morally reprehensible sympathy with fascism, Justin's hatred and suspicion of England springs from legitimate causes. Dolly, who like Rima is one of the play's privileged voices, explains:

> DOLLY. Justin does love his country, Alec.
> ALEC. So he must hate mine?
> DOLLY. Sometimes he must, yes. In the years you lived here, did you not find that out?
> ALEC. No I didn't. I never will. Do you want to see Hitler win, Dolly? (*Dolly* 39)

Dolly does not. She welcomes the English and American soldiers to her kitchen, and supports Alec's enlistment in the army; but even she cannot countenance Shaw's suggestion that Churchill should violate Ireland's independence and newly won territorial integrity by re-taking the Treaty Ports. She tells Alec, 'if you and your Allies invade Ireland, I will be the first to put a bullet through your brain' (66). Dolly's actions are thus roughly consonant with official Irish policy during the Emergency: de Valera rigorously maintained formal neutrality, withheld the ports and kept up friendly relations with the German ambassador; but he sanctioned constant practical collaboration with the Allies. Throughout the war Ireland's neutrality towards Great Britain, and later America, was benevolent. For example, downed British fliers were returned home via the North of Ireland, while Germans were interned for the duration of the war. Irish intelligence services co-operated extensively with both the British and the Americans.[10] Numerous Southern Irish men and women volunteered for the British army, and Justin's support for the Nazis was not widely shared. Many later commentators condemn Ireland's neutrality policy unequivocally: Neil Jordan claims that it 'led to much that was sinister, much that was ridiculous' (*Nightlines* ix); but McGuinness approaches his subject with restraint. Although his play includes a scene set after the war is over, he makes no cheap capital out of de Valera's notorious visit to the German ambassador on the death of Hitler. Nevertheless, *Dolly West's Kitchen*, which received an ecstatic reception in London, was not uniformly well reviewed in Ireland.

Although Justin's hysterical tirade against Alec in Act One may suggest that the play is destined to become a rerun of the familiar Ireland versus England grudge match, McGuinness opens out the political playing field by acknowledging Ireland's place in a complex system of international alliances. Jamie O'Brien, whose grandfather came from Donegal, represents Irish America, a constituency initially opposed to American involvement in the war. Marco Delavicario's Italian origins might have made him reluctant to oppose Mussolini. But neither Jamie nor Marco has hesitated to join up: they are more American than hyphenated. America, in the war after Pearl Harbour, and closely allied with Ireland's ancient enemy, complicates purist nationalist calculations, and a stage Englishman looks different when he appears in the company of two young Americans. Once again, McGuinness lays out his political themes through sexual analogies. The *Irish Times* reviewer took issue with this technique:

> [T]he author wants to compare and contrast the loyalties and enmities in the dinner party with the loyalties and enmities of the parties engaged in, or neutral in the world war. Here he falls into a logical fallacy which is ultimately lethal to his drama. Sexual love or hate is not comparable to love or hate of country, so that to compare . . . the resolution of sexual relationships with the end of the war is merely sentimental. (Nowlan)

If this assessment were correct, we might have to conclude that much of the Irish drama we have looked at is 'merely sentimental'. I would reject this conclusion, along with the implied denigration of sentiment as a political and theatrical force. When Benedict Anderson categorizes nationalism with kinship and religion he indicates that love of one's country is closer to passion than to intellectual allegiance. The familiar analogy between sexuality and nationality that McGuinness uses to structure his play does not depend on a 'logical fallacy', and it is inherited from the Irish dramatic tradition.

Rima's bizarre social inspiration bears fruit when the outrageously camp Marco defuses the tension between the English and Irish officers by encouraging Justin to recognize and act on his own homosexuality. McGuinness links Justin's extreme nationalism and moral isolationism with hyper-masculine self-assertion and homophobia, as his classic opening exchange with Marco demonstrates:

> MARCO. . . . I am an American soldier. I am most emphatically not wearing lipstick. A little rouge, yes. No Nazi's going to bitch about my bone structure.
> JUSTIN. Do you know what the Nazis do to men like you?
> MARCO. Why the fuck do you think I'm fighting them? (*Dolly* 33)

Marco sees camp femininity as compatible with courage, and is fighting Hitler not only for the sake of justice and liberty, but also for the right to wear high heels. From that moment Justin is captivated. As in *Someone Who'll Watch over Me*, the deconstruction of his conventional ideas about gender frees an Irishman from his obsessive aggression towards the English, although in *Dolly West's Kitchen* the 'ancestral' enemies do not forge a personal bond like the one Edward eventually shares with Michael. In what may be a veiled metaphor for American intervention in the current peace process, as well as in World War II, Marco redirects Justin's intense energy away from Alec and towards himself. The theatre critic of *The Scotsman* argued that 'McGuinness's need to suggest links between sexual repression and neurotic forms of nationalism is sometimes a shade desperate and unconvincing' (McMillan), and perhaps Justin's swift 'conversion' is rather schematic. But the schema itself is not original to McGuinness. The connection between neurotic nationalism and sexual repression has been current in Irish drama ever since O'Casey put Rosie Redmond up against Padraig Pearse.[11]

The unrepressed and irrepressible Rima, who astounds the assembled company by wanting to know what men do together in bed, dies halfway through the play; but she directs all of its subsequent developments. At Rima's urging, Alec finally asks Dolly to marry him. The resolution of the old, unsatisfactory relationship between Dolly and Alec results in a queer and middle-aged version of the national romance. Alec unites elements from every strand of the stage English tradition. McGuinness signals his self-conscious participation in that tradition when his character becomes stereotypically stiff and apologetic:

ALEC. If I am causing any offence whatsoever, I assure you . . .
DOLLY. Alec, stop acting the Englishman. (*Dolly* 24)

Moreover Ned, who is fond of Alec, offers him the defining accolade without which no stage English character is complete: 'Alec, you're as decent an eejit as ever looked over a half-door' (24). Though the war has brought him back from abroad to enlist, he is not a career officer, and Dolly finds it 'hard to imagine Alec in uniform, following orders. He was always his own man'. But Ned quickly and accurately fits him back into the stereotype: 'Alec's not the kind of man to shirk his duty to his country' (14). Alec is a benevolent hibernophile after the model of Yolland, who was entranced by the scenery of the West, and of Tom Broadbent, who wanted to play golf on it:

ALEC. . . . God, the White Strand. I do believe it's one of the great sights on this earth.
NED. You've seen a fair few of them, Alec.
ALEC. But it is truly magnificent on a clear day. When I was walking past the golf course at Lisfannon, I got it into my head, Neddy, we might play a few holes there. (42)

Dolly remembers that in his student days Alec spent little time in England: 'When we were at Trinity, he never took a holiday back there. Even Christmas he spent wandering through the blizzards in the west of Ireland' (14). Probably he went to the Aran Islands on an ethnographic expedition: his current job is to explain the peculiarities of the Irish to American GIs. Dolly even forces him to admit that he calls the Southern Irish 'the natives'. He announces himself with an imitation of Synge, delivered in an unconvincing brogue: 'Excuse me, lady of the house, but would you have a cup of tea for a stranger?' (16). He is still, as his lamentable stage Irish impersonation proves and as Justin reminds him, a stranger in the house.

Alec's originality as a stage Englishman lies not in his personality, which is McGuinness's witty and self-conscious compound of all the previous formulae, but in his verbal bluntness about sexuality, an area where he seems to have more experience and fewer inhibitions than his predecessors. (Since the liberated sixties, the stage Englishman has blossomed in the erotic department.) Alec tells a story about his travels in Tibet that must be the first description of bestiality on the Irish stage:

ALEC. We were about to hit the sack, when this little girl – six or seven – she arrived with her yak. It was all decorated with bells and ribbons. We patted it and told her it was a lovely yak. She made it clear the yak expected more than patting.
DOLLY. She thought you were going to –
ALEC. Yes, with a yak.
DOLLY. You've had your fair share of dogs –
ALEC. That's enough. We got rid of her and the yak, or so we thought. She was

back five minutes later with a younger yak that had no need of bells or ribbons.
We sent that one packing as well, but I'm sure that somewhere in Tibet there's
an ageing yak sipping gin with smeared lipstick thinking those bloody English
turned me down for a younger model.
DOLLY. Jesus, I'm ageing with the yak. (18–19)

The parable is not hard to decode, especially when Dolly teasingly introduces
their good-looking teenaged maid Anna as 'our yak'. Re-creating the scene
between Captain Molineux and Claire at the opening of *The Shaughraun*, Alec
duly makes a classic stage English pass at Anna the comely colleen. Like
Molineux, he gets his comeuppance when Anna rebuffs his impertinent kiss:
'You're an old man – old enough to be my father. (*She points at the dirty potato
water.*) That's what you look like to me. Dirty' (44). In a witty and surely
deliberate allusion to Claire's impersonation of a butter-churning dairymaid,
she then douses the offender with a glass of milk. Turning decisively away
from old England towards young America, Anna eventually heads off to the
States with Jamie O'Brien.

The characters' ages, which McGuinness specifies in the cast list, are politically significant. It is the thirty-something Dolly rather than the teenager
born after Independence who has unfinished business with Alec the dirty old
man. After Anna's dairy dismissal, Alec and Dolly are free to explore the possibilities of a mutual desire that is both queerly unfixed and a little past its
prime. Though her crack about dogs may be unfounded, Dolly has privileged
insight into Alec's previous sexual tastes:

> ALEC. . . . the fresh smell of cock has not been to my liking since I was fifteen.
> DOLLY. You had a fling with a man in your twenties.
> ALEC. I was drunk.
> DOLLY. It went on for three months.
> ALEC. I was very drunk. (19–21)

Perhaps because of her knowledge of Alec's ambiguous sexuality, Dolly did
not declare her love for him, but she has never desired anyone else: 'The day
I set eyes on you, I wanted you. Since you left me, I've been with you. Can
you say the same?' (67). Alec cannot, but he is willing to consider a creative
sexual compromise:

> ALEC. . . . If I ever asked you to marry me, you would run a mile.
> DOLLY. I'm standing still, Alec.
> (*He takes Dolly's hand. He moves it through his legs, up to both his breasts.
> He kisses her hand.*)
> What do you want? Woman or man?
> ALEC. Both.
> DOLLY. You can have that. (*She kisses him violently.*) (67–8)

We do not know whether Dolly plans to get in touch with her own androgyny or whether she will leave Alec free to follow his homoerotic desires within the structure of an unconventional union, but the marriage itself is not in doubt. On one level this sexual interchange is simply the unorthodox resolution of an unfinished personal history, and Dolly agrees to live in England with Alec 'for you. Not your country' (84). Nevertheless, McGuinness's creatively queer variations on the gendered national allegory are impossible to ignore. In the bisexual Alec, McGuinness combines the heterosexual Englishman of Boucicault, Shaw and Friel with the homosexual (or perhaps bisexual) Englishman of *The Crying Game* and his own ambiguously oriented Michael from *Someone Who'll Watch over Me*. Although he retains the transnational marriage plot and the connection between Englishness and maleness, he reverses the convention that the English man must proposition the Irish woman, for it is Dolly who makes the running. In the final marital configuration of characters, an Irishwoman still mediates between an Irishman and an Englishman: Dolly brings the nationalist Justin and the soldier Alec into positive relation as brothers-in-law, just as Claire connected her Fenian brother Robert with her British army husband Molineux. Justin's neutrality and isolationism cannot withstand the introduction of an Englishman into the West 'family'. But the power-shifts caused by Southern Irish independence and the birth of feminism are manifested both through Anna's rejection of and Dolly's pursuit of Alec: Irish women are now free to manage their own relationships with the former colonizer on equal terms.

In the last scene of the play, when the soldiers return to Buncrana after the war to renegotiate and ultimately confirm the sexual arrangements that were made before they went away, there is tension to be dispelled between those who fought and those who stayed at home. In helping to defeat Hitler, the bisexual Alec, the camp queen Marco and the straight Jamie have also saved Ireland. Free from historical guilt, the two Americans directly reproach the Irish males with their inaction: Marco tells Justin, 'You always knew you were safe so you let us suffer for you' (77), while Jamie taunts Ned: 'We knew how to win a war rather than sit on the sidelines shitting ourselves' (79). Justin and Ned respond with cathartic violence: they demonstrate that they are not physical cowards, but they offer no intellectual rationale for their position of neutrality. Alec, suffering from a bad case of Major Doryan's shellshock, makes no recriminations and can speak to no one except Dolly. What he has seen at the liberation of the death camps has shifted his stage English taciturnity towards catatonia and transformed his perspective on the world: 'Children. Dead children. Burned off the face of the earth. Millions' (83). In giving this apocalyptic vision to the Englishman instead of the Americans, McGuinness weights the ethical scales in favour of the old enemy, and sets up an audacious reversal of the balance of historical pain. The Holocaust renews the wanderer Alec's devotion to his own country, because, while Ireland has had, in Lee's words, 'a relatively cosy war' (*Ireland* 233), England has suffered materially in the struggle against moral evil: 'It's my home. I need to go home. What's been inflicted on it. It's hungry. Bombed, broken, lost. England, on its knees. Poor country'. His new-found English patriotism is protective and defensive rather than supremacist; Napper Tandy's 'poor old Ireland' has become poor old England. From an Irish perspective England on its knees, spent by the effort of combating Hitler, is England at its most attractive, and even though Dolly cannot share Alec's patriotic sentiments, she is willing to live there. She is not, however, willing to submerge her individual identity as an Irishwoman to do so: 'No, Alec, I won't love it. They won't love me. I'll make sure of that. That is your country. Yes, it has suffered. Yes, it's on its knees. But I am not. All right, I'll stand by you. But I'll be standing on my own two feet. And I'll be doing it for you. Not your country' (Dolly 84).

McGuinness, a university lecturer in English literature, is well aware of the conversation about gender and nation that has been carried on in Irish studies since the late eighties. He leaves the outward structure of both the matrimonial and the homosocial tropes of union intact, but he radically transforms their content. Dolly is his attempt to employ the marriage paradigm in the service of peace and national reconciliation without either submerging the woman in the symbol, using her as a means of exchange between men or mapping the conventional relations of matrimonial power onto the English/Irish connection. The marriage between Dolly and Alec is an alliance between equals, not the absorption of one by the other. Between men there is reconciliation, but no affection. Justin drops his hostility to Alec, and even accepts his gift of a bottle of whiskey, admitting grudgingly 'They have their uses, the Brits' (70). But the offer of whiskey, an intertextual echo and reversal of the scene on the beach between Ffolliet and Molineux in *The Snaughraun*, takes place offstage, and after their first angry confrontation we never see the Englishman interact directly with the Irishman. Between in-laws a ceasefire is required; to demand good feelings would be Utopian.

In *Dolly West's Kitchen*, as in several of his previous plays, McGuinness intensifies dramatic emotion by his bold use of complete texts from canonical English literature and hymnology. These familiar works, most of which have achieved popular cultural status through either the Protestant Church or the school curriculum, provide a strategy of emotional border-crossing that matches McGuinness's desire to violate the integrity of sexual, religious and national boundaries. In *Carthaginians*, Walter de la Mare's English poem 'The Listeners', memorized by countless schoolchildren both in the North of Ireland and the rest of the United Kingdom, brings to mind the names of the Catholic dead of Bloody Sunday. In *Someone Who'll Watch over Me*, the Anglican George Herbert's poem 'Love' persuades the Catholic Edward to nourish himself once more. The moving climax of *Observe the Sons of Ulster* is set up when the soldiers prepare to go over the top by singing an English hymn, 'Heaven Is My Home', composed by Sir Arthur Sullivan in 1872. 'Heaven Is My Home' explicitly disavows the idea of an earthly fatherland, but the hymn with which McGuinness chooses to end *Dolly West's Kitchen* is the ultimate English patriotic anthem, 'I Vow to Thee My Country', written by Sir Cecil Spring-Rice in the closing months of World War I. This emotional hymn, with its lovely setting from Holst's *The Planets*, is often sung at weddings, and is thus appropriate to Dolly and Alec. Its sentimental popular associations were recently increased because it was Princess Diana's favourite, and was played at both her wedding and her funeral. McGuinness's unabashed exploitation of sentiment is reminiscent of Boucicauldian melodrama (melodrama, of course, means drama with music). Alec recites the first verse:

> I vow to thee, my country, all earthly things above,
> Entire and whole and perfect the service of my love.
> The love that asks no questions, the love that stands the test,
> That lays upon the altar, the dearest and the best.
> (*He sings.*)
> The love that never falters, the love that pays the price.
> The love that makes undaunted – the final sacrifice. (84)

It is a measure of McGuinness's success with his character and his careful choice of hymn-text that Alec does not at this moment seem to reaffirm the worst kind of English jingoism. England at the end of the war had indeed paid a high price for freedom; both her own and that of other small nations like Ireland. But whatever English moral superiority Alec may indirectly be claiming through the first verse of the hymn is neutralized by Dolly's recitation of the second verse, which, like 'Heaven Is My Home', moves the direction of the sentiment to 'another country', one without flags or frontiers:

> And there's another country, I've heard of long ago,
> Most dear to them that love her, most great to them that know.
> We may not count her armies, we may not see her king,
> Her fortress is a faithful heart, her pride is suffering,
> And soul by soul and silently, her shining bounds increase,
> And her ways are ways of gentleness and all her paths are peace. (85)

In this final scene, Alec and Dolly are outside the kitchen set, alone on the seashore. As they recite and sing the hymn, we see that inside the kitchen another secular agape, more successful than the disastrous one with which the play began, is being enacted. From the exterior Alec repeats the words 'gentleness' and 'peace' in counterpoint with Dolly's sister Esther, who calls to them from inside, 'Dolly, Alec, the lamb's ready', and instructs the others: 'Pour the wine, Justin. Pass the bread, Anna' (85). Within the warmth of the kitchen, the sacrificial lamb and the bread and wine of the Mass confirm the relationships of Justin and Marco, Anna and Jamie: in political terms, the agape cements the alliance between the Irish and the Americans, gay and straight. Outside, things are not so certain. Twice Alec asks 'Is the war over,

Dolly?' and twice she replies, 'I hope so'. On that hope, the play ends. This conclusion resonates with mingled optimism and pessimism: unlike the char acters, the audience knows that although the World War is over the Troubles in the North are yet to come, and that British soldiers will return to the streets of Derry in less attractive roles than the one played by Alec. Invoking the immediate present as well as the recent past, however, McGuinness uses the dinner party to remind us that the play was written after the peace agreement concluded on Good Friday 1998. He puts paschal lamb on the menu not only to mark the end of war shortages, but to highlight the current political mean-ing of the Easter sacrifice: the Good Friday Agreement returns power from Westminster to the North of Ireland and mandates the sharing of that power between Unionists and Nationalists. If the new Assembly survives the numer-ous challenges to its existence, Dolly's cautious hopefulness will be justified. In any case, Rima would certainly have preferred lamb to mackerel.

'BRITS BEHAVING BADLY'
From Bourke to Jordan

Few dramatic traditions are without their counter-movements, and my account of the drama of reconciliation would be incomplete without an acknowledgement of its shadow. Boucicault, Shaw, Behan, Friel and McGuinness all address mixed audiences: Irish, English and American. All demonstrate varying degrees of impatience with what Gibbons and Kiberd call, presumably to distinguish it from the approved version, 'narrow-gauge nationalism' ('Dialogue' 30, *Inventing* 144). Their liberal humanist or socialist politics lead them to emphasize fraternity between peoples and their representatives, and to absolve individual Englishmen (though not the imperial system) from colonial guilt in relation to Ireland. But when the radical dramatist P. J. Bourke produced historical melodramas for almost exclusively nationalist Irish audiences in the years before the Easter Rising, he placed the military stage Englishman in the formulaic role of the 'heavy': as greedy, lustful and cruel as the Irish hero was noble, patriotic and unselfish. Although Boucicault's parables of reconciliation were far more dramatically influential than Bourke's nationalist propaganda, some echoes of the latter's straightforward antagonism may be found in twentieth-century Irish drama and film, and we are occasionally presented with a genuine English villain. Not surprisingly, this tendency has increased since 1969 and manifests itself in a number of recent dramas and films about the conflict in the North of Ireland, culminating in Neil Jordan's historical epic about the earlier Troubles of the nineteen twenties, *Michael Collins* (1996). As liberal English support for military withdrawal has increased, censorship has grown weaker and the fledgling Irish film industry has become more self-confident; a number of film-makers have braved the negative box-office consequences of unflattering representations of the colonizer.

In Bourke's *When Wexford Rose* (1910) and *For the Land She Loved* (1915), dramas about the failed rising of 1798, the simple patterns of good and evil characteristic of melodrama exactly reflect the adversarial colonial situation. Bourke retains the gendered analogy in which the English male pursues an Irish woman, and recasts the pursuit as rape or attempted rape. In both cases the villain's motive is primarily financial rather than sexual, which accords with standard melodramatic practice and highlights the economic dimension of colonialism. The interest of these plays, which make Boucicault look like Shakespeare by comparison, lies not in their wooden stagecraft, repetitious plotting and unintentionally hilarious dialogue, but in their reversal of traditional gender roles.[1] The *aisling* model, established by the Gaelic bards as an allegory for the plight of Ireland after the defeat of the Jacobites, represents the lovely woman who is Ireland, the *spéirbhan*, as helpless to resist the advances of the colonizer. Aogán Ó Rathaille's 'Gile na Gile' ('Brightness Most Bright'), one of the most famous exemplars of the genre, says bluntly that while imprisoned by the 'goblins' (code for the English) the poet was forced to watch the violation of his beloved: 'a lumbering brute took hold of my girl by the breasts'. The poem's coda, which is called 'The Knot', pessimistically reiterates the sexual dimensions of the colonial allegory:

> Pain, disaster, downfall, sorrow and loss!
> Our mild bright, delicate, loving, fresh-lipped girl
> with one of that black, horned, foreign, hate-crested crew
> and no remedy near till our lions come over the sea. (*An Duanaire* 151–3)

The bitterness of defeat finds its most charged expression in the language of male sexual jealousy: the rape of the woman signifies the emasculation of her man. Using the pre-existing formulas of melodrama Bourke sets up a scenario that initially resembles the *aisling*, but he reinvigorates the passive or dying heroine.[2] As Cheryl Herr notes, Bourke's plays reflect his immediate historical situation: he was writing not only in an actively revolutionary Dublin, but also at the height of the suffrage agitation. The 'remedy' that the *aisling* poet seeks in vain is discovered by the rebel dramatist in the physical courage and ingenuity of the women of 1798. Some of these women were real and some imagined, but all of them challenge the formulaic representation of Ireland as a helpless maiden.

When Wexford Rose, which resembles *Arrah-na-Pogue* in all but its theatrical effectiveness, sets up two pairs of lovers, the rebel gentleman Donal O'Byrne and his beloved Grace Bassett, who take after Beamish MacCoul and Fanny Power, and their servants Ned and Kitty, who are poor relations of Shaun the Post and Arrah. The relationship between the patriots Donal and Grace is triangulated not by a self-denying character like Boucicault's amiable O'Grady, but by the irredeemably wicked Colonel Needham, the 'Commander of the ancient Britons', who is determined to possess both the orphan Grace and her considerable fortune. Sexual, financial and political motives coincide, and Needham is given the standard dialogue of a melodramatic villain: 'Curse the jade! Once more she has given us the slip' (*Wexford* 266). His 'nefarious machinations' (268) occupy the foreground of the plot, which is based on episodes from the uprising of 1798 in Wexford: the rebels' victory at Oulart Hill and their defeat at Arklow. The real Colonel Needham was the victor at the siege of Arklow and one of the commanders when the rebels were definitively crushed at Vinegar Hill.[3] The fictional Needham's major antagonists, however, are not soldiers, but women. When Grace expresses her envy for Irishmen who are fighting to free their country, Donal tells her that she should stick to 'a sphere of action more suited to your strength' and patronizingly calls her 'the best little woman in Ireland' (268). For a little woman, however, Grace does quite well; first she holds off the English officer Colonel Foote with a stiletto, and then in a climactic confrontation with Needham she tears herself from his amorous embrace and shoots one of his men. At the end of the play, as Donal and Grace prepare to leave Ireland for France, Needham falls into their power and is condemned to be executed. The villainous Englishman is not even permitted to die bravely. He grovels to Grace, begging her to spare his life, but she consigns him to the firing squad with unsentimental alacrity: a reversal of both gendered and national relations of power that was, of course, a piece of inspirational wish fulfilment on Bourke's part.

Grace, moreover, is outdone in energy and fighting spirit by Kitty, who spends the play 'goin' round fightin' like a man' (*Wexford* 281). Kitty and her friend Mary Doyle, known to the troops as 'the Rebel hussies' (274) become expert with sword and gun. Mary Doyle is a historical figure, remembered for her gallantry at the battle of New Ross. A chronicler of 1798 described her as 'an amazon named Doyle, who marched with the insurgent army and bore herself as gallantly as the most courageous man' (quoted in Ann Kinsella 191). In the play we hear how the literate and determined Mary 'proved herself as half a dozen men at the battle of New Ross' (*Wexford* 284), where she occupied herself with conserving weapons and ammunition:

> Bravin' the storm of bullets from the redcoats above, she leaped into the pass of death and cutting the ammunition belts from the dead bodies of the fallen redcoats, she flung the belts back to our men . . . The boys in their hurry were leavin' behind a small cannon we had brought with us & that proved very useful. But my bould Mary sat herself on the barrel & declared she wouldn't stir a step from the place unless we brought her dear little gun along with us. (285)[4]

We also see her fight a duel with Colonel Foote and run him through with her sword. When Mary is finally shot her killer is a woman, the treacherous but equally spirited Irish informer Croppy Biddy, herself a legendary historical figure.[5] Croppy Biddy, a gendered variation on the long melodramatic tradition of the Irish male informer, is the most powerful character in the play. From the start she mocks, dominates and financially out-manoeuvres her English paymaster Colonel Needham; at the end she is executed by his side. The unusually prominent role accorded to women in *When Wexford Rose* alters the symbolic balance of power of the colonial allegory. When an Englishman's designs are foiled primarily by the women he seeks to possess or dominate, the *aisling* story as national metaphor has undergone a radical change.

As its title indicates, *For the Land She Loved* is also a play that refuses the image of Ireland as a passive maiden, since the patriot who gives her life for her country is Betsy Gray, the heroine of Ballynahinch, who was celebrated as 'Ulster's Joan of Arc' (Bartlett 67; Ann Kinsella 194). At Ballynahinch 'She led us on through that fire of hell that came from the enemy's guns, an' for ten hours it was as hot as hell sure enough. . . . We were led as men were never led before by a girl' (*For the Land* 353–4). Bourke retains the battle episode as the climax of the play, but forces Betsy's legend into the familiar melodramatic mould of the love triangle. She is engaged to the rebel hero, Robert Monro, but she is pursued and at one point almost raped by the cruel and duplicitous Colonel Johnston, an English villain who covets her money and goes to ridiculously repetitive lengths to secure her hand. As if one triangle were not enough, Bourke adds a second: Lady Lucy Nugent, daughter of General John Nugent, the commander of the King's Troops in Ulster, loves and pursues Betsy's fiancé Robert Monro. Lady Nugent is an energetic and enterprising female villain, always ready with a dastardly plot and handy with both the gun and the sword. At the beginning of the play she shoots and kills Betsy's father; at the end, in a striking reversal of gender roles, she fights a duel with Betsy over Robert Monro. She is more than the equal of her English ally Colonel Johnston. Both of these sexual predators express imperial claims on Ireland through their desire for an Irish lover, but both are rebuffed. Robert and Betsy are determined not to concede, either sexually or politically. Although Lady Nugent's father, General Nugent, keeps foiling the designs of his despicable subordinate officer, his conventional role as honourable stage Englishman seems to be inserted more to ensure an endless sequence of narrow escapes than to hint at any possibility of reconciliation between England and Ireland.

The modern Irish dramatist who was most indebted to melodrama for his inspiration and structure was Sean O'Casey. In *Juno and the Paycock* (1924) O'Casey revised Tom Broadbent's comic sexual conquest of the 'Irish heiress' Nora into an unpleasant melodramatic episode, Bourkian rather than Boucicauldian in tone, that turns out badly for almost everyone concerned. A more calculating predator than Shaw's genial Broad*bent,* O'Casey's tall and handsome Englishman Charlie *Bent*ham (the reverse consonance of their names suggests a conscious connection) makes love to Juno Boyle's daughter Mary and displaces her Irish suitor, the trade unionist Jerry Devine. Unlike Larry Doyle, Jerry Devine minds being thrown over, and O'Casey makes it clear that, although Jerry's humanity is not equal to the acceptance of another man's child, the match Mary is forfeiting would have been adequate. Shaw's romantic Broadbent has no need for, or interest in, the forty pounds a year of which his beloved Nora is so proud, but the aptly named utilitarian Bentham is an economic predator (though not a very clever one, as his mistake in drawing up the will suggests). He pursues Mary for the money he thinks she is about to inherit. Once he discovers that his own incompetence has ruined the Boyle family and there is nothing further to be gained in Ireland, he disappears to England, abandoning his pregnant girlfriend and her rapidly splintering family to their fate. O'Casey's stage directions do not specify Bentham's nationality, but in Alfred Hitchcock's 1930 movie version of the play he was played as an Englishman by the British actor John Longden. Though Bentham's obsession with theosophy may be a satirical dig at AE, whom O'Casey despised, his name, his speech patterns and his eventual place of refuge mark him as a symbolic representative of the rulers of Ireland. Boyle even mocks him as 'his Majesty, Bentham' (*Three Plays* 33).[6] The allegory of British withdrawal is clear: the breakup of Juno and Joxer's marriage mirrors the civil war that claims the life of their son, and 'his Majesty' takes no responsibility for the consequences of his economic or sexual wrongdoing. Susan Harris reads Bentham's drawing-up of the faulty will as 'standing in for the Treaty', an equally flawed document (*Bodies* 259). Abrupt decolonization leaves the Irish family/nation in a terrible 'state o' chassis'. Despite his refusal of nationalism and insistence on class and economic analysis, O'Casey follows Boucicault and Shaw in presenting the relationship between England and Ireland in gendered terms: gender is the stereotypical formulation that persists the longest, even in the hands of socialist or women playwrights.[7]

The behaviour of Bentham the English seducer is the model for the duplicitous Englishman Joe Conran in Anne Devlin's *Ourselves Alone* (1986). Conran replaces an Irishman in the affections of the Irish heroine Josie, gets her pregnant, and then disappears back to England, betraying both her and the cause he has pretended to support. When Josie says of herself and the child she is carrying 'you don't have to worry about me, Joe. I have two hearts' (*Ourselves* 79), Devlin alludes to Juno Boyle's affirmation that, despite Bentham's disappearance, Mary's half-English child will be well looked after because 'it'll have two mothers' (*Three Plays* 71). Bentham the sexual cad is a representative of English colonialism by analogy only; Conran, however, is directly modelled on the SAS undercover operative Captain Robert Nairac. Nairac was a living, breathing stage Englishman, an English Catholic with a history degree from Oxford, who was described by his teachers as 'a romantic' (Dillon, *Dirty War* 162). Lieutenant Yolland's abduction by the Donnelly twins may have been suggested by Nairac's disappearance in South Armagh in 1977. Like Yolland he was supposedly engaged in mapping: one of the covert SAS detachments to which he belonged was posing as 4 Field Survey Troop, Royal Engineers (Bradley 44; Dillon 164–5). After he went missing, his sister told reporters, 'Since he has always loved Ireland and the Irish, it is ironic that he may have died while trying as a volunteer to contribute to peace in Ireland' (Bradley 47). The contributions of the SAS to peace in Ireland are apparent only to the British, whose newspapers portrayed Nairac as a gallant idealist murdered by the IRA. The government encouraged this interpretation by awarding him a posthumous George Cross.

Friel's fictional Lieutenant Yolland resembles the Nairac constructed by sentimental English newspaper propaganda: he is a soldier-romantic and hibernophile. Devlin's Joe Conran, who claims Anglo-Irish descent but whose education, army training and English mother mark him as more Anglo than Irish, is modelled on the historical Nairac, a much less attractive figure. The connection between Nairac, Friel and Devlin can plausibly be made because his bizarre story was prominently featured in the media, and many other writers took it up. In *The Romans in Britain* (1980) English playwright Howard Brenton represented Nairac as Captain Thomas Chichester, an SAS assassin who passes himself off as Irish by singing 'a few rebel songs in the local pub' and pretends to be a gunrunner selling communist weapons to the IRA. A fellow British army officer describes him as 'a maverick . . . And a romantic and a bloody menace' (76–7). The IRA man who is Chichester's target, and who ultimately orders his execution, is more precise: 'you're either a madman, or an intelligence officer with the Special Air Services Regiment' (99). A sardonic quatrain by Paul Muldoon lampoons the spurious 'Irish' credentials of someone who was born not with a silver spoon in his mouth, but with a mink hood on his rain jacket:

> A mink escaped from a mink-farm
> in South Armagh
> is led to the grave of Robert Nairac
> by the fur-lined hood of his anorak. (*Quoof* 28)

The resemblances between the real Nairac and Devlin's fictional Conran are extremely close. Like Nairac, Conran attended Ampleforth, the English Catholic public school that was a breeding ground for SAS men. Nairac went to Oxford, Conran to Cambridge: both were enrolled at Sandhurst, the upper-class English officer-training academy, and both posed as engineers. Yolland is a genuine romantic, 'A soldier by *accident*' (Friel, *Translations* 30) who dislikes the army; and both Nairac and Conran infiltrated the IRA by pretending to be someone like Yolland, someone who derives from the stage tradition of the English hibernophile. From the same upper-middle-class background as Yolland, Conran is nevertheless married to Rosa, an urban version of the colleen Maire, 'A wee hussy from the Bogside' (*Ourselves* 51). The fictional Conran seeks an interview with the notorious British counter-terrorism expert Brigadier Frank Kitson; the historical Nairac, trained in Kitson's school of Counter Insurgency Operations, may have directed loyalist death squads, including the one that perpetrated the Miami Showband massacre. He frequented the bars in the borderlands of South Armagh, affecting a Belfast accent and proclaiming his allegiance to the Official IRA. He was nicknamed 'Danny Boy', because he sang Irish ballads and rebel songs at the pub microphone. The stage Englishman, the Oxford hibernophile, put on a bizarre performance as the stage Irishman. His act ran for thirty months before he was abducted and killed by the IRA.

When he arrives in the North of Ireland as an undercover agent to track down IRA chief Cathal O'Donnell, Devlin's fictional Joe Conran immediately becomes the lover of Josie, a working-class IRA volunteer from West Belfast. To complete the Shavian cross-national triangle, Conran's seduction of Josie rekindles the passion of her neglectful former lover, who is Cathal O'Donnell himself. As usual, the Englishman initially triumphs in the erotic contest; more obviously than usual the Irishwoman's function is simply to facilitate the circulation of desire between two men. Remembering Sedgwick's definition of desire as the 'glue, even when its manifestation is hostility or hatred . . . that shapes an important relationship' (Sedgwick 2), we may argue that Conran's desire was never for Josie herself but for the man whose place in her bed he has usurped, his male victim and psychic double O'Donnell. O'Donnell in some measure reciprocates this desire: he believes in Conran's act and is the last to accept that his erotic rival is also a double agent and an informer. O'Donnell has seen *Translations* once too often: instead of suspecting Conran's social background and army contacts and eliminating him at once, he makes a fatal literary–critical misjudgement. Taken in by the stage English credentials of this unlikely IRA recruit, he declares confidently: 'It's really very simple. He's a romantic' (*Ourselves* 71).

No more a romantic than Nairac was, Conran is a cold-hearted spy who impregnates and abandons Josie, sets up the capture of O'Donnell and betrays a huge IRA arms shipment to the Irish security police. As the pre-Rising years produced the English villains of Bourke, so the post-hunger strike phase of the Troubles and the British shoot-to-kill policy prompted Anne Devlin's treacherous Anglo-Irishman.[8] Devlin adopts the myth of the Wild Irish Girl and the English lover who makes the cause of Ireland his own, but she suggests that its foundation lies in exploitation and violence, rather than benevolence. She also breaks the traditional mould by eliminating the inevitable Irish informer in favour of an English one: Conran combines the roles of colonizer and traitor. Devlin is no supporter of the IRA, who are seen as callous abusers of their foolishly loyal women, and her upbringing as the daughter of the Northern trade unionist Paddy Devlin is reflected in her awareness of the importance of class; nevertheless, she produces in Joe Conran one of the most treacherous Englishmen on the twentieth century Irish stage.

Three films by the writing team of Jim Sheridan and Terry George expand the critique of the stage Englishman. *In the Name of the Father* (1993), which fictionally documents the abuses meted out to the Guildford Four and the Maguire Seven by a corrupt and incompetent British judicial system, confronts the innocent Irish victims with a whole range of despicable English males: savage interrogators and brutal prison officers, suavely duplicitous policemen, venal lawyers and culpably blind old judges. The 'heavy' villain – the man who oversees the extortion of confessions from the Irish prisoners, deliberately suppresses their only alibi, lies repeatedly on the witness stand and refuses to act when the real IRA bombers claim responsibility for blowing up the Guildford pub – is called Inspector Dixon. The irony here (which will be lost on an American audience) is that the longest-running police serial on English television, *Dixon of Dock Green* (1955–76), embodied all the most comforting and reassuring features of the British law in the figure of its fatherly hero, the honest and plainspoken Inspector Dixon. The film's Inspector Dixon (played, ironically, by the leftist actor Corin Redgrave) turns this well-loved character inside out, and reveals that the justice of which the English people were once so proud is a dishonest and cruel sham. Smiling policewomen serve birthday cake and cups of tea in the corridors while young Irish prisoners are being tortured in the interrogation rooms. The smooth, wealthy and well-spoken Dixon embodies this disjunction between comfortable English surfaces and sinister depths. He allows lower-class, thuggish Brits and a policeman from Belfast (Ger McSorley) to play bad cop until Gerry Conlon is reduced to a dribbling wreck. Then, moving in with a pseudo-fatherly embrace, some superficial psycho-babble ('let it all out, let out all the hatred') and the talismanic cigarette, he gets the confession he wants.

The eventual confession of the real bomber lays bare the extent of Dixon's anti-Irish racism. The Belfast policeman admits that his strong-arm tactics failed to elicit the truth from the Guildford Four. 'They didn't do it', he says; but Dixon responds, 'They all did it'. As 'The Men Behind the Wire' has it, 'Being Irish means they're guilty / So we're guilty one and all'. Stung by this negative reflection on what is, after all, his own ethnicity, the policeman replies 'I'm going back to Belfast', but Dixon is unrepentant, and the film implies that he has support in high places. When he is finally defeated in court, he says to his unidentified superiors, 'Don't try and make me the fall guy for the whole British Establishment', but that in fact is what Sheridan's film does. In the interests of dramatic economy and simplicity, Dixon stands in for the numerous Englishmen who were complicit in the state-sanctioned abuse of the Guildford Four, the Maguire Seven and the Birmingham Six. Like the original Dixon of Dock Green, he is a symbol of British justice.

Sheridan and George were attacked in the British press because their film, while billing itself as a true story, is constructed according to conventional Hollywood principles: it employs a few easily recognizable characters, omits or simplifies numerous details in order to maintain the forward thrust of the narrative and alters others to increase the power of the father/son relationship and the dramatic suspense of the climax.[9] The demonizing of Dixon is balanced by the insertion of a fictitious sequence in which the IRA bomber, Joe McAndrew, inflicts terrible burns on the head warder. Gerry Conlon writes that IRA prisoners differ from other inmates in their superior discipline and do not get involved in 'grudge attacks on screws or other prisoners' (Name 159). Sheridan deliberately ignored Conlon's own testimony in order to distance his innocent protagonist from the violent tactics of the IRA.

> No one objected to one distortion we were guilty of, which was showing the IRA burn a prison officer. That never happened, but no one has complained. Why? Because our biggest distortion was to show that violence doesn't work. If you look at history, all reality tells us the opposite. But I'm glad to be guilty of that distortion because, even if violence does achieve its ends, it's not worth it. (Quoted in Woodworth)

Although Sheridan never claimed that the film was a documentary, many British critics condemned its numerous manipulations of fact, whatever their aesthetic or political implications (Jenkins, Tookey). As the McAndrew sequence suggests, however, Sheridan is an equal-opportunity distorter. The police and the IRA may be presented as mirror images of one another (both get their way by threatening to kill the families of their enemies), but the need to give an English audience an emotional foothold in the film also leads Sheridan and George to glamorize the role of at least one 'decent' English character; not a man this time, but a woman.

In the Name of the Father begins with Gerry Conlon telling his female solicitor, Gareth Pierce, 'I never thought I'd trust an English person again'. A film that attempts, quite successfully, to 'bring the entire British legal system into disrepute' has an English heroine, played by the compelling Emma Thompson, fighting for justice for the Guildford Four. Like Dixon, she is simplified into a symbol. As she challenges the representatives of the elderly male British establishment, her youth and her gender align her with the Irish Others whom she is defending. Nevertheless, her apologetic and self-deprecating style (she says 'sorry' incessantly), her Oxford accent and many of her character attributes mark her as a female exemplar of the better qualities of the stage Englishman. In her persistence, truthfulness and common sense she embodies Arnold's 'energy with honesty'. Her motivating force is an 'English' obsession with fair play, and Dixon's refusal to grant a compassionate release to the dying Giuseppe Conlon (whom he knows to be innocent) threatens her belief in English magnanimity. Early in their relationship Gerry Conlon tells her, 'I don't understand your language. Justice. Mercy. Clemency. I literally don't understand what those words mean'. Gareth, who upholds the old standards of decency that the British judicial establishment has discarded, is later forced to agree with him: 'They ought to take the word compassion out of the English language', she exclaims.

Gareth's propensity for emotional outbursts in the court, her sensitivity and the intuitive sympathy with which she handles both Giuseppe and the initially hostile Gerry combine to feminize the traditional virtues of the stage Englishman. After a few outings as a homosexual (The Crying Game, Someone Who'll Watch over Me), the decent chap has turned into a woman. In the eighties, however, the rise to power of Margaret Thatcher provided both the left-wing English and the Irish film industries with a new model: an ostensibly female stage English villain, who, despite her electric blue suits, her ladylike handbag and her stiffly-waved hair, competes in the virility stakes with her opponents, whether they be black immigrants, English miners, Argentine generals or Irish hunger strikers. Her over-schooled plummy tones appear in ironic counterpoint to the scenes of eviction at the beginning of Hanif Kureshi's Sammy and Rosie Get Laid (1987), and are used to similar effect in the introduction to Ken Loach's Hidden Agenda (1990). Sheridan and George borrow the tactic for the start of their film on the Irish hunger strikes, Some

Mother's Son (1996). The peaceable words of St Francis of Assisi, 'Where there is discord, let us sow harmony', sound grating in the mouth of one who was to escalate the conflict in Ireland; and while St Francis fed the birds, Margaret Thatcher allowed ten men to starve themselves to death rather than show any signs of feminine 'weakness' herself. After the opening shot of the blue suit she does not appear again in person, but her surrogate throughout the film is a nasty young government hack called Farnsworth, who presents the PM's 'new approach' to a sceptical War Room: 'Isolation. Criminalization. Demoralization. . . . There is no war. There is only crime'. Thatcher's puppet Farnsworth is another Dixon, a 'heavy' villain who is supposed to channel the audience's dislike and distrust; but where Dixon exuded an aura of solid masculinity Farnsworth's short stature, wavy hair and prissy speech patterns constantly remind us of the Iron Lady he serves.

From the start, Farnsworth is opposed by the Good Englishman Harrington, a career diplomat from the Foreign Office who has had experience as an observer in the Northern prisons and who mistrusts the new policy. 'We're really going to fuck it up', he prophesies; and fuck it up they do. Harrington's role as the internal opposition is better judged in dramatic terms than Farnsworth's villainy, which at moments is so ludicrously overstated as to be funny. Thatcherism can bring out the worst in left-wing directors (think of the implausible cabal of Thatcherite Tories in *Hidden Agenda*),[10] perhaps because no fiction can match the reality. Harrington fares better, not only because we recognize his long and honourable stage English ancestry ('I have never cheated anyone in my life'), but also because he gets some of the best political lines. When Farnsworth justifies his dishonest tactics on the grounds that 'this is war, not diplomacy', Harrington replies swiftly, 'I distinctly remember you saying it wasn't a war'. The audience remembers it too, and the intellectual duplicity of Thatcher's criminalization policy is nakedly exposed – by an Englishman. Harrington's risky attempt to end the hunger strike by brokering a good-faith deal with the Sinn Féin representative Danny Boyle costs him his career: he is foiled at the last minute by Farnsworth's blackmail photographs of their clandestine meeting. The English do not talk to terrorists. (It has recently been revealed that they did so all the time.) In Thatcher's new England decency no longer pays; despite the Prime Minister's lip service to Victorian values, all the old ethical standards have gone. Harrington is there to measure the loss, and his defeat by Farnsworth reveals the moral deficiencies of British policy.

When the middle-class mother Kathleen (Helen Mirren) says 'Thirty thousand people voted for Bobby Sands; that's more than voted for Thatcher', she claims democratic legitimacy (the ballot box rather than the Armalite) for the nationalist position. The Republican mother, Annie (Fionnula Flanagan), admits that 'We never had much use for the ballot box ourselves', but she involves Kathleen in Sands's election campaign with the line, 'This isn't violence, it's an election'. In all of their films Sheridan and George attempt to steer a political middle course between the constitutional and the physical force varieties of Irish nationalism. They condemn violence, but they show why Irish people have felt the need to use it. Gerry Conlon's politicization by the IRA man Joe McAndrew is not erased by the incident with the warder; it is simply re-directed towards non-violent protest, the letter-writing campaign advocated by his pacifist father Giuseppe. In their ceasefire film *The Boxer* (1997), Sheridan and George present the disciplined containment of violence as their central metaphor: ex-IRA man Danny attempts to channel antagonism between the Catholic and Protestant communities into a non-sectarian boxing club. The film's brief excursion to England, in which Danny fights in a luxurious London dinner venue for the entertainment of a roomful of braying Brits, presents him with a symbolic challenge: does he stop fighting when his opponent is obviously hurt, or continue, as the English referee insists that he must? Danny chooses to lose the bout rather than inflict any more damage on his Nigerian opponent. His choice not only establishes the parameters within which boxing is compatible with honour and outside of which it degenerates into meaningless cruelty, but also offers a message to the IRA bosses who are considering the merits of a ceasefire. A loss of face is preferable to continued bloodshed. The English setting of this scene, however, and the ethnic identities of the Irish and Nigerian pugilists, suggest that in the aftermath of Empire the English are still exploiting their former colonial subjects as circus animals. Danny's mentor Ike compares the pugilists to 'performing monkeys'. Like the violence in the North of Ireland, the violence the two boxers perform is orchestrated by the imperial ringmaster.

Conversely, Sheridan's English characters assume that personal hatred, rather than principled opposition to oppression, is the psychological motor for Republican violence. Dixon suggests that Gerry Conlon bombed the Guildford pub because he hates all English people. (As we see, it is Dixon and, by implication, the English establishment who feel that way about the Irish.) In order to refute this crude assumption, *Some Mother's Son* interrupts its narrative with a gratuitous but politically conciliatory scene. When Kathleen tries to teach Annie how to drive on the beach, their car gets stuck in the sand. After a cheerful group of British soldiers, sexist but helpful ('Stand aside, ladies'), rescue it from the advancing tide, Annie reluctantly admits, 'I don't hate them all, you know'.

Neil Jordan's *Michael Collins* (1996), which resembles the Manichean melodrama of P. J. Bourke rather than the reconciliatory project of Boucicault, directly engages the question of Irish hatred, admitting its existence while blaming the British for producing it. Collins declares flatly, 'I hate them. Not for their race. Not for their brutality. I hate them because they've left us no way out. I hate whoever put a gun in young Ned Tannin's hand. I know it's me, and I hate myself for it. . . . I hate them for making hate necessary' (*Michael Collins* 135). Jordan abandons his previous exploration of love between national enemies to concentrate on the love between Irishmen who chose different sides in the Civil War. He replaces the cross-national male triangle of *The Crying Game* with an all-Irish erotic configuration: Eamon de Valera comes between Michael Collins and Harry Boland. Their English adversaries, led by the suavely vicious, well-groomed and efficient Soames, embody only the negative aspects of the stage English stereotype. While Sheridan and George's films received a mixed welcome in England, *Michael Collins* caused an uproar in the conservative British press.

The turbulent reception accorded to Jordan's film emphasized the political significance of what was, in aesthetic terms, a well-acted, visually attractive, occasionally over-obvious and rather too swiftly paced bio-epic: *Gandhi* at warp speed in the rain. In Ireland it caused a popular sensation and was widely hailed as the most important Irish film ever made. Never mind that it was made with American money: the Irish creative talent, the location shoots with Irish extras and the nationalist subject matter won it a certificate of authenticity, together with a lenient certification from the Irish censor. From English Tories, Irish revisionist historians and the Unionists of Northern Ireland, on the other hand, it attracted passionate condemnation. (British movie reviewers generally liked it.) Released in October 1996, when the 1994 IRA ceasefire had been broken by the bomb at London's Canary Wharf and the peace process was suspended by a thread, the film was read as a reckless intervention into the political situation in the North. An editorial in the conservative *Daily Telegraph* entitled 'Warners' profit, Ulster's loss' compared Jordan's representation of the British with the representation of Jews in anti-Semitic propaganda, thus equating Irish nationalists, both past and present, with the Nazis. Apparently convinced that movies make things happen, the *Telegraph* quoted Yeats's famous lines, 'Did that play of mine send out / Certain men the English shot' (*Poems* 345), and demanded that this 'inflammatory film' be withdrawn ('Warners'). The tabloid *Daily Mail* billed it as a 'morally repugnant film glamorizing the IRA terrorist Michael Collins' which 'sees the English solely as villains, conquerors and brutes' and provides 'another excuse for the ethical lepers of Hollywood, arguably . . . the most dangerous people on Earth, to propound yet more of their pro-terrorist fantasies'.[11] The writer had clearly never seen *Patriot Games* (1992), an anti-terrorist fantasy that is far more representative of Hollywood's attitude to the IRA than *Michael Collins*.

Irish revisionist historians who take a sceptical view of what they consider the mythic simplicity of the nationalist historical narrative, and who therefore resist negative depictions of the British, also took issue with the film (Byrne). Ruth Dudley Edwards noted that Connolly was not kicked as he lay wounded on a stretcher after the surrender in 1916 (although she could not have denied that he was taken to his subsequent execution on a similar stretcher). Irish historian Paul Bew assaulted Jordan for anachronisms like the scene in which a Northern Irish policeman with an unmistakable accent arrives in Dublin to sort out the incompetent Southern locals. 'A bit of Belfast efficiency is what they need', he snorts, and jumps into his car, which promptly explodes. Bew points out that, while car bombs feature prominently in the repertoire of today's IRA, they were unheard of in Collins's Ireland: 'The terrorist technology of the present is thus gratuitously inserted into the "heroic" past of Irish history. Back to the Future it may be, history it ain't' ('History'). From a strictly occupational perspective, the Disabled Police Officers Association of Northern Ireland took a similar view of the scene (Harnden). Echoing the *Telegraph's* equation of Irish nationalism with Nazism, and going into rhetorical overdrive, Bew claims that Jordan's formal homage to *The Godfather*, in which Collins's assassinations of the English villain Soames and his Secret Servicemen (the Cairo gang, a 'mob' that rivals the Apostles) are intercut with his *nuit blanche* with Kitty in the Gresham Hotel, 'is close to that cruel self-absorption spliced with sentimentality that is characteristic of fascist art' ('History'). There is certainly shock value in the way that the brutal assassinations are offset by Kitty's fingering of a rose and conclude with her line, 'Flowers delivered. Do you think they got the message?' but the perennial association of love with death is hardly the exclusive prerogative of fascism. Jordan's reference to *The Godfather*, moreover, is a double-edged political sword. In *In the Name of the Father*, Sheridan uses a prison showing of the movie to tar several of his characters (the English crime boss Ronnie, the head warder Barker, and the IRA man Joe McAndrew) with the Mafia brush. Shots of the ageing Don (Marlon Brando) talking with his son Michael Corleone lead into and facilitate McAndrew's violent attack on Barker, after which Gerry Conlon rejects all potential godfathers and returns to his biological father Giuseppe. The popular description of the IRA as the 'Godfathers of terrorism', like the criminalization policy, identified political violence with organized crime. *The Godfather* is thus a negative symbolic identification which risks rubbing off even on Michael Collins, whose responsibility for the elimination of the English Secret Servicemen is unflinchingly presented by Jordan as the bloodiest episode in a sanguinary career.[12]

But Jordan's Collins is so carefully prevented from killing anyone himself, and so often compelled to worry about the moral implications of violence, that one suspects the presence of the airbrush. He repeatedly asks his various accomplices 'could you handle it' or 'could you bear it', and before every bloodbath he humanely gives his young assassins the chance to opt out (*Michael Collins* 126). No one ever does, of course, but Jordan absolves them in advance because they regard violence as such a distasteful necessity. Collins's Apostles pick off 'legitimate' British targets one by one, praying before they do so and invoking the blessing of God on their victims as they open fire; the Tans, on the other hand, massacre Irish civilians in random swathes. The Irish are also allowed to tell the audience that the killing is, in Ned Broy's words, 'pulling me to ribbons' (*Michael Collins* 149), while the British are not permitted to confide their scruples, supposing they have any, to the camera.

Despite Jordan's careful sanitization of Irish violence, and the fact that it is a trifle difficult to equate the British in Ireland with the victims of the Holocaust, the 'fascist' or 'Nazi' analogy applied to Jordan by Bew and the *Daily Telegraph* proved attractive for other Irish critics unsympathetic to the nationalist position, like former Workers' Party member Eoghan Harris:

> Stylistically, in Susan Sontag's terms, Michael Collins is a neo-fascist movie. The power of the images, like Leni Riefenstahl's, sweeps away our critical barriers. . . . And if our media and academics were not so numbed by nationalism, they would see the movie is racist – all the Brits are bastards. That is bad history, bad morals and bad art. (Eoghan Harris)

The invocation of Riefenstahl makes a tendentious analogy between Michael Collins and Hitler. Harris ignores the fact that the figure who demonstrates a neo-fascist contempt for democracy, proclaims his readiness to wade through Irish blood and harbours a mystical conviction that he embodies the spirit of the nation is not Collins but Eamon de Valera, who takes over as the film's lead villain when the British depart.

Harris is on stronger ground when he notes that 'all the Brits are bastards', as indeed they are, though they are mostly anonymous and unindividualized. The Tans do what a Tan's gotta do: they roar through the streets in their Crossley tenders, answering rotten vegetables with lethal gunfire, and they slaughter unarmed football supporters at Croke Park. The elite Cairo gang look briefly sinister before being comprehensively rubbed out. Only Soames, their leader, has a 'character'. He is upper-class, sharply dressed and patronizingly charming to the Irish chambermaid who betrays him. Where Molineux gave Claire a symbolic crown, Soames gives Rosie half a crown and keeps her up to the mark in matters of personal hygiene: his last words are 'Clean sheets, Rosie' (*Michael Collins* 160). Like his unfortunate counterpart from Belfast, he is impatient with Southern Irish inefficiency. His peremptory relationship with Collins's double agent Ned Broy neatly symbolizes the power disparity between colonizer and colonized: 'Thank you, Boy. That will be all', he says in his clipped tones, as if to a native servant. 'It's Broy, sir', replies Ned wearily. Their last exchange is quietly sinister:

> SOAMES. Sufficient unto the day the evil thereof. Eh, Boy?
> BROY. Yes, sir.
> SOAMES. Or is it Broy?
> BROY. Broy, sir. (*Michael Collins* 153–4)

Soames is the evil that is sufficient unto the day, which is to be Broy's last. Later that night, the English villain orders the half-hanging of Collins's spy in order to elicit information. His sadistic use of torture is accompanied by a racist witticism: 'That's the trouble with the Irish; they sing at the drop of a hat, but when you ask them to talk they won't'. The audience is thus primed to observe his assassination on the following morning with equanimity, if not with pleasure.

The major objections to *Michael Collins*, more vehement than those that greeted *In the Name of the Father*, sprang from the fact that, after years of negative Irish stereotypes, the representational shoe was now on the other foot. If his countrymen appear 'solely as villains, conquerors and brutes', it is naturally an English journalist's duty to discredit the historical accuracy of *Michael Collins*. Most of the objections that were raised look generically naive. A film that covers six years of complex history must inevitably simplify, condense and omit, in order to produce an aesthetically satisfying structure peopled by a recognizable group of central characters. Like Sheridan, Jordan is creating a highly mediated representation of events, not a documentary. All but the most unreflective filmgoers, or those who reject what they call 'faction' altogether, will be ready to accept changes or omissions as inevitable: it is the contemporary political ends that such changes serve which precipitate controversy.[13] In the diary that prefaces his screenplay, Jordan himself worries about fusing all of Collins's double agents into the figure of Ned Broy and killing him off in the Castle on the night before Bloody Sunday, when in fact he lived to a ripe old age. Because Clancy, McKee and Clune, the three men whom the British did kill in the Castle, had no previous role in his plot, he substituted Broy, whose character was already well established. Jordan consoled himself with the thought that 'Shakespeare did far worse with Holinshed' (*Michael Collins* 14), but ironically his aesthetically motivated substitution of a single known victim for three anonymous ones (surely an improvement from the don't-blame-the-British point of view) competed with the car bomb and the Croke Park massacre as a focus for complaints about historical inaccuracy.

Jordan also defends his exclusion of the Treaty negotiations and Collins's affair with Lady Hazel Lavery on the reasonable grounds that to take the film to London would have doubled its cast and its length. Considering the lack of interesting women in the film, Lavery's absence is a pity, but the topic of her romance with Collins and her role in securing his assent to the Treaty had already been fictionalized in the 1936 Hollywood film *Beloved Enemy*, which turns the American-born Lavery into an Englishwoman. Given his previous interest in love between those on opposing sides of a conflict, this saccharine melodrama (which allows Collins to recover from the assassination attempt in order to marry his upper-class English admirer) might have offered Jordan a heterosexual model of Irish/English relations. Instead, he maintained both his narrative drive and his uncompromisingly negative view of the British by eliminating Hazel Lavery and permitting the notorious womanizer Collins a single female beloved: the Irishwoman Kitty Kiernan.

In terms of its political reception, as well as its structure, the film falls into two halves: the War of Independence culminating in the Treaty, and the subsequent repudiation of the Treaty by de Valera that led to the Civil War. The

British objected only to the first half of the movie, which ought, the *Daily Mirror* observed, to be renamed 'Brits Behaving Badly' (Parsons). The question of how badly the Brits did in fact behave during the Irish struggle for independence was answered according to the political prejudices of the observer: consequently the liberal British press did not attack *Michael Collins* with the same energy as the Tory organs, although the *Independent* suggested that 'Jordan's depiction of the British enemy leans towards a mythic simplicity' (Jackson). The arch right-winger Paul Johnson fulminated that 'The *Guardian*, a paper specially written for people who hate England and the English – who hate themselves, in fact – gave generous space last week to Neil Jordan'. After establishing that a liberal British viewer who likes *Michael Collins* necessarily hates herself, Johnson goes on to lay the blame for the film on Hollywood, which represents 'plain, unmitigated evil' (Johnson). Indeed, if Palace Pictures, the small English company with which Jordan worked earlier in his career, had produced *Michael Collins*, it might have been a different movie. The global power of Warner Brothers permitted Jordan to disregard English opinion as well as English sources of funding.

Both English and Irish opinion was engaged by Jordan's use of an armoured car during the worst British atrocity depicted in his film, the massacre of unarmed spectators in Croke Park. This powerful scene favourably impressed the reviewer of the Sinn Féin paper *An Phoblact*, leaving him with 'a sense of anger and frustration that no history lesson ever matched' (quoted in R. D. Edwards). In fact the soldiers used only their guns, a less visually powerful (but no less effective) way of killing twelve people and wounding sixty-four more. Jordan's use of the British armoured car may be defended on aesthetic grounds: at Croke Park its sinister swivelling gun turrets depersonalize the agents of the massacre, and symbolize the superiority of British firepower during the whole of the War of Independence. It also enables a striking visual parallel when Collins later borrows the vehicle from the British to use against his fellow Irishmen, the anti-Treatyite Republicans holed up in the Four Courts. But Sinn Féin's approval of *Michael Collins* (an approval which, as I argue in Chapter 9, is based on a superficial appreciation of its politics) lent credence to the conservative and revisionist contention that the movie was no more than Provo propaganda.

Other cinematic episodes that represent British imperialism in an unflattering light (the massacre at Amritsar in *Gandhi*, for example) have caused fewer outcries: it was the parallel between the past and the present that unleashed the storm of protest over *Michael Collins*. The Croke Park massacre came to be known as 'Bloody Sunday'; the most emotive memory of the recent Troubles is of another Bloody Sunday, 30 January 1972, when British paratroopers killed thirteen unarmed people during a protest march in Derry. Jordan acknowledges in his diary that 'the movie is like a prism that reflects every development of the recent situation' (*Michael Collins* 83): the guerrilla warfare between the IRA and the British that began in 1969; the emergence of Gerry Adams as a Collins lookalike, a former freedom fighter who now wants to negotiate; the 1994 ceasefire; the frustrating peace negotiations; and the split between the members of the IRA who bombed Canary Wharf and the Lisburn barracks early in 1996, and those in Sinn Féin who were still committed to the possibility of a settlement.

Because Collins commanded the Irish Republican Army in a successful guerrilla war, the British tabloids perceived him as a poster boy for the Provos. In fact the contemporary Irish Republican Army, which is descended from the 'Irregular' faction that broke away from Collins's organization and repudiated the Treaty he had signed, might well view Collins as the betrayer of the Republic that was proclaimed in 1916. But they would also find it difficult to identify with the upholder of that Republic, Collins's rival Eamon de Valera, who suppressed the IRA with merciless thoroughness once he rose to power. On Jordan's hostile representation of de Valera (which I discuss at greater length in Chapter 9), the Irish revisionists and the British critics of the film were mostly silent, presumably because they were delighted to see the symbol of the Republic so thoroughly discredited.

Principles of structure, in which parallels and contrasts of character give aesthetic shape to the narrative, fuse with Jordan's evident dislike of de Valera to reinforce a pre-existing political myth: the tragedy of the betrayed lost leader, the hero cut down in his prime. Neeson's charismatic performance makes it difficult for the audience to resist Collins's point of view, or even to consider the revisionist claim that the War of Independence won no more than a settlement that was bound to come in any case. The Collins we are left with at the end of the film, however, is no longer a ruthless guerrilla, but an advocate of peace and a statesman who upholds the democratically expressed will of the majority. Jordan was aware that, at the time he died, the historical Michael Collins was busy supplying guns to Catholics in the North (*Michael Collins* 66), but he suppresses this fact in order to claim that his hero died while trying 'to take the gun out of Irish politics'. In the contemporary Northern context, Jordan's alteration of the facts sends a relatively uncontroversial message: if violence was originally necessary in order to get the attention of the easily distracted British, it is now time for it to stop.

The outraged myopia which caused the conservative British press to overlook Jordan's pacific contemporary agenda in order to excoriate his 'hysterically anti-British film' (Parsons) suggests that the moderation previously shown by the majority of Irish dramatists and film-makers in their representation of the colonizer must have lulled some English audiences into the delusion that their role in Ireland had been relatively benevolent. Without a Harrington or a Gareth Pierce to embody British decency, they were forced to contemplate an entirely hostile vision of themselves. They did not like what they saw.

PART TWO

CARTHAGINIANS OR COWBOYS:
ANALOGY, IDENTITY, AMBIGUITY

ROMANS AND CARTHAGINIANS
Anti-colonial Metaphors in Contemporary Irish Literature

I

Analogy – the discovery of a likeness between two apparently discrete things – is the imaginative process by which metaphors are constructed. Genealogy – the claim that a likeness is inherited – is often equally imaginative, despite its historical pretensions. Unlike a simile, a metaphor is a dynamic comparison in which the properties of the two things compared are fused rather than juxtaposed, and the energies of metaphor can be harnessed in politics as well as in poetry. Marx noted the reliance of the French revolutionaries on historical models supplied by republican Rome, their need to deck their radical enterprise in the retro fancy dress of togas and laurel wreaths. During the same historical period, the first Celtic revivalists also looked back to the classical world for dynamic comparisons, but they constructed Irish identity in opposition to imperial Rome, which to them looked uncomfortably like the British Empire. Some Anglo-Irish antiquarians identified with Rome's defeated enemies, the Carthaginians. Others, despising Rome as the utilitarian exponent of power and plumbing, envisaged the Irish as latter-day Greeks, overwhelmed by Roman military might but intellectually and culturally superior to their conquerors. During the second Celtic Revival, and in the years leading up to Independence, some Irish nationalists saw their identity as an oppressed but chosen people reflected in the story of Moses in Egypt: the Irish then became pseudo-Israelites. All of these analogies can be found in play at the same historical period, or even in the same text; what reconciles their potential contradictions is their shared investment in being Not Rome. If the effective use of metaphor is commonly privileged as the gold standard of good poetry, the ability to see one's own political predicament mirrored in that of others might be called the gold standard of the politics of empathy. When the Other with whom the Irish choose to identify is a long-dead civilization this practice of retro-empathy may bolster native pride, but it requires no exertion in the present. When the chosen group is engaged in its own contemporary struggles, as are African and Native Americans, the identification produces a politics of imaginative solidarity with the potential for practical action.

Frank McGuinness's play *Carthaginians* (1986) uses the historical relation between Rome and Carthage as a metaphor for the recent struggles between

Britain and the nationalist community in the North of Ireland.[1] 'I am Carthaginian. This earth is mine, not Britain's, nor Rome's' (17), says one of the characters. The play, an elegy for thirteen Irish civilians murdered by British paratroopers on Bloody Sunday in Derry,[2] depends on an analogy between Ireland and Carthage that, since the eighteenth century, has helped to focus imaginative Irish resistance to British rule, and intensified when British troops came to the North in 1969. To isolate the Carthage analogy is not to assert its unique importance or to exhaust the subtleties of the works in which it appears, but to demonstrate the evolving political and literary significance of the Irish choice of oriental and Semitic origins. The myth of Carthaginian descent was originally invoked to counteract the degrading English insistence that Irish ethnic characteristics derived from the savage Scythians.

Once a great civilization, Carthage was so effectively obliterated after the Third Punic War that our evidence about it comes mostly from Rome, its conqueror. Feminized by defeat, the Carthaginians were 'the Others of ancient history, the vanquished rather than the victors' (Moscati 11). In contemporary Irish literature the Rome–Carthage motif functions in complex and variable ways: as origin myth, colonial parable and site of intersection between nationalism and sexuality. It passes between writers in interchanges that have been enabled by the intimacy of the Northern literary scene and the former cultural dominance of the Field Day Theatre Company of Derry.[3] McGuinness's play revises representations of Rome and Carthage that had already appeared in Seamus Heaney's *North* (1975) and in Brian Friel's Field Day play *Translations* (1980). Heaney and Friel draw on a historical tradition in which medieval genealogy, antiquarian philology and literary texts combine to construct an oppositional identity for the colonized Irish.

One term of the metaphor, the substitution of the Roman for the British empire, has wide currency. Long before Britain had an Empire, medieval historians forged a genealogical parallel between Rome and London via their supposed common ancestor, Troy.[4] In his influential *Histories of the Kings of Britain* (c.1136), the chronicler Geoffrey of Monmouth asserts that Brutus, great-grandson of the Trojan prince Aeneas, the legendary founder of Rome, first settled the island of Albion. (Geoffrey got his information from an earlier and even less reliable text, the ninth-century *Historia Britonum*.) To keep alive the memory of his origins, Brutus named his capital city Troynovaunt, or New Troy (*Histories* 22). Geoffrey's version of the story is celebratory, for the Trojans find in Britain a site for the re-creation of their ruined original home. Giraldus Cambrensis reports in his *Expugnatio Hibernica* (Conquest of Ireland) that the Norman invader Robert Fitz-Stephen encouraged his English soldiers to remember their proud origins: 'We derive our descent, originally, in part from the blood of the Trojans' (*Historical Works* 200). *Sir Gawain and the Green Knight* rehearses the Trojan genealogy as a prelude to describing the subsequent glories of Arthur and his court, but its opening image of Troy in flames and its slippery allusion to Aeneas's treachery render it less clearly affirmative (1). The myth of Trojan descent may be used to celebrate the distinguished classical origins of the British, but it also foreshadows the inevitable downfall of Arthurian civilization. The close of the *Alliterative Morte Arthure*, which asserts that the dead Arthur was descended from Priam (157), reminds its audience that, while Troy was ancient and Priam noble, Troy was eventually burned and Priam defeated.

In England itself the inherited rhetorical figure was modified by changing historical circumstances, as the medieval Trojan story was gradually replaced by a more factually plausible emphasis on England's Anglo-Saxon, Teutonic origins. During the English Renaissance and Enlightenment, Rome's importance as a positive classical model did not depend upon a spurious genealogy, but by the beginning of the eighteenth century the growing importance of the British Empire increased the temptations of analogy. In the nineteenth century Rome came to stand for two different concepts: decadence and empire. For some, it evoked Christians thrown to the lions, unspeakable sexual and gastronomic orgies and the trope of inevitable decline.[5] For others, Rome's eventual fall was less significant than the imperial *pax Romana* that preceded it. The introduction to a 1948 edition of Tacitus' *Agricola* illuminates the British political unconscious at work: 'It was the destiny of Rome to rule the world, the destiny of the high-born Roman to share in that great task. . . . We may think of Tacitus as something like an officer of the Indian army and an Indian Civil Servant rolled into one' (Mattingly 8–9). The rhetoric that locates Tacitus in Cawnpore implies that Britain was also 'destined' to rule the world.

For Irish writers, naturally, the triumphalist Troy–Rome–London sequence had primarily negative associations. *Carthaginians* begins with music: the dying lament of Dido, the legendary founder and queen of Carthage, from Henry Purcell's opera *Dido and Aeneas*. Revising Virgil's imperial foundation narrative, Purcell depicts the Trojan ancestor of the Romans as a sexual betrayer whose quest for 'Italian ground' cost his lover her life. Dido, not her faithless suitor, is Purcell's central figure. 'When I am laid in earth,' Dido sings, 'remember me' (75). Remembering the abandoned Dido rather than the successful Aeneas and his colonizing descendant Brutus, McGuinness invokes alternative mythical origins that avoid the Troy–Rome–London axis altogether. His strategy is not original: numerous medieval vernacular poets had contested the *Aeneid*'s patrilineal assumptions in order to focus on its female protagonist (Desmond 2).

The story of how the Irish enlisted the Carthaginians as progenitors demonstrates the manipulation and gendering of genealogy by a colonized people. Giraldus Cambrensis, writing in 1187 to justify the territorial ambitions of Henry II, established the English practice of constructing the Irish as barbarians.[6] Instead of training a critical counter-gaze on the metropolis, where there was plenty of barbarism to be found, Irish writers concentrated on refuting ethnic slurs. While their efforts to counter British assumptions of superiority risked substituting one racist myth for another, the Carthaginian story is a Mediterranean hybrid rather than an appeal to Celtic racial purity. Moreover, Carthaginians compose only one thread in the complex pattern of anti-colonial discourse: as I have already noted, the Irish also compared themselves to the Jews and the Greeks, other civilized peoples crushed by Roman efficiency. Irish writers reframed the English opposition between civilians and barbarians as a struggle between colonial power and Celtic culture, or between masculine brutality and feminine sensibility.

The gendered dimension of the Carthaginian metaphor, which is associated primarily with the defeated queen Dido rather than with the equally famous warrior Hannibal, stands out more clearly when it is seen to revise and complement an earlier myth of origin that derives the Irish from a less agreeable oriental people, the warlike and masculine Scythians. In the programme for his own production of *Carthaginians* (Druid Theatre Company, 1992), McGuinness included an abridged passage from Edmund Spenser's *A View of the Present State of Ireland* (1596) describing the Scythian origin of the Irish mantle ('Programme'; Spenser 50–2). For Spenser, Ireland's Scythian ancestry helps to explain its present depravity; but the Scythians had not always been so negatively represented. At the beginning of the twelfth century, while Geoffrey of Monmouth was celebrating the Trojan roots of British history, Irish scribes were copying down the *Lebor Gabála Erenn* (Book of the Taking of Ireland), a mythological account of Irish prehistory that reaches back to the Flood. According to this native genealogy, at a time when Albion could claim no more than the odd giant, Ireland had been occupied for millennia by a series of peoples: the Formorians, the Fir Bolg, the Tuatha Dé Danaan and finally the Milesians. The Milesians, who were supposedly descended from Noah's son Japhet, originated in Scythia. Subsequently they wandered through Egypt, moved to Spain and arrived at last in Ireland. In the *Lebor Gabála* Carthage is not mentioned, and Scythia as a point of origin appears ethically neutral. Scythians are neither heroic nor despicable, merely ancient: perhaps the oldest people in the world.[7] They are not represented as skeletons in Ireland's genealogical closet.

Renaissance ethnographers, however, used the Scythians, a nomadic oriental people who inhabited the steppes north of the Black Sea between 600 BC and AD 300, as a metaphor for barbarity.[8] According to the fourth book of Herodotus' *History*, the Scythians drank the blood of their enemies, scalped them and used their skulls as goblets. Their burial customs, which involved the slaughter and impaling of servants and horses, were indubitably macabre (303–7). They were also wealthy connoisseurs, sagacious warriors, skilled riders and successful pastoralists (Rice 21–3): Marlowe depicts Tamburlaine the Scythian shepherd as both brutal and magnificent. When Lear rejects Cordelia, however, Shakespeare perpetuates only the negative stereotype:

> The barbarous Scythian,
> Or he that makes his generation messes

To gorge his appetite, shall to my bosom
Be as well neighboured, pitied, and relieved
As thou my sometime daughter. (*King Lear*, 1.116–20)

'Generation' may mean parents or children, but in this context Lear is metaphorically casting himself as Cordelia's next meal. To eat one's family is to break the ultimate western taboo, as the story of the house of Atreus reveals. Herodotus explicitly denied that the Scythians were cannibals, claiming that the Man-Eaters, a neighbouring clan, were 'the only one of these people who eat human flesh' (319). Shakespeare, however, may have drawn on the popular legend of St Andrew, who, on finding the Scythians eating their enemies, supplied them with the Eucharist instead.[9] (Presumably symbolic cannibalism provided a satisfactory replacement for the literal kind.) In 'On Cannibals' Montaigne repeats as common knowledge the idea that the ancient Scythians ate their prisoners 'for nourishment' (113). Montaigne has kind words for the Brazilian cannibals who are the main subject of his essay, refusing to believe that 'there is anything barbarous or savage about them, except that we all call barbarous anything that is contrary to our own habits' (108). He prefers their custom of roasting and eating enemies after they are dead to the tortures inflicted upon living bodies by his fellow Frenchmen (113). But Montaigne is the intelligent exception, the commentator who judges barbarism in the metropolis more harshly than barbarism at the periphery. Since the Scythians had no alphabet, they left no writings to disturb the prejudices of later commentators. Largely forgotten except for rhetorical purposes, they lived on as English cultural shorthand for Otherness: war-loving, bloodthirsty and masculine eaters of human flesh.

Did the Scythians' poor reputation among Elizabethan writers derive from their alleged ancestral relation to the Irish? The Greek geographer Strabo 'says in his fourth book that the Irish are a man-eating people' (Keating 9), and Giraldus Cambrensis repeats the accusation. Worse, they ritually consume their dead fathers: in this they resemble Shakespeare's Scythians.[10] (The name of Shakespeare's Caliban, the original inhabitant of an island that is geographically located in the Mediterranean but imaginatively situated in the Atlantic New World, is a nearly perfect anagram of the word 'cannibal'; and Prospero's island is related by analogy to Spenser's Ireland.)[11] Cannibalism is a universally useful denominator of Otherness (to eat human flesh is to be by definition inhuman), and the Irish were demonized by reference to their supposed progenitors. Spenser claims that the Scythian origins of the Irish are the most influential determinant of their savage customs. Although he dismisses as implausible the English 'Tale of Brutus, whom they devise to have first conquered and inhabited this land' (65), Spenser swallows the equally implausible Scythian story whole. He imagines the barbarian hordes sweeping down to the coast, 'where enquiringe for other countryes abroade, and gettinge intelligence of this Countrye of Irelande, findinge shippinge convenient, [they] passed over thither, and arived in the North parte thereof, which is now called Ulster' (66).

The Scythians are a crucial component of Spenser's negative ethnography: the sharks in the Irish gene pool. Irish mantles, hairstyles, battle cries, and keens are all identified, and deplored, as Scythian (81–101).[12] What most disturbs the civilized English poet about both the nomads of the steppes and the wild Irish, however, is their practice of moving their cattle from place to place according to the season (81–3). This ostensibly inoffensive habit is fatal to the intentions of the colonizer, since it produces a nation of wandering men who have no settlements to defend, and who can move their families and property around with them. Herodotus recounts admiringly how the Scythians frustrated the invading forces of the great empire of Darius the Persian by retreating rapidly, destroying food supplies and filling in the wells behind them (323–6). Nomads make good guerrillas. Giraldus Cambrensis had established an opposition between pasture and husbandry, and a connection between civilization and settlement, that was to resonate through hostile accounts of the Irish in succeeding centuries:

> They are a wild and inhospitable people. They live on beasts only, and live like beasts. They have not progressed at all from the primitive habits of pastoral living.
>
> While man usually progresses from the woods to the fields, and from the fields to settlements and communities of citizens, this people despises work on the land, has little use for the money-making of towns, contemns the rights and privileges of citizenship, and desires neither to abandon, nor lose respect for, the life which it has been accustomed to lead in the woods and countryside.
> (*History* 101–2)

The connection of nomadic habits with savagery and lack of culture reflects the prejudices of men with fixed addresses and expansionist ambitions. (In the nineteenth century Darwinian evolutionary theory was brought into play to produce an equally damning genealogy for the Fenian Irish: not Scythians, but simians.)

When Irish writers realized that, as Sydney Owenson (later Lady Morgan) wrote, 'It has been the fashion to throw an odium on the modern Irish, by undermining the basis of their ancient history, and vilifying their ancient national character' (3: 14n), they sought to reinterpret and revalue, rather than deny, their Scythian pedigree. In the 1630s Geoffrey Keating observed indignantly that English commentators on Ireland were like dung beetles, ignoring the flowers in their eagerness to roll in the shit (5). He defended Ireland against the ultimate 'barbarian' slur, the allegation of cannibalism: according to Keating there was only one cannibal in Ireland, and, since she was known as Eithne the loathsome, the habit was evidently not sanctioned (9–11). On their Scythian origins, Keating repeated Herodotus' story of the defeat of the Emperor Darius, and praised the gallantry of the nomads. He also noted that the Scythians 'had heard of the power of the Romans, and (yet) had never felt it' (229). In this they indeed resembled the Irish, for 'the Romans . . . had no control over Ireland, but it . . . was a refuge to the other territories to protect them from the violence of the Romans' (17). To those like David Hume who saw the Romans as the fount of civilization, the absence of the legions was a disaster that condemned the Irish to centuries of ignorance and underdevelopment; the Irish, on the other hand, considered themselves fortunate.[13] If a likeness existed between the Scythians and the Irish, it lay in their happy escape from the tyranny of Rome.

In 1788 the French scholar Jean-Jacques Barthélemy reversed the civilian–barbarian opposition in his influential and frequently republished description of the imaginary travels of Anacharsis, a virtuous Scythian anthropologist who observes the peculiar customs of his decadent Greek neighbours (Bernal 1: 185–6). This reversal of stereotypical attributes has become a standard, almost formulaic, rhetorical strategy in subsequent Irish writing. Maria Edgeworth, for example, whose letters reveal that she had read *Anacharsis* (McCormack, 'Introduction' xx), evoked and revalued the Irish origin myth in her novel *The Absentee* (1812). In the course of a tour through Ireland, Lord Colambre visits the home of the learned Irish antiquarian Count O'Halloran and is shown into his study. There he discovers, among other oddly assorted animals, an eagle, a white mouse and a bowl of goldfish. The Count, who has read his Herodotus, explicates the significance of his peculiar menagerie by alluding to certain mysterious gifts that the Scythians sent to Darius the Persian invader. He tells the obnoxious Englishwoman Lady Dashfort, 'a mouse, a bird, and a fish, are, you know, tribute from earth, air, and water, to a conqueror –' (116).[14] With conscious irony, he modifies Herodotus' account Herodotus reports that along with the animals the Scythians also sent five arrows, and that Darius fled Scythia because he was persuaded that the gifts were not in fact tributes to a conqueror but a warning that, unless the Persians could fly like birds, swim like fish or burrow like mice, they would soon find themselves full of holes (Herodotus 327–8). The recondite reference to Herodotus is lost on the vulgar Lady Dashfort, but she is shortly forced, Darius-like, to retreat from Ireland in discomfiture. Lord Colambre, who is better read than the English 'invader', shows his proficiency in the discourse of origins by capping Count O'Halloran's Greek allusion with a Shakespearean reference. The animals may be tributes to a conqueror, he says, 'But from no barbarous Scythian!' (Edgeworth 116). The educated and courtly Count, 'Scythian' because he is Irish, is nevertheless no barbarian. Resisting the idea of the Irish as virile savages, Edgeworth represents the two men as highly civilized, although the Count (a portrait of her friend the antiquarian Sylvester O'Halloran) may also be seen as slightly absurd.

Edgeworth, a propagandist for the Union and the mingling of cultures she hoped it would foster, locates the epitome of virtuous Irishness in her gentle and cultivated heroine, the patriotically named but genetically English Grace

Nugent.[15] Although her role is to plead for the absentee Clonbrony parents to return to their Irish estate, and eventually to marry their son Lord Colambre, this desirable union is delayed by the need to unravel the suspicious circumstances of her birth, discover her wealthy English grandfather and establish her as a legitimate heiress. The comic agent of her good fortune is Count O'Halloran's rare Irish greyhound, which is named after Carthage's most famous and successful general, Hannibal. Grace's suspicious and reclusive grandfather Mr Reynolds is a fanatical dog lover. When Colambre and O'Halloran seek admittance to his house, Mr Reynolds's desire to meet the hound prompts him to let them in. He later admits that, without Hannibal, he would have turned them away and never learned that Grace was his granddaughter. Thus Hannibal both legitimizes and enriches the 'Irish' heroine.

Hannibal the greyhound, Edgeworth's antiquarian in-joke, shows that genealogical thinking was taking a new direction. While Keating and Edgeworth rehabilitated the Scythians, Irish scholars constructed an alternative history, in which the Scythian influence was not disavowed but mediated through a better known and reputedly less obnoxious oriental people, the Semitic Phoenicians. In the eighteenth century, philology served national pride as scholars argued that the Irish language originated with Noah's son Japhet in Scythia, spread to the Phoenician cities on the eastern coast of the Mediterranean (modern Lebanon) and from there reached Carthage, the great Phoenician colony on the north coast of Africa. Carthaginian merchants brought the language to Spain, and then, according to the eighteenth-century antiquarian and philologist General Charles Vallancey (a British army engineer who was, paradoxically, one of the leading figures of the first Celtic Revival), to Ireland. (See Fig. 1) This linguistic trajectory followed (more or less) the story of Irish origins outlined in the narratives of the *Lebor Gabála* and provided the Irish tongue, and indeed the Irish people, with an oriental pedigree distinct from the genealogy of the Anglo-Saxons, whose language had Teutonic origins (Leerssen, 'Edge' 95–102; Vallancey iii–x). Moreover, the cultured Phoenicians, who were credited with the invention of the alphabet, were ethically and aesthetically preferable to barbarous and illiterate Scythians. This originary claim on writing resonates in Owenson's *The Wild Irish Girl* (1806), where the nationalist Father John argues that 'Ireland, owing to its being colonized from Phoenicia, and consequent early introduction of letters there, was . . . esteemed the most enlightened country in Europe' (2.69).

Although the 'Phoenician Scytho-Celtists', as they were called, included many Ascendancy figures like Sir James Ware, Sir William Betham and the English-born Charles Vallancey (Leerssen, 'Edge' 99–101; Vance 226–7), their theory of the separate origins of the Irish language had nationalist implications. This theory, which declared Ireland's linguistic independence, dominated Irish philology until the end of the eighteenth century, when the crushing of the nationalist rising against English colonial rule in 1798 and the subsequent Act of Union led to its demise (Leerssen, 'Edge' 102–3). Among

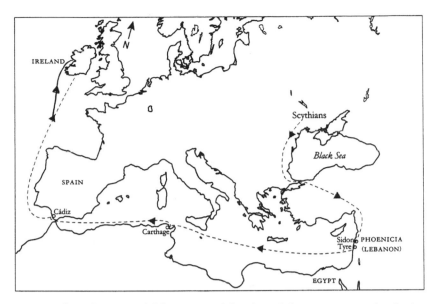

Fig. 1. *Eighteenth-century philologists argued that the Irish language originated in Scythia and came to Ireland via Phoenicia, Carthage and Spain*

European philologists, however, Phoenicia was of interest less because it might have spawned Irish than because of its contested relationship to Greece. Martin Bernal attributes the late-nineteenth-century decline of 'Phoenicianism' to anti-Semitic German classical scholars who wanted to keep Greece purely Aryan and therefore denied that Semitic Phoenicians and Black Egyptians had been its original colonizers (1: 337–66). Attempting to counteract hostile stereotyping by self-exoticization, the Irish aligned themselves with the Phoenicians – who despite their reputation as explorers and merchants also belonged to the category of 'feminine' orientals or 'effeminate' Semites – only to be drawn into yet another negative discourse of ethnicity.[16]

While the theories of the Phoenician Scytho-Celtists lost scholarly ground in the early nineteenth century, they retained considerable popular acceptance. In *Don Juan*, Byron jokingly describes the stage Irish phrase 'a broth of a boy' as 'Punic', explaining that

> The antiquarians, who can settle time,
> Which settles all things, Roman, Greek or Runic,
> Swear that Pat's language sprung from the same clime
> With Hannibal and wears the Tyrian tunic
> Of Dido's alphabet. (Canto 8, Section 23)

In a footnote to this passage Byron refers to Charles Vallancey and Sir Lawrence Parsons (917). His information probably came from his friend the Irish poet

Tom Moore or from his reading of Owenson, whose novel *The Wild Irish Girl* bristles with antiquarian allusions to the Phoenicians. The moral education of Owenson's English hero, Horatio, consists in shedding his crude preconceptions about ethnicity and gender: 'Whenever the *Irish* were mentioned in my presence, an *Esquimaux* group circling round the fire blazing to dress a dinner or broil an enemy, was the image which presented itself to my mind' (1: 36). Broiling one's enemy for dinner is standard Scythian stuff, and the analogy between the Irish and the Native Americans had been used since Elizabethan times to suggest that both participated in a state of nature that was ripe for colonial conquest (Gibbons, *Transformations* 151–3).[17] Instead of savage male cannibals, however, Horatio discovers in the West a beautiful young girl who knows Latin and plays the harp. His conversion by Glorvina, the paradoxically civilized wild Irish girl, involves a crash course on Phoenician Scytho-Celtism:

> Behold me then, buried amidst the monuments of past ages! – deep in the study of the language, history, and antiquities of this ancient nation – talking of the invasion of Henry II as a recent circumstance – of the Phoenician migration hither from Spain, as though my grandfather had been delegated by the Firbalgs to receive the Milesians on their landing. (*Irish Girl* 2: 8–9)

References to 'Phoenician progenitors' (2: 183) and footnotes on Vallancey (1: 61–2n) punctuate Owenson's text.[18] She retrieves the origin of the Irish keen from Spenser's brutish Scythians and reassigns it to the Israelites and the Phoenicians: 'for the pathetic lamentations of David for the friend of his soul, and the *conclamatio* breathed over the Phoenician Dido, has no faint coincidence to the *Caoine* or funeral song of the Irish' (3: 46n). The shift from Scythian barbarity to Phoenician lamentation also signals a change in gender coding. Warlike Scythian cannibals epitomize masculinity, but Owenson, following the eighteenth-century *aisling* poets, portrays Ireland as a *spéirbhan*, a beautiful maiden.[19]

In nineteenth-century British hands this fusion of Ireland with the feminine had dubious consequences. Arnold claims that the 'sensibility of the Celtic nature, its nervous exaltation, have something feminine in them, and the Celt is thus peculiarly disposed to feel the spell of the feminine idiosyncrasy; he has an affinity to it; he is not far from its secret' (*Lectures* 347). He illustrates what he calls 'the sheer, inimitable Celtic note' in poetry by quoting Shakespeare's description of Dido from *The Merchant of Venice*:

> 'in such a night
> *Stood Dido, with a willow in her hand,*
> *Upon the wild sea-banks, and waved her love*
> *To come again to Carthage*'. (5.1.9–12; quoted in Arnold, *Lectures* 379)

For Arnold, these lines epitomize the feminine sensibility of the Celts: they are 'drenched and intoxicated with the fairy-dew of . . . natural magic' (380).[20] It suits his argument that Shakespeare's Lorenzo deprives Dido of her fury, softening her into a pathetic figure waving a willow branch, the emblem of deserted love. Virgil's Dido vehemently curses Aeneas and prophesies the eternal enmity between the Romans and the Carthaginians that was enacted in the three Punic Wars; Shakespeare's Dido, on the other hand, merely begs Aeneas to return. Arnold, who wanted to send 'a message of peace to Ireland' (386), may have been unaware of the local political implications of the Dido story, but he used it to stereotype the Celts as passive feminine victims and romantic failures.

For Irish writers, however, the Phoenician metaphor retained imaginative currency as a figure of difference and resistance as long as the British occupied Ireland. In 1907 James Joyce reaffirmed Vallancey's outdated theory of the Phoenician origin of the Irish language (I discuss this in detail in the next chapter), and even history textbooks continued to suggest that the connection between Ireland and the Orient was factual, not metaphorical. Edward D'Alton opens his 1913 *History of Ireland* with the story of Phoenician colonists from Spain discovering tin in Britain and Ireland. Later their Carthaginian cousins arrived too: 'The Carthaginians were as daring, as skilful in navigation, and as keenly anxious to acquire wealth by commerce as their kinsmen of Spain or Phoenicia, and in an expedition under Himilco they discovered those famous Tin Islands which they had long sought for in vain' (2). Although the opening chapters of many out-of-date Irish history books refer to Scythia, Phoenicia or Carthage,[21] it is surprising to discover that as late as 1922 Oxford University Press was prepared to lend its imprimatur to the following assertions:

> Everything points to the conclusion that Ireland was discovered by the Phoenicians. . . . They were the greatest mariners in the ancient world. Long before Rome was founded they had passed, from their settlements in the eastern basin of the Mediterranean, at Tyre and Sidon, beyond the straits of Gibraltar into the Atlantic. Spain with its rich deposits of silver belonged to them, so too did the tin mines on the coast of Cornwall, which they called the Cassiterides. From Cornwall they passed in time to Ireland, attracted thither by its rich gold-fields, its purple-bearing shells, and the pearl oysters that lined its coast and freshwater lakes. Wherever the Phoenicians went they established their factories, generally on some island near the mainland or on some strongly fortified headland. Some of these factories or settlements, like that of Dun Aengus on the Isle of Aran in Galway Bay, are still in existence to testify to the skill and enterprise of these ancient merchant sailors. . . . What form of religion the earliest inhabitants of Ireland, the Ernai, professed we cannot certainly say, but there can be little doubt that, after they fell under the influence of the Phoenicians, their religion became that which is definitely associated with the erection of megalithic structures such as dolmens, pillar-stones, and stone circles. Two ideas underlie this religion – the idea of immortality and the idea of the sun as the generating principle of all things. The system culminated in the worship of Baal. In Ireland the worship of Baal assumed under Celtic influences the form of religion known as Druidism. (Dunlop 8–9, 12)

Vallancey's linguistics might be discredited, but the historical influence of the Phoenicians on early Ireland and its religious practices could still be asserted in respectable academic circles.

II

When the British withdrew from the South of Ireland in 1922, leaving the Protestants in control of the partitioned North, the metaphorical narrative of British Romans and Irish Carthaginians lost some of its political relevance. During the 1960s, when the Catholics in the North began to agitate for the civil rights they had been denied under the rule of the Protestant majority, they challenged not the British government but the Irish Protestant Unionists, who wished to retain their dominance in the province and the link with Britain that secured it. This third force was not compatible with the binary structure of the metaphor. After the explosion of violence between Catholic and Protestant communities in 1969, however, British soldiers returned to the streets of the North, and in 1972 direct rule from Westminster replaced the parliament at Stormont. Northern nationalists argued that the Troubles derived from British colonialism and the legacy of partition rather than from Irish sectarianism. Evidence for this thesis seemed overwhelming when, on 30 January 1972, the Parachute Regiment killed thirteen innocent people during a civil rights march in Derry.

The Southern poet Thomas Kinsella responded to the Widgery Report, an egregious and now discredited piece of whitewash that exonerated the 'paras' and blamed the victims, with a satirical poem whose clanging octosyllabic couplets announce his deliberately propagandistic intention: 'One changed one's standards, chose the doggerel route, and charged', he wrote (*Fifteen Dead* 58). 'Butcher's Dozen' reverses the political agenda of Aeneas' descent into Hades, which permitted him to hear his father Anchises prophesy the glories of imperial Rome. Kinsella journeys through the underworld of the Bogside to hear the stories of the murdered Catholic men. His poem speaks not of the future, but of the rubble left behind when the English imperialists leave: 'An Empire-builder handing on. / We reap the ruin when you've gone'. Anchises foretold the ascendancy of Julius and Augustus Caesar; but the British pseudo-Caesars have departed, if only from the Republic. Echoing the Latin tag familiar to every schoolchild, Caesar's '*Veni, vidi, vici*', Kinsella enforces the analogy between Roman and British imperialism:

> You came, you saw, you conquered. . . So.
> You gorged – and it was time to go.
> Good riddance. We'd forget – released –
> But for the rubbish of your feast,
> The slops and scraps that fell to earth
> And sprang to arms in dragon birth.

> Sashed and bowler-hatted, glum
> Apprentices of fife and drum. (*Fifteen Dead* 18)

The Protestants of the Six Counties, like the legendary warriors that sprang from the dragon's teeth sown by Cadmus, are the neo-colonial leftovers of Empire.

For Kinsella the Roman analogy seems cognate with the anti-British impulse, as if automatically evoked by a new outbreak of the old imperial brutality. With the polarity between native oppressed and foreign oppressor once more established in the North, the viability of a binary metaphor re-emerged. Seamus Heaney, a Northern Catholic who originally saw the conflict as 'an internal Northern Ireland division', a struggle between the Catholic minority and its Protestant rulers, decided during the writing of *North* (1975) that 'the genuine political confrontation is between Ireland and Britain'. Heaney says that he 'never had any strong feelings . . . about the British army', yet he represented it in his verse as a Roman legion ('Unhappy' 62). In 1980 the Catholic dramatist Brian Friel joined Stephen Rea, a Protestant actor, to found the Field Day Theatre Company, a Northern group whose stated aims were to promote the cultural unity of Ireland and to mediate between nationalism and unionism (Richtarik, *Acting* 7). Nevertheless, Field Day's opening production was Friel's play *Translations*, which avoids mention of the Protestant tradition and evokes the binary opposition between Carthage and Rome to indict the British destruction of Gaelic culture. Many commentators now associate Field Day with the 'green' or nationalist positions it has always tried to complicate through social and economic analysis. No matter how carefully nuanced the company's productions, pamphlets and public statements might be, the anti-colonial positions of its most powerful directors (Heaney joined the board in 1981) logically require a politically united Ireland: a desirable ideal, but not one to which a Unionist would subscribe (Richtarik, *Acting* 90–1, 110, 135–7, 145). In 1985, for reasons that have never been fully explained, Field Day rejected Frank McGuinness's play *Observe the Sons of Ulster Marching towards the Somme*, a critical but sympathetic exploration of the historical roots of Unionist antipathy towards Irish reunification (Richards 142–3). McGuinness, a Northern Catholic, suggested in a 1986 interview that the company 'associates itself very strongly with the colour green' and asked, 'Don't you think art is more colours than green?' (quoted in J. Fitzgerald 63). In *Carthaginians* (1986), which he withdrew from production by Field Day (Roche 277), McGuinness uses the story of Dido to 'reflect the rainbow', to engage with Irish problematics of gender and sexual orientation that, in his view, Field Day has elided (quoted in J. Fitzgerald 63, 65).

Heaney, who says he is proud that 'My passport's green' ('Open Letter' 25), and who in 1977 described his poetry as a 'slow, obstinate, papish burn' ('Unhappy' 62), rediscovered the Romans as a metaphor for the British army after Bloody Sunday. In the last section of Heaney's poem 'Kinship' (1975),

Tacitus, the Roman ethnographer of the British and the Germans, is called to witness what seems at first to be an internal religious conflict. Heaney establishes a detached position above the fray on the 'ramparts' of Derry so that Tacitus can 'observe' and the soldiers can 'stare' at the sectarian slaughter:

> And you, Tacitus,
> observe how I make my grove
> on an old crannog
> piled by the fearful dead:
>
> a desolate peace.
> Our mother ground
> is sour with the blood
> of her faithful,
>
> they lie gargling
> in her sacred heart
> as the legions stare
> from the ramparts.
> Come back to this
> 'island of the ocean'
> where nothing will suffice.
> Read the inhumed faces
>
> of casualty and victim;
> report us fairly,
> how we slaughter
> for the common good
>
> and shave the heads
> of the notorious,
> how the goddess swallows
> our love and terror. (*North* 45)

Heaney's Tacitus is both a representative of Rome and a detached anthropologist. In his *Germania*, Tacitus describes how German tribes worship Nerthus, Mother Earth, 'In an island of Ocean', afterward drowning all the slaves who have participated in the ritual. The ceremony takes place in a sacred grove, where 'The sacrifice in public of a human victim' marks the moment when 'the nation had its birth' (132–3). Heaney constructs an analogy between the German and the Irish tribes by locating his own sacred 'grove' on a *crannóg*, which is an Irish word for a dwelling on an island in a lake. He self-consciously uses these 'primitive' German rites as analogues for killings committed by and inflicted on contemporary Republican devotees of the Irish goddess Kathleen ni Houlihan, which themselves repeat and derive from the nation-founding sacrifice of the patriots who died for the Republic in the Easter Rising.[22] In 'Easter 1916' Yeats had warned that 'Too long a sacrifice / Can make a stone of the heart' and asked, 'O when may it suffice?' (*Poems* 181). Heaney's pessimistic answer, 'Nothing will suffice', may appear to align him with Conor Cruise O'Brien, who argues that an 'Unhealthy Intersection' between the literary rhetoric of patriotic martyrdom and the political claims of Republican nationalism helped to produce the Troubles (3–8). The 'atavistic' violence of blood sacrifice has been, according to Heaney, 'observed with amazement and a kind of civilized tut-tut by Tacitus in the first century AD and by leader-writers in the *Daily Telegraph* in the 20th century' ('Mother Ireland' 790).

But Heaney's analogy between 'primitive' ritual murder and death on the streets of Derry is not intended to delegitimize his nationalist 'tribe'. His juxtaposition of Tacitus with the right-wing British newspaper the *Daily Telegraph* suggests that the negative connotations of the Roman trope, though less obvious than in 'Butcher's Dozen', are still at work. If the Romans are positioned solely as 'civilized' anthropological observers, the reader may overlook their complicity in producing a neo-colonial situation where the Irish barbarian 'tribes' murder each other in the name of religion. But with the line 'a desolate peace', Heaney expands his condemnation to include the staring legions, and those who sent them. In Tacitus' *Agricola* the British chief Calgacus denounces the Roman invaders of his country: 'Robbery, butchery, rapine, the liars call Empire; they create a desolation and call it peace' (80). Ironically, the formerly colonized Britons now play the role of colonizers in contemporary Ireland: they have assumed the mantle of their Roman oppressors. Heaney describes the Troubles as a gendered struggle between the feminized Catholics who serve Kathleen ni Houlihan and a 'male cult whose founding fathers were Cromwell, William of Orange and Edward Carson'. The male godhead is figuratively Roman, 'incarnate in a rex or caesar resident in a palace in London' (*Preoccupations* 57).[23] The peacekeeping 'legions' that 'stare from the ramparts' as Catholics and Protestants kill each other have been sent to Derry to keep the warring natives apart; but British imperialists themselves have created the desolation that their conservative leader-writers now haughtily deplore.

Heaney's defence of his 'barbarian' nationalist community in the face of Tacitus' 'civilized tut-tut' is not an endorsement of Irish sacrificial violence, but neither is it an admission of Tacitus' right to moral superiority.[24] Ireland's 'faithful' who lie 'gargling / in her sacred heart' are victims not only of local 'atavism', but of Horace's supposedly 'civilized' Roman platitude: 'Dulce et decorum est / Pro patria mori'. Heaney chooses the unmistakable word 'gargling' to remind his readers of Wilfred Owen's rejection of Horace:

> If you could hear, at every jolt, the blood
> Come gargling from the froth-corrupted lungs,
>
> . . .
>
> My friend, you would not tell with such high zest
> To children ardent for some desperate glory,
> The old Lie: Dulce et decorum est
> Pro patria mori. (*Poems* 55)

Heaney quotes these lines in an essay praising Owen for bearing honest witness to human suffering (*Government* xiii–xvi), and they suggest a deliberate riposte to critics who have accused him of condoning Republican violence:[25] it is not 'proper' to die for your country. Writing of his own local war, Heaney argues in 'Kinship' that blood spilt on the 'mother ground' is not sweet, 'dulce', but 'sour'.

In the poetry of *North* Heaney does not question the validity of the familiar analogy between Irish nationalism and femininity, nor the complementary assignment of masculinity to the powerful. For him, Carson's 'male cult' of unionism logically derives from the British masculinity represented by Cromwell and King Billy. Heaney's essentialist gendering of the 'mother ground' intersects with the Irish origin myth in 'Bog Queen' (1972), a poem that literalizes the familiar topos of the land as a woman's body by producing a real corpse.[26] According to P. V. Glob, 'The first properly documented account of a bog body comes from County Down in Ireland'. A woman dug up on Lord Moira's estate had 'a sort of cape worn on one shoulder and passing under the opposite arm. This cape was worked in different materials and colours and had a border into which motifs were woven in a fine technique. It was supposed to have come from the East, and to have been brought in by the Phoenicians' (103–4). Since the body was found in 1781, the provenance of the textile must have been suggested by the contemporary Carthaginian craze. Juxtaposing the Phoenician cape with the woman's breasts, Heaney gives erotic nationalist resonance to Glob's neutrally descriptive account:

> My sash was a black glacier
> wrinkling, dyed weaves
> and phoenician stitchwork
> retted on my breasts'
>
> soft moraines. (*North* 33)

Although Glob argues that the woman was Danish, Heaney shows her becoming one with the aboriginal landscape. The breasts into which the Phoenician stitchwork has soaked are 'moraines': mounds of earth left behind by glacial action. While dreaming of her native Baltic amber, she is 'digested' by local 'roots' into a version of Kathleen ni Houlihan, the embodiment of rebel Ireland (*North* 32–3). Heaney uses the Phoenician origin myth to establish Irish national claims to county Down, now a part of the United Kingdom.[27] He translates Glob's factual statement that Lady Moira 'paid well' to obtain the woman's Phoenician garments (Glob 103) into the rhetorically loaded phrase 'a peer's wife bribed him', which suggests Anglo-Irish appropriation of the land. His conflation of the queen's black sash with the glacier itself suggests her ancient right to the earth, as opposed to the upstart political claims symbolized in Protestant popular culture by the Orange sash. The queen's resurrection is violent and macabre, but the poem's concluding image hints at hope:

> I rose from the dark,
> hacked bone, skull-ware,
> frayed stitches, tufts,
>
> small gleams on the bank. (*North* 34)

The woman's Phoenician stitchwork may be frayed, but the 'small gleam' of national identity that it embodies is reborn out of the bog.

The first section of *North* combines Arnold's vision of Ireland as feminine with Yeats's emphasis on the mythical sacrificial mother for whom men die.[28] Roman men and women wearing Phoenician stitchwork sustain the gendered pattern of the metaphor. Heaney's Phoenicia is not uniformly associated with women, however: in his poem 'Freedman' from the second section of *North*, the speaker who wears purple dye is male. Yet he is feminized by his subordinate subject position within the colony.[29] In this poem the Romans are Irish Unionists kept in power by, and therefore metaphorically indistinguishable from, the British. Heaney's ironic epigraph is taken from R. H. Barrow's celebratory text *The Romans* (1949), an old-fashioned endorsement of Roman character and values that reads like a displaced encomium on the British temperament. The Roman was honest, thrifty, patient, long-suffering and brave. He also owned slaves, but, in the passage Heaney quotes, Barrow puts a positive spin on the practice: 'slavery comes nearest to its justification in the early Roman Empire: for a man from a "backward" race might be brought within the pale of civilization, educated and trained in a craft or a profession, and turned into a useful member of society' (Barrow; quoted in *North* 61). Barrow's use of the metaphor 'beyond the pale', which commonly referred to the 'backward' natives outside the Pale or English settlement around Dublin,[30] helps Heaney establish his parallel between Roman slaves and Irish Catholics:

> Subjugated yearly under arches,
> Manumitted by parchments and degrees,
> My murex was the purple dye of lents
> On calendars all fast and abstinence. (*North* 61)

The arches under which Heaney's speaker is 'subjugated' are the Protestant triumphal arches erected annually to commemorate the battle of the Boyne. According to Bill Rolston, they 'took on the significance of ancient yokes, reducing to the status of subjects all nationalists who could not avoid passing under them' (Rolston ii). The Barrow quotation connects these manifestations of Orange popular culture with the triumphal arches built by slaves to celebrate the victories of Roman emperors. This yearly reminder of the speaker's previous emasculation and enslavement, however, is balanced by his education and training: he is a 'Freedman' who has been 'Manumitted by parchments and degrees'. Heaney was one of the first generation of Northern Catholics to take advantage of the provisions of the Education Act of 1947, and he was awarded a first-class degree in English at Queen's University Belfast. The punning phrase 'by degrees', however, suggests not only his paper qualifications but also the painful slowness of his manumission.

The status of a freedman in Rome, according to Barrow, was equivocal: he was neither enslaved nor free but 'freed'. Augustus worried about the increasing numbers of freedmen: 'In his opinion, manumission – and manumission turned the ex-slave into a Roman citizen eligible for any and every post – was doing harm: and he reorganized the methods of granting freedom, instituting a status of lesser rights as a kind of probation' (Barrow 100). The poem evokes with precision the injustice of the 'lesser rights' accorded to Catholics in Northern Ireland, the driving force behind the civil rights movement. 'Freedman' might, indeed, be called a 'civil rights' poem. The speaker's Phoenician identity is established by his reference to colour: 'My murex was the purple dye of lents / On calendars all fast and abstinence' (*North* 61). The production of purple dye was crucial to the Phoenicians, whose name is cognate with the Greek word *phoinix*, which means purple-red (OED, s.v. 'Phoenician').[31] The pigment came from a mollusc called the murex. Although in Roman times 'Tyrian purple' symbolized the civil and religious power of emperors, senators and priests (Mazza 554), Heaney's purple, claimed by the possessive adjective in the phrase 'my murex', relates the speaker to Phoenician producers rather than to imperial Roman consumers.

Doubling the metaphor, Heaney fuses his 'Phoenician' with his Catholic identity.[32] Unlike imperial purple, liturgical purple, the colour of Lent, is the garb of second-class citizens, the emblem of both religious and civil deprivation:

> 'Memento homo quia pulvis es'.
> I would kneel to be impressed by ashes,
> A silk friction, a light stipple of dust –
> I was under that thumb too like all my caste. (*North* 61)

The Church enjoins fasting and abstinence on its adherents; those who obey the Church are automatically designated as inferior by the state. Heaney takes a Joycean view of his position as a Northern Irish Catholic. Stephen Dedalus declares himself the servant of two masters, '[T]he imperial British state . . . and the holy Roman catholic and apostolic church' (*Ulysses* 1.643–4). Heaney's speaker is 'subjugated' by the smudge of ashes 'impressed' on his forehead by the priest on Ash Wednesday: 'I was under that thumb too like all my caste'. This mark of the speaker's service to holy Rome designates him a political untouchable in the eyes of the Unionist establishment, the 'groomed optimi' of imperial Rome:

> One of the earth-starred denizens, indelibly,
> I sought the mark in vain on the groomed optimi:

> Their estimating, census-taking eyes
> Fastened on my mouldy brow like lampreys. (61)

The Protestants in the North, who depend on demographic superiority for continued dominance, worry about the increasing numbers of Catholics, just as Augustus worried about freedmen. Not until Heaney's speaker rids himself of the Catholic caste mark by acquiring the transnational status 'poet' can he escape the bloodsucking gaze of the 'groomed optimi':

> And poetry wiped my brow and sped me.
> Now they will say I bite the hand that fed me. (61)

To escape, the speaker must reject the visual identifiers of religion and ethnicity and refuse the cultural performance of Ash Wednesday, a refusal that will be interpreted as betrayal.

Although Heaney's analogy between Britain and Rome is echoed by his Field Day colleague Brian Friel in *Translations* (1980), Friel's 'Romans' speak no Latin. The English officers Lancey and Yolland, who come to Donegal as part of a British ordnance survey team charged with anglicizing the local Irish placenames, are ignorant of the classics. Although British officers would probably not have been so undereducated,[33] their ahistorical ignorance is necessary for Friel's polemical reversal of the stereotype of English civilians and Irish barbarians.[34] Friel's local characters, who learn Latin and Greek in the hedge school that provides the setting for the conflict between new and old linguistic traditions, are astounded by the officers' lack of culture. The study of classical tongues proves that the Irish are, as the interpreter Owen says, '"*civilised*" people' (28). Latin is not shunned as a vehicle of imperialism, but revered as the language of Horace, Ovid and Virgil. Although quotations from Homer dominate the opening of the play, the pastoral Virgil of the *Georgics* more than holds his own, and even provides a farming suggestion that would have helped to moderate the effects of the coming Famine: 'Black soil for corn. *That's* what you should have in that upper field of yours – corn, not spuds' (19). The negative metaphorical connection between England and Rome therefore unfolds only gradually, against the linguistic grain of the text. Yet the Latin spoken by Irish characters in their attempts to communicate with the strangers connects Friel's British soldiers with Heaney's 'legions': the colleen Maire says to Yolland, '*Tu es centurio in . . . exercitu Britanico*', 'You are a centurion in the British army' (50, 70); and after the brutal Lancey threatens to kill all the livestock and evict the villagers if Yolland, who has been abducted and presumably murdered, is not found, Hugh the Irish schoolmaster comments, '*Edictum imperatoris*', 'The decree of the commander' (66, 70).

Hugh then recalls how he and his old friend Jimmy set out for Sligo during the rebellion of 1798 'with pikes across their shoulders and the *Aeneid* in their pockets'. Pike and epic text are metonymically linked. The time and the town evoke Yeats and his play about patriotic sacrifice, *Cathleen ni Houlihan* (1902),[35] and Hugh emphasizes the connection: 'I had recently married my goddess, Caitlin Dubh Nic Reactainn'. Leaving one Cathleen to follow the call of another, as Yeats's sacrificial hero Michael Gillane left his betrothed Delia Cahel to join the rebels (*Plays* 87–8) and as Aeneas abandoned Dido, Hugh set out for the revolution under the sign of Virgilian *pietas*: 'And to leave her and my infant son in his cradle – that was heroic, too'. After a session in the pub, however, Hugh 'got homesick for Athens, just like Ulysses', and returned to his wife without using his pike. Friel thus associates foundational acts of self-sacrifice and epic heroism with Virgil (and Yeats), and credits the Ulysses of Homer (and Joyce) with love of hearth and home: 'Our *pietas*, James, was for older, quieter things' (*Translations* 67).

The high cost to others of *pius Aeneas'* epic determination is established at the close of the play, when Hugh twice recites Virgil's description of Juno's fruitless hopes for Carthage:

> *Urbs antiqua fuit* – there was an ancient city which, 'tis said, Juno loved above all the lands. And it was the goddess's aim and cherished hope that here should be the capital of all nations – should the fates perchance allow that. Yet in truth she discovered that a race was springing from Trojan blood to overthrow some day these Tyrian towers – a people *late regem belloque superbum* – kings of broad realms and proud in war who would come forth for Lybia's [*sic*] downfall. (68)

Hugh stumbles in his translation as he realizes that the destruction of Carthaginian culture by the Romans prefigures the destruction of Gaelic culture by another people sprung 'from Trojan blood': the English descendants of Aeneas' great-grandson Brutus. Overcome with emotion, Hugh cannot complete the reference to the destruction of Carthage, which was particularly vindictive: after the Third Punic War the Romans razed the city and 'a plough was drawn over the site and salt sown in the furrow, to signify that it was to remain uninhabited and barren for ever' (Warmington 208). Not content with material destruction, the Romans dispersed the Carthaginian libraries among neighbouring African princes, and the Punic language gradually died out.

Yet the lines of the *Aeneid* that describe by analogy the destruction of Irish culture and the Irish language are literary touchstones for Hugh: verses that he knows by heart. He cannot repudiate Latin without denying a portion of himself, for Latin is the only language in which he can compose poetry (*Translations* 42). Similarly, Friel cannot repudiate English without losing most of his audience. The symbolic connection between Virgil's poetic Latin and Friel's dramatic English is underlined by Hugh's acceptance of loss and his tentative assertion of new linguistic possibilities, which also reflects current debates about the place of Irish in the modern world (see Toolan). Hugh recognizes the need to appropriate the anglicized placenames, to 'make them our own' (66), and he agrees to teach English to Maire, the would-be emigrant to America. Faced with the erosion of Irish and the inexorable growth of English as a world language, Friel and his Field Day colleagues have decided to follow Joyce, and to affirm the compensatory command of the defeated over the tongue of the conquerors. Stephen Dedalus's debate with the English Dean of Studies about the provenance of the term 'tundish', which the priest takes to be an Irish dialect word, is often cited to suggest the abjection consequent upon the loss of a native tongue. Stephen thinks: 'The language in which we are speaking is his before it is mine. . . . My soul frets in the shadow of his language'. But when Stephen later looks it up, he discovers that the word is not Irish at all, but 'good old blunt English'. Although he did not know it at the time, he was right when he joked that a funnel 'is called a tundish in Lower Drumcondra . . . where they speak the best English' (*Portrait* 204–5). 'What did he come here for', Stephen now irritably wonders, 'to teach us his own language or to learn it from us?' (274).[36] The Dean of Studies is ignorant of his own mother tongue, and the best English is indeed spoken in Lower Drumcondra. In a similar spirit Heaney has argued, 'English is by now not so much an imperial humiliation as a native weapon' (quoted in Arkins 208–9). The final linguistic irony of Friel's quotation from Virgil is that it is presented in translation: Latin is now as moribund as the British Empire (Kearney, 'Language Plays' 134).

When the issue is language, then, appreciation of the *Aeneid* can accompany deprecation of Aeneas and his imperial mission; thus Friel's play ends with Virgil's lines presaging disaster, not with Lancey's promised razing of the village.[37] In *Carthaginians* McGuinness memorializes an atrocity that really took place, the massacre on Bloody Sunday in Derry; but he too complicates the anti-British resonance of the Rome–Carthage trope. Like both Joyce and Heaney, McGuinness exploits the religious as well as the political dimension of the Roman metaphor, although in comparison to Friel he weights the analogy differently: his Rome is Catholic before it is imperial. McGuinness's Carthaginians, a group of deprived and damaged people who are awaiting the resurrection of the dead in a Derry graveyard, inhabit a city that was enslaved by the Holy Roman Church long before it was invaded by British paratroopers. In a dialogue with Greta, one of the women who believes that the dead will rise, the ex-quizmaster Paul establishes that Derry is 'Part of a great empire':

GRETA. British Empire?
PAUL. The British Empire is dead.
GRETA. The Roman Empire?
PAUL. Roman Catholic Empire. This city is not Roman, but it has been destroyed by Rome. What city did Rome destroy?
GRETA. Carthage.
PAUL. Correct. Two points. Carthage. (*Plays* 310; differs from *Carthaginians* 17)

But if the British Empire is dead, the Union is not, and Paul also objects to its territorial claims: 'I am Carthaginian. This earth is mine, not Britain's, nor Rome's' (*Carthaginians* 17). To be Carthaginian, then, is to reject both the Union and the prospect of 'Rome rule' offered by the Catholic South: a prospect that Northern Protestants dread. McGuinness writes that

> Irish Catholics are shaped by the authority of Rome, which can be an excep-
> tionally destructive force. *Carthaginians* looks at the acceptance of that author-
> ity in Ireland, at what happens to a people who move the centre of authority
> away from their own country. . . . When you do that you are handing author-
> ity to an empire which will destroy you ultimately. (Quoted in Pine, 'Frank
> McGuinness' 30)

McGuinness's hostility to 'Roman' Catholicism emerges in Paul's arcane remark, 'Do you know who I blame for the state of this town? . . . St Malachy' (*Carthaginians* 15). Saint Malachy, twelfth-century Archbishop of Armagh and the unofficial patron of Derry, brought early Celtic Christianity under the rule of the Vatican and imposed the Latin liturgy.[38]

Yet McGuinness refuses to perpetuate the idea of defeat conveyed by the story of Rome's triumph. His Dido, although rejected by Hark, a homophobic former member of the IRA, is not a suicidal victim but a resourceful and creative gay man who openly defies the Catholic proscription of homosexuality, as McGuinness has done through his own outspoken work. (Members of the Irish clergy publicly condemned *Innocence*, his play about Caravaggio.) The dramatic energy of *Carthaginians* emanates primarily from its gay hero, who queers the gendered binary that constructs colonizers as male and colonized as female.

McGuinness supplements the Dido story with numerous allusions to high and popular culture, beginning with Dido's dying lament from Purcell's *Dido and Aeneas*. This English opera, in which Dido is the star and Aeneas plays a notably feeble dramatic and musical role, has been read as a political commentary on the Glorious Revolution of 1688, a coded warning of the disaster that would ensue if William of Orange (Aeneas) continued to neglect his wife, Queen Mary (Dido).[39] Whether or not this hypothesis is correct, the connection between Aeneas and William had wide currency in the seventeenth century: the publisher Tonson retouched the illustrations to Dryden's translation of the *Aeneid*, hooking Aeneas's nose to make it resemble the King's.[40] McGuinness's citation of Purcell's opera thus equates the Trojan empire builder Aeneas with King Billy, hero of the Northern Protestants. The Irish political resonance of this somewhat arcane reference to William of Orange is augmented if we remember that Purcell's opera was first performed in 1689, the year of the siege of Derry.

McGuinness first published the script of *Carthaginians* in 1988, identifying it as 'the text of the first day in rehearsal' (5).[41] The version he included in the first volume of his *Plays* (1996), however, contains some significant changes. In the first edition the stage directions extend the Carthage reference by superimposing on contemporary Derry three alternative locations: Neolithic Ireland, England in the 1980s and Old Kingdom Egypt. The scenery is a palimpsest, and its most striking feature is 'A large pyramid, made from disposed objects' that is intended as a locus for resurrection: 'Through here the dead will find their way back to this world. When I'll finish, they'll rise, the dead' (24). There are no stage directions in the second edition, but Paul is still constructing his pyramid. The symbolic connection of the Phoenicians with Egypt, a civilization that dominated them politically, is historically accurate. Egypt also has an independent place in the Irish origin myth: the Milesians, whose journey begins in Scythia, sojourn in Egypt before arriving in Ireland. Both Carthage and the pyramids, then, are aligned with Derry as places of death that may become places of rebirth. Paul wants to go to Carthage and would 'like to see the pyramids'. 'I'm building a pyramid', he says, 'But I'm no slave. I am Carthaginian' (17).

The superimposition of Egypt upon Carthage also occurs in McGuinness's source text, the *Aeneid*. Virgil's epic encodes the problems that his patron Augustus had experienced with a real Egyptian queen: Cleopatra, like Dido, had lured a Roman from his historical destiny. Virgil's fictional account of Carthage was an allegory, a *roman-à-clef* for those who would recognize in the narrative of Dido and Aeneas the struggle between Augustus and his lieutenant Antony, whose oriental mistress detained him in Alexandria when his imperial and sexual duty lay elsewhere (see Bono; Desmond 31–3). McGuinness elaborates the parallel not only through Paul's pyramid but also through his line of questioning in the quiz game:

> PAUL. . . . Dido's team, in the 1963 film, Cleopatra, a well-known couple –
> DIDO. I know this. Elizabeth –
> PAUL. – Taylor and Richard Burton were the leads. Cleopatra died by means of an asp bite. What was the name of the asp? (*Carthaginians* 56)

Elizabeth Taylor and Richard Burton provided a tabloid version of the stories of Antony/Aeneas and Cleopatra/Dido. The gay writer Paul Monette, who describes his 'Liz Taylor fetish' as something that 'marked me as a budding queen' (65), records his fascination when 'the *Cleopatra* scandal erupted. Liz and Eddie and Richard and Sybil, every day a new revelation' (67). Dido's eagerness to answer the quiz question about Liz as Cleopatra suggests his identification with the star as gay icon, a female female impersonator whose exaggerated performance of womanliness exposes gender as masquerade.[42] Pushing a pram while wearing pale blue Doc Martens and a pink scarf or cross-dressing in '*a long, flowing skirt, a loose blouse, thick-rimmed glasses, boots, and a beret*' (*Carthaginians* 33), Dido is a figure of high camp.

During the quiz game, Paul demonstrates his own obsession with the story of Carthage and Hark ties it firmly to Dido's transgressive gender identity:

> PAUL. Easy one. Which queen of Carthage ruled there until deserted by Aeneas?
> DIDO. Dido, Queen of Carthage.
> HARK. Dido, queen of Derry.
> DIDO. At least I admit it, sunshine.
> HARK. Bitch, bitch. (57)

Dido, who is both an 'opera queen' and a queen from Purcell's opera,[43] rejoices in these complex identities. In the second edition of the play McGuinness adds a new quiz question that first suggests and then rejects Dido's connection with the essentialist stereotype of 'Celtic' femininity established by Matthew Arnold:

> PAUL. Identify the source of these lines:
> > The moon shines bright in such a night as this
> > When the sweet wind did gently kiss the trees
> > And they did make no noise, in such a night –
> GRETA. It's *The Merchant of Venice*.
> PAUL. Correct.
> GRETA. In such a night
> > Stood Dido with a willow in her hand
> > Upon the wild sea banks and waft her love
> > To come again to Carthage.
> DIDO. How flattering. Thank you, Greta. Piss off.
> GRETA. I remember it from A-level. (*Plays* 361)

As I previously noted, Arnold used these particular lines from Shakespeare to illustrate 'the sheer, inimitable Celtic note' in poetry. Rejecting the connection with both Arnold's defeated Celt and Shakespeare's victimized queen, Dido shows himself unimpressed by Greta's quotation ('How flattering. . . . Piss off').

Dido prefers to complicate the conventional markers of gender. He enjoys pressing flowers, a hobby he ironically describes as 'Very butch' (*Carthaginians* 15). He enters singing the lines about dying flowers from 'Danny Boy' and at the end of the play he scatters pressed flowers on his sleeping friends. He received his name from a man who gave him red roses, symbols of feminine sexual passion:

> DIDO. . . . I met him when I was wandering the docks.
> MAELA. Was he a sailor?
> DIDO. Likely. I didn't ask. He came up to me carrying red roses and he gave them to me. He said his name was John. He told me he was from Lebanon. (28)

Modern Lebanon is ancient Phoenicia, whose people settled Carthage. John reincarnates the drowned Phoenician sailor from Eliot's *The Waste Land*, in which 'Death by Water' alludes to resurrection (64, 75). In the name of the earth he laments the violence of the Troubles and rejects blood sacrifice: 'I am a peaceful earth, give me not your dead'. Then, Dido reports, 'He smiled and called me Dido' (*Carthaginians* 29). Dido's Carthaginian and queenly identity, appropriately conferred by a Phoenician sailor, involves the rejection of war and the replacement of homosocial masculinity (on which war depends) by a homoerotic carnival. Dido longs 'to corrupt every member of Her Majesty's forces serving in Northern Ireland. . . . It's my bit for the cause of Ireland's freedom' (11). Were it to be successful, Dido's 'war effort', the seduction of pretty blond soldiers from Newcastle, would subvert conventional masculine and nationalist subject positions in the interests of peace. It would also enlist Dido in the tradition of homosocial or homoerotic Irish/English relationships that I have analysed in the first section of this book. His camp identification with the feminine, however, involves a potentially essentializing vision of women as peacemakers, a vision which is more marked in the first than in the second version of the text. Greta's care for the dying bird at the beginning of the play is explained by the Irish name for Derry, Doire Colmcille ('Columba's oak grove'), which is related through the saint's name to the Latin for dove, *columba*, 'The bird of peace' (50). The 'gentle' dead flowers (15) that Dido collects and scatters associate him with the women and with the dying bird. In the first version Hark tells him 'You're a woman' (19), shortly after an antiphonal question-and-answer session that valorizes the feminine:

> HARK. The women never leave.
> PAUL. They're women.
> HARK. Better than men?
> PAUL. Who?
> HARK. Women?
> PAUL. Women.
> HARK. Women. (18)

Hark's observation that 'the women never leave' connects the watchers in the graveyard with the women who in 1981 established a peace camp outside the American air force base at Greenham Common to protest the situating of cruise missiles in Britain: they were still encamped when the play opened. The play's original stage directions included 'Three plastic benders, of the type used by the women at Greenham Common'. These 'benders', tents made of plastic sheeting stretched over branches, are exclusively feminine symbols, since the Greenham women excluded men from the camp (Harford and Hopkins 5, 31–4). Wendy Shea, the designer of the first production, did not incorporate the benders in her set,[44] and the exchange about women between Hark and Paul is cut from the later edition of the play. Nevertheless, the stage directions remain in the first edition of the text as evidence of McGuinness's original thinking about women and the peace movement. Although the connection of neo-colonial violence in Derry with the global violence threatened by atomic weapons is politically suggestive, the Greenham reference was perhaps too ephemeral, while the later version of the play is stronger for its omission of the bald claim that women are better than men.

The gendered significance of the benders was originally supposed to be reinforced by visual reference to the megalithic passage graves in the Boyne valley at Knowth, Dowth and Newgrange. The stage directions stipulate that 'The outline of a row of graves should be suggested . . . [which] should resemble in their shape and symbols those of the grave chambers found at Knowth'. At Knowth there was an annual 'vigil of the dead' (Eogan 40), which echoes the vigil kept by McGuinness's contemporary characters. There are other relevant connections: in his 1770 account of Newgrange the antiquarian Thomas Pownall referred to it as 'the great Pyramid' and claimed that the carvings he saw there were Phoenician (238, 259). (Dunlop's idea that Neolithic monuments were vestiges of the worship of Baal was obviously quite common.) Although their exact meaning is unknown, the circles and spirals that adorn the burial stones of Knowth, Dowth and Newgrange are popularly interpreted as female symbols, vaginas or breasts, perhaps placed there in homage to 'the death-goddess worshipped for so long in the Mediterranean world' (Mitchell 38; Herr 24–32). Again, McGuinness's first design idea was abandoned, which suggests either that Wendy Shea found the Boyne spirals too hackneyed (they are omnipresent on jewellery, pottery, textiles and advertisements for Irish products) or that McGuinness himself had second thoughts about the implications of using them.

McGuinness has said that he wishes to highlight 'great areas of experience, female experience' (quoted in J. Fitzgerald 65) previously ignored in Irish theatre. His revisions of this play, however, suggest his increasing awareness of the dangers of essentialism and the pitfalls of a too-naive goddess worship. He also complicates and challenges stereotypes of maternal femininity through the figure of Juno, the patron of Carthage, 'an ancient city which, 'tis said, Juno loved above all the lands' (*Translations* 68). Dido's transvestite play, 'The Burning Balaclava', contains several parodies of Juno Boyle's famous lament over her dead son from O'Casey's *Juno and the Paycock*:

> What was the pain I suffered, Johnny, bringin' you into the world to carry you to your cradle, to the pains I'll suffer carryin' you out o' the world to bring you to your grave! Mother o' God, Mother o' God, have pity on us all! Blessed Virgin, where were you when me darlin' son was riddled with bullets, when me darlin' son was riddled with bullets? Sacred Heart o' Jesus, take away our hearts o' stone, and give us hearts o' flesh! Take away this murdherin' hate, an' give us Thine own eternal love! (*Three Plays* 71–2)

Doreen, one of the characters from 'The Burning Balaclava', has a pet cocker spaniel called Charlie. When Charlie is shot by a British soldier, Doreen wails 'Little did I think that the pain I had bringing him into the house would be anything like the pain I have carrying him out of it'. Mrs Docherty, a Derry mother 'tormented by the troubles' and fanatically devoted to the Sacred Heart (*Carthaginians* 34), sees her favourite statue smashed in a hail of gunfire and demands, 'Son, son, where were you when my Sacred Heart was riddled with bullets?' On being informed that he was in the pub with his Protestant girl-friend she replies, 'Take away these quick pints' (39, 41, 42). Through this mockery, McGuinness distances himself both from O'Casey's sentimental over-estimation of Irish motherhood and from the essentialist myth of Mother Ireland. McGuinness's Juno figure, the Derry mother Mrs Doherty, is revealed as a hidden source of violence. Like Yeats's Cathleen ní Houlihan or Joyce's Old Gummy Granny, Mrs Doherty thrives on the bloodshed: 'I depend on the dying. . . . I knit all the balaclavas' (42).

McGuinness also mocks the social construction of masculinity through the comic destruction of the phallus. As a cigar it is smoked, as a banana it is devoured, as a sausage it is pulped, as a plastic water pistol it is chewed up. Hark confronts Dido in a mock military interrogation: 'Is there anything between your legs? . . . Is the united Ireland between your legs? What hap-pens when cocks unite? Disease, boy, disease. The united Ireland's your dis-ease' (20). (See Fig. 2) Hark's carefully staged 'performance' of British hostility to the IRA combines with his own genuine homophobia to produce a deadly metaphor of the Republican and homosexual phallus as the carrier of politi-cal AIDS. Dido, however, refuses all phallic metaphors, negative or positive: 'I know how to use what's between my legs because it's mine. . . . Some people here fuck with a bullet and the rest fuck with a Bible, but I belong to neither' (21). Neither woman nor man, as those categories are commonly understood, Dido is a biological male who performs the peacefulness traditionally associ-ated with women and re-codes femininity as the strength to survive.

After an elegiac litany of the names and addresses of the young men killed on Bloody Sunday has produced a transfiguring moment of light and bird-song, Dido rewrites the metaphor inscribed in his name, which ought to define him as a deserted and self-destructive victim of imperialism. Instead he determines to move on: 'it is time to leave Derry'. McGuinness is careful to stress that Dido's decision does not imply betrayal: 'While I walk the earth, I walk through you, the streets of Derry. If I meet one who knows you and they ask, "How's Dido?" Surviving. How's Derry? Surviving. Surviving. Carthage has not been destroyed' (70). Against Virgil's tragedy of Dido, queen of Carthage, and against Cato's famous declaration, 'Delenda est Carthago' ('Carthage must be destroyed'), Dido, queen of Derry, asserts both personal and communal survival. *Carthage*, he says, means 'new city' (57). Indeed, in pre-Virgilian tradition Dido was primarily honoured as the city's founder, not pitied as Aeneas' forsaken lover (Desmond 25–6). Quoting Purcell's Dido, McGuinness' Dido begs, 'Remember me' (70).

Purcell's librettist Nahum Tate was notorious for his dislike of unhappy endings; he even rewrote *King Lear* to save Cordelia. Although he could not rescue Dido, Tate refused to end with her prophecy of endless war between Rome and Carthage or with her violent suicide. Before stabbing herself on the funeral pyre, Virgil's Dido curses Aeneas and his descendants: 'From my dead bones may some Avenger arise to persecute with fire and sword those settlers

Fig. 2.   *Hark to Dido: 'Is the united Ireland between your legs?' Conor McDermottroe (Hark) and Pat Kinevane (Dido) in Druid Theatre Company's 1992 production of* Carthaginians, *directed by Frank McGuinness. (Photo: Amelia Stein).*

from Troy' (*Aeneid* 116). Purcell's Dido, who dies more peacefully of a broken heart, specifically forbids reprisals:

> When I am laid in earth may my wrongs create
> No trouble in thy breast.
> Remember me, but ah! forget my fate. (*Dido* 75)

McGuinness maintains that for the Troubles to end the dead must be buried unavenged, though not forgotten.

McGuinness's reference to Knowth in the original stage directions suggests that he shares his desire to rewrite the unhappy endings of classic texts with Seamus Heaney, who in his poem 'Funeral Rites' dreams of restoring 'the great chambers of Boyne' and of preparing a sepulchre 'under the cupmarked stones' for the victims of the troubles. To emphasize his longing for an end to reprisals, Heaney alters the outcome of Njal's saga, imagining the hero Gunnar joyfully at peace in his megalithic tomb, 'though dead by violence / and unavenged' (*North* 16–17). Similarly altering Virgil and Purcell, McGuinness outdoes Nahum Tate as Dido escapes the graveyard and his textually ordained fate. Purcell ends his opera with a chorus commanding cupids to 'scatter roses on her tomb' (*Dido* 75), but McGuinness inverts this conclusion as Dido scatters flowers on his sleeping companions. Dido's last word, 'Play' (70), appropriately signifies his skilful manipulation of the historical meanings and gender positions assigned to the Carthaginians by earlier Irish writers.[45]

III

The persistence of a political analogy, even such an academic or classical one as this, preserves for a colonized or formerly colonized culture imaginative parallels that acquire new currency at moments of historical crisis. In the nineteen seventies and eighties, working in the context of re-awakened conflict in the North of Ireland, Heaney, Friel and McGuinness gave the story of Rome and Carthage new literary and political life, mediating between its antiquarian origins and more popular expressions of Irish resistance. Their work revived the related idea of Troy, homeland of Aeneas and origin of Rome, as an analogy for Britain. In Anne Devlin's 1994 play *After Easter*, a hostile encounter between a Northern nationalist and the British army encapsulates the process of denigration and intellectual compensation that originally produced the trope. The British soldiers call the Irishman 'Paddy' and 'thicko micko'. In response to these stereotypical ethnic insults, he shouts 'Down with Troy!' Apparently none of the Irish characters on the stage are mystified by this learned imprecation (52–3), which establishes the character who uses it as a 'civilized' person, not a 'thicko micko', and attributes street currency to a high-cultural literary allusion. Sinéad O'Connor and the Cranberries, both of whom use Yeats's poem 'No Second Troy' as the basis for popular songs (O'Connor's 'Troy' and the Cranberries' 'Yeats's Grave'), appear to be aware of the colonial significance of London as Troynovant, the Second Troy.[46] Whether Yeats himself was similarly aware is uncertain; if he was, his rhetorical question about the nationalist revolutionary Maud Gonne, 'Was there another Troy for her to burn?' (*Poems* 91), would have to be answered in the affirmative.

In 'Quatrain without Sparrows, Helpful Bells or Hope' (1984), Thomas McCarthy invokes the contemporary political force of the analogy between Troy and England. He adapts an eighteenth-century Irish epigram attributed to Eoghan Rua Ó Súilleabháin, who uses Troy merely as one among several other departed civilizations. Ó Súilleabháin's poem reads:

> The world laid low, and the wind blew – like a dust –
> Alexander, Caesar, and all their followers.

> Tara is grass; and look how it stands with Troy.
> And even the English – maybe they might die. (*An Duanaire* 194–5)

McCarthy retains the anti-English thrust of the poem, and focuses his adaptation upon the contemporary situation in Ulster. Dropping the mention of Tara, which would confuse the political issue, he identifies the Irish with the Greek Alexander, the English with fallen Troy:

> My world has been laid low, and the wind blows
> Alexander's ashes and all who killed for us.
> Troy is gone. And Ulster's wild sorrow,
> It too, like Troy, like the English, it too will pass. (*Non-Aligned Storyteller* 33)

The line 'Alexander's ashes, and all who killed for us' indicates, as Ó Súilleabháin's quatrain does not, that the author is aware of historical wrongs on both sides. Although his quirky title refuses to offer 'Sparrows, Helpful Bells, or Hope', McCarthy uses the fall of Troy to suggest the inevitability of British withdrawal from the North of Ireland. Time will put an end to the conflict, even if nothing creative or joyful happens in the interim. As I suggested at the beginning of this chapter, the story of Troy can signify either the origin of two great empires or the certainty of their degeneration. Many post-war English texts concern the end of Britain's imperial role: John Osborne's *Look Back in Anger*, David Hare's *Plenty*, Paul Scott's *Staying On*, Kazuo Ishiguro's *Remains of the Day* and Philip Larkin's 'Homage to a Government', to name only a very few. England's continuing importance to the Irish is out of line with her relative impotence elsewhere in the world.

The title of Frank McGuinness's play about Shakespeare and Spenser in Ireland, *Mutabilitie* (1997), emphasizes this idea of ineluctable imperial decline: Mutabilitie's barely contained rebellion against Cynthia (Elizabeth) is the last episode of Spenser's unfinished *Faerie Queene*.[47] McGuinness's Shakespeare is a gay Catholic who has tired of the theatre and come to Ireland to ask Spenser to help him get a job in the civil service. Imitating his own character, Prospero, Shakespeare conjures a group of defeated Irish characters to perform a masque lamenting the Fall of Troy:

> I call upon
> The broken towers of Troy, Troy
> That fell, Troy most desolate. (*Mutabilitie* 76)

But the fate that the Irish bewail as they speak for Hecuba, Cassandra, Priam and his sons is not their own: the symbolic message of the masque is directed at Queen Elizabeth, who despite her motto *Semper Eadem* (always the same) must be taught that 'This earth is Mutabilitie'.

> Great Gloriana, learn from Troy,
> Your kingdom's but a paltry toy.

Great Gloriana, none are saved
When spirits rise from out their graves. (78)

McGuinness's play bears out the prophecy contained in the masque: it ends
with Spenser setting fire to his own castle and fleeing the country, accidentally
leaving one of his children behind as 'a hostage' (100).

The image of this young English hostage, who will be fostered kindly by
the Irish characters, is the only gleam of redemption in an otherwise bleak
play which ends without sparrows, helpful bells or indeed much hope. But
another text that deals with the fall of Troy has cornered the political market
in poetic optimism. Seamus Heaney changed the title of Sophocles' drama
Philoctetes to *The Cure at Troy*, and the Field Day Theatre Company staged his
version of the play in October 1990. *Philoctetes* tells how its eponymous hero
is abandoned by his Greek companions on the way to Troy because they cannot tolerate the stench of his incurably infected foot. Learning that without
his miraculous bow, which was given to him by Hercules, the Trojans will
never be defeated, Ulysses and Neoptolemus return to try and persuade
Philoctetes to accompany them to Troy. A line-by-line comparison reveals that
Heaney did not have to alter much of the original text to turn *Philoctetes* into
a parable about the situation in the North. In 'Whatever You Say, Say Nothing', Heaney had already established the parallel between the Northern
Catholics and the Greeks:

> half of us, as in a wooden horse
> Were cabin'd and confined like wily Greeks,
> Besieged within the siege. (*North* 60)

It is therefore easy to see in the cave-dwelling and chronically ill Philoctetes
the plight of the Catholic minority community: abandoned by the South and
enduring inferior housing, poor hygiene, a restricted diet and inadequate
medical attention. Or, with rather more effort, we might read Philoctetes'
sense of betrayal, his resentful refusal to surrender his weapon and his culti-
vation of a siege mentality as a reference to the extreme Loyalists. Presumably
it was on this reading that Derry wits based their alternative title for the play:
'Ulcer Says No' (Taylor).

Despite the trickery of Odysseus, the honest Neoptolemus (helped by a
nudge from Hercules himself) finally convinces the reluctant 'wild man' (*Cure*
12), who has been nursing his hatred and bitterness for years, that he must
cease to feed on his own wound and learn to cooperate with his fellow Greeks.
Heaney uses the symbolic opposition between Greece and Troy to urge the
paramilitaries to come in from the cold and work together to create a new
political situation that will represent a moral victory over England. Unfortunately the destruction of Troy, which is the ultimate goal of Sophocles' play, is
not exactly congruent with Heaney's desire for reconciliation between Irish fac-
tions and a negotiated settlement with the British. He gets over this difficulty

by inventing a markedly therapeutic title (not the more familiar *Fall of* but the *Cure at* Troy), and adding a Chorus of his own which establishes that his primary concern is not with the destruction of the Trojans but with healing between the Greeks, clearly identified as the IRA and the RUC:

> A hunger striker's father
> Stands in the graveyard dumb.
> The police widow in veils
> Faints at the funeral home.
>
> History says, Don't *hope*
> *On this side of the grave.*
> But then, once in a lifetime
> The longed-for tidal wave
> Of justice can rise up,
> And hope and history rhyme. (*Cure* 77)

These lines impressed the newly elected President of the Republic, Mary Robinson, who said in her inaugural speech two months later, 'May I have the fortune to preside over an Ireland at a time of exciting transformation when we enter a new Europe where old wounds can be healed, a time when, in the words of Seamus Heaney, "hope and history rhyme"' (Finlay 160).

Although Mary Robinson's election indeed ushered in a decade of social change and increased prosperity in the South, in the bleak Northern context of 1990 Heaney's phrase seemed like whistling in the dark. But the relative abstraction of these particular lines made them almost as politically flexible as Yeats's 'Things fall apart; the centre cannot hold' (which I discuss in 'Reading Yeats in Popular Culture'). In 1992 Mary Robinson used them again to press for action on the famine in Somalia, and a broadcasting mishap on ABC's *Good Morning America* enormously inflated their international currency:

> Mrs. Robinson remarked: 'I think perhaps if I could just use the words of Seamus Heaney, the Irish poet. He says "History says don't hope on this side of the grave. But then, once in a lifetime . . ."' Her voice was cut off and that of a man in an advertisement cut in with the words '. . . one of these rolls of paper towels can clean up a lot more than the others, because it gives you so much more to work with'. (O'Clery, 'President')

Apologizing to President Robinson and to irate callers, ABC's Nancy Snyderman later completed the lines in front of *Good Morning America's* three million viewers. During a press conference after her meeting with the UN Secretary-General, another penitent reporter from ABC asked her to repeat the Heaney quotation: 'The President did so, concluding an impassioned account of conditions in Somalia with the words: "I call for that tidal wave of justice to rise up so that hope and history can rhyme in Somalia"' (O'Clery, 'President'). No publicist could have hoped for more favourable exposure.

The IRA ceasefire of August 1994 provided a context in which Heaney's words could resonate more fully, and the *Observer* quoted them to mark the anniversary of the ceasefire in August 1995 (Hugill). During his momentous visit to Ireland in the autumn of 1995, just after Heaney had been awarded the Nobel prize, President Clinton quoted from *The Cure at Troy* in Derry, in Belfast and finally in Dublin, where he said, 'We live in a time of immense hope and immense possibility, a time captured, I believe, in the wonderful lines of your poet, Seamus Heaney, when he talked of "the longed for tidal wave of justice can rise up and hope and history rhyme"' (O'Regan). His allusion was repeatedly echoed in editorials and headlines by the Irish media ('Rhyming'; Holland; MacDubhghaill). When he got back home Clinton used Heaney's phrase for the title of his re-election campaign book, *Between Hope and History* (1996). Since Clinton comes from the town of Hope, Arkansas, the quotation is a felicitous pun, and he tells us proudly that Heaney's manuscript of these words hangs in the Oval Office (175). The metaphor, it seems, has come full circle: out of the antagonistic analogy between Troy and Britain has emerged a political mantra for hope and healing. The current Northern Ireland Assembly owes a great deal to Clinton's commitment to the cause of peace. If it survives the constant challenges to its existence posed by the issues of policing and decommissioning, if, in another line from *The Cure at Troy*, 'a crippled trust might walk' (81), the Irish stories of Troy, Rome and Carthage may finally lose their metaphorical urgency and become antiquarian footnotes once again.

PHOENICIAN GENEALOGIES AND ORIENTAL GEOGRAPHIES
Language and Race in Joyce and his Successors

In his 1907 Trieste lecture, 'Ireland, Island of Saints and Sages', James Joyce affirms Vallancey's pseudo-historical genealogy of the Irish language, which he claims 'is oriental in origin, and has been identified by many philologists with the ancient language of the Phoenicians' (*Critical Writings* 156). In the previous chapter I discussed the anti-colonial significance of this outdated linguistic theory. I now turn to the geographical and ethnic implications of a concept that connects Ireland with the Semitic Orient and Arab north Africa rather than with neighbouring 'mainland' Britain.

Although Edward Said defines Orientalism as 'a Western style for dominating, restructuring, and having authority over the Orient' (*Orientalism* 3), Lisa Lowe suggests that Orientalist strategies are 'not exclusively deployed by European or colonial rule, but articulated . . . by a variety of dominant and emergent positions on the discursive terrain' (12). Postcolonial critics who perceive the negative impact of British imperialism as the determining factor in Ireland's history are sympathetic to analogical links between the Irish and other 'emergent' ethnic groups.[1] It has become an academic cliché to quote Roddy Doyle's Jimmy: 'The Irish are the niggers of Europe' (*The Commitments*).[2] Critics like Declan Kiberd, who use the work of Fanon to chart Ireland's emergence from colonial oppression, through a necessary nationalism, towards an ultimate but not yet achieved liberation, explicitly claim kin with the people of colour for whom Fanon's theory was originally developed. In the film Jimmy has a line on that too: 'We're a Third World country, what can you do?' Revisionists, however, assert that Ireland was a beneficiary as well as a victim of Empire, and that geographical proximity, common language and skin colour, and shared prosperity, link the Irish more closely with their 'dominant' British neighbours than with other postcolonial societies.[3] Ireland is, in David Lloyd's phrase, an 'anomalous' state (*Anomalous* 3).

bell hooks's response to *The Crying Game* provides an exemplary illustration of the interpretative consequences of this anomaly. Jordan parallels Fergus the white IRA man with Jody the black British soldier: though enlisted in opposing armies, both are 'emergent' products of British colonialism. Fergus's repressed homoerotic desire for both Jody and his black 'girlfriend' Dil suggests an emotional analogy between these white and black Others. As

Fergus tells Dil Jody's parable of the scorpion and the frog, we understand that Jody and Fergus share the same 'nature': they are trusting frogs, not predatory scorpions. hooks, however, reads Fergus's story as a 'dominant' rhetorical move:

> As the film ends, Fergus as white male hero has not only cannibalized Jody, he appropriates Jody's narrative and uses it to declare his possession of Dil. . . . This paradigm mirrors that of colonialism. It offers a romanticized image of the white colonizer moving into black territory, occupying it, possessing it in a way that affirms his identity. (hooks 59)

While Neil Jordan and Stephen Rea saw Fergus as a portrait of the IRA man as disenfranchised subject, alienated by the colonial presence of the British in the North (Rea 9), the black American feminist hooks sees the power differentials between white and black, masculine and feminine, as more important than the power differential between Brits and Paddies. To her, Fergus is not a member of an 'emergent' ethnic group, just plain 'white folks' (hooks 62). Frank McGuinness's play *Someone Who'll Watch over Me* and Colin Bateman's novel *Divorcing Jack* also depict close relationships between an Irishman and a sympathetic black male. Nevertheless, all three black men (Jody, Adam and Charles Parker) are killed halfway through the narrative. Evidently the authors could not imagine an ending that would incorporate a person of colour, especially one who exists more for analogical than for realistic purposes.

Analogies, then, are slippery things: one man's sympathetic identification is another woman's 'cannibalistic' appropriation, and the construction of aesthetic parallels that elide historical differences or asymmetries of power may appear racist or falsely totalizing. The same analogy may also be deployed to opposing political ends. On the positive side, however, imaginative connections between emerging cultures can be used to demonstrate that the postcolonial condition is widely shared, to destabilize essentialist conceptions of national identity, and to energize political action. While they may not facilitate a rigorous intellectual analysis of colonialism, they operate, as does most popular culture, through the power of empathy, which can be a potent mobilizing force. For artists, the creative freedom to seek parallels that cross ethnic or temporal boundaries increases the potential range and complexity of literary or cinematic metaphors.

Analogies were among James Joyce's favourite aesthetic devices. In a well-known essay, Seamus Deane argues against their political usefulness:

> The pluralism of his [Joyce's] styles and languages, the absorbent nature of his controlling myths and systems, finally gives a certain harmony to varied experience. But, it could be argued, it is the harmony of indifference, one in which everything is a version of something else, where sameness rules over diversity, where contradiction is finally and disquietingly written out. ('Heroic Styles' 56)

Yet Joyce's absorbent analogies express ideals more specific than 'diversity' and 'contradiction'. His transnational and transhistorical 'Orientalism' is the formal strategy most consistent with his rejection of what he called 'the old pap of racial hatred', his pacifism and his self-definition as a 'socialistic artist' (*Letters* 2: 167, 89).

In the bad old days, when Joyce was an apolitical modernist, 'Ireland, Island of Saints and Sages', source of the Phoenician genealogy, was rarely cited. Now that he has become an Irishman once again, it is ubiquitous. But the lecture is itself an anomalous document, claimed by some critics as evidence that Joyce was fed up with Irish politics, by others as testimony of his political extremism. Herring uses it to prove that 'the plight of Ireland left him cold and somewhat bored' (6), Colin McCabe to argue that by 1907 'Joyce's interest in Irish politics [had] waned' (165). Reading Joyce through the lens of the contemporary Northern Troubles, however, Costello claims that all Joyce's Trieste writings evince 'extreme' nationalism, and show that 'Even in distant Austria he remained true to the politics of his father and John Kelly, the politics that still impose upon unhappy Ulster the burden of revolutionary violence and community hatred' (273). Vincent Cheng cites anti-British passages to demonstrate that Joyce is not 'an apolitical colonial author' (6) but omits his bitter reflections on Irish self-betrayal, epitomized by Dermot McMurrough's invitation to Strongbow and the Irish parliament's vote for the Union. 'From my point of view', Joyce writes, 'these two facts must be thoroughly explained before the country in which they occurred has the most rudimentary right to persuade one of her sons to change his position from that of an unprejudiced observer to that of a convinced nationalist' (*Critical Writings* 162–3). Only Emer Nolan emphasizes rather than ignores Joyce's contradictions, citing his 'ambiguities and hesitations' as evidence of 'the uncertain, divided consciousness of the colonial subject' (130).

In 1906–7 Joyce was feeling warmer than usual about Ireland (Ellmann 239), and the lecture demonstrates his desire to mitigate the harshness of *Stephen Hero* and the earlier stories of *Dubliners*. Yet he remains sceptical about revivalist claims for Ireland's Catholic virtue and Celtic purity, and about the practical effectiveness of her revolutionary organizations. He condemns the British Empire, and considers rebellion justifiable, but he cannot see 'what good it does to fulminate against the English tyranny while the Roman tyranny occupies the palace of the soul' (*Critical Writings* 173).

Joyce's Orientalist genealogy of the Irish language is an attempt to undermine the 'Roman tyranny' by challenging the primacy of Catholicism in Ireland. His tendentious linguistics subvert the pious patriotic cliché embodied in his lecture title, 'Island of Saints and Sages':

> This language is oriental in origin, and has been identified by many philologists with the ancient language of the Phoenicians, the originators of trade and navigation, according to historians. This adventurous people, who had a

monopoly of the sea, established in Ireland a civilization that had decayed and almost disappeared before the first Greek historian took his pen in hand. It jealously preserved the secrets of its knowledge, and the first mention of the island of Ireland in foreign literature is found in a Greek poem of the fifth century before Christ, where the historian repeats the Phoenician tradition. The language that the Latin writer of comedy, Plautus, put in the mouth of Phoenicians in his comedy *Poenulus* is almost the same language that the Irish peasants speak today, according to the critic Vallancey. The religion and civilization of this ancient people, later known by the name of Druidism, were Egyptian. The Druid priests had their temples in the open, and worshipped the sun and moon in groves of oak trees. In the crude state of knowledge of those times, the Irish priests were considered very learned, and when Plutarch mentions Ireland, he says that it was the dwelling place of holy men. Festus Avienus in the fourth century was the first to give Ireland the title of *Insula Sacra*; and later, after having undergone the invasions of the Spanish and Gaelic tribes, it was converted to Christianity by St Patrick and his followers, and again earned the title of 'Holy Isle'. (*Critical Writings* 156)

According to Joyce, then, the Irish language is Phoenician, and Irish religion and civilization are descended from the Egyptians. Since Phoenicia was a client state of Egypt, Joyce's conflation of the Milesian with the Carthaginian origin myth is reasonably coherent. In 1884 the nationalist historian David Power Conyngham wrote, 'The Milesians had their origin from the Scythians, and their customs and literature from the Egyptians. As these were the most polished of ancient nations, the Milesians brought with them to Ireland their laws, their religion, and their literature' (24–5). Those Egyptians, 'polished' by the historian's desire to keep Irish origins squeaky clean, are the source of Ireland's pre-Christian religious practice.

Ireland's 'Saints and Scholars' are usually identified as the monks who kept Christian piety and learning alive in Europe during the Dark Ages. Joyce's 'Sages', on the other hand, are Egyptianized Phoenicians who got to Ireland a century ahead of St Patrick and the saints and subsequently metamorphosed into Druids. The genealogical question of who first sanctified Ireland (and with what kind of sanctity), though apparently abstruse, carries an ideological charge. In the nineteen thirties Yeats justified the unorthodox sexual and religious views of his heretical Irish hermit Ribh with the conjecture that 'Saint Patrick must have found in Ireland, for he was not its first missionary, men whose Christianity had come from Egypt, and retained characteristics of those older faiths that have become so important to our invention' (*Variorum Poems* 837). Yeats needs 'those older faiths' as allies against the Catholic theocracy of the newly founded Free State; he therefore uses Egypt, and his Egyptianized sage Ribh, to dispute the axiomatic primacy of St Patrick. In his battles against censorship and for divorce and reproductive rights, the poet openly inhabited the awkward political space reserved for anti-Catholic Irish nationalists. But why would Joyce, who claimed that he had left Ireland in order to fly by the nets of nationality, language and religion, use the Phoenicians to reproduce – albeit with a subversive twist – the familiar nationalist *topoi* of Ireland's superior antiquity, literacy and sanctity? Is his deadpan promulgation of Vallancey's long-exploded theories serious or tongue-in-cheek?

Joyce's attitude to the language fluctuates, even as he celebrates its putative Oriental ancestry. In *Stephen Hero* he satirizes Hughes, Stephen's Gaelic League instructor (modelled on Joyce's teacher, Padraig Pearse); and in 1906 he told Stanislaus that his distaste for the language revival prevented him from calling himself a nationalist (*Letters* 2: 187). But the next year, delivering 'Ireland, Island of Saints and Sages' to an Irredentist Triestine audience, who were Italian speakers unwillingly marooned in the Teutonic desert of the Austro-Hungarian empire, he represents the Gaelic League with only a touch of his usual irony: 'The members of the League write to each other in Irish, and often the poor postman [is] unable to read the address' (*Critical Writings* 156).[4] Perhaps in deference to the Italian nationalist politics of his listeners, Joyce is uncharacteristically positive about the language. He even effects a geographical reversal by which the Aran Islands, usually depicted as the backward fringes of the continental landmass, become what he calls the 'pickets of the vanguard of Europe, on the front of the eastern hemisphere' (*Critical Writings* 155). This geographical inversion, which re-maps the Aran Islands as the frontline rather than the backyard of Europe, resonates with Molly Ivors's invitation in 'The Dead': 'will you come for an excursion to the Aran Isles this summer? . . . It will be splendid out in the Atlantic' (*Dubliners* 189).

The Atlantic Ocean may be construed as a barrier or an opportunity: the end of a continent or the beginning of a sea journey. (The sea journey, known as the *immram* or rowing about, structures numerous medieval Irish narratives and has persisted as a model into the twentieth century: Yeats's *The Shadowy Waters* is an *immram*, and Paul Muldoon's poem 'Immram' is a postmodern variation on the genre.) Joyce occasionally praised the 'ingenuous insularity' of the Irish (*Letters* 2: 166) but usually saw the ocean as a geographical impediment to intellectual advancement. In *Stephen Hero* he describes his protagonist as 'living at the farthest remove from the centre of European culture, marooned on an island in the ocean' (199), and he frequently refers to his compatriots as 'the islanders' (39, 57). He laments that Ireland is

> *an island* . . . the inhabitants of which entrust their wills and minds to others that they may ensure for themselves a life of spiritual paralysis, *an island* in which all the power and riches are in the keeping of those whose kingdom is not of this world, *an island* in which Caesar . . . confesses Christ and Christ confesses Caesar that together they may wax fat upon a starveling rabblement.
> (*Stephen Hero* 151; my italics)

Stanislaus agreed: he called the Irish the 'lying, untrustworthy, characterless inhabitants of an unimportant island in the Atlantic' (*Dublin Diary* 64). Despite nationalist complaints about Ireland's loss of population, Joyce's story 'Eveline' endorses emigration: better Buenos Aires (even though 'Buenos Aires' may be code for the life of an expatriate prostitute)[5] than a celibate existence at the mercy of an abusive father, the life of a 'passive . . . helpless animal'. Not to get on the boat is to refuse both the risk and the promise of living fully: 'All the seas of the world tumbled about her heart. He was drawing her into them: he would drown her' (*Dubliners* 34, 254–5n). Bolder than Eveline, though equally phobic about immersion, Joyce 'sailed' to Trieste, metaphorically retracing the route first by travelled by the Phoenicians, an 'adventurous people, who had a monopoly of the sea' (*Critical Writings* 156).

But in 1907 Britannia ruled the waves. In the face of imperialism, nationalists defined Ireland's insularity not as a condition of deprivation and isolation, but as a God-given physical indicator of her right to independence. The ideological importance of being surrounded by water is manifest in the recently deleted Article 2 of the Constitution: 'The national territory consists of the whole island of Ireland, its islands and the territorial seas' (*Bunreacht* 4). Tom Paulin's poem 'States', in which the narrow North Channel enforces the 'natural' separation between the North of Ireland and the State to which it belongs, the United Kingdom, laments the violation of Article 2, the cancellation of geography by politics. Paulin's speaker reproves a British soldier who is being ferried across 'the dark zero waste' to Belfast in order to police an artificial Union. He argues that

> Any state, built on such a nature,
> Is a metal convenience, its paint
> Cheapened by the price of lives
> Spent in a public service. (*State* 7)

Paulin implies that this 'state' is unnatural, made of 'metal' not earth and rocks, because its constituent parts are divided by water.

Yet in *The Personality of Ireland* (1973) the influential Belfast geographer Estyn Evans challenges 'the naive conception of geography's place in history apparently held by some pious nationalists who see Ireland as a God-given island which was predestined to be the home of a single nation' (xii). Evans rejects the nationalist interpretation of Irish history as the story of a racially pure Celtic people reclaiming from their conquerors a nation tidily contained within a sea-bound physical territory. In *Ulysses* Leopold Bloom is also sceptical about the politics of natural boundaries: he swiftly expands his initial definition of 'a nation' as 'the same people living in the same place' to encompass the same people 'living in different places' (12.1422–9); an elastic approach to geography which is dictated by his diasporic Judaism.

Like Joyce, Evans often equates insularity or 'islandness' with narrow-mindedness isolationism. But he also points out that insularity can mean exactly the opposite: islanders use boats, and sea travel used to be easier than travel across a large landmass. In the past, Ireland's insularity meant openness to other cultures, since 'islands are accessible from all directions' (*Personality* 20). Joyce's Phoenician model depends on a 'diffusionist' theory of cultural development, which posits the physical migration of languages and peoples, usually from East to West. The alternative model, the 'autochthonous' or independent development of cultures, is more attractive to romantic nationalists, who prefer the idea of nations uncontaminated by the genetic material of their neighbours. The idea that insularity signals not the 'autochthonous development' of an indigenous civilization, but rather accessibility and receptivity to foreign influences, is antithetical to the concept of Celtic racial purity promulgated by such Irish-Irelanders as Moran, Pearse and Corkery. In 'Ireland, Island of Saints and Sages', Joyce adopts the diffusionist position that the Irish were hybrids, 'compounded of the old Celtic stock and the Scandinavian, Anglo-Saxon, and Norman races . . . with the various elements mingling and renewing the ancient body' (*Critical Writings* 161).

Whether it is serious or strategic, Joyce's Orientalist assertion of exotic (and factually dubious) Phoenician–Semitic and Egyptian–African origins balances his condemnation of Irish insularity. It also challenges the Unionist view that Ireland's geographical proximity to Britain must determine its political destiny. The western and south-western coasts of Ireland have excellent harbours, and an 'Atlantean' geography, which connects the Irish with the seafaring coastal peoples of Morocco and Spain, contests the idea of Ireland as West Britain, a small island in the shadow of a larger neighbour through whom all continental influences must be mediated. In Joyce's geography of the margins, Ireland is not simply an 'insular' backwater whose cultural retardation is a function of its situation 'behind' Britain and its distance from the imperial centre, but is linked by the Atlantic Ocean with many other, and older, cultures.

Though Phoenicians make no appearance in Joyce's story, Vincent Cheng correctly argues that we must relate 'Ireland, Island of Saints and Sages' to 'The Dead', composed in the same year (130). Like the lecture, 'The Dead' foregrounds questions of antiquity, geography and language. Cheng reads both texts as indictments of the failures of empire and patriarchy (128–47), but if his stimulating interpretation ignores some striking passages from the essay, it also removes some of its 'ambiguities and hesitations'. Gabriel's complex interaction with Miss Ivors, for example, precludes any univocal reading of the language politics of 'The Dead'.

Molly Ivors is introduced, through Gabriel's eyes, as 'a frank-mannered talkative young lady, with a freckled face and prominent brown eyes. She did not wear a low-cut bodice and the large brooch which was fixed in the front of her collar bore on it an Irish device' (*Dubliners* 187). Gabriel stereotypes her as a New Woman: verbally bold but prudish and forbiddingly plain (those 'prominent' brown eyes become 'rabbit's' eyes later in the story). Though he first describes her as a 'young lady', her assertive language politics confound Gabriel's traditional gender categories: 'Of course the girl or woman, or whatever she was, was an enthusiast' (191).[6]

Miss Ivors's twice-repeated insistence that because Gabriel writes for the *Daily Express* he is a 'West Briton' frames their encounter in geographical terms. In between, their conversation fluctuates abruptly between cordiality and hostility. After attacking its place of publication she admits to liking the offending review, and extends her invitation to Aran, a move that would translate Gabriel from West Britain to the West of Ireland. Gabriel's refusal, however, elicits a stern public 'cross-examination' about his holiday preferences, culminating in the pointed question, 'haven't you your own language to keep in touch with – Irish?' Gabriel is so stung by this interrogation that he declares, 'Irish is not my language' and exclaims that he is 'sick of my own country' (188–90). Whether or not publication in the *Daily Express* is a reliable indicator of West Britonism, Miss Ivors's initial indictment of Gabriel has gained in credibility.

All the negative diction applied to Miss Ivors as a woman who dares to be frank, opinionated and talkative (she has 'critical quizzing eyes', she is full of 'propagandism' and her manner is 'heckling' [191–2]) is mediated through Gabriel's limited consciousness. Gabriel does not know much about women, especially New ones. His famous speech in praise of Irish hospitality is initially conceived as a hypocritical riposte to Miss Ivors and '*the new and very serious and hypereducated generation that is growing up around us . . .* Very good: that was one for Miss Ivors. What did he care that his aunts were only two ignorant old women?' (193). Miss Ivors's credit with the reader is strengthened by Gretta's longing to accept her invitation, and by Gabriel's discourteous rejection of his wife's desire to revisit Galway. If it were not for her precipitous departure from the party, Gabriel's negative assessment would be enough to establish Molly Ivors as a minor heroine of 'The Dead', the first person to point out that, in geographical terms at least, 'The time had come for him to set out on his journey westward' (225).

But she does leave the party early, and in defiance of the conventions of hospitality refuses even 'a pick' of the Morkans' food, wounding the sensibilities of her youngest hostess: 'I am afraid you didn't enjoy yourself at all, said Mary Jane hopelessly'. After her departure, 'Mary Jane gazed after her, a moody puzzled expression on her face' (196). Miss Ivors's rejection of Gabriel's pseudo-chivalric offer to accompany her home and her breezy exit, punctuated by laughter and the pointedly Irish valediction, '*Beannacht libh*', conflate feminist independence with linguistic politics; but in asserting her own autonomy she also snubs Mary Jane, a woman who has sacrificed herself in order to become the 'main prop' of her elderly aunts. In the dispute between the New Woman, the 'old maid' and the wife-and-mother (for Gretta too attempts to uphold the conventions by persuading Molly Ivors to stay) our sympathies are divided. When Gabriel makes his speech celebrating 'the tradition of genuine warm-hearted courteous Irish hospitality' (a tradition Joyce felt he had neglected in his earlier stories),[7] the thought that Miss Ivors 'had gone away discourteously' gives him renewed self-confidence; and this time he is not represented as a hypocrite (204).

Joyce's attitude towards the standard-bearer of the Irish language in 'The Dead' is therefore not easy to decode. Cheng sees her as 'something [Gabriel] fears and has repressed, denied, or sold out: his "Irishness", that unruly, romantic, wilder, less cultured, less civilized, and uncolonizable self which . . . seems to be represented here by Gretta and Michael Furey and the West of Ireland' (138). But Cheng's representation of 'Irishness' as wild, romantic, uncultured and uncivilized ignores the fact that the journey westward may also symbolize regression. To some critics Michael Furey's death, the pathetic self-immolation of a dying boy from the unromantic gasworks, suggests the futility of sacrifice for Kathleen ni Houlihan, and his ghost signifies the dead hand of the past (J. W. Foster, *Fictions* 160–1). Moreover Miss Ivors, an educated, sexless and urban young woman, makes an odd representative of the wild romance of the uncultured West, and her proposed 'excursion' suggests cultural tourism rather than a return to authentic, 'uncolonizable' origins. Her travelling companion Kathleen Kearney (the daughter of 'A Mother') epitomizes the manipulative pretensions of Miss Ivors's Gaelic League milieu:

> When the Irish Revival began to be appreciable Mrs Kearney determined to take advantage of her daughter's name and brought an Irish teacher to the house. . . . Soon the name of Miss Kathleen Kearney began to be heard often on people's lips. People said that she was very clever at music and a very nice girl and, moreover, that she was a believer in the language movement. (*Dubliners* 135, 310n)

Joyce satirizes this Celtic revivalist culture in *Stephen Hero*, when Stephen takes up Irish at the behest of Emma Clery, whom he worships physically but despises intellectually. He joins her Gaelic League class but fails to command her exclusive attention and, when he is feeling particularly lonely, discovers that 'Emma had gone away to the Isles of Aran with a Gaelic party' (167). Here the journey westward is undertaken by a young woman whose 'distressing pertness and middle-class affectations' (72) irritate Stephen so much that he tries to persuade her to sleep with him once and then part with him for ever (203). The Aran Islands are the tourist destination of both the flirt and the prude: Miss Ivors is Emma Clery turned inside out. If 'the ladies' are 'The best helpers the language has' (*Portrait* 239), their journey westward invites conflicting interpretations.

Indeed, the end of 'The Dead' is a political Rorschach blot for Joyceans. Joep Leerssen agrees with John Wilson Foster that the journey westward is deathly, Michael Furey is another Count Dracula and the past is a nightmare from which no one can escape (J. W. Foster, *Fictions* 142–74; Leerssen,

Remembrance 228, 288n). But Seamus Deane endorses the views of Cheng, Gibbons (*Transformations* 144–7), and Nolan (34–6) when he claims that 'an actual space for liberation open[s], in the west of Miss Ivors and Michael Furey' (*Strange Country* 95).[8] If we look to 'Ireland, Island of Saints and Sages' for help, Joyce's apparent pride in the ancient Oriental provenance of the Irish language seems to bear Deane out, but in the closing moments of his lecture Joyce undermines the value of mere antiquity: 'If an appeal to the past . . . were valid, the fellahin of Cairo would have all the right in the world to disdain to act as porters for English tourists'. But they do not, because 'Ancient Ireland is dead just as ancient Egypt is dead' (*Critical Writings* 173).

There is, however, a geographical key to Joyce's protean ability to have it both ways: not Miss Ivors's romanticized Aran, but Gretta's Galway, the busy seaport in the West that leads back East via Spain and Gibraltar to the Mediterranean from which the Phoenicians came, and to which Joyce himself had fled. In 'Ireland, Island of Saints and Sages' Joyce sketches a preliminary map that disturbs the topographical essentialism of the Irish-English dialectic and anticipates the cultural hybridity of *Ulysses*, which imaginatively superimposes the Mediterranean basin upon the city of Dublin. Both Bloom and Stephen prefer 'a continental to an insular manner of life, a cisatlantic to a transatlantic place of residence' (*Ulysses* 17.21–2).

In Friel's *Translations*, Hugh tells the English mapmaker Yolland that he has never heard of Wordsworth, poet of the English landscape: 'I'm afraid we're not familiar with your literature, Lieutenant. We feel closer to the warm Mediterranean. We tend to overlook your island' (41). Although Irish weather resembles English weather far more closely than that of the Riviera, Friel discards climatological kinship and physical propinquity in favour of linguistic and cultural affinity. This neglect of the proximate in favour of the exotic follows the same analogical reasoning as Joyce's Phoenician story, and depends on a similar appeal to the distant past. The phrasing of Hugh's speech suggests that Brian Friel has read Estyn Evans, who argues that 'The land that was to become Ireland . . . lay near the edge of another ocean in far earlier geological time, for it was never far from the fluctuating margins of that warm mediterranean ocean (Tethys) of which the Mediterranean Sea is a remnant' (*Personality* 21). Evans's geology is metaphorically related to Friel's linguistics, for in *Translations* the Irish can speak the languages of the warm Mediterranean, Latin and Greek, while the English speak only English and are themselves regarded as 'insular'.

In 'Ireland, Island of Saints and Sages', Joyce emphasizes the Mediterranean connection by stressing Ireland's historically well-attested relationship with Spain, first mentioned in the pseudo-histories of the twelfth-century *Book of Invasions*. As I have noted in the previous chapter, this mythical native account of how Ireland was peopled provides the opening of many pre-twentieth-century antiquarian and historical texts and, as Maria Tymoczko has convincingly demonstrated, Joyce did not have to know the original in order to know its contents (24–36). Although the *Book of Invasions* was used by anti-imperialists to privilege Ireland's distinctive history and superior antiquity, it is, ironically, a record of successive military conquests by Mediterranean peoples. Joyce's assertion that, via its clients the Phoenicians, Egypt was one of the matrices of Irish culture derives from the Irish origin myth of the sons of Milesius. The ancestors of Milesius moved from their native place, Scythia, to Egypt, where their leader Niul married Scota the Pharaoh's daughter. They were expelled from Egypt for helping the Jews to make their Red Sea getaway, and subsequently migrated through Greece into Spain. 'If the Jews are on their way back to Palestine, could not the Irish be prevailed on *antiquam exquierer matrem* [to seek their ancient mother] and emigrate in search of Scota, Pharaoh's daughter?' asked Bishop Stubbs (quoted in Curtis, *Anglo-Saxons* 82). Leopold Bloom, who is associated throughout *Ulysses* with Masonic signs and insignia,[9] belongs to a brotherhood that derived much of its symbolism (including the pyramid with the eye at its apex that still appears on the American dollar bill) from Egypt. Accused of sexual assault by the maid Mary Driscoll, Bloom is defended by J. J. O'Molloy on the grounds that 'such familiarities as the alleged guilty occurrence [are] quite permitted in my client's native place, the land of the Pharaoh' (*Ulysses* 15.945–7). Bloom is dubbed 'that bloody freemason' by the nationalist Citizen (12.300), and vilified by his Irish-Ireland antagonists as a foreigner; but in the light of the *Book of Invasions*, his Masonic connections suggest that the shortest way to Tara is via the Great Pyramid of Giza.

Joyce's 'Egypt', however, is a sliding political signifier. In the context of J. F. Taylor's famous allegory of the Irish as Israelites in the house of bondage, the Egyptians represent the British. The Egyptian high priest sneers, 'You are a tribe of nomad herdsmen: we are a mighty people' (7.846), and in the Circe episode Joyce represents the English King Edward VII 'robed as a grand elect perfect and sublime mason with trowel and apron' (15.4454–5). On the other hand, Egypt's place in the ancient Irish genealogy combines with its status as the origin of Druid wisdom and its present abject state ('The masters of the Mediterranean are fellaheen today' [7.911]) to make it a sympathetic colonial analogy. The paradox by which Egypt can stand either for the British oppressor (the high priest) or the victim of British oppression (the fellahin) demonstrates the protean slipperiness of the analogical method. Joyce slyly undermines the nationalist interpretation of J. F. Taylor's parable when Bloom twice misquotes his father's prayer, 'brought us out of the land of Egypt and into the house of bondage' (7.208–9, 13.1158–9). This inversion implies that the house of bondage is Ireland itself, and that the ancestors of Milesius would have done better to remain with the Pharaoh (Tymoczko 32).

Instead, after spending many years in the Iberian Peninsula the Milesians left Spain for Ireland and banished the Tuatha Dé Danaan to their fairy forts. With a straight face Joyce told his Trieste audience how the Irish churchman Sedulius was sent to Spain to settle an ecclesiastical dispute:

but when he arrived there, the Spanish priests refused to listen to him, on the grounds that he was a foreigner. To this Sedulius replied that since he was an Irishman of the ancient race of Milesius, he was in fact a native Spaniard. This argument so thoroughly convinced his opponents that they allowed him to be installed in the bishop's palace at Oreto. (*Critical Writings* 159)

Spaniards are usually considered to be European, but until the end of the Middle Ages most of southern Spain was controlled by Moors from north Africa, who were dark-skinned and of mixed Arab and Berber descent. As Joyce's portrait of Molly Bloom emphasizes, the Moorish and Sephardic Jewish presence in southern Spain has left exotic oriental traces: Gibraltar-born Molly has a 'jewess looking' mother, from whom she inherited her Moorish blood and 'Moorish' eyes (*Ulysses* 13.969, 13.1114).

The Moorish–Iberian–Irish connection evoked during Molly's reminiscences of Gibraltar is prehistoric. Contemporary archaeologists researching the origin of Irish passage tombs like Newgrange and Knowth observe that such tombs are found 'mainly in the countries bordering the Atlantic littoral' (Harbison 56, 82). Ireland's Atlantic connections were later sustained by commerce: Yeats's great-great-grandfather, 'trading out of Galway into Spain', and his great-grandfather, the 'Old merchant skipper that leaped overboard / After a ragged hat in Biscay Bay' (*Poems* 101), were following an ancient shipping route, memorialized today by the Spanish Arch on the quays in Gretta's birthplace, Galway. But the Phoenician–Semitic and Egyptian–African connections that Joyce posits in his lecture and develops in *Ulysses* are less susceptible of proof. From Carthage, Phoenicia's north-African colony, an explorer named Himilco sailed through the Pillars of Hercules (of which Molly's Gibraltar was supposedly one), along the Atlantic coasts of Spain and France, and maybe reached the British Isles. But even if it could be established that Carthaginian sailors carrying Egyptian cultural baggage came over the sea to Irish harbours, it is impossible to determine whether they stayed or what they left behind. Contemporary Irish archaeologists seldom mention them. Until the era of historical revisionism, however, it was customary to begin with the Phoenicians. As we have seen, in 1922 Dunlop claimed Dun Aengus as a Phoenician settlement and interpreted Irish dolmens and megaliths as remnants of the worship of Baal (8–12).

Joyce attributes his Phoenicianism to the antiquarian General Charles Vallancey, who, as I noted in the previous chapter, traced a westward movement of language and people from Scythia via the Phoenician cities of the eastern Mediterranean to Carthage, Spain and Ireland. Although Vallancey was a General in the British army, Leerssen comments on the 'strong . . . anti-English subtext' of the Phoenician model (*Remembrance* 74). Basing his argument on innumerable false etymologies, Vallancey gives Irish a Semitic, Oriental and north-African pedigree which distinguishes it from Indo-European, origin of the Teutonic languages from which Anglo-Saxon, the language of the colonizer, was derived (Leerssen, 'Edge' 91–102).

Vallancey got panned even in his lifetime, but his ideas, discredited in the philological community by the triumph of the Indo-European paradigm, still had popular currency in late nineteenth-century Ireland. Whether or not Joyce believed them, they dovetailed with other theories that attracted him. For example, Victor Bérard argued in *Les Phéniciens et l'Odyssée* (1902–3) that, although Homer was Greek, his mariner Ulysses was a Semitic Phoenician (Seidel 4–8). In his *Handbook of Homeric Study*, Father Henry Browne, who was one of Joyce's teachers at UCD,[10] promulgated the gospel according to Bérard. With alarming frankness he emphasized the contemporary racial significance of Bérard's theory: 'the Phoenicians were the Semites of the West, and . . . to discuss the history and the importance of Phoenician activity in early times is to enter upon the question as to the debt which we Aryans owe *to a people whom we are naturally inclined to hate*' (182, my italics). Despite Browne's enthusiasm for the Phoenician hypothesis, orthodox Homeric scholars regard it as eccentric: in picking Vallancey and Bérard as his authorities Joyce situates himself within an appropriately heretical tradition.

Martin Bernal, whose Afrocentric *Black Athena* argues that the influence of Nubian Egypt and Semitic Phoenicia on Greece was downplayed by nineteenth-century German philologers with an ideological investment in Aryan racial purity, sees the neglect of Bérard as an anti-Semitic academic conspiracy (1: 337–66). Leopold Bloom, a peripatetic Jew whose ethnic identity is uncertain (his mother was a Gentile; he is uncircumcized and he has been baptized), who fantasizes about the Orient, and who is subjected to the racial hatred of Irish nationalists, embodies (among many other things) Joyce's affirmation of cultural hybridity through the myth of wandering Ulysses, the Semitic Phoenician. Bloom and Stephen compare Hebrew with Irish:

> What points of contact existed between these languages and between the people who spoke them?
>
> The presence of guttural sounds, diacritic aspirations, epenthetic and servile letters in both languages: their antiquity, both having been taught on the plain of Shinar 242 years after the deluge in the seminary instituted by Fenius Farsaigh, descendant of Noah, progenitor of Israel, and ascendant of Heber and Heremon, progenitors of Ireland. (*Ulysses* 17.745–51)

The point of this arcane parody of Vallancey's linguistics emerges in the final parallel between the Jews and the Irish, which is a political one: they await 'the restoration in Chanah David of Zion and the possibility of Irish political autonomy or devolution' (17.759–60).

Analogical, genealogical and linguistic connections between the Irish and the Jews were, of course, commonplace. J. F. Taylor's speech 'advocating the revival of the Irish tongue' evokes Moses *bearing in his arms the tables of the law, graven in the language of the outlaw*' (*Ulysses* 7.795–96, 7.868–69). But although the Irish Famine has been equated with the Holocaust, contemporary Israel is no longer an appropriate political model of 'the outlaw', so the artistic and theoretical stock of alternative genealogies of 'bondage' has risen. The Milesian hegira is reinflected to stress its north-African sectors, emphasizing the connection of the Irish with Islamic Moors and, by a longer and more imaginative associational stretch, with sub-Saharan Africans and their descendants the American slaves.[11]

Several nineteenth-century Irish history books assert that Ireland's shores were 'the resort of Vikings, not from Scandinavia, but Africa' (Ferguson 1), and that these Africans were Carthaginian pirates known as the Formorians (Conyngham 20).[12] In Yeats's play *Deirdre* (1907), the treacherous King Conchubar's messenger, executioner and soldiers are Libyans, described as physically sinister 'dark men, / With murderous and outlandish-looking arms' (*Plays* 175). Yeats's negative depiction of his Libyan mercenaries reminds us that representational connections between Ireland and the 'darkness' of Spaniards, Moors, Arabs, Egyptians or Africans are double-edged.

Nineteenth-century colonial commentators found it inconvenient that, despite their African pedigree and prognathous facial angles, the Irish remained stubbornly white. Charles Kingsley's notoriety in Irish studies has been secured by his well-known description of the inhabitants of Sligo: 'to see white chimpanzees is dreadful; if they were black, one would not feel it so much' (Kingsley 111). Carlyle's solution to Kingsley's visual dilemma was simple: 'Black-lead them and put them over with the niggers' (quoted in Hackett 227); and English cartoonists attempted to follow his prescription by turning the native Irish origin myth against itself.[13] In the cartoon reproduced in Fig. 3, Milesian Spain provides the crucial link in the genealogy that derives the Irish from African Negroes:

> The Iberians are believed to have been originally an African race, who thousands of years ago spread themselves through Spain over Western Europe. . . . The skulls are of low, prognathous type. They came to Ireland, and mixed with the natives of the South and West, who themselves are supposed to have been of low type and descendants of savages of the Stone Age, who, in consequence of isolation from the rest of the world, had never been outcompeted in the healthy struggle of life, and thus made way, according to the laws of nature, for superior races. (quoted in Bornstein 176a)

The geographical progression from Africa through Spain to Ireland 'blackens' the Irish by association.[14]

In *Ulysses*, however, Stephen's meditation on the Moorish origins of mathematics reverses the Christian image of the Redeemer as a light shining in darkness to affirm the creative genius of two 'dark men', the Jewish philosopher Moses Maimonides and his Islamic contemporary Averroes, who both worked in Spain:

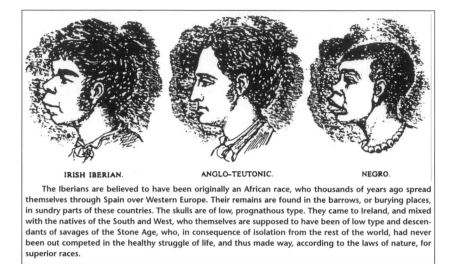

IRISH IBERIAN.   ANGLO-TEUTONIC.   NEGRO.

The Iberians are believed to have been originally an African race, who thousands of years ago spread themselves through Spain over Western Europe. Their remains are found in the barrows, or burying places, in sundry parts of these countries. The skulls are of low, prognathous type. They came to Ireland, and mixed with the natives of the South and West, who themselves are supposed to have been of low type and descendants of savages of the Stone Age, who, in consequence of isolation from the rest of the world, had never been out competed in the healthy struggle of life, and thus made way, according to the laws of nature, for superior races.

Fig. 3. 'The Iberians are believed to have been originally an African race.' Frontispiece, H. Strickland Constable, Ireland from One or Two Neglected Points of View, 1899.

> Across the page the symbols moved in grave morrice, in the mummery of their letters, wearing quaint caps of squares and cubes. Give hands, traverse, bow to partner: so: imps of fancy of the Moors. Gone too from the world, Averroes and Moses Maimonides, dark men in mien and movement, flashing in their mocking mirrors the obscure soul of the world, a darkness shining in brightness which brightness could not comprehend. (2.155–60)

Joyce reclaims both the Spanish and the African associations of the word 'Moor' in order to assert the Irish claim to intellect and civility against the pejorative 'barbaric' stereotype promulgated by the English press. His brother Stanislaus apparently accepted the prognathous slur: 'It is annoying that I should have a typically Irish head; not the baboon-faced type, but the large, square low-fronted head of O'Connell' (*Dublin Diary* 21). But Joyce, who had also noticed 'the baboon-faced Irishman that we see in *Punch*' (*Stephen Hero* 69), chose to revise and revalue that familiar cartoon stereotype. In 'The Dead', the drunken Freddy Malins resembles Kingsley's 'white chimpanzee': 'His face was fleshy and pallid, touched with colour only at the thick hanging lobes of his ears and at the wide wings of his nose. He had coarse features, a blunt nose, a convex and receding brow, tumid and protruded lips' (*Dubliners* 184–5). The prognathous Freddy may look like a loser, but his genuine and emotional appreciation of Aunt Julia's song suggests his capacity for empathy (Norris 497). In a subtle associational move, Joyce gives Freddy his finest moment when he praises 'a negro chieftain singing in the second part of the Gaiety pantomime who had one of the finest tenor voices he had ever heard' and defends him against Bartell D'Arcy's indifference: 'And why couldn't he have a voice too? asked Freddy Malins sharply. Is it because he's only a black?' (*Dubliners* 199).[15]

Freddy's defence of the Negro chieftain is not an aberration in the Joyce canon. Vincent Cheng notes that Leopold Bloom, despite exotic fantasies borrowed from the discourse of Orientalism or the practice of 'blackface' minstrels like Eugene Stratton, nevertheless thinks critically about his own (and his culture's) racist stereotypes and preconceptions (169–84). The anonymous narrator of the Cyclops episode, however, does not. He reports that the barmen are reading a newspaper account of a lynching: '*Black Beast Burned in Omaha, Ga.* A lot of Deadwood Dicks in slouch hats and they firing at a Sambo strung up in a tree with his tongue out and a bonfire under him. Gob, they ought to drown him in the sea after and electrocute and crucify him to make sure of their job' (*Ulysses* 12.1324–8). Though the narrator is not particularly sympathetic to the 'Sambo', his casual use of the word 'crucify' connects the black lynching victim with Christ and anticipates Bloom's assertion that 'Christ was a jew like me' and the Citizen's threat to 'crucify' him (12.1808–9). Anti-Semitism and colour prejudice unite in the discourse of the Citizen, who calls Bloom a 'whiteeyed kaffir' (12.1552). Underscoring the analogical connection between his own people and black Americans, Bloom himself notes that Jews are being 'sold by auction in Morocco like slaves or cattle' (12.1471–2).

II

Almost half a century later, the comparison between Northern Catholics and Southern slaves gained considerable currency during the civil rights campaign that preceded the outbreak of the Troubles. Michael Farrell, one of the leading student activists of People's Democracy, writes:

> The whole civil rights movement drew inspiration from the black civil rights movement in the United States. Its anthem was 'We Shall Overcome'. . . and at the first march from Coalisland to Dungannon in August 1968 one of the speakers had declared to loud applause: 'We are the white negroes of Northern Ireland'. ('Long March' 57)

In the sequence from *North* (1975) that compares victims of sacrificial violence preserved in the bogs of Jutland with victims of the Troubles, Seamus Heaney uses the literal blackness of the ancient bog bodies to construct a triple analogy between murdered prehistoric Danes, contemporary Irish Catholics and lynched American slaves. In the savage context of the years between 1972 and 1975, Heaney jettisoned the optimism of 'We Shall Overcome' in favour of a more sombre anthem. He borrowed the title of one of his bog poems, 'Strange Fruit', from Billie Holiday's signature song, which has

been called 'a declaration of war . . . the beginning of the civil rights movement' (Ahmet Ertegun, quoted in Margolick 17). 'Strange Fruit', which was
written by a Jewish Communist schoolmaster, Abel Meeropol, addresses the
subject of lynching with brutal directness. As in Joyce's newspaper account
from Omaha, Georgia, the victim is shot, hanged, and burned:

> Southern trees bear a strange fruit,
> Blood on the leaves and blood at the root,
> Black body swinging in the Southern breeze,
> Strange fruit hanging from the poplar trees.
>
> Pastoral scene of the gallant South,
> The bulging eyes and the twisted mouth,
> Scent of magnolia sweet and fresh,
>
> And the sudden smell of burning flesh!
> Here is a fruit for the crows to pluck,
> For the rain to gather, for the wind to suck,
> For the sun to rot, for a tree to drop,
> Here is a strange and bitter crop.
>   (Lewis Allan [Abel Meeropol], quoted in Margolick 15)

Heaney alludes to Holiday's song directly in his title, and obliquely in his
opening line, which presents a different but equally bitter crop: 'Here is the
girl's head like an exhumed gourd' (*North* 39). Heaney's 'strange fruit' is native
neither to Jutland nor to Ireland, but the gourd (or squash) grows in the
American South and has a special resonance in the musical culture of slavery.
The song 'Follow the Drinking Gourd' instructed runaway slaves how to
escape to the North by observing the stars in the constellation Ursa Major.

Heaney's cross-cultural reference to Holiday governs many of the details
of his poem. The fruit metaphor is continued in his description of the head:
'Oval-faced, prune-skinned, prune-stones for teeth'. The blackness of a wrin-
kled prune modulates into the blackness of the peat from which she was dug:
'Her broken nose is dark as a turf clod'. As in 'Strange Fruit', the victim is on
display; Holiday's 'pastoral scene of the gallant South' becomes Heaney's
destructive museum 'exhibition'. In both song and poem the act of ritual
killing is presented in its full moral and physical horror: the victim is 'murdered', not sacrificed, and both voyeurism and veneration must be resisted:

> Murdered, forgotten, nameless, terrible
> Beheaded girl, outstaring axe
> And beatification, outstaring
> What had begun to feel like reverence. (*North* 39)

If we read 'Strange Fruit' in conjunction with Holiday's text, descriptive
details from Heaney's other bog poems take on a wider American resonance:

the Grauballe man 'seems to weep / the black river of himself', the Bog Queen's sash is like a 'black glacier', the victim in Punishment has a 'stubble of black corn' on her head and a 'tar-black face' (*North* 35, 33, 37–8). In 'Freedman' Heaney is explicit about slavery, although he translates it to an older culture: the Northern Catholics stand in relation to the Northern Protestants as newly emancipated but not fully enfranchised former slaves stand in relation to the 'groomed optimi' who run imperial Rome.

Heaney's Black analogy is subtle rather than prominent, but the vision of the Catholic nationalists as the 'white negroes' of the North has become widespread in contemporary Irish popular culture. Several West Belfast murals, one in honour of Nelson Mandela, one juxtaposing the women of Cumann na mBan with the Southwest African People's Organisation and the PLO (See Fig. 4), another associating Irish women with blacks, Muslims and Native Americans (Rolston 58, 49, 51), take up the analogy in directly political terms. In *The Crying Game* the IRA man Fergus bonds with both the black soldier Jody and his black 'girlfriend' Dil; in *Someone Who'll Watch over Me* the Irishman Edward is in love with the black American Adam; in Jim Sheridan's *In the Name of the Father* Gerry Conlon, wrongly imprisoned in an English jail for the Guildford bombing and initially ostracized by the other white prisoners, finds his first and most steadfast ally in an Afro-Caribbean man. Benjamin Bailey invites Gerry to share the happy (and obviously symbolic) task of consuming the British Empire, a huge jigsaw puzzle saturated in LSD. In his autobiography Gerry Conlon asserts that 'in prison the blacks and Irish have good relations' (*Name* 125), and remembers how 'in the cricket – which I became interested in because I had many West Indian friends in prison – I'd

Fig. 4. *Solidarity between Women in Armed Struggle.*

be crowing when England were "black-washed" in a Test series' (*Name* 199). Interviewed in Washington, Sheridan and Conlon forecast that the movie would resonate with Americans, as 'this is a nation with a long history of successful struggle for civil rights . . . Conlon expects black Americans will be particularly able to relate to his experience' (O'Clery, 'In the Name'). In Sheridan's later film, *The Boxer*, the Irish hero's grotesquely humiliating bout in a London dinner club is fought against a black Nigerian. His refusal to beat his opponent into a pulp in order to satisfy the English promoter is not just an adherence to the rules of the game, but a symbolic act of solidarity with a fellow victim of colonialism and race prejudice. In a similar spirit, Sinéad O'Connor calls herself a Rastafarian, and Bono of U2 accepts the sobriquet 'White Nigger' as a compliment (Hewson 190).

It is tempting to subsume the connections between Ireland, Africa and the Middle East into the political agenda of the IRA. The West Belfast murals do so unhesitatingly: a Beechmount Avenue gable end painted in 1982 shows a member of the PLO and a member of the IRA standing side by side with their hands on the same rocket launcher: the caption reads 'PLO IRA one struggle' (Rolston 50; see Fig. 5). But this alignment is contested. In his 1983 television documentary *Atlantean: An Irishman's Search for North African Roots*, independent film-maker Bob Quinn revives Joyce's Phoenician story to assert that the Irish are not Celts, but part of an 'ignored culture of maritime peoples' from the Atlantic seaboard who 'owe more to the immense artistic and religious traditions of North Africa and the Middle East than to any European tradition'. The fact that one of Quinn's Irish-language film projects was funded by Official Sinn Féin, a Marxist group that split from the Provisionals and renounced the armed struggle, suggests that his anti-Celtic and anti-Catholic origin myth is at least partially shaped by contemporary anti-Provo politics. Quinn rejects the colonialist idea of Ireland as a geographical appendage to the 'mainland' but, like Joyce, he is hostile to what he sees as the nationalist Celtic orthodoxy produced by the Gaelic Revival: 'Once the Irish adopted "Celt" as a working title, they carried it to its logical conclusion. Not only did they base an insurrection on the idea, they founded an independent state as a result. To maintain consistency they were obliged to interpret the name racially' (27). Quinn objects to the multiple historical exclusions necessitated by 'the political urge to force a unified national image' (56).

Like Joyce, Quinn uses analogy to extend the geographical range of Irishness and to detach it from Celticism and Roman Catholicism. *Sean-nós* singing sounds like Moroccan or Nubian music, Irish illuminated manuscripts resemble Islamic ones, certain grammatical and lexical features of the Irish language suggest not the Indo-European family but the Hamito-Semitic group, and the elaborate knitting patterns found on Aran resemble Egyptian Coptic religious art. By foregrounding himself as an eccentric researcher with an axe to grind and a bee in his bonnet, however, Quinn undermines the generic truth-claims of documentary. He mocks his own 'tenuous connections', admitting that he

Fig. 5. *PLO/IRA One Struggle*

was inclined to credit outlandish ideas provided they fitted his thesis. He might be satirizing Vallancey, for whom a spurious etymological resemblance was enough to prove that 'Pat's language sprung from the same clime / With Hannibal, and wears the Tyrian tunic / Of Dido's alphabet' (Byron, *Don Juan*, Canto 8, Section 23).

Despite his tone of self-parody, Quinn pillages some respectable authorities, including Heinrich Wagner, Professor of Celtic Philology at Queen's University, Belfast. Like Estyn Evans, whom he admires greatly,[16] Quinn is intrigued by Wagner's conclusion that 'many peculiar features of Insular Celtic, rarely traceable in any other Indo-European language, have analogies in Basque, Berber, Egyptian, Semitic and even in Negro-African languages' (quoted in Evans 45; see Quinn 85–9). Quinn's determination to hybridize the Celtic myth by crossing it with ancient Oriental and north African influences also derives from Evans, who writes:

> We get a very restricted view of the Irish people by thinking of them as 'Celts', overlooking not only the productive mingling of many varieties of historic settlers but also the substantial contribution of older stocks who had peopled the land in pre-Celtic times and absorbed its nature. It is not only writers of popular history and political propaganda who pursue the Celtic myth. Some Celtic scholars have been guilty of the very crime with which they reproach English historians of medieval Ireland, of treating the country as though nothing of significance had happened there before. The history of early Celtic Ireland has been written in much the same imperialist spirit as that in which the history of Roman Britain used to be written, as though the natives were conscious of their inferiority and anxious to receive the benefits of civilization. (Evans 45)

Quinn is not the only Celto-sceptic who has adopted Evans's ideas. Evans's learned but accessible work made him a hero to many non-geographers who reject what they see as essentialist nationalist ideology and are hostile to Republican practices and aspirations.

The poet Paul Durcan studied archaeology at Cork under M. J. O'Kelley, 'excavator of Newgrange, who re-introduced me to the reality of my native land, to the poetry of geography, anthropology, geology, folklore, and to the name and work of E. Estyn Evans'. Durcan later contributed a foreword to the 1992 paperback edition of Evans's *The Personality of Ireland*, which was originally published in 1973 during the worst of the Troubles. Durcan regards this text as a 'small wisdom book' ('Foreword' viii). In his poem 'Before the Celtic Yoke', he connects the bloodshed of the seventies with the ideology of an imperialist Celticism that matches in violence anything perpetrated by the Normans or the Elizabethans. 'Before the Celtic Yoke' (1976) stands in political contrast to Heaney's 'Ocean's Love to Ireland' (1975),[17] which also envisages geographical conquest in anthropomorphic and gendered terms.

Heaney's 'imperialist' comes from the traditional nationalist rogues gallery: he is the Elizabethan buccaneer Sir Walter Ralegh, who, with other Englishmen from Devon and Somerset, appropriated land in Munster in the late 1560s:

> Speaking broad Devonshire,
> Ralegh has backed the maid to a tree
> As Ireland is backed to England
>
> And drives inland
> Till all her strands are breathless.

In 1580 the Pope and Philip II of Spain combined to send a small force of Spaniards and Italians to assist Irish rebels who were protesting the plantation of Munster. After this force had surrendered, Ralegh and Sidney helped the English Deputy Lord Grey de Wilton to massacre them at the Fort of Smerwick (called in Irish Dún-an-óir or Fort of Gold):

> Smerwick sowed with the mouthing corpses
> Of six hundred papists, 'as gallant and good
> Personages as ever were beheld'.

Heaney is quoting Edmund Spenser, Grey's secretary, who recorded the massacre and subsequently allegorized his master as Artegall in *The Faerie Queene*. The literary might of England is equated with sexual and political barbarity: Sidney, Ralegh and Spenser beat the 'iambic drums' of English that signal linguistic as well as physical conquest.

> The ruined maid complains in Irish,
> Ocean has scattered her dream of fleets,
> The Spanish prince has spilled his gold
>
> And failed her. Iambic drums
> Of English beat the woods where her poets
> Sink like Onan. (*North* 46–7)

Heaney's poem is saturated with semen: Ralegh's phallic 'crest' 'runs its bent / In the rivers of Lee and Blackwater', while the Spanish prince 'has spilled his gold' and the defeated Irish bards, like Onan, spill their seed upon the ground. This despondent nationalist poem equates massacre, the loss of territory and the extinction of the native tongue with unfruitful ejaculation. Sexual infertility presages the cultural barrenness that followed the extirpation of the Gaelic aristocracy that had patronized the poets.[18] In contrast, the last line of the poem reminds us that the potent Englishman Ralegh was rewarded by the Queen with the grant of even more Irish land: his estates in Munster eventually totalled over forty thousand acres, 'ground possessed and repossessed.'[19]

In Durcan's poem, as in Heaney's, Ireland appears in the all-too-familiar guise of a woman repeatedly raped by invaders; but, while Heaney reproduces the Jacobite formula of the *aisling*, Durcan moderates its anti-English political force.

> What was it like in Ireland before the Celtic yoke –
> Before war insinuated its slime into the forests of the folk?
>
> Elizabethan, Norman, Viking, Celt,
> Conquistadores all:
> Imperialists, racialists, from across the seas,
> Merciless whalesback riders
> Thrusting their languages down my virgin throat,
> And to rape not merely but to garotte
> My human voice. (*Teresa's Bar* 45)

Both Heaney's and Durcan's poems are descended from the ancient Irish lament, 'The Old Woman of Beare', which established the image of the island as a woman's body caressed and then abandoned by the ocean. From a feminist perspective there is little to choose between them, but they express diametrically opposed political positions. 'Before the Celtic Yoke' revises the *aisling* formula to suggest that the nationalist grievance against England looks petty in the context of previous invasions, including that of the Celts themselves: in a double sexual pun he claims that 'these are but Micky-come-latelies'. Heaney's ruined maid complains in Irish, but in Durcan's view Irish is only one among many languages of conquest. His island speaks an older, 'primal tongue':

> My vocabularies are boulders cast up on time's beaches;
> Masses of sea-rolled stones reared up in mile-high ricks
> Along the shores and curving coasts of all my island;
> Verbs dripping fresh from geologic epochs;
> Scorched, drenched, in metamorphosis, vulcanicity, ice ages.
>
> (*Teresa's Bar* 45)

Durcan's long geologic perspective and anti-Celtic thesis reflects his opposition to what he sees as the irredentist and 'insular' nationalism of the Provisional IRA. He writes that Estyn Evans's historical geography 'enabled me . . . to articulate suspicions I had been having for many years about the murderous mythologies of an Irish racial purity' ('Foreword' viii). The present-day IRA does not, so far as I know, found its opposition to the Loyalists on doctrines of racial purity, although such doctrines were certainly a part of the early history of Irish nationalism.

Durcan records an encounter with a distinguished nationalist academic at Cork who claimed 'that while Evans was a competent geographer he was a "crypto-Unionist"' ('Foreword' viii). Contemporary historical geographers disagree: they read Evans as the exponent of a timeless rural culture that chimes with de Valera's pastoral idyll or Corkery's 'Hidden Ireland' (Whelan 60–4). In the light of these clashing assessments of Evans's political significance, we must approach *The Personality of Ireland* in its immediate context. Because he has experienced what he calls 'the evil happenings in Northern Ireland' (x), Evans contests the Republican claim to the Six Counties, using historical geography to reach political conclusions. He asserts that the last landbridge between Ireland and Britain, submerged a mere ten thousand years ago by the glacial melt at the end of the Ice Age, ran between Ulster and south-western Scotland, across the sea that Tom Paulin, speaking from the opposite political perspective, posits as a permanent, immutable boundary. 'Ancient Caledonian mountain girders, eroded to their roots but often reinforced by granite cores, cross Scotland and the northern part of Ireland' (Evans 20). The words 'girders', 'reinforced', 'roots' and 'cores' have an ideological as well as geographical resonance. Not only is Ulster physically identified with Scotland, it is 'naturally' separated from the rest of Ireland by a boundary of glacial deposits, little hills called drumlins. Although Evans admits that there are some drumlins in the West of Ireland that are 'not particularly Protestant', he nevertheless suggests, 'When you see the big drumlins . . . you may expect to hear the noise of the big drums in the month of July' (30–1). Perhaps that distinguished nationalist academic in Cork was onto something after all: Evans's language implies that geography is destiny, and that destiny in the North of Ireland marches to the beat of the lambeg.

Like any colonized nationalist, Evans grants primary title to the land to those who were there first, but unlike Joyce and his Semitic Phoenicians, or Patrick Pearse and the Celtic Gaels, the Belfast geographer goes back eight thousand years in search of his originary moment. The first human inhabitants of the island, 'pioneers of Upper Palaeolithic ancestry *whose descendants have the best claim to be called Irishmen*', came 'into the north-east across the North Channel' (32, my italics).[20] By implication, these Palaeolithic proto-Unionist 'pioneers' (approving word) guarantee the rights of their contemporary Ulster descendants to their Protestant drumlins. In this extremely long view, the colonial plantations of the seventeenth century merely reunited the Lowland Scots with their long-lost cousins, who had 'the best claim to be called Irishmen'. Before we dismiss these fantasies of origin as harmless professorial word-spinning, we should remember the antiquarian loyalist paramilitaries: Ian Adamson has recruited the Cruithen, ancient Pictish inhabitants of Ulster, into the ranks of the UDA, and Andy Tyrie has demanded that the Fenians repatriate Cuchulain, 'ancient defender of Ulster from Irish attacks over 2000 yrs ago', as an East Belfast mural has it (Rolston 17).

The Personality of Ireland is a revisionist text: it reacts against the nationalist version of Irish history by reinterpreting Irish geography. The impulse for Evans's rebuttal of Celticism was provided by the Troubles, which he attributes not to the demand of a disenfranchised Catholic minority for social and political justice, but to the claim of Irredentist nationalist ideologues that the boundary of the state must coincide with the boundary of the nation. That claim, implicit in Article 2 of the Southern Constitution, was not the original inspiration behind the Northern Ireland Civil Rights Association, which sought an end to political, social and economic discrimination against the minority Catholic population. If the 'insular' idea of a united Ireland gained renewed currency as the Troubles worsened and the IRA revived, it was fuelled by the violence of the Unionist and British response to NICRA's legitimate demands. At the beginning of the century Joyce had some reason to worry about myths of racial purity, but both Evans and Durcan conjure straw nationalists out of the ghosts of Moran and Pearse.

Durcan's volume, *O Westport in the Light of Asia Minor* (1975), makes numerous connections between Ireland and Africa, but at the same time it challenges the political identification between Catholic nationalists and black freedom fighters. 'Black Sister' identifies a young woman sitting in the lounge of an Irish hotel with her counterpart on the television screen, who emerges

> Out of missionary fields into a country courthouse,
> Machine-gun firing from your thigh, and freedom
> On your dying lips.

The speaker recognizes, however, that the oppressive 'missionary fields' of Africa are financed by Irish collection plates, and represents the young woman as the victim of Irish rather than colonial racism. Her boyfriend's father,

> Though no niggard to mission fields at Sunday Mass
> Is not standing for his son to hitch up with a black bitch
> Even if she's a Catholic virgin.
> She's black; and therefore a whore.
> And electric mammy, than whom there is no more fearsome
> Drum-beater for black babies,
> Collapsed when she glimpsed the sun dancing halo round your head.
>
> (*Westport* 40)

Collecting for black babies in Africa is one thing; a black daughter-in-law who might produce some in Ireland is quite another. According to Durcan, institutional Catholicism and racism are two sides of the same coin. He refuses the virgin/whore polarity by representing the woman both as an Eve 'seductive as the tree of knowledge' and a black Madonna with an 'afro halo'. She beckons him towards an 'ambiguous' encounter.

In the surreal 'Two History Professors Found Guilty of Murder', Durcan again dismantles the political analogy between Republicans and blacks. Two 'green, green, green' nationalist academics called Columba A. and Columba B. Cantwell are found guilty of chopping up their Caribbean colleague Jesus Trinidad, because, as they explain to his wife:

> Apart from the fact that your husband
> Was a disgustingly intelligent West Indian, a Witty Wog,
> He had consistently encouraged his students to ascertain the true facts
> Of the history of Ulster, despite constant warnings not to do so.
>
> (*Sam's Cross* 27)

The 'true facts' of the history of Ulster, presumably, would not sustain the idea of the IRA as blood brothers of the ANC. The two nationalist historians are found guilty of imposing a 'final solution', but the judge, Columba C. Cantwell, gives them a suspended sentence. A racially homogenous Irish society, in which everyone has the same Gaelic saint's name and the same satirical surname, closes ranks against the 'foreigner' Jesus Trinidad. Neither Church nor state can accommodate the black sister with the 'afro halo' or the black brother with the Christ-like name. To claim political solidarity with them is 'Cant'.

Durcan is not always so stridently one-sided: Irish racism is contrasted with Irish humanity in 'The Limerickman Who Went to the Bad'. A Limerick member of the British Lions rugby team, who naively claims that he has come to segregated South Africa 'to play football not politics', is assaulted by a fellow Limerickman:

> I was not surprised to find out later that he was a spoilt priest
> And that no sooner had he landed in South Africa
> Than he had started co-habiting with a coloured skivvy. (*Westport* 65)

Although the racist speaker is too dim to get the point, his countryman's attack is a principled protest against the sporting apartheid in which the British Lions team is participating. It is significant that his assailant is a 'spoilt priest': for Durcan true religion is always askew of the Church.

In 'Dún Chaoin', a poem dedicated to '*Bob, Angela, and Rachel, in Nigeria*', Durcan's speaker visits 'a bar at the world's end' in Ireland's most westerly parish, a part of the Irish-speaking Gaeltacht, and makes a surreal epidermal association between Nigeria and West Cork. The barman, 'more native to the place than the place itself', is described as 'A big blue man' (*Westport* 67). The Irish phrase *fir gorm*, or blue man, means native of Africa, a little-known fact that appears both in Quinn's *Atlantean* and in Stuart Gilbert's book on *Ulysses*. Gilbert cites an early Irish chronicle that describes a group of Moorish prisoners who were brought to Ireland as 'the blue men of Erin', and notes the numerous references to Moors in Joyce's novel, from *Othello* to Morris (or Moorish) dances and Molly's Moorish eyes (Gilbert 63–4). Quinn also has a long section on the Oriental provenance of the Morris dance, and his documentary opens with a stick dance in an Egyptian park.

Durcan claims that in *The Personality of Ireland* Estyn Evans 'is "Dancing at Lughnasa" '. He makes this connection with Brian Friel's 1990 play because Evans 'had an instinctive as well as intellectual grasp of the affinity between Gaelic Ireland and African culture' ('Foreword' ix). Evans indeed argues that Irish folk customs and beliefs concerning cattle 'find parallels in North Africa, Western Asia and the ancient East' and suggests that they are remnants of a 'pre-Celtic' culture. He also finds traces of 'pre-Celtic' rituals in the Irish harvest festival of Lughnasa (Evans 48). Although for Evans, Durcan and Quinn 'pre-Celtic' is not a politically neutral term, Friel, who does not share their anti-Republican agenda, calls Lughnasa a Celtic festival (*Dancing* 1). At Friel's Lughnasa bonfires the villagers drink, dance and 'drive their cattle through the flames to banish the devil out of them' (16). A boy is nearly burned to death while 'doing some devilish thing with a goat – some sort of sacrifice for the Lughnasa festival' (35). Although the orthodox Catholic Kate Mundy is horrified by this pagan blasphemy, she joins her four sisters in a bout of frenzied dancing to the Irish music of Marconi the wireless (which Maggie originally wanted to call Lugh). Their dance parallels the 'Ryangan' ceremonies described by their brother Father Jack, a missionary who has been sent home from Africa because he has 'gone native'. At harvest time, Jack tells them, the Ryangans also light bonfires, drink, dance and sacrifice goats: 'the Ryangans are a remarkable people: there is no distinction between the religious and the secular in their culture. And of course their capacity for fun, for laughing, for practical jokes – they've such open hearts! In some respects they're not unlike us' (48). Instead of saving the souls of African lepers, the Irish missionary has come home a convert to the worship of the Great Goddess Obi. Like Durcan's 'spoilt priest' who lives with a 'coloured skivvy' in Johannesburg, Father Jack has abandoned religious imperialism. He has the approval of his author, the audience and even of the pious Kate, who, although she is sacked from her job by the parish priest because of her brother's apostasy, is eventually reconciled to his pursuit of 'his own distinctive spiritual search' (60).

As I noted at the beginning of this chapter, the contemporary currency of the analogy between the Irish and black Americans may be measured by the near-canonical status of this passage from Roddy Doyle's *The Commitments*:

> – The Irish are the niggers of Europe, lads.
> They nearly gasped: it was so true.
> – An' Dubliners are the niggers of Ireland. The culchies have fuckin' everythin'.
> An' the northside Dubliners are the niggers o' Dublin. – Say it loud, I'm black
> an' I'm proud. (*Commitments* 9)[21]

To those who reject the idea that Ireland is a postcolonial country because the inhabitants are white, Jimmy suggests that blackness is not a condition of the epidermis but a state of 'soul', a function of culture rather than race. He intends to bring black soul to the working people of northside Dublin. After watching a video of James Brown in action, his friend Dean asks nervously, 'Don't you think we're a bit white?' but Jimmy is sure that skin colour is less important than commitment. He makes it clear, however, that the politics of his analogy do not lead towards Fianna Fáil, the Labour Party, or the Worker's Party. 'Party politics, said Jimmy, – means nothin' to the workin' people. . . . Soul is the politics o' the people' (39). Although 'The Irish are the niggers of Europe' may have a broadly anti-colonial resonance, Jimmy is not primarily interested in the symbolic kinship of the oppressed Irish with former slaves. He wants the musical self-assertion of American blacks to energize the Dublin working class: 'Rednecks and southsiders need not apply' (11). The Commitments are 'black' because they are proletarian, not just because they are Irish.

Jimmy's mentor Joey the Lips, who claims to have played with all the American soul greats, says that his biggest regret is that 'I wasn't born black' (125). Joey's pigment envy leads him to ideologically suspect conclusions. He argues that Charlie Parker, who was 'a beautiful, shiny, bluey sort of black' (a *fir gorm*), 'had no right to his black skin' because the polyrhythmic modernist jazz he played to white intellectuals, unlike the soul music of James Brown, lacked populist emotion: 'Jazz is for the mind' (125–6). Joey unwittingly replicates the familiar stereotype: blacks have rhythm and feeling but no intellectual capacities. Moreover, the language of Doyle's characters is casually racist (the film censored the word 'nigger' but it is used freely in the book, even as the characters claim to be against racial discrimination), and they accept crude assumptions about such things as penis size: 'the blackies . . . got bigger gooters than us' (38).

The end of *The Commitments*, which, unlike the 'niggers of Europe' passage, is seldom cited, questions Jimmy's attempt to forge solidarity between the Irish working classes and the descendants of African slaves. After the demise of the original band, some of the former Commitments decide to regroup. They plan to abandon black soul in favour of its political antithesis, 'Dublin country'. Country music is what the culchies like; it is 'Man's music' (162). The girls will be wearing "tha' Dolly Parton sort o' clobber. Yeh know, the frilly bits on the elbows an' tha' sort o' shi'e', and Mickah, the new lead singer, will call himself 'Tex Wallace'. Jimmy spells out the ideological meaning of this dramatic change of musical direction:

> No fuckin' politics this time either. – But, yeh know, Joey said when he left tha' he didn't think soul was righ' for Ireland. This stuff is though. You've got to remember tha' half the country is fuckin' farmers. This is the type o' stuff they all listen to. – Only they listen to it at the wrong speed. (164)

At the end of the film Doyle's analysis of the incompatibility between the Irish and the African-American experience is elided, and even reversed. Bernie, the former Commitmentette who joins a country-and-western band, is said to have sold out. But at the end of the book Jimmy hopes that 'Dublin country' or 'country-punk' will provide a hybrid crossover between the young urban unemployed and the conservative culchies who idolize Garth Brooks and Dolly Parton (165): a homegrown and less ambitious ideological project.

Doyle's book suggests that the analogy between the Irish and the African-Americans is well meaning but inappropriate: it reinscribes both ethnicities within the suspect rubrics of 'timeless' primitivism, emotionalism and rhythm. Freddy Malins's sympathetic insistence that the Negro singer must be allowed to have a voice is more reasonable than Jimmy's failed attempt to appropriate that voice for Ireland. Moreover, in light of the dismal history of Irish-American hostility to African-Americans chronicled by Noel Ignatiev in *How the Irish Became White*, the analogy is historically misleading. When she came to America to raise funds for People's Democracy, Bernadette Devlin McAliskey was horrified by the racism she encountered among Irish-Americans, because her political education in the Northern Irish civil rights movement had convinced her that Irish and blacks everywhere should be on the same side of the barricades. The vision of the Catholics as the white Negroes of Northern Ireland failed to take into account the actual interactions between the Irish and the Blacks in North America.

Doyle's irony is directed against the kind of literalism that prompted McAliskey to hand over her keys to New York to the Black Panthers ('Playboy Interview' 86), or that directly equates the IRA with the ANC. A more generous reading of the politics of empathy governing the identification between colonially subjugated cultures and ethnicities might found itself instead on Frederick Douglass's sympathy for the starving Irish peasantry and Daniel O'Connell's support for the abolition of slavery. A literary, as opposed to literal, interpretation of the analogy is easier to defend. In such a reading, Joyce's Semitic hero, his Moorish heroine, Friel's Father Jack, Durcan's 'blue man', and Quinn's idiosyncratic researcher may be seen as performing what Luke Gibbons has called 'lateral journeys along the margins which short-circuit the colonial divide' (*Transformations* 80); and the Phoenicians, legendary voyagers along those Mediterranean and Atlantic margins, provide a mythical map of the route to ethnic hybridity. As Joyce says in 'Ireland, Island of Saints and Sages', 'What race or what language . . . can boast of being pure today? And no race has less right to utter such a boast than the race now living in Ireland. Nationality . . . must find its reason for being rooted in something that surpasses and transcends and informs changing things like blood and the human word' (*Critical Writings* 165–6).

'JOHN WAYNE FAN OR *DANCES WITH WOLVES* REVISIONIST?'
Analogy and Ambiguity in the Irish Western

I

Numerous contemporary Irish writers and film-makers have chosen to restage the games of 'Cowboys and Indians'[1] that filled the magazines, popular fiction and cinema screens of their youth. Though the heyday of the picture house is over and the Western itself is a moribund genre, videos and old movies on television have ensured the long afterlife of the classic Western in contemporary culture. The American West is an image bank on which novels about boyhood like Roddy Doyle's *Paddy Clarke Ha Ha Ha* and Pat McCabe's *The Butcher Boy*, and even high cultural works like Paul Muldoon's long poems 'The More a Man Has' and 'Madoc', draw freely. The Western in Irish quotation appeals to nostalgia, whether for the confident masculine bravado of the cowboy winners or the poetic appeal of the Indian losers, or for both at once: the protagonist of *The Butcher Boy* fantasizes himself as John Wayne in the legendary 'Take 'em to Missouri' scene from Howard Hawks's *Red River*, but he also prays to the Manitou in the Indian persona of Bird Who Soars (P. McCabe 8, 50). The genre lives on in the privileged sphere of male memory and in the pleasurable illusion of the wide-open spaces of America.

Its currency, however, is not a politically uniform one. As I have noted in the previous chapter, postcolonial theorists who see the negative impact of British imperialism as the determining factor in Ireland's history have encouraged analogical links between the Irish and other ethnic groups who have endured colonial rule or, in the case of Native Americans, centuries of internal oppression. But the imaginative construction of postcolonial Irish identities by analogy with the mythic world of the American Western produces multiple political ambiguities and reveals how discourses of race, gender and colonialism can intersect, run parallel or violently collide. An Irishman's release from colonial constraint may entail the expropriation of a Native American, or, to put it another way, one man's liberation may be another woman's oppression.

To start with, most Irish consumers of popular culture identify with what ought to be, from a postcolonial point of view, the 'wrong' side: they root for the cowboys and the US Cavalry rather than for the Native Americans. Much of Ireland was (and still is) a cattle and horse culture. Spenser denigrated the

Irish because they were a people who, like the nomadic Scythians, moved around with their herds rather than settling in one place. To claim and celebrate the cowboy ethos of the American West is to challenge retroactively the contempt of Giraldus for Irish pastoralists: 'They live on beasts only, and live like beasts. They have not progressed at all from the primitive habits of pastoral living' (*History* 101). The anti-colonial valence of the identification of the Irish with the cowboys is laid out in Brian Friel's *Making History*. Mabel Bagenal, who has abandoned her English heritage to embrace the Gaelic world of her husband Hugh O'Neill, discusses her way of life with her sister Mary, who remains a part of the 'New English' culture:

> MARY. They have no orchards here, have they?
> MABEL. No, we haven't.
> MARY. Mostly vegetable growing, is it?
> MABEL. We go in for pastoral farming – not husbandry; cattle, sheep, horses. We have two hundred thousand head of cattle here at the moment. (21)

Mary rejects Mabel's analysis as a defensive cover for her husband's lack of 'civility', and invokes the Gaelic failure to engage in husbandry as a justification of English colonial conquest: 'You talk about "pastoral farming" – what you really mean is no farming – what you really mean is neglect of the land. And a savage people who refuse to cultivate the land God gave us have no right to that land' (24). Hugh O'Neill himself takes up the opposition between ranching and farming as a metaphor for the political difference between Irish and English civilization when he debates whether he should lend his support to the 'Fermanagh rebel' Maguire, or to Mabel and Mary's brother Henry 'Butcher' Bagenal, the Queen's Lord Marshal of Ireland:

> The old dispensation – the new dispensation. My reckless, charming, laughing friend, Maguire – or Our Henry. Impulse, instinct, capricious genius, brilliant improvisation – or calculation, good order, common sense, the cold pragmatism of the Renaissance mind. Or to use a homely image that might engage you: pasture – husbandry. But of course I'm now writing a cliché history myself, amn't I? Because we both know that the conflict isn't between caricatured national types but between two deeply opposed civilizations, isn't it? (28)

Hugh is anachronistically self-conscious about the dangers of Arnoldian national stereotyping, but he lets the 'pasture – husbandry' metaphor stand as emblematic of the clash of incompatible cultures.

Seamus Deane has suggested that the need to construct a coherent national identity begins in the experience of loss and fragmentation.[2] In America, Irish emigrants nostalgic for their origins invented genealogical connections that would bridge the estranging Atlantic with what Angela Bourke has called 'the silken thread' of cultural continuity and survival.[3] The theme of the 1998 North Texas Irish Festival was 'Celts to Cowboys', and the 14th annual Cowboy Poetry Gathering in Elko, Nevada, celebrated the Irish and Welsh origins of the genre. The organizer stressed the link between 'what cowboy poetry is today in this country and where it came from, that old bardic tradition'. Imaginatively connecting the ancient Irish bull-stealing epic *The Cattle Raid of Cooley* to the cattle theft that causes the *Gunfight at the OK Corral*, he added: 'The Irish can lay claim to what is apparently the first use of the word "cowboy". The reference was in 10th century literature – although the connotation was more of a rustler than a ranch hand.'[4]

Where culture was concerned, the transatlantic corridor turned out to be a two-way street. Emigration produced interrelated groups of consumers on both sides of the Atlantic, and Irish products, once absorbed into popular American culture, were easily re-exported. The sensational melodrama of Dion Boucicault directly influenced the syntax of the early American cinema,[5] and Fintan O'Toole argues that country-and-western 'had its roots in the Irish music brought to the Southern states by the hard men who built the railroads' (*Mass* 100). O'Toole neglects the contribution of the folk ballads of England and Scotland, but the Irish have certainly re-embraced country music with far greater enthusiasm than the English or the Scots. Hollywood Westerns and American country songs have permeated twentieth-century Irish popular culture, providing violent or sentimental images of a cattle-raising world elsewhere. These images were attractive in their difference from the pious frugality of de Valera's ideal Republic; they also functioned as emblems of success within the Irish diaspora. The superficial semantic and geographical correspondences between the American frontier and Synge's Western World were seductive but somewhat misleading. Luke Gibbons argues that, while the American West was the proving ground of rugged individualism, the Irish West was the site of imagined community (*Transformations* 24). Such distinctions, however, were lost on ordinary readers and cinemagoers, who embraced the form, and the analogy, with enthusiasm.

Even Yeats in his old age read little but detective stories and novels about the Wild West, a curious fact that might nuance our reading of his epitaph: 'Horseman pass by'. Although *Riders of the Purple Sage* makes an unlikely intertext with 'Under Ben Bulben', Sean O'Casey recalls Yeats admitting that 'I turn for shelter and rest to Zane Grey and Dorothy Sayers'. O'Casey was surprised by Yeats's lowbrow tastes, though appreciative of his frankness: 'But Yeats is quite open and honest about it anyway; though Sean thought it odd entertainment for a poet' (*Inishfallen* 195). Well before Yeats's death, movies had captured the popular imagination. English speaking, and without an indigenous cinema of their own, the Irish provided a voracious market for the Hollywood product. By 1930 there were 265 cinemas in Ireland, and though the Irish bishops lamented the morally degrading influence of foreign films, Westerns, which kept women firmly in their place and eschewed overt sex, mostly escaped the censor. The Antient Concert Rooms, once the haunt of Celtic Revivalists like Yeats himself, was transformed into a cinema: 'That place is a picture house now of course', says Shanahan in Flann O'Brien's 1939 satire *At Swim-Two-Birds*: 'plenty of the cowboy stuff there. The Palace Cinema, Pearse Street. Oh, many a good hour I spent there too' (281). Stretching the 'silken thread' of cultural identity across the Atlantic from the *Táin* to the OK Corral and back again, O'Brien fuses Irish with Hollywood epics by staging a Dublin street brawl as a cattle raid at the Circle N ranch (73–83) and orchestrates a bizarre episode in which a Pooka, a good fairy, and the wanderer Mad Sweeney encounter two cowboys called Shorty Andrews and Slug Willard (163–87).

Some of the Irish fascination with the Western may be explained by the fact that the master of the genre, John Ford, born Sean Aloysius O'Feeney, habitually exploited his Irish origins and rebel sympathies.[6] After filming Liam O'Flaherty's Civil War novel, *The Informer* (1935), and O'Casey's Easter Rising play, *The Plough and the Stars* (1936), Ford did not return to Ireland as a setting and subject until *The Quiet Man* (1952). Nevertheless his cavalry trilogy, *Fort Apache* (1948), *She Wore a Yellow Ribbon* (1949) and *Rio Grande* (1950), is full of characters with Irish names and antecedents, full-blown stage Irish behaviour (usually involving Victor McLaglen and excessive quantities of alcohol) and sentimental or martial Irish melodies.[7] Ford takes advantage of the historical fact that many of the 'melting pot' troopers in the US cavalry were Irish, and his cavalrymen ride to tunes like 'Garry Owen' and 'The Girl I Left Behind Me'. (Legend has it that the Seventh Cavalry adopted 'Garry Owen' as its regimental tune after General Custer heard the melody sung by a drunken Irish soldier.)

Rio Grande depicts the struggle between Lieutenant-Colonel Kirkby Yorke (John Wayne) and his estranged wife Kathleen (Maureen O'Hara) over their son Jeff, who has enlisted in his father's cavalry regiment after flunking out of West Point. Kathleen, who has not seen her husband for fifteen years, comes to his post in order to buy Jeff out of the army. The couple are tenacious in their advocacy of incompatible values: he is dedicated to his job as an Indian fighter, while she tells her son 'what makes soldiers great is hateful to me'. He is a Yankee, she a Southerner, and their estrangement dates from the American Civil War, now fifteen years in the past. Ford's fiction intersects with history through the figure of General Philip Sheridan, who plays a role in the movie. After the Union had suffered several defeats in the Shenandoah Valley, General Ulysses Grant sent Sheridan there in 1864. After winning decisively at Opequon Creek and Fisher's Hill, Sheridan withdrew from the Valley, burning mills, barns and crops behind him. Among those entrusted with carrying out his scorched-earth policy were Kirkby Yorke and his faithful Sergeant Quincannon (Victor McLaglen), and among the old plantations they burned was that of Kirkby's aristocratic wife, Kathleen. Unsurprisingly, the couple have not spoken since.

When Kathleen arrives at Yorke's post in Texas, attraction and repulsion are evenly balanced. She accuses him of obsession with duty; he snaps back that she trades on her hereditary privilege. Still unreconciled, they embody the democratic North and the aristocratic South; and behind the American political allegory a shadowy Irish one may also be discerned. Sheridan's destruction of Kathleen's plantation evokes not only Sherman's burning of Atlanta in *Gone with the Wind* (1939), but also the IRA's burning of Anglo-Irish Big Houses during the Troubles. Sheridan, who is at the post when Kathleen arrives, was in reality a first-generation Irish immigrant with strong Fenian sympathies. According to Sergeant Quincannon, Bridesdale Plantation has been in Kathleen's family 'since that grand Irishman Sir Walter Ralegh first smoked a pipe'. Via the unlikely medium of the 'Mick Sergeant', Ford slips in a complex geographical and political allusion. Sir Walter Ralegh was no Irishman, but a planter; Queen Elizabeth rewarded him for his service in Ireland by granting him vast estates in Munster. He is thought to have brought tobacco and the habit of pipe-smoking back to England from Virginia, the colony he founded in America. The Shenandoah Valley is in Virginia, and perhaps the crop 'the arsonist' Quincannon burned in Kathleen's barns on the orders of the 'Fenian' Sheridan was tobacco. Like Scarlett O'Hara, Kathleen the Southern Belle (played by Maureen O'Hara with a definite lilt in her voice) has Irish roots, but she comes of Ascendancy planter stock.

Her national identity is emphasized by the soundtrack, which establishes the song 'I'll Take You Home Again Kathleen' as her leitmotif. Presumably at the sentimental Quincannon's prompting, the regimental singers (played by the legendary country music group The Sons of the Pioneers) serenade Yorke and Kathleen with this song, which is considered the quintessential expression of the Irish emigrant's desire to return to her birthplace (alas, it was written by an American schoolteacher in Illinois when his wife took a trip to New York):

> I'll take you home again, Kathleen
> Across the ocean wild and wide
> To where your heart has ever been
> Since you were first my blushing bride.
> The roses all have left your cheek.
> I've watched them fade away and die
> Your voice is sad when e'er you speak
> And tears bedim your loving eyes.
>
> Oh! I will take you back, Kathleen
> To where your heart will feel no pain
> And when the fields are fresh and green
> I'll take you to your home again!

As Yorke and Kathleen stand uncomfortably side-by-side to receive the full impact of this unabashed sentimentality, he disclaims the song: 'This music is not of my choosing'. 'I'm sorry, Kirkby,' she replies, 'I wish it had been'.

Sheridan's Irish rebel heritage is also confirmed through music. After a dinner in which Kathleen toasts the US cavalry as her 'only rival', The Sons of the Pioneers return to entertain the General with a performance of the Fenian ballad 'Down by the Glenside.'[8]

'Twas down by the glenside,
I met an old woman,
A plucking young nettles;
She ne'er saw me coming
I listened awhile
To the song she was humming,
'Glory O, glory O,
To the Bold Fenian men!'

'Tis fifty long years
Since I saw the moon beaming
And strong manly forms,
Their eyes with hope gleaming
I see them again,
Sure, through all my days dreaming,
'Glory O, glory O,
To the Bold Fenian men!'

I passed on my way,
God be praised that I met her,
Be life long or short
I shall never forget her;
We may have great men,
But we'll never have better.
'Glory O, glory O,
To the Bold Fenian men!'

Sergeant Quincannon is so overcome by these patriotic sentiments that he is forced to resort to his handkerchief. Though less emotional than Quincannon, Sheridan too is visibly moved by the musical evocation of anti-colonial struggle in the service of the 'old woman', Mother Ireland. To have this song performed in 1879 is an anachronism: it was written by Brendan Behan's uncle, Peadar Kearney, around the time of the 1916 rebellion, which was, as the song says, 'fifty long years' after the Fenian rising of 1867. Nevertheless it makes Ford's point economically: Sheridan, the scourge of Shenandoah, would have made common cause with the IRA when it came to burning out the Ascendancy planters. United by their ethnic origins, Sheridan and Kathleen are nevertheless divided by class, gender and the struggle over slavery, as were many Irish immigrants; and Ford's ethnically inflected perspective suggests that we see the American Civil War as a reflection of Irish political dissension.

An irony not noted in *Rio Grande* itself, but implicit in the historical circumstances on which it draws, is that while the Union troops that Sheridan commanded were ostensibly fighting on behalf of the black slaves who worked plantations like Kathleen's, after the war those cavalry regiments went on to help obliterate another ethnic underclass, the Native Americans. Ford addresses this paradox directly in *Cheyenne Autumn* (1964), when the Secretary for the Interior appeals on behalf of the American Indians to a senator who has lost an arm at Gettysburg: 'You'd never even seen a Negro slave. All you knew was that they were human beings with the rights of human beings. And it was worth an arm to you'. To be consistent, the Secretary implies, the senator should now act to halt the harassment of the Cheyenne, although it has been ordered, as Ford reminds us, by Sheridan himself. Fintan O'Toole might have been thinking of Sheridan's double political identity when he wrote that

> The great American myth, of course, is the myth of the taming of the wilderness, the conquering of the uncivilised Indian by the civilised white man. The Irish played more than their fair part in this process. But that role remains crucially ambivalent. The ambivalence comes from the fact that the Irish are not, in this dichotomy, either/or, they are both/and. They are natives and conquerors, aboriginals and civilisers, a savage tribe in one context, a superior race in another. (*Ex-Isle* 67)

In *Rio Grande* (though not in all of Ford's works) there is no place for empathy with the Indians, who are represented as drunken and savage killers of women and would-be murderers of a wagonload of innocent children. Sheridan denied having said that 'the only good Indian is a dead Indian', but the aphorism has always been attributed to him. His behaviour after the Civil War, when he applied to the Plains tribes the brutal tactics that had pacified the Shenandoah Valley, suggests that he earned the attribution.

In *Rio Grande* gender too is a battlefield, as Kathleen's domestic and pacifist 'feminine' values are pitted against Kirkby's puritanical fidelity to military duty. The quasi-Oedipal narrative, in which Jeff the mother's boy is detached from her female influence, stands up to his bullying father and symbolically proves his manliness during a skirmish in which Yorke receives what initially appears to be a fatal wound, faithfully reflects the construction of traditional masculine gender roles. Men need to be men in order to protect the women and children. Kathleen is forced to give up her opposition to her son's choice of career, and at the end of the film we see her girlishly twirling her parasol in rhythm as, on Sheridan's orders, the troopers parade to 'Dixie'.[9] The North and the South are in harmony, the boy Jeff has become a man decorated for courage, the husband has his compliant wife back and the Fenians are in charge of the cavalry. Irishness and patriarchy triumph in unison.

They do so again in Ford's most famous Irish film, *The Quiet Man* (1952). Herb Yates of RKO pictures permitted Ford to film this movie about an Irish-American boxer returning to his birthplace only on condition that he made *Rio Grande* first: Yates thought that the Irish subject would be a loser and wanted another Western in the can as insurance. In consequence, *Rio Grande* is a shadow anticipation of *The Quiet Man*, with the same major casting – Wayne, O'Hara, McLaglen – and many of the same dynamics, especially the stormy relationship between the taciturn Wayne and the stubborn O'Hara, who again embody diametrically opposed value systems. Ford gestures to this resemblance when 'I'll Take You Home Again Kathleen' makes a cameo appearance as Wayne and O'Hara sit together by the fire after their less than satisfactory wedding. More strikingly, the scene from *Rio Grande* in which Kirkby Yorke returns to his tent to find Kathleen concealed in the shadows and passionately embraces her precisely anticipates in choreography and body language the episode from *The Quiet Man* in which Sean Thornton discovers Mary Kate hiding in his cottage and gives her the famous kiss that taught ET how humans behave in the grip of passion. This kiss travels from the American West to the West of Ireland and back again, to be registered by a bemused alien and re-enacted by two Californian children. Spielberg even maintains the stereotypical connection between Irishness and alcohol by having a drunken ET see *The Quiet Man* on television after drinking a six-pack of Coors.

Fintan O'Toole argues that, 'Ford's real Ireland is Monument Valley, the American desert landscape that has all the qualities of timelessness, freedom from history and social amnesia that the Irish romantic movement always sought in the West of Ireland' (*Mass* 141). On the other hand, Robert Ray and Gary Wills think of *The Quiet Man*, which is set in Connemara, as a disguised Western (Wills 249). Exploiting Wayne's established screen persona, Ford takes many of the cowboy and cavalry tropes (hard riding, hard drinking, taciturnity, nostalgia for a vanished past and cathartic fist fighting) from Monument Valley back to Ireland. But, unlike most traditional Westerns, *The Quiet Man* centres on a woman's control of her sexuality. As Luke Gibbons has pointed out, the American and Irish myths of the West are ethically distinct: here Ford shows us American individualism in confrontation with the established mores of a Connemara community.

The returned Yank, Sean Thornton, who once boxed under the name of 'Trooper Thorn' (the cavalry reference is deliberate), has abandoned his successful career after inadvertently killing a man in the ring. He falls in love with the local 'spinster' Mary Kate Danagher, but fails to understand the matrimonial customs of her traditional Irish village. Although he succeeds in wedding her, she refuses to consummate the marriage until her brother Squire Danagher (a surly Victor McLaglen) hands over her dowry. Thornton is not interested in the money and does not appreciate that Mary Kate's identity is symbolically invested in her financial autonomy. Without the fortune, she tells him, 'you don't have myself'. In her turn, she misinterprets his refusal to challenge Danagher as cowardice. When, after their first night of passion, she runs away from him because she cannot stand the 'shame' of her position as a woman without a fortune married to a man without courage, he drags her back across the fields by the scruff of her neck to confront her brother. Danagher hands over the cash and Mary Kate helps Thornton to burn it: not money but her pride was at stake.

Because the modernizing Yank is ultimately forced to accept the traditional meaning of the dowry as the guarantee of an Irish countrywoman's independence and dignity, Gary Wills argues that, '*The Quiet Man* is a far more interesting study of indigenous rights than Ford's "pro-Indian" *Cheyenne Autumn*' (250). Wills's reading, which would make all the inhabitants of Inisfree Indians by analogy, conflates gender (Mary Kate and her 'right' to a dowry) with ethnicity (the Indians and their 'rights' to the land). But what this tempting identification leaves out is the male triumphalism of the scene in which Thornton manhandles Mary Kate in front of the approving people of Inisfree. The price she pays for the acknowledgement of her identity as a properly married woman is public humiliation and physical abuse, which, alarmingly, she accepts without complaint. Her momentary possession of her 'rights' restores her self-respect, but the only use she makes of her liberation is to return home as 'the woman of the house' and cook Thornton's supper. Until he gives full rein to the violence he has previously eschewed, Thornton himself is not man enough to keep sexual possession of his woman. When he finally asserts himself against Danagher in the Donnybrook, the vicar, the protestant Bishop and two Catholic priests sanction his behaviour. Even the Churches believe that heterosexual masculinity, which depends on violence, must be kept up. Thornton, the playboy of two Western Worlds, subdues not his da but his brother-in-law, and a right to the chin replaces the blow of a loy, but Ford's yoking of violence and sexuality is closely modelled on Synge. In both *Rio Grande* and *The Quiet Man* O'Hara's fiery persona is allowed to hold centre stage for just long enough to surprise and please an audience accustomed to quieter women, but by the conclusion she is firmly re-enclosed in the domestic family hierarchy, while the men kill Indians or beat each other senseless in the proper masculine way. The shrew has been tamed and, like the hag in Chaucer's *Wife of Bath's Tale*, Mary Kate gets the sovereignty she desires only to hand it back again.

Most classic Westerns, indeed, are concerned with the construction of dominant white masculinity at the expense of its female as well as Native American Others.[10] Although there are exceptions like the Wild West imagery of the rock band U2, Irish investment in the image of the Stetson-wearing cowboy and the related genre of country-and-western music tends to be rural, conservative and connected with the traditional nationalist politics of Fianna Fáil. As I mentioned in the previous chapter, after the original Commitments break up, the new group abandons its radical attempt to produce 'black' soul music in favour of a new, composite style that their manager Jimmy christens 'Dublin country'. They plan to dress the girls like Dolly Parton and their singer Mickah adopts the stage name Tex Wallace. Jimmy justifies his choice on the grounds of demographics; after all, he says, 'half the country is fuckin' farmers', and culchies prefer country.

The country-and-western craze continues today (Garth Brooks is massively popular in Ireland),[11] but it peaked in the late sixties and the seventies: the glory days of the country dancehalls. Many of these dancehalls were owned by Albert Reynolds, later the leader of Fianna Fáil, who, 'while he was minister in charge of telecommunications, appeared on television in a cowboy suit and Stetson singing *Put Your Sweet Lips A Little Closer to the Phone*' (O'Toole, *Mass* 85–6). Despite his Western wear, Reynolds's phone song indicates that much 'country' music has little to do with the range: the 'western' in 'country-and-western' was a synthetic product of the singing cowboys of thirties Hollywood. Country songs, derived from traditional Irish, Scottish and English ballads, reflected the often cruel narratives of their originals and the actual hardships of life in Appalachia. They still feature cheatin' hearts, crimes of passion, bad divorces, finding Jesus, losing Mama and standing by your man: lots of tears and the occasional smile. But however cattle-free the content of the lyrics, the cowboy trimmings of Nashville are ubiquitous.[12]

Tom Murphy's play, *Conversations on a Homecoming* (1985), takes place in the early seventies in a Tuam pub called 'The White House'. It features a 'returned Yank', Michael, who unlike Sean Thornton has no cowboy or cavalry attributes: the Western tropes are attached to a man who stayed at home, the 'stupid and insensitive' small businessman Liam who 'affects a slight American accent' and is frequently called a 'cowboy' by the other characters. One derogatory meaning of the word 'cowboy' is a worker who does a shoddy job without proper qualifications, and in this sense it suits Liam, who is 'a farmer, an estate agent, a travel agent . . . owns property' (*Plays: Two* 4) and also puts up makeshift partitions. (Though the play makes no mention of his voting habits, he looks like a stereotypical supporter of Fianna Fáil: a farmer and small businessman in the rural West of Ireland.)[13] Unlike the other participants in the homecoming party, Liam is doing well financially and is set to buy up the pub and marry the landlord's daughter. Murphy uses the gombeen man's cowboy persona to represent the cultural and economic Americanization of Irish life. Although the progressive liberal dreams fostered by John Kennedy and espoused by JJ, the publican of 'The White House', have turned sour and the boom produced by the modernization programme of Seán Lemass is in retreat, the ersatz ethos of country-and-western has saturated the culture. Liam's fake American accent is stronger than Michael's authentic one, and when he is sufficiently well oiled he sings a maudlin country song in which his 'tear drops fall' over his dead pony (69–70).

Fintan O'Toole argues that the Irish embrace of country music was not entirely meretricious: he sees it as a response to the cultural domination of the Beatles, a quasi-political choice of America over England (*Mass* 101–2). Murphy takes a more negative position: he relates Liam's cowboy persona directly to his nationalist politics, which are unsympathetically represented.[14] The play is set in the early years of the Troubles, and Liam admits to having thought seriously of going up North to 'Shoot us a few Prods' (*Plays: Two* 13), and he mouths slogans about 'A minority Catholic group being oppressed'. He is not the only one to have entertained these fantasies, but no one else uses phrases like 'No border', 'Faith and Truth', and 'racial memory' (47–9). Through Liam, Murphy alludes to the arms scandal of 1970, in which Charles Haughey, Neil Blaney and Kevin Boland lost their seats in the Fianna Fáil cabinet because of their supposed complicity in an attempt to supply guns to the Catholics in the North.[15] Liam the gombeen man, whose Mercedes 'doesn't need a clutch' (9) and whom Tom accuses of being 'only a fuckin' bunch of keys' (72), is a faint provincial shadow of the flamboyant Haughey, whose high living and taste for fast cars was legendary. Tom, a critical and reflective (though also cynical and drunken) schoolmaster, posits a direct connection between Liam's affected cowboy melancholia and his attitude to the North:

> [T]he real enemy – the big one! – that we shall overcome, is the country-and-western system itself. Unyielding, uncompromising, in its drive for total sentimentality. A sentimentality I say that would have us all an unholy herd of Sierra Sues, sad-eyed inquisitors, sentimental Nazis, fascists, sectarianists, black-and-blue shirted nationalists, with spurs a-jinglin', all ridin' down the trail to Oranmore. (67)

Tom's friend Junior also connects Liam's sympathy for the IRA with his Western persona when he mockingly tells him, 'Keep the faith, cowboy!' (78).

During the sixties in the US similar political critiques contributed to the decline of the Hollywood Western itself: *Butch Cassidy and the Sundance Kid* and Peckinpah's *The Wild Bunch*, both made in 1969, are elegies for a genre that could not survive the interrogation of masculinity and Manifest Destiny initiated by feminism, the civil rights movement and Vietnam. Peter Ormrod's low-budget film *Eat the Peach* (1986), whose script was originally by Stewart Parker, examines the Irish obsession with this fading Western mythos through a minor character called, after his trademark cowboy footwear, Boots. Boots is a short, middle-aged, paunchy fellow who boasts about his experiences in the States, extols showbiz and private enterprise and never appears without his Stetson. He encourages the American dream of the two protagonists, who, like Elvis Presley in *Roustabout*, build a motorcycle wall of death in their bleak rural community and seek commercial sponsorship. Although this sounds like an outlandish exaggeration of the Irish mania for American icons, the film is based on a true story.

The bar in which Boots listens to his favourite country music is called 'The Frontier', and his local frontier is the Border. Unlike the political gunrunners of 1970, Boots takes clandestine goods in the opposite direction. He is employed by the brother of the local (surely Fianna Fáil) TD to smuggle petrol and whiskey from the North into the Republic. Boots's employers have purely financial motives: British prices are lower than Irish ones. Boots attempts to cast an aura of Western glamour over the mundane task of economic smuggling: as he drives a milk lorry full of illicit gasoline along a minor, unpoliced route he remarks, 'a useful wee road this, the Navajo trail we call it'. When he is caught watering the smuggled whiskey, his boss says threateningly, 'Boots – you're some cowboy – it'll be a while before you ride again'. In hospital after the ensuing punishment beating he hands over his precious boots to his friend Arthur for safe keeping and makes a poignant confession: 'I wanna level with you – I've never been to the United States'. Replies Arthur, to the plangent twang of a steel-stringed guitar: 'Everybody knows that, Boots'. 'Everyone?' asks Boots in pathetic amazement. Boots's transparent macho identification with the West has been nurtured by a dying form; a form that even in its heyday was structured by nostalgia, since the real frontier was closed before the first celluloid cowboy got his spurs. Ormrod's gently comic film permits us to feel sorry for Boots, but Murphy's Tom is unrelenting about such adolescent cultural fantasies: 'And Danny O'Toole up the road thinks he's Robert Mitchum and he only five feet two? . . . And Danny O'Toole is winning the west for us?' (*Plays: Two* 52). Tom sees all American dreams, John Kennedy's no less than Jim Reeves's, as irrelevant and damaging, and dismisses the easy connection between the Western and the West of Ireland: 'we are such a ridiculous race that even our choice of assumed images is quite arbitrary' (54).

II

If the cowboys and the cavalry are beginning to seem arbitrary, the contrary imaginative identification of the Irish with the Native Americans, which began in the sixteenth century as a staple trope of anti-Irish propaganda,[16] has recently been given a new spin by Ireland's belated entry into the arena of postcolonial discourse. The title poem of Paul Muldoon's collection *Meeting the British* is set during the French and Indian War, which ended in 1763 with the defeat of France and the annexation of Canada by Britain. British victory in this conflict established it as the world's foremost imperial power. The poem's Native American speaker is identified as an ally of the French, in whose language he calls out, but he is 'meeting' the British to negotiate a treaty or a ceasefire, traditionally marked by the smoking of the peace pipe. Ominously, neither the British General Jeffrey Amherst nor the Swiss mercenary Colonel Henry Bouquet 'could stomach our willow tobacco', and the gifts they offer in exchange symbolize the viral holocaust that decimated the Native American people after the first contact: 'They gave us six fishhooks / and two blankets embroidered with smallpox' (*Meeting* 24).[17] The Irish, soon to be allied with the French in the rising of 1798 and later to be wiped out during the Famine, were also headed for defeat at the hands of the Empire.

With characteristic obliquity, Muldoon leaves the reader to make the connection between the two; other writers are less subtle. Fintan O'Toole asks:

> How did we get . . . from the idea of national cultural distinctiveness to the desire not just to be somebody else, but to be a different race, and an oppressed one at that? And why do you find, in works by younger Irish writers from urban communities, conscious usage of imagery linking the Irish not just to the blacks but to the Indians, a linkage that is sometimes playful and comic, but sometimes serious and almost literal. (*Black Hole* 56)

Part of the answer lies in the permeable boundaries between postcolonial theory and literary culture. Playwrights like Friel and McGuinness incorporate elements of academic discourse into the texture of their imaginative work: Friel's contact with Seamus Deane on the board of Field Day and McGuinness's position as a university teacher keep them at the centre of critical developments. The debate over revisionist and postcolonial versions of Irish history, moreover, is carried on in the opinion columns and letters pages of the *Irish Times*, as well as in learned journals.

In Belfast the Republican muralists juxtapose Native American with Irish women, and depict a Native American chief against the background of the American flag with the caption 'Our struggle: your struggle' (Rolston 51, 53, 59). The transethnic political solidarity implied by the Irish/Native American analogy has both academic and commercial promoters. A California company called Reality Tours sells excursions to Ireland that promise accommodation in 'Belfast's bustling Falls Road community' and offer 'the unique opportunity to visit political prisoners inside the infamous Long Kesh Prison'. Tourists will participate in the annual Doolough to Louisburgh Famine Walk, 'which is always led by representatives of the Choctaw nation of America to honour their donation of $170 in 1847 for Irish famine relief.'[18] That touching donation from one dispossessed tribe to another represents the most positive side of the Irish/Native American equation, but it was only in the wake of postcolonial theory, with its examination of the shared experience of dispossession of indigenous peoples all over the globe, that the story of the Choctaw gift was retrieved from the historical archive and used to energize contemporary political action.[19]

Nevertheless, the Irish experience of eviction and famine, characterized by embittered emigrants as English genocide, haunts the margins of a much earlier work, Boucicault's 'American' play *The Octoroon* (1859), which despite its sympathetic portrayal of Southern slave owners clearly condemns the institution of slavery and inspired horror among advocates of racial separation (Fawkes 106–11, 128–30). Boucicault himself played the part of Wahnotee, a Native American chief who speaks no English and communicates through grunts and incomprehensible patois. Boucicault's creation of this almost silent role suggests that he knew that the Irish were commonly compared to the Native Americans by English colonizers interested in representing both peoples as savages needing civilization or extirpation.[20] As I have already noted, Peter Brooks highlights 'the text of muteness' in melodrama, arguing that 'extreme physical conditions' such as muteness or physical disability evoke 'the extremism and hyperbole of ethical conflict and manichaeistic struggle' (56). Like the Irish, the almost mute Wahnotee belongs to a 'nation out West' (*Plays* 143) that has been dispossessed of its territory and savagely reduced in numbers. He shares with the stage Irishman a taste for liquor, an affectionate heart and the capacity for violence; and in performance the 'Irishness' of Boucicault's own stage persona must have inflected the character.

Wahnotee's love for Paul, a young black slave who is murdered by the wicked Yankee overseer M'Closky, symbolically unites Native American and negro as victims of the 'manichaeistic struggle' between white and dark races. Because, like an Irish-speaking peasant, he cannot understand his accusers or deny his guilt, Wahnotee is nearly lynched by a white crowd who wrongly suspect him of Paul's murder. His 'trial' exemplifies melodrama's use of the mute role to signify 'the defencelessness of innocence' (Brooks 60). The good overseer, Scudder, protests: 'Here's a pictur' for a civilised community to afford; yonder, a poor ignorant savage, and round him a circle of hearts, white with revenge and hate, thirsting for his blood' (*Plays* 172). Boucicault's memorable phrase '*white* with revenge and hate' momentarily reveals the intensity behind his otherwise moderate and cautious indictment of slavery and dispossession. As I have already noted, in the nineteenth century the Irish were frequently categorized as less 'white' than the English, and contemptuously compared to Africans (Allen 29–30). Radicals sympathetic to each other's causes made the same comparison with the opposite ethical inflection: after touring Ireland in 1845 Frederick Douglass claimed that Irish peasants were more miserable than black slaves, while the Irish leader Daniel O'Connell supported abolition (Bornstein 172–4).

Boucicault often kept the choicest theatrical morsels for himself: Wahnotee is given the crucial task of stalking and slaughtering the white villain, the racist overseer. In America the killing occurred offstage, presumably because it was too inflammatory, but in England and Ireland it formed part of a sensational concluding 'grand Tableau' that included an exploding riverboat. At home, Boucicault confided the spectacular operation of justice to the dispossessed native. The prominence of pantomime and tableau in popular melodrama affords the spectator 'the opportunity to see . . . emotions and moral states rendered in clear visible signs' (Brooks 62). As the red man in full warpaint avenges the murder of the black man by stabbing the white oppressor, Irish members of the audience might see in this racialized moral pantomime a displaced image of their own revolt against the colonizer.

Boucicault was ahead of his time. At the beginning of this century the identification of the Irish with Native Americans was either a racial slur or an omen of defeat. 'It was Joe Dillon who introduced the Wild West to us', says the narrator of James Joyce's short story, 'An Encounter'. Despite sharing a surname with the famous white marshal Matt Dillon, Joe plays Indian rather than cowboy. His Wild West consists of Indian battles, all of which are crowned by his fierce 'war dance of victory': 'He looked like some kind of Indian when he capered round the garden, an old tea-cosy on his head, beating a tin with his fist and yelling, "Ya! Yaka, yaka, yaka!"' The comic papers in which Joe Dillon and his younger brother Leo find their Western stories are published in England, but the politics of the Indian identification are anti-British. In school, Leo Dillon is reproved for reading 'The Apache Chief' instead of translating his Roman history. Given the common analogy between the Roman and the British empires, the substitution of Geronimo for Caesar as a role model implies a defiance of the political status quo. Although the narrator prefers American detective stories containing 'fierce and beautiful girls' and represents himself as a 'reluctant Indian' who fears Joe Dillon's ferocious energy, still 'The adventures related in the literature of the Wild West . . . opened doors of escape' (*Dubliners* 11–12).

Not for the Native Americans, however, and not for the main characters of this depressing story. Joyce presents the idea of escape as a delusion. Like the most famous Apache chief, Geronimo, who was eventually confined on a reservation and ended up selling souvenir photographs of himself at the World's Fair, Joe Dillon, the Indian victorious only in fantasy, is doomed to enter the reservation of the priesthood. His brother Leo hasn't even the spunk to join in the Indian 'adventure' that the protagonist organizes for himself and a friend. That adventure, moreover, turns out to be a dismal affair that climaxes in a disturbing quasi-paedophiliac 'encounter' with a 'queer old josser' whose masturbatory fantasies involve whipping little boys:

> He said that if ever he found a boy talking to girls or having a girl for a sweetheart he would whip him and whip him; and that would teach him not to be talking to girls. And if a boy had a girl for a sweetheart and told lies about it then he would give him such a whipping as no boy ever got in this world. He said that there was nothing in this world he would like so well as that. He described to me how he would whip such a boy as if he were unfolding some elaborate mystery. He would love that, he said, better than anything in this world; and his voice, as he led me monotonously through the mystery, grew almost affectionate and seemed to plead with me that I should understand him.
> (*Dubliners* 19–20)

Joyce not only empties the Wild West of its potential romance, he hints that its all-male epic battles serve as a disguise for homoerotic sado-masochism and a disavowal of the 'fierce and beautiful girls' that the narrator enjoys in detective novels. Joe Dillon's vocation to the priesthood may be more intimately connected with his passion for the Wild West than his 'incredulous' friends suppose.

Seamus Heaney also uses the Native Americans as emblems of defeat in his poem 'Hercules and Antaeus', but between the publication of *Dubliners*

(1914) and that of *North* (1985) the political weight attached to the analogy has changed. When Heaney spent a year in California in 1970–1,

> The whole atmosphere in Berkeley was politicized and minorities like the Chicanos and Blacks were demanding their say. There was a strong sense of contemporary American poetry in the West . . . rejecting the intellectual, ironical, sociological idiom of poetry and going for the mythological. I mean everyone wanted to be a Red Indian, basically. (Quoted in Morrison 59)

When Heaney returned, the Troubles were escalating and he too made comparisons between his own 'tribe' and the expropriated Native Americans. In local political terms Antaeus, the giant who drew his strength from 'contact with the soil' (Yeats, *Poems* 321) represents 'resistance and black powers / feeding off the territory'. Antaeus stands for 'atavism', a word that is often used as negative code for the IRA's attachment to the past, but, although his defeat is predetermined by the myth, Heaney divests it of all traces of Joycean squalor. Hercules lifts Antaeus

> into a dream of loss
>
> and origins – the cradling dark,
> the river-veins, the secret gullies
> of his strength,
> the hatching grounds
>
> of cave and souterrain,
> he has bequeathed it all
> to elegists. Balor will die
> and Byrthnoth [*sic*] and Sitting Bull. (*North* 52–3)

Balor was the Formorian giant destroyed by the Tuatha Dé Danaan at the battle of Moytura, and Byrhtnoth was the Saxon chief defeated by the Vikings at the battle of Maldon. Like them, Sitting Bull is elegized by Heaney as a symbol of 'loss and origins': all were indigenes dispossessed by invaders. The figure of the 'sleeping giant' and the concomitant dream of lost origins is belittled at the end of the poem as 'pap for the dispossessed', but the mythic and historical figures Heaney chooses as analogies for Northern Catholic resistance evoke something more pungent than baby food.

Balor and the Formorians represent darkness, the 'black powers' defeated by Lugh, the god of Light. The words of Byrhtnoth's loyal thane Byrhtwold have come to epitomize fortitude in the face of overwhelming odds: 'The spirit must be the firmer, the heart the bolder, courage must be the greater as our strength diminishes'. Sitting Bull is an equally formidable figure for 'resistance': he bitterly hated the white man and fought tenaciously to maintain the territorial rights of the Sioux nation. After these rights had been violated by the gold rush in the Black Hills of South Dakota, Sitting Bull won a famous victory against Lieutenant-Colonel George Custer at the battle of Little Bighorn (1876); but the decline of the buffalo herds and the consequent famine eventually forced him to surrender to US forces. Fourteen years later, when the rise of the revolutionary Ghost Dance movement alarmed the government, Sitting Bull was killed by Native American policemen who had been sent to arrest him. Heaney, who has confessed to 'nostalgia' for Antaeus, once defined his poetry as a 'slow obstinate papish burn, emanating from the ground I was brought up on' ('Unhappy' 62–3). That obstinate 'ground' belongs to Antaeus, and by analogy to Sitting Bull.

The story of Sitting Bull, however, cannot be too seamlessly aligned with the victimization and resistance of the Irish. In 1885 he exhibited himself in the Wild West Shows of Buffalo Bill Cody, who went to considerable rhetorical lengths to claim Milesian descent (O'Toole, *Black Hole* 64–5). When Sitting Bull was shot, he was wearing an Irish holy medal round his neck: not a gesture of solidarity with another dispossessed people, but a war trophy taken from the Irish soldier Captain Myles Keogh, who was killed by the Sioux at the battle of Little Bighorn. At the beginning of John Ford's *She Wore a Yellow Ribbon*, news arrives of the slaughter of Custer's troops, the legendary Seventh Cavalry. Captain Nathan Brittles (John Wayne once more) visits his wife Mary's grave to tell her the sad news about the death of his friend 'Myles Keogh – that happy-go-lucky Irishman'. Brittles remembers how Keogh used to waltz with Mary, and admits that he was jealous of the Irishman's rhythm: 'Never could waltz myself'.

The oblique and complex linkage between Myles Keogh and Sitting Bull, both killers and both victims, indicates that, while the Irish may seem like savages to the WASP establishment, to the Native Americans they are just part of the cavalry – as indeed many of them were. It was no accident that the equation of a good Indian with a dead one clung to the Irish cavalry officer Philip Sheridan. Nathan Brittles is an older man than Kirkby Yorke, however, and his view of the Indians is more nuanced. While he defines the young braves who are excited by the defeat of Custer and eager for blood as 'hostiles', in the last hours before his retirement he confronts an aged Native American chief, Pony that Walks, and appeals to him to control his people. Both of them are too old for war, he says. Although the hospitable Pony that Walks would be delighted to spend his own retirement hunting buffalo and smoking pipes with Nathan Brittles, he cannot command his younger followers, and a massacre is averted only by Brittles's stampeding of their horses. The film nevertheless leaves us with the image of a 'good Indian', and without the numerous 'dead Indians' that the plot seemed to promise.

John Ford uses the paradox by which the Irish could be 'a savage tribe in one context, a superior race in another' (O'Toole, *Mass* 134) as an important subtext of *Fort Apache* (1949), his highly fictionalized treatment of Custer's last stand. In this film, Sergeant-Major O'Rourke (Ward Bond), a non-commissioned Irish officer who won a Medal of Honour in the Civil War and who dies beside his foolish and stubborn commanding officer Colonel Thursday (Henry Fonda) in a hopeless charge against the Apaches, is loosely modelled on the real Irish soldier Myles Keogh. The Romeo and Juliet romance plot involving O'Rourke's son Michael and Thursday's daughter Philadelphia may seem extraneous to the film's main historical purpose, but it is central to Ford's defence of the Irish troopers against the eastern snobbery of the military establishment. Colonel Thursday can hardly believe that Michael, the son of an Irish regular soldier, went to the elite officer school West Point, and is horrified by his cross-class courtship of Philadelphia. When Michael notes correctly that a marauding band of Indians must be Mescaleros, because 'Apaches carry off their dead', Thursday replies with a sardonic and back-handed appreciation of his familiarity with native customs: 'It speaks a knowledge of the savage Indian which I am sure you did not acquire at the military academy'. To clarify the ethnic force of his insult he adds, 'In taking my daughter riding without bespeaking my permission you have been guilty of behaviour more consistent with a savage Indian than an officer and a gentleman'. To the WASP Thursday, Michael (cinematically framed beside his Irish father to receive the ethnic insult) might as well be a 'breech-clouted Indian'.

Ford mocks Thursday's racism during a scene in which the dignified and subtle Apache chief, Cochise, introduces his allies to the white men: next to the inevitable Geronimo stands one Setanta, who is identified as a Mescalero. Setanta, of course, is the boyhood name of the Irish hero Cuchulain. This Irish/Indian analogy, however, although it acknowledges the complexity of the Irish position as both oppressors and oppressed, is not part of a sustained critique of the genocidal practices of the US cavalry. By the end of the movie, the rash and arrogant Thursday has been reconstructed as a fallen hero and Michael has not only married his daughter, but also adopted his role as Indian fighter. Ambiguity remains, however. Throughout the movie we have seen Thursday, the Custer figure, as wrongheaded, hasty and racist. Ford acknowledges that the creation of his legend may be politically expedient, 'good for the country', but the film has shown us an alternative version of the truth.[21]

However problematic the politics of the Western may be, and however sham or sentimental John Ford's 'professional' Irish identity may seem, his awareness that the exploited of one continent have readily assimilated with the exploiters of another nuances his representations both of the Irish and of the Native Americans. His last Western, *Cheyenne Autumn* (1964), an under-rated predecessor of *Little Big Man* (1970) and *Dances with Wolves* (1990), recounts the desperate flight of a group of Cheyenne from their forced exile in Oklahoma back North to their home in the Black Hills.[22] Ford's comment on *Cheyenne Autumn* is better known than the film itself:

> I had wanted to make it for a long time. I've killed more Indians than Custer, Beecher and Chivington put together, and people in Europe always want to know about the Indians. There are two sides to every story, but I wanted to

show their point of view for a change. Let's face it, we've treated them very badly – it's a blot on our shield; we've cheated and robbed, killed, murdered, massacred and everything else, but they kill one white man, and, God, out come the troops. (Quoted in Bogdanovich 104)

The idea that there are two sides to every story is easy to ridicule as a classic liberal humanist position. Within the Western genre, however, liberal humanists are rare, and Ford's asymmetrical balance between genocide and the murder of one white man suggests that he is ethically ready to designate the whites as 'worse'. Opinions differ as to whether Ford succeeded in giving the Indian 'point of view' in *Cheyenne Autumn*, but he avoided some of the most obvious pitfalls associated with an attempt to depict the historical victims.

For example, while Kevin Costner's Lakota Sioux actors speak their own language, his film has subtitles. Ford wanted his two leading Cheyenne characters to be played by the Monument Valley Navajos with whom he had worked so often, but this desire was frustrated by commercial considerations.[23] Nevertheless, the Cheyenne speak their lines (a lot of them) without subtitles, so that the audience is forced to experience the difference of Native American culture:

> Since lack of communication was one of their chief causes of trouble, it would be ridiculous to show them speaking the national language . . . The Indians, as a people, are to be portrayed as Indians . . . unable to speak English or to communicate their thoughts to the Whites, but magnificent in their stoical dignity.
> (Notes for the film, quoted in Sinclair 198)

'Magnificent in their stoical dignity' sounds ominous: to move from bloodthirsty savage to Noble Savage is merely to exchange a negative for a benevolent stereotype. But Ford avoids this simplistic substitution by depicting the Cheyenne as fatally divided among themselves by sexual jealousy. This tragic division, which leads their chief Little Wolf to kill the son of his comrade Dull Knife and exile himself from the community, comes at the end of the film, 'when the nation was safe'. No sooner do the few remaining Cheyenne win the right to stay on their ancestral lands than they break apart internally. The reference to the Irish Civil War is not difficult to discern.

Cheyenne Autumn is a long, complex and uneven film which tried the patience of the critics in 1964.[24] The popular success of the equally lengthy *Dances with Wolves* in 1990 suggests that Ford, like Boucicault, was ahead of his time in his effort to represent the Native Americans more fairly.[25] Much of the film's complexity arises from Ford's use of multiple analogies between the Cheyenne and other persecuted ethnic groups. As we have already seen, a former Union soldier who gave his arm to liberate black slaves is urged to defend the Native Americans. The equation between the two groups is strengthened when the Secretary of the Interior addresses a portrait of Abraham Lincoln with the question, 'Old friend, old friend, what would you do?' In the background, the tune of 'John Brown's Body' evokes the abolitionist revolt at Harper's Ferry and gives him a definitive answer. Among the numerous whites who sympathize with the plight of the Cheyenne is a Polish enlisted man who identifies the US cavalry as 'Cossacks'. Cossacks, he says, 'kill Poles just because they're Poles, like we kill Indians just because they're Indians'.

The officer who eventually imprisons the helpless tribe in a freezing warehouse is a cultured Prussian called Oscar Wessels, who has a library of German books on Indian life and culture but justifies his inhumanity to the Cheyenne as obedience to 'orders'. Wessels was indeed the name of the officer in command at Fort Robinson, and Ford shows it to us twice on a signboard; this unusual visual emphasis reminds us that the *Horst Wessel Lied* was the Nazi anthem. Ford's analogy between the reservation and the final solution is strengthened when the Quaker heroine Deborah asks Wessels, 'then you don't believe that the Indians should be wiped off the face of the earth along with the buffalo?' Wessels says no, but his subsequent behaviour leads to a massacre, as the desperate Cheyenne break out of the warehouse in which they have neither food nor heat.

To complete Ford's ethnic spectrum of good and evil, a drunken Irish doctor sobers up enough to operate on a wounded Cheyenne child and is the only man at Fort Robinson willing to confront the Prussian officer, whom he arrests, in a knowing reversal of the Irish stereotype, for alcoholism. The doctor forges a symbolic link between the Cheyenne and the Irish when he observes that they 'sound like a thousand banshees out there keening over the grave of Cuchulain'. The obliteration of a non-English-speaking culture at the hands of imperialists has native resonance for Ford: he apologizes to the American Indians by identifying them with his own dispossessed 'tribe', as well as with Blacks, Jews and Poles. His apologia is marked by a shrewd self-irony: a newspaper editor decides that, instead of continuing to excoriate the Cheyenne as 'bloodthirsty savages', it is time to 'grieve for the noble red man'. The market demands a change of pace; he will 'sell more papers that way'. Ford thus anticipates and hopes to forestall a similar political critique of his own film.

Ford's complex legacy may be discerned in *Into the West*, a 1994 film directed by Mike Newell and scripted by Jim Sheridan (See Fig. 6). Near the beginning of the film the heroes, two young traveller brothers called Tito and Ossie, are watching a classic Western scenario on television: cowboys defend a circle of covered wagons as Indians swoop around on their horses and the cavalry ride to the rescue. Ossie asks Tito, 'Was there a Wild West in Ireland?' and Tito replies, 'There still is, on the other side of the mountains'. 'Then are the travellers Indians?' asks his brother. 'No', says Tito, presumably identifying the covered wagons with the travellers' caravans, which they physically resemble, 'we're the cowboys'.

The rest of the film tests and gradually discredits Tito's assumption that the travellers are the cowboys, and therefore on the winning side. The racism

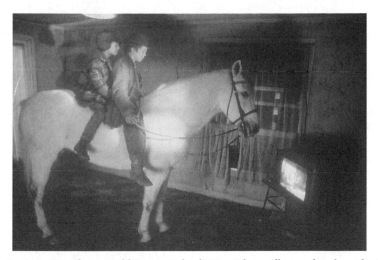

Fig. 6. *Ossie: 'Was there a Wild West in Ireland?' Tito: 'There still is, on the other side of the mountains.' Ossie: 'Then are the travellers Indians?' Tito: 'No, we're the cowboys'.*

habitually shown towards them by Southern Irish 'settled people' echoes the racism of white settlers, including those of Irish descent, towards the Native Americans. Tito's grandfather insists, 'We're travellers, we don't belong here with the settled people'. He wants his son-in-law to return from his urban high-rise slum to Connemara, to the old ways. The film parallels the Irish epic of Finn and the Fianna with the epic of the American West. The white horse that follows the old man from the Connemara coast to Dublin is both the magic steed that carries Finn's son Oisín to Tír na nÓg (hence its name) and the Lone Ranger's faithful Silver. Twice, the boys call 'Hi Ho, Silver!'; the second time the horse rears as Silver used to do. When Tír na nÓg is stolen by a corrupt and racist police officer, sold to an equally corrupt businessman and finally repossessed by the boys, their flight on its back towards the sea is both a journey to fairyland and a Western adventure. As the boys catch sight of the Wicklow Mountains Tito cries, 'It's the Rockies'.

Earlier, while the children are looking through the Western section at their video store, Tito says, 'We've seen all these cowboys. Have to have a new one'. At that moment they notice the stolen Tír na nÓg on the store's television screen and begin a 'new' cowboy movie scripted by themselves. On the counter of the store a video copy of Jim Sheridan's *The Field* is prominently displayed. Although Sheridan also wrote the screenplay for *Into the West*, this brief intertextual allusion is not merely a vanity moment: it is substantive. *The Field* takes place in the setting to which the boys are headed, Connemara, and it chronicles the violent animosity between the cowman (or cowboy?) Bull McCabe and a group of travellers. While McCabe struggles to buy his rented grazing field for the sake of the younger generation, his son Tadgh cares nothing for the land and plans to go on the road with the traveller girl Katy.

Although the travellers in *The Field* are represented as drunken, quarrelsome and abusive to their children, they are also free of the curse of the famine field. Bull says, 'they lost their footing on the land during the Famine and they'll never get it back again'. Katy, however, has no desire to own the earth, and nor does Tadgh, who nevertheless pays the price for his father's single-minded obsession with 'settlement'. Bull's cows carry his last surviving son with them as, in a fit of despairing madness, he stampedes them over a cliff. Sheridan recasts the story of Cuchulain's killing of his only son as a homicidal cattle-drive. Being a 'cowboy' is the opposite of being a traveller.

Sheridan and Newell sustain the ambiguities of their Western analogy by constant reference to *Butch Cassidy and the Sundance Kid*, which Tito watches on a neighbour's television through a hole in the wall. In a neat visual pun, he sees Butch Cassidy survive a challenge to his leadership of the 'Hole in the Wall Gang'. This brief sequence reminds us that Butch and Sundance are not really 'cowboys' and certainly do not ride with the cavalry: they are outlaws, and, like the Western genre itself, their days are numbered. 'That's an old filum, that', says the neighbour Mrs Murphy. *Butch Cassidy and the Sundance Kid* constantly highlights the displacement of tradition by modernity: Butch and Sundance are out of date. The film opens with Butch casing a bank; as the camera traces the closing of impressive modern locks, he asks what happened to the old building. 'It kept getting robbed', snarls the security guard. 'But it used to be so pretty', laments Butch. The bicycle he rides in the goofy 'Raindrops' musical sequence is also a harbinger of the change that will eventually destroy them: to Sundance he calls out, 'Meet the future; the horse is dead'. But after their flight from the professional posse organized by Mr E. H. Harriman and their decision to leave for Bolivia, Butch tosses aside the bike with the words, 'The future's all yours, you lousy bicycle'. The travellers operate at the same interface between traditional modes of life and the pressures of the modern world. Images of the horse-drawn caravan juxtaposed with the underbelly of a jet plane, or of the boys leading their horse into the elevator of a run-down tower block in Ballymun, emphasize the fact that, like Butch and Sundance, the travellers and their horses are anachronisms.

When the children, mounted on Tír na nÓg, flee from police pursuers towards the West of Ireland, their journey is closely modelled on the tracking sequence in which Butch and Sundance, also riding a single horse, attempt to outrun the Pinkerton posse. The boys translate a striking silhouette shot of foxhunters rising over the horizon into Western idioms: 'What's that?' asks Ossie. 'That's OK, it's the cavalry', replies Tito. 'No it's not, it's the posse', cries Ossie. If they were the cavalry, the figures on the horizon would represent rescue and escape, as at the end of Ford's *Stagecoach*. As the posse, however, they are the modern hunters who will eventually drive Butch and Sundance out of the country altogether, towards their deaths in Bolivia. Tito and Ossie have trouble with definitions: when they find out that, like Butch and Sundance, there is a price on their heads, they exclaim, 'now we're real cowboys'; but what the reward confirms is that they are now real outlaws. The boys are pursued both by the police and by their father, who enlists the uncanny tracking skills of the traveller Kathleen in an attempt to reach them before the law does. As Kathleen squats down to feel the ground, her body language evokes the moment when Butch and Sundance observe that the Pinkerton posse owes its preternatural adhesiveness to the brilliance of a famous Indian scout, Lord Baltimore. Through choreography, Newell establishes that the female traveller and the Indian share the same mystical gift, though Kathleen's tracking is benign while Lord Baltimore has crossed over to the side of the law.

Tito nevertheless tries to sustain the cowboy fiction: when the brothers attempt to go to a hotel and are turned away with the manifestly hostile question 'Are ye travellers', he answers 'No, we're cowboys'. Taking refuge in a cinema instead, they watch a scene from *Back to the Future 3*, in which the time-travelling DeLorean runs straight into an Indian charge set in John Ford's Monument Valley. Like most Westerns, this brief episode construes the Native Americans as the enemy. By the end of *Into the West*, however, Tito's confidence in his cowboy identity has been shaken, and he repeats his brother's earlier question, 'Are the travellers cowboys or Indians, papa?' Papa's response is evasive, but, since the film's depiction of anti-traveller racism suggests that travellers are Indians in relation to the settled community, the Southern Irish must be the cowboys. As we have seen, this identification is familiar, but, in a postcolonial context, not necessarily positive. The travellers are white Others who have been 'blackened' by a previous group of white Others, the Irish. (Eastern European immigration is currently creating an analogous situation.) While it is Utopian to expect that the experience of racism would, by ideological inoculation, prevent the victims from spreading the contagion themselves, *Into the West* uses the cowboy metaphor to indict the indifference or hostility of the Southern state towards a marginalized sector of its own population.

III

If the Southern Irish are often the cowboys, Britain's continued presence in the Six Counties may explain why minority Northern Catholics frequently identify with the Native American underdogs: Bobby Sands used to sign himself 'Geronimo', and there is a Geronimo mural inside Long Kesh prison, where he died on hunger strike.[26] We have already noted the Republican muralists' contribution to the currency of this identification, and Paul Muldoon's long poem, 'The More a Man Has', constructs an analogy between a Native American trickster figure, an Oglala Sioux, and an IRA man on the run. But in *Divorcing Jack*, his 1995 thriller about the Troubles, Colin Bateman suggests the ambiguous character of the analogy even in the Northern context. Anticipating the imminent escalation of hostilities between rival paramilitary groups, an Alliance Party spokesman says pessimistically:

'You'll see . . . political figures progressively eliminated from both sides of the paramilitary line and then we'll be down to a straightforward game of cowboys and Indians'.

'Which is which?'

'Depends on your point of view really. Depends whether you're a John Wayne fan or a *Dances with Wolves* revisionist'. (84)

Most Northern Catholics, even if they begin as John Wayne fans, end up as *Dances with Wolves* revisionists. John Montague's short story, 'The Oklahoma Kid', starts with a memory of the narrator's childhood in County Tyrone and his identification with the white men: 'It was my Cowboy period' (*Occasion* 13). The boy shares his passion for tales of the Wild West with a number of older countrymen, who, like him, are thrilled at the prospect of attending a cowboy movie. Together they arrange a trip to the local town to see Cagney and Bogart in *The Oklahoma Kid* (1939), taking with them the local eccentric, a 'smallish, rather dusty-looking man who always sported a green hat with a large chicken feather stuck under the band [which] . . . made him look like an aging Indian brave' (20). Papa, who is the antithesis of modernity, has never seen a film and cannot distinguish cinematic imagery from real life. His loud and unstoppable commentary irritates the British soldiers, with whom the cinema is crowded, and eventually gets the whole group of farmers ejected. Soldiers and townspeople alike despise them as 'country-looking idiots' (27). Seventeen years later, however, the narrator arrives in the real Oklahoma City, USA, and meets a man in a cafeteria:

He seemed rather disreputable, his hat jammed on his head, his jaws masticating ceaselessly. Yet he also seemed somehow familiar – that great nose, that coppery tint (noticeable even under a day-old beard), those wise eyes of legend.

'I'm a Cherokee from Tulsa', he said, with what I took to be both fatalism and pride. 'What part of Oklahoma do you come from?'

'From Oklahoma City', I said involuntarily, 'County Tyrone', and choked with a mixture of joy, shame and ridiculous conceit. (28)

This mixture of joy, shame and ridiculous conceit captures the psychic state of a John Wayne fan evolving into a *Dances with Wolves* revisionist: Papa's embarrassing garrulity and naive ignorance of cinematic conventions are transformed into 'those wise eyes of legend'.

Those who romanticize the wisdom of the Native American elders, however, risk consigning them to an ethnic museum in which their qualities are essentialized and fossilized even as they come to be defined by their ultimate defeat. Focusing on the masochistic connotations of finding the Indians more attractive than the cowboys, Frank McGuinness satirizes the Northern Catholic identification with Native America in *Carthaginians*, his play about the Troubles. Hark, an ex-IRA man who was not brave enough to volunteer for the hunger strike, Seph, who informed on his IRA comrades, and Paul, a neurotic and dysfunctional quiz show moderator, engage with the sceptical hero Dido on the subject of childhood games:

> HARK. Nothing like a good western.
> DIDO. When you were a kid, Hark, playing Cowboys and Indians, which were you?
> HARK. The Indian.
> DIDO. You get weirder by the minute.
> HARK. What's wrong with Indians?
> DIDO. They always got beaten.
> HARK. Not always.
> SEPH. I liked the Indians as well. Their head-dresses were great.
> HARK. They had the best words.
> PAUL. Firewater.
> HARK. Medicine man.
> SEPH. Peace pipe.
> PAUL. Great words. Like poetry. (*Carthaginians* 65–6)

Masquerading as Matthew Arnold, McGuinness produces an ironic description of the Irish/Indians as a picturesque and colourful people addicted to firewater, magic, quaint ethnic costumes and poetry, who went forth to battle but nearly always fell. The Arnoldian chorus is voiced by a bunch of assorted male losers; but Dido, a politically non-aligned gay man, thinks that to identify with those who always got beaten is 'weird'. McGuinness uses the interchange as a criticism of the IRA, whom he sees as still motivated by Pearsian rhetoric of heroic but futile self-sacrifice. As we have seen, Dido is determined to revise the depressing historical analogy suggested by his own name into a narrative of optimism.

Dido also critiques the Western's affirmation of violence as the guarantor of white heterosexual male identity by evoking the genre's most famous showdown, the end of *High Noon*. Playing a principled sheriff facing four murderous gunslingers without any support from his craven community, Gary Cooper walks alone down the empty street to the film's theme song, 'Do Not Forsake Me O My Darling'. This song has become a synecdoche for the whole movie, just as the phrase 'High Noon' is synonymous with 'showdown'. Dido uses a cassette recording of the tune to set up the final ludicrous bloodbath of his parody Troubles play, 'The Burning Balaclava'. If it is weird to sympathize with the Native Americans, Dido finds the trigger-happy macho mentality he attributes to the gunmen on both sides of the conflict in Derry even less attractive. 'Do Not Forsake Me O My Darling' is musical code for 'a man's gotta do what a man's gotta do'.

The Snapper, a movie concerned with the politics of gender in the South rather than with sectarian animosity in the North, also uses this unmistakable song to make fun of traditional assumptions about masculinity. Despite the pregnant Sharon's repeated assertions that she can look out for herself, her brother is anachronistically determined to defend his sister's honour. After he has heaved a dustbin through the window of her seducer and been dragged away in a squad car, we see his father Dessie leaning grimly on the gate as a neighbour satirically whistles the opening bars of 'Do Not Forsake Me O My Darling'. (When the family go to the police station to bail him out, the musical citation is reinforced by a visual reference to *High Noon*'s recurrent motif, a clock face in close-up.) The allusion, significantly, is exchanged between two middle-aged men: the Western is shorthand for only one part of the community. Dessie sings about the streets of Amarillo during his hair-raising dash through the streets of Dublin to get Sharon to the hospital, and his cultural references are drawn from outdated Western television shows. But while Dessie is yodelling 'Rolling, rolling, rolling, keep them dogies rolling, Rawhide', his children are going to discos and watching *Top of the Pops*. Dessie's urban family is not unique. In Roddy Doyle's *Paddy Clarke Ha Ha Ha*, Paddy's wife-abusing father likes Hank Williams and watches cowboy films and *The Virginian* on television (87–9, 65, 209). In reaction, his son prefers Geronimo to Daniel Boone and plays Indians and cowboys instead of cowboys and Indians (54–7, 147). In *In the Name of the Father* a tripping Gerry Conlon mocks his father Giuseppe's confidence that justice will eventually be done and they will be released from jail. As Giuseppe recites the Hail Mary, Gerry asks, 'Are you praying for the Seventh Cavalry?' and then attempts a derisive imitation of the troopers' bugle call. The white male Western hero belongs to the older generation.

When *High Noon* is used by a woman, therefore, it becomes part of a sustained critique of an outdated ethos of masculinity, and the effect of that violent ethos on Northern Irish political life. When that woman is a Southern Protestant who lives in the North and defines herself as a supporter of Republicanism, the critique is necessarily oblique and complex. Jennifer Johnston's dramatic monologue *Mustn't Forget High Noon* (1989) evokes the voice of Billy Maltseed, who interweaves the symbolism of Northern Protestantism – especially King Billy on his white horse – with images derived from the Westerns he used to watch with his father, an old man who now lies dying. His father

> [r]eally fancied himself as Jimmy Stewart. He liked to think of himself as a hero. I always had to do the bad parts. The ones who got killed. The Red Indians, the rustlers, the bad eggs.
> Naw.
> He let me be Chief Sitting Bull.
> I won that time.
> My mother never believed the Indians won the Battle of Little Big Horn.
> You can't be right, she said after we'd acted it out for her. (*Three Monologues* 36)

In the context of the Troubles, Chief Sitting Bull, a Catholic by analogy, is a Janus-faced icon. A Northern Protestant remembers that he won the battle of Little Bighorn, but, as we have seen, a Northern Catholic like Seamus Heaney is more likely to reflect that he was wiped out in the end. Johnston equates Sitting Bull's victory over Custer at Little Bighorn with the coming defeat of Unionism, the return of the oppressed:

> I remember sitting with him one evening watching that film . . .
> *Custer's Last Stand* and on to the screen comes this guy on his white horse and said to him . . .
> *Dada is that King Billy?*
> He took a hold of my arm like he was going to break it.
> *God almighty will you whisht, son. It's General Custer and don't you go making a show of me, asking stupid questions like that . . .*
> I'd like to have seen King Billy on the pictures.
> The battle of the Boyne would have made a great picture.
> . . .
> Great name.
> Little Big Horn.
> The Battle of the Boyne.
> Derry, Enniskillen and the Boyne. (37)

In juxtaposing Custer with King Billy, and his defeat at Little Bighorn with the Protestant victory at the battle of the Boyne, Johnston's Billy unconsciously turns a litany of past victories into an omen of failure. The Native Americans won that time, and the Native Catholics will win next time. The Protestants are making their Last Stand.

As we learn from his wife's monologue, Billy's own last stand is imminent: after he joins the Protestant paramilitaries he is assassinated by the IRA. Although his family has been on his farm for 'over two hundred years', Billy cannot pass his inheritance to a son, because he is infertile. He is thus deprived of Protestant patriarchal continuity, strikingly figured as three generations of males watching Western videos together. The Western plays a crucial part in the production of a masculinity that will go down fighting rather than attempt political negotiation or compromise.

> . . . and we'd have sat there, the son and I, and we'd have watched them all, like I did with the old man.
> *Stagecoach.*
> *They Died with Their Boots On.*
> *Gunfight at the OK Corral.*
> *Drums Along the Mohawk.*
> *Destry.* Yes. *Destry.*
> . . .
> The old man could have watched too.
> He'd have liked that.
> And *High Noon.*
> Mustn't forget *High Noon.*
> *Do not forsake me O my darling.* (44)

But the Protestants are about to be forsaken. *High Noon* pits one man against four, and depicts those who fail to help him as traitors and cowards; it is an apt metaphor for 'Not an Inch' and 'No Surrender'. Johnston began work on her monologues just after the 1985 Anglo-Irish Agreement, which established consultations between the Republic and the British on the administration of the North. Loyal Unionists regarded this, rightly, as the thin end of the wedge: their feeling of desertion and betrayal was palpable.

Moreover, this is a woman's critique of a man's film and a male culture, in which ethnic and political ironies intersect with gendered ones. As boys, both Billy and his gun-toting, trigger-happy friend Sammy 'wanted to marry Grace Kelly'. In *High Noon* Kelly plays Amy, the woman whose Quaker abhorrence of violence causes her to abandon Cooper as he prepares to gun down his enemies.

> *Do not forsake me O my darling . . .*
> You could never have a woman like that, I said to him, never in a month of Sundays.
> *. . . on this our wedding day . . .*
> Never.
> People like us . . .
> *Do not forsake me . . .*
> Anyway I was right, wasn't I?
> She married that French prince.
> Oh aye.
> Anyway, she's a Taig. (40–1)

Taig or not, Grace Kelly's angelic-looking blonde, who ultimately stands by her man, accepts the necessity for violence and shoots one of Cooper's antagonists in the back, becomes an idol for Sammy and Billy. Neither of them mentions the other woman in the film, Cooper's former lover, a feisty, experienced and heavily made-up Mexican saloon-owner played by Katy Jurado. To fantasize about a blonde Taig is pushing the envelope: an independent woman of colour is inconceivable as an object of desire.

Kelly the Taig princess is more acceptable to the Ulster patriarchy than Marlene Dietrich, the brassy saloon singer from *Destry Rides Again* who helps her corrupt lover to fleece innocents in the wild town of Bottleneck until Destry, played with disarming innocence by Jimmy Stewart, comes to wipe off her make-up, clean up her act and win her heart. Frenchy's knowing vulgarity, exhibitionist singing style and cavalier assumption of equality with 'the boys in the backroom', appals Billy's puritanical father:

> *Destry Rides Again.*
> Jimmy Stewart . . . a real good guy.
> See what the boys in the backroom will have and tell them I'm having the same.
> I remember the old man getting all worried at the beginning of the film . . .

thinking this was going to be an unsuitable one for me.
Bad women.

. . .

. . . he said *That Stewart is a great fellow.*
We'll tell your mother all about him. Hey?
We'll keep our mouths buttoned about . . .
Frenchy, I said, just to let him know I was clued in.
Frenchy. (*Three Monologues* 36)

The Maltseeds, father and son, conspire to obliterate Dietrich and her up-front, almost parodic sensuality from a movie they want to remember as belonging to the real good guy, Jimmy Stewart. In so doing they are conforming to the protocol established by the movie itself, which exhibits and enjoys the 'bad woman' Dietrich, only to kill her off so that Destry can eventually marry a nice, boring young virgin who has been hanging about since the beginning of the plot. Frenchy, who stops a bullet meant for Destry, sacrifices her vividly unsuitable self so that the 'real good guy' can make a respectable match.

Johnston shows father and son employing the familiar Madonna/whore dichotomy in order to emphasize the gendered as well as the political limitations of Unionist culture: a Frenchy is impossible in the Presbyterian context. In the less urgently polarized culture of the Republic, Neil Jordan uses *Destry Rides Again* as a framing metaphor for a private Oedipal fantasy that unconsciously perpetuates the politics of gender critiqued by Johnston. Despite his liberal attitude to eroticism, Jordan's pastiche also operates to exorcise the Frenchy figure, the sexual older woman. In 1939, when *Destry* was made, Jimmy Stewart was thirty but looked younger, while Dietrich's make-up could not conceal her thirty-nine years. In *The Miracle*, Jordan exploits the age disparity between Stewart and Dietrich to play with the Western convention in which the sexual, often foreign woman is killed or displaced in favour of the virginal, natural-looking blonde.

Jordan's adolescent hero is called Jimmy. He and his friend Rose, who make a hobby of inventing stories about people they do not know, shadow Renee Baker, 'a woman of a certain age' who is paying a summer visit to the seaside town of Bray. Jimmy insists that Renee must be French, and her blowsy sensuality and faded glamour (in an era of tights she wears stockings, which makes her, as Jimmy says, 'old-fashioned') directly evokes Dietrich. So, though Bray is hardly Bottleneck, a young 'Jimmy' becomes increasingly obsessed by an older 'Frenchy'. When he discovers that Renee is a Hollywood actress who has come to Dublin to star in a musical version of *Destry Rides Again*, these hints become direct quotations. In several scenes we see Renee playing Dietrich playing Frenchy, even down to the removal of Frenchy's make-up. The famous 'See what the boys in the backroom will have' musical sequence is lovingly parodied. Although Rose tells Jimmy that Renee is 'menopausal', and Renee herself says she is 'too old', Jimmy goes to church to pray for a 'miracle': he wants to seduce Renee before summer is over.

Jordan's adaptation of the *Destry* plot is suggestive without being exact. Destry is preceded by his father's reputation as a straight-shooting lawman, and initially disappoints the sheriff because of his refusal to carry a gun. Jimmy's father, an alcoholic saxophone player, is constantly badgering Jimmy to pick up his saxophone so they can play together. When Renee enters this world of fathers, sons and instruments, it gradually becomes clear that Jimmy's desire is taboo not merely because she is 'too old', but because she is really his mother, who abandoned him when he was a baby. If she is a whore, it is because she has slept with his father, who has dismissed her from his life by telling their son she is dead.

The bad woman, the woman who wanted to live her own life and there-fore abandoned her child, cannot now be loved as a mother: she is either a phantom or a taboo sex object. Jimmy tells Renee that his mother is dead; Renee repeats the remark to her dresser; Rose speculates that Renee herself is a ghost. The only compliment Jimmy pays Renee on her performance as Frenchy is 'you died well'. Through some suggestive crosscutting, Jordan indi-cates that the 'miracle' does occur, that Destry 'rides' again in the Irish sense, but the satisfaction of Jimmy's incestuous desire serves as a secular exorcism. Like Frenchy, in whose bloodstained death costume she twice appears to Jimmy, Renee takes herself out of the story, and her son returns to the unmade-up, natural Rose. Jordan evidently thinks that the bad mother cannot go home again, except as a ghost: for her, emigration is a kind of death.

The Western, then, does not offer much of an identity foothold for women on either side of the Border: the difference between Jordan and Johnston is that Johnston critiques the exclusion of Frenchy, while Jordan colludes with it. The imperialism of the classic Western is easier to subvert than its misog-yny. The male children in Neil Jordan's *The Butcher Boy* impersonate Geron-imo and Sitting Bull, and Francie's father plays the theme tune of *The Lone Ranger* on his trumpet, but Francie's chronically depressed mother has no place in either of these mythical frontier narratives. A trope that is complex, shifting and ambiguous in its relation to national or political allegiances is rarely so in relation to gender.

PART THREE

REVIEWING LITERARY AND POLITICAL CANONS

READING YEATS IN POPULAR CULTURE

The mass culture of the electronic age is frequently characterized, especially by contemporary devotees of Adorno, as an agent of hegemony, a tool for the manufacture of political consent. Advertisements, television, Hollywood movies, popular music and most newspapers and magazines are seen as vehicles of the ruling ideology: financed by global capital, driven by the power of the market and designed to promote passive consumerism. Certainly mass culture is more visible than culture created by 'the people'. Folksong, street games, poetry slams and other communal rituals, all of which require an oral rather than a print or electronic medium and highlight performance rather than consumption, may continue to flourish, but they are necessarily less potent as agents of ideological saturation than television or the Internet. Yet it seems pointless, as well as elitist, to attempt to defend the barricades of ethical, aesthetic and political value erected to distinguish both 'high' and 'folk' art from the manipulative inauthenticity of commercial 'mass' culture. One of the numerous challenges of cultural studies is to discover if and how new media, new technologies and the new habits of spectatorship they have created can meaningfully incorporate and transform the classics of the past. Antony Easthope has argued persuasively for a practice of cultural studies that, instead of replacing the analysis of the canon with analysis of, say, advertising or soap operas, recognizes 'a necessity to read high and popular [texts] together' (167). The boundaries between 'high' and 'low' culture are too porous to be strictly policed.

Indeed, bizarre and interesting things happen on boundaries. In a recent issue of the magazine *UFO Universe*, a long and surprisingly well-informed article on Yeats uses 'Leda and the Swan' and 'The Second Coming' to demonstrate that the poet foresaw 'not only the modern phenomenon of alien abductions, but also the coming of alien/human hybrids and even the sighting of a Sphinx-like face on Mars' (Chambers).[1] In this contemporary context, Yeats's 'shape with lion body and the head of a man' (*Poems* 187) occupies the same cultural space as reports of paranormal cattle-maiming in New Mexico and speculation about the American government's secret collaboration with extraterrestrials. Such a collocation of Yeats and UFOs may offend the purists, but it is entirely appropriate. Rationalist intellectuals deride popular millenarianism, but Yeats never met a supernatural manifestation he did not like, or at least investigate, and throughout his life his interest in the occult was as New Age as that of any Southern Californian theosophist.[2] 'The Second Coming' and the alien abduction scenario both attempt to make sense of a universe apparently spinning out of control, to explain the unexplainable by reference to a paranoid system of secret knowledge. Perhaps because so many of the terrible events of the twentieth century seem to defy rational explanation, 'The Second Coming' is currently one of the best-known poems in the English-speaking world. So many writers, politicians, journalists, advertisers and cartoonists regularly cite it that William Safire has suggested its number should be retired ('Politicians').

Yeats's presence in contemporary popular culture, as a non-verbal icon or a source of poetic allusions, may reflect either a modernist or a postmodernist aesthetic. In the modernist aesthetic, subscribed to by Yeats himself, meaning may be elusive and difficult but close attention will usually uncover it. In the unified modernist work (and indeed in the modernist *reading* that most of us still practise), the text signifies all over: every detail is important, and therefore some knowledge of the original is indispensable to the interpretation of a literary allusion. Although at the dawn of the age of mass media traditional culture was already fragmented, high modernist artists clung to the heritage of Western civilization: T. S. Eliot's 'heap of broken images' (*Poems* 63) or Ezra Pound's 'two gross of broken statues' (*Personae* 188). If we do not know *The Tempest* or *Tristan und Isolde*, for example, our understanding of *The Waste Land* will be impoverished. To a modernist writer or reader, it matters that we recognize Yeats as the source and authorial guarantor of phrases such as 'Things fall apart', 'the centre cannot hold', or 'Slouches towards Bethlehem'.

Contemporary postmodernist culture, on the other hand, has supposedly abolished the 'depth' model of literary and cultural enquiry. Terry Eagleton satirically paraphrases the postmodern ethic: 'if only we could kick our metaphysical nostalgia for truth, meaning and history . . . we might come to recognize that . . . fragments and surfaces [are] all we ever have, kitsch [is] quite as good as the real thing because there is in fact no real thing' (*Against* 143). In this view, the shards of culture that we unearth can never be reassembled into a statue and Yeats's phrases float free of their origin in his poem. In the absence of any meaningful historical sense, our references to the classic works of the past function as pastiche (depthless and mechanical copying) rather than intertextuality (the production of significance out of the relationship between two discrete texts and contexts). If this is so, we might ask why anyone should refer to Yeats at all; critics hostile to postmodernism would doubtless answer that, while the poet's relation to meaning and truth (that is to history and ethics) has vanished, his status as a commodity fetish has never been higher. Without having to read him, American consumers understand that the postmodernist 'Yeats' signifies cultural capital.

Indeed, the Sears advertisement in Fig. 7 demonstrates the use of a volume of Yeats's poetry as a fashion statement. The headline 'Come see the *softer* side of Sears' pairs with the androgynous cuteness of the young male model to suggest that reading poetry is not a macho activity. Since this is a

Fig. 7. *The Softer Side of Sears.*

'Back to School Sale' the target audience is the sensitive college kid, the kind who buys the *Collected Poems* rather than using the Norton Anthology. For this good-looking lover of verse, and for all those who would like to emulate his cool, Yeats's poetry must be equated with the purchase of 'colorful cotton henleys' and 'this happenin' suede vest'. Poets and readers of poetry are individualists, so the prospective consumer is urged to 'Be yourself. Make a statement'. Should he worry that being himself might expose him to ridicule, he is reassured that Sears has 'the right look'; and the volume of Yeats guarantees the rightness of the look by demonstrating that Sears knows the right poet. Nothing indicates that either the advertisers or the model have actually perused the contents of the book. 'Poetry' and 'Yeats' have a value independent of the meaning of words.

Shaken loose from his historical context and used to promote suede vests to college-age youth, Yeats as icon fits comfortably into the mass culture of postmodern America that is censured by Eagleton and Jameson. In *The Bridges of*

Madison County (1995), Francesca (Meryl Streep) and Robert (Clint Eastwood) also make use of what we may call the Sears Yeats: she drops an unattributed misquotation from the 'Song of Wandering Aengus', 'when white birds [it should be moths] are on the wing', into an invitation to dinner, he recognizes the line as belonging to Yeats, and we see a brief shot of her (like the Sears model) clutching the *Collected Poems*. They both know the right poet, though perhaps not all that well. When they meet again, he continues the 'Song of Wandering Aengus' (mis)quotation game with 'the silver apples of the moon, and [sic] golden apples of the sun'. In case we missed the point, she promptly names the poet and supplies the title, while he continues: 'Good stuff, Yeats . . . music, economy, sensuousness, beauty, magic, all that appeals to my Irish ancestry'. This breathtakingly banal list has all the resonance of a Sears catalogue: the commodity on display is Irishness, and the come-on is romance.

Not all the consumerist versions of Yeats are equally depthless or deracinated, however. When the Irish put the poet's face on the twenty-punt note, were they celebrating the tourist revenue that he continues to generate or remembering that he was an actively engaged chairman of the committee that created newly independent Ireland's first and most handsome metal coinage? Surely profit and history are here symbolically and aptly allied. That banknote (affectionately nicknamed a 'Yeat' by the poet's descendants) has been retired, but, from his summer school in Sligo to the tea towels, T-shirts and coffee mugs imprinted with his image or a few lines from his verse, Yeats permeates the culture the Irish sell to foreign tourists,[3] and even to themselves. Journalism about the Troubles in the North could hardly survive without reference to 'Easter 1916'; depending on the writer's attitude to the IRA, either 'a terrible beauty is born' or 'too long a sacrifice can make a stone of the heart'. The audio-visual presentation at the Pearse Museum in Dublin is called 'This Man Kept a School', which must strike visitors unfamiliar with 'Easter 1916' as a distinctly peculiar title. Irish academics are equally in Yeats's linguistic debt: the respected historian Joe Lee uses 'The Second Coming', written in 1919, to explicate the post-independence years, which in fact contradicted Yeats's prophecy of political apocalypse: 'It was due in a large measure to him [Cosgrave] that things did not fall apart, that the centre did hold, that not so many but so few of the rough beasts slouching through the Ireland of the twenties would reach their blood soaked Bethlehems' (Lee 174). Lee's allusion is tightly bound to the context of the original, but the philosopher Richard Kearney deftly moves the poem away from its material origins towards the more abstract world of theory: 'After deconstruction, we are told, the centre cannot hold' (*Postnationalist* 62).

Yeats is not the only literary source for merchandisers and academics: James Joyce, as much the presiding spirit of Dublin as Yeats is the avatar of Sligo and Gort, rivals him in the memorabilia stakes, and has even usurped his place on the banknotes.[4] Other writers, like Synge, have acquired a summer school of their own. The 'heritage' industry has attracted considerable hostility: like the film versions of Jane Austen and E. M. Forster, Irish interpretative centres are deplored as pap for the culturally dispossessed.[5] The universal chorus of praise for the Famine Museum at Strokestown, however, suggests that it is not so much the existence of heritage centres that is problematic, but the political angle at which their contents are displayed, or the effect of their placement on the landscape they purport to explicate.[6] And, as the difference between the failed Celtworld theme park and the successful museum at Strokestown demonstrates, the economic and ideological uses to which the Irish past can be put are infinitely variable. As a former Director of the Yeats Summer School in Sligo, I find myself unable to condemn unequivocally the commercialization of the Irish literary heritage. Like most of those who originally produced it, I am glad when literature sells, even gladder if a stray poem lodges in the luggage of an otherwise indifferent traveller. The idea that 'high art' should remain uncontaminated by money is a Romantic fiction. Regrettably or not, tourism is a fact of Irish life; and literary tourism highlights an aspect of Ireland's past that is as real as the passage grave at Newgrange, and less fragile. The planned simulacrum of Newgrange will, like Lascaux Two, divert the flow of tourist traffic and prevent the destruction of the 'aura', to use Benjamin's term, of the original. But most tourists will still be conscious of missing Newgrange One. The experience of reading Yeats's poetry, on the other hand, does not depend on the possession of a first edition, and is immeasurably enriched by an acquaintance with Ireland.

One of the charges most often levelled against the exploitation of cultural capital is that it leads to a vulgarization and trivialization of 'high art'. The use of classical music or images in television advertising incenses some critics;[7] similarly, Helen Vendler argues that 'ripping a line or two out of a poem' is like 'cutting off the head of the Apollo Belvedere'.[8] But it is necessary to discriminate between types of exploitation. Shakespeare pointed out long ago that poems are inherently less vulnerable to tourist depredations than artefacts such as passage graves or ecologically sensitive natural treasures like the Burren:

> Since brass, nor stone, nor earth, nor boundless sea,
> But sad mortality o'ersways their power,
> How with this rage shall beauty hold a plea,
> Whose action is no stronger than a flower? (Sonnet 65)

Shakespeare's answer is that 'in black ink my love may still shine bright'. Perhaps 'I will arise and go now' inscribed on a coffee mug was not precisely the immortality that Shakespeare had in mind, but as long as the royalties are paid the poetic damage is hard to calibrate. One might even invoke the principle that there is no such thing as bad publicity: acquaintance with a truncated phrase could induce curiosity about the whole poem. At the more intellectual end of the exploitation scale, the various summer schools are even

harder to censure, since their aim is to deepen rather than fragment or trivi-
alize the experience of literature. Though the competing attractions of Guin-
ness and scenery should not be underestimated, most literary tourists do not
attend summer schools in order to avoid reading the works of the featured
writer, whoever he (usually he) may be.

Sometimes, of course, the iconic Yeats is used in spectacularly inappropriate contexts: for example, there used to be a daycare centre in Sligo called 'The
Stolen Child' whose proprietors had surely never read that slightly sinister
poem about a little boy abducted by the fairies. ('The Stolen Child' was more
aptly quoted on Dublin posters warning the public about cot death.)[9] But
sometimes the context is perfectly apropos, as when the line 'I will arise and
go now, and go to Innisfree' was used to caption the home page of the North
West Tourist Guide on the World Wide Web.[10] Yeats, who was one of the first
poets to broadcast on the radio, would have been delighted by his presence in
cyberspace, and indeed 'The Lake Isle of Innisfree' was among the texts he
chose to transpose from print into the new audio technology. As one of his
most famous and best-loved poems, it was a felicitous choice for the new popular medium. The volume in which it appears, *Poems 1895*, which was
reprinted fifteen times in Yeats's lifetime, continued to satisfy the taste of the
poetry-buying public long after he had published his more difficult modernist
work.[11] And its appeal has lasted: in a 1999 *Poetry Ireland* poll, 'The Lake Isle
of Innisfree' headed the list of one hundred favourite Irish poems (Dorgan).

'The Lake Isle of Innisfree' taps into the perennial longing for a peaceful
life close to nature, a longing also exploited by the producers of holiday
brochures and the purveyors of second homes, and of course by the tourist
promoters of the West who placed it on their website:

> I will arise and go now, and go to Innisfree,
> And a small cabin build there, of clay and wattles made:
> Nine bean-rows will I have there, a hive for the honey-bee.
> And live alone in the bee-loud glade.
> . . .
> I will arise and go now, for always night and day
> I hear lake water lapping with low sounds by the shore;
> While I stand on the roadway, or on the pavements grey,
> I hear it in the deep heart's core. (*Poems* 39)

This longing is strongest when the speaker is standing, as Yeats was, 'on the
roadway, or on the pavements grey' of urban London. Ironically, Yeats's immediate inspiration was a futuristic piece of advertising, 'a fountain in a shop
window which balanced a little ball upon its jet'. This modern mechanical
device intersected with his intense homesickness for Sligo to produce the
auditory illusion of 'lake water lapping with low sounds by the shore' (*Autobiographies* 153). According to the poet's daughter Anne, Sligo 'represented a
kind of Shangri-La' to the Yeats children because their mother's loathing of

London and longing for her native place permeated the household.[12] Yeats borrowed his opening cadence from the prodigal son, who on deciding to return to the house of his father announces: 'I will arise and go'. It seems appropriate, then, that Irish Ferries' newest vessel on the route between Dublin and Holyhead is called 'The Isle of Innisfree'. Though the boat probably carries more tourists and emigrants than returning natives, the symbolic wish encoded in its name, as in the poem itself, is for Ireland's expatriate children to come home.

An ingenious English advertisement prompts the production of a high cultural artefact, which in its turn promotes the services of an Irish ferryboat. This sequence suggests the inevitable hybridity of cultural processes, and the impossibility of placing a cordon sanitaire around the verbal icon. For good or ill, art and consumerism have things to say to each other. Yeats's Shangri-La has contributed richly to the Bord Fáilte mystique of Ireland, particularly the West, as a rural Eden in which the stressed-out foreign vacationer can find that most elusive and precious of commodities, the peace that 'comes dropping slow'. Consequently Yeats is sometimes accused of nurturing a false consciousness that refuses to recognize Ireland's urban modernity and locates her essential identity somewhere west of the Shannon and before the Industrial Revolution. In this he is linked with Eamon de Valera, an equally iconic figure, though one who currently generates somewhat less tourist revenue: in 1999 his summer school attracted only five participants (Ruane).

But the pastoral has always been a consciously 'fake' genre. Created by cosmopolitan Latin poets like Virgil and Theocritus as an imaginary break from the pressures of life at the imperial court, it was born well before the Industrial Revolution gave us something we really needed to get away from. Pastoral is so hackneyed as to have generated, as long ago as the Renaissance, the anti-pastoral, which reminds the weekend shepherd of bad weather and the nasty habits of real sheep. People who make their living in the country are seldom romantic about it. Even Thoreau, whose rural retreat at Walden Pond provided Yeats with his blueprint for the simple life and the oddly specific detail of the 'nine bean-rows', stayed in his own 'small cabin' for only a couple of years, and the second season he neglected his beans, which accordingly failed to come up.

The persistence of pastoral has less to do with the longing for different material conditions of life than it does with desire itself, which is created and sustained by absence. As Socrates says in Plato's *Symposium* (76–7), we cannot desire what we already possess; desire is therefore always displaced onto the thing we cannot have. He might have been talking about marketing strategies. In his poem 'Essential Beauty', Philip Larkin brings Plato's ideal forms into direct relation to the culture of advertising and its teleology. The 'domestic pastoral' contained in the idealized images of comfort and wellbeing used to sell tea, butter or cigarettes does not merely pain the viewer by contrast with his own imperfect and unbeautiful life, it actually beckons through perfection towards oblivion. 'Dying smokers' are granted a vision of the woman whose unattainable image prompted them to purchase a particular brand, 'Smiling, and recognising, and going dark' (*Whitsun* 42). In an urban culture, peace, solitude and natural beauty are metaphors for the impossible perfection that cannot be achieved except in death, the ultimate return home – to heaven or the mother's womb, according to your Christian or Freudian interpretative bias.

In *The Loved One* (1948) Evelyn Waugh satirically relocates 'The Lake Isle of Innisfree' to the American never-never land, California, where it becomes a part of popular funerary culture. In Whispering Glades, Waugh's parody of Forest Lawn cemetery, burial plots on the Lake Isle command the top prices. As the boatman says, 'they've certainly got it fixed up poetic. It's named after a very fancy poem. They got bee-hives. Once they had bees too, but folks was always getting stung so now it's done mechanical and scientific; no sore fannies and plenty of poetry' (82). Once again we can follow a trajectory from the mechanical fountain in urban London, via Yeats's deliberately constructed Irish pastoral, back to Waugh's buzzing beehives, in which the narrator sees 'a tiny red eye which told that the sound-apparatus was working in good order' (83–4). The artifice of the Lake Isle in Whispering Glades, like Yeats's golden bird in 'Sailing to Byzantium', is the artifice of eternity.

Waugh's intention is comprehensively satirical: both Yeats's fantasy island and its literal-minded American simulacrum are being sent up. Whispering Glades is an expensive thanatological theme park and, in Waugh's early-postmodern vision of California, poetry and Irishness are commodities that can be produced by machines. The boatman observes that, although the original customers for the Lake Isle's luxury plots were supposed to be Irish-Americans, 'it seems the Irish are just naturally poetic and won't pay that much for plantings [burials]' (82). Unlike the 'good style Jews' who can afford to purchase their last home in a holiday paradise, Waugh's Irish are savvy consumers who can recognize the difference between natural and artificial poetry. Only foreigners are taken in by the Celtic kitsch.

The pastoral myth of the West of Ireland as a maternal heaven is similarly satirized in John Ford's classic 1952 movie, *The Quiet Man*, in which the name 'Inisfree' (spelt with only one 'n') becomes a synecdoche for an entire landscape. Shot mostly on location, the film juxtaposes picturesque images of the village of Cong, the mountains of Connemara and the beaches near Clifden as if these widely scattered places were all in easy walking distance of each other, and calls them 'Inisfree'. Ford's violence to topography tells an imaginative truth about the way a literary artefact has become the lens through which outsiders see the West. In its turn, his film has coloured the landscape it reorganized: the Connemara location of a famous scene is now called 'The Quiet Man Bridge'.

The film opens with the appearance of a stranger who confounds the expectations of the Irish. For the locals, Inisfree is not a symbol of paradise but a source of income: a place where tourists come to take photographs and catch trout. An American who arrives with a sleeping bag instead of a camera or a fishing rod is an anomaly. As Sean Thornton (John Wayne) steps out of the railway carriage and into a world governed by conversation rather than the need to keep the trains running on time (post-Mussolini this stereotypical Irish failing becomes a virtue), an absurdly tangential and long-winded discussion about the best way to get to Inisfree keeps the title of Yeats's famous poem in the forefront of the audience's mind. The former Abbey actor Barry Fitzgerald finally rescues Wayne. 'Inisfree? This way', he says, with a brisk flourish of his carriage whip. The layers of Yeatsian allusion are doubled, at least for those who recognize Fitzgerald as someone who starred in the theatre Yeats helped to found. As Wayne and Fitzgerald trot away the camera pans deliberately across the sceptical faces of the locals, one of whom asks dubiously, 'I wonder, now, why a man would go to Inisfree?'

The opening of Ford's film thus challenges the opening line of Yeats's poem; but like the poem and its namesake the ferryboat, Ford's film also deploys the myth of reverse emigration, of coming home to Ireland. The 'quiet, peace-loving man' of the title, an Irish-American burnt out on life in Pittsburgh and haunted by a tragic accident in the boxing ring, is determined to return to the Irish cottage where he was born. Like Yeats's mother Susan Pollexfen, Sean Thornton's mother has kept alive in her child the dream of their lost origins: 'Ever since I was a kid living in a shack near the slag heaps my mother told me about Inisfree and White O' Morn. Inisfree has become another word for heaven to me.' The locals view things differently: 'Inisfree is far from being heaven, Mr Thornton', says the sardonic widow Tillane, from whom he buys the cottage.

The Quiet Man is a brilliant exercise in having it both ways. It provides a satirical commentary on the cultural ideology of forties and fifties Ireland, as epitomized in de Valera's much derided vision of his country as

> the home of a people who valued material wealth only as the basis for right living, of a people who were satisfied with frugal comfort and devoted their leisure to the things of the spirit – a land whose countryside would be bright with cosy homesteads, whose fields and villages would be joyous with the sounds of industry, with the romping of sturdy children, the contests of athletic youths and the laughter of comely maidens, whose firesides would be forums for the wisdom of serene old age. (*Speeches* 466)

Ford's fantasy West is at once gorgeously 'authentic' (real Technicolor green fields, golden sands, the comeliest of maidens) and cheerfully subversive (the serene elders get up off their deathbeds at the prospect of a fight, the priests are all compulsive gamblers and there is nothing frugal about the alcohol consumption). Ford anticipates the present debate on tourism and heritage centres when the widow Tillane asks Sean Thornton if he plans to turn White O'

Morn into a national shrine to the Thornton family and charge admission. Paradoxically, the economy of the present-day village of Cong is sustained in part on its representation as 'Inisfree', a place that never was, and there is indeed a Quiet Man Heritage Cottage which 'will give the visitor a total Quiet Man experience. Designed as a replica of "White-O'Mornin" [sic] Cottage, all furnishings, artefacts and costumes are authentic reproductions'.[13]

Whatever an authentic reproduction may be, the phrase suits the film perfectly. White O' Morn was always a heritage cottage. Thornton is determined to recreate his birthplace in the image of his exiled mother's dream, and the film projects the white thatched cottage as a fantasy return to the womb. As he works to spruce up the picture-perfect outside, painting the woodwork a clichéed bright green, the Anglican vicar and his wife pay him a visit. Mrs Playfair, an unlikely metacritic of film aesthetics, recognizes that the cottage, which was indeed built on a Hollywood set and looks remarkably unreal, is a simulacrum, kitsch rather than the real thing. In a layered moment of irony she exclaims, 'It looks just as Irish cottages ought to, but so seldom do. And only an American would have thought of emerald green'. Postcard Ireland, the Emerald Isle, signifies primarily to people who do not live there: it is a product of emigrant nostalgia and tourist demand. Like White O' Morn itself, it is always already a replica.

Together with round towers, high crosses, castles and monasteries, the thatched cottage remains a dominant feature of the marketable landscape, outnumbered in contemporary photographic catalogues only by the façades of pubs.[14] In Neil Jordan's *The Butcher Boy* (1997), the hero Francie runs away from small-town Ireland to Dublin, and while he is in the city he buys for his mother a plaster model of one of these 'cosy homesteads', an urban fantasy of everything his own squalid Irish home is not. When the colleen who sits playing the harp outside the thatched cottage comes to surreal life as the notoriously transgressive rock star Sinéad O'Connor (who also plays the Virgin Mary), the joke is at the expense of de Valera's 'comely maidens' and the stereotypical national image, the woman with the harp.[15]

The Quiet Man, which foregrounds pub façades and Celtic crosses and even features the bottom of Yeats's tower in a semi-disguised visual quotation, is itself a catalogue of romantic 'Images of Ireland' that are exploited and undermined at the same time. Sean Thornton is even more impractical than the Yeats of 'Innisfree': instead of 'frugal' beans, he plants extravagant roses round his 'small cabin' in honour of his mother, who evoked them constantly in her memories of the cottage. The symbolic connection of roses with fantasy is continued throughout the film: when his new wife Mary Kate (Maureen O'Hara) refuses to consummate their marriage because her dowry has not been paid, Thornton in his turn refuses to plant vegetables, although he continues to nurture his rose garden. No children, no cabbages. To Mrs Playfair, however, a flower is just a flower. She offers Thornton a pot plant as a housewarming gift and even accompanies it with a line of poetry, but the line she chooses, 'A primrose by a river's brink', is deliberately anti-poetic. She misquotes 'Peter Bell', one of Wordsworth's dullest poems. The Reverend Playfair's pedantic correction of her rhyme-word, '"brim", not "brink". The next line ends with "him"', indicates that Ford's literary allusion is precise enough to take the weight of a modernist reading, demands, indeed, that we go and look it up. For Wordsworth's Peter Bell, nature is empty of symbolic meaning:

> A primrose by a river's brim
> A yellow primrose was to him
> And it was nothing more. (64)

Challenging Thornton's conviction that the shortest way to heaven is via Inisfree, Ford's invocation of Peter Bell's materialism exposes and undercuts the maternal fantasy represented by the roses and the emerald-green cottage door. Mrs Playfair's dismissal of the imagination, 'Poets are so silly, aren't they? I do hope you aren't one, Mr Thornton', teases not only Wordsworth, but also Yeats and his romantic disciple the Quiet Man. Mrs Playfair trenchantly reminds Thornton that dreams are nourished in the foul rag-and-bone shop of the heart: the best fertilizer for roses, she says, is horse manure.

Yeats is not the only writer of the Irish Renaissance whom Ford lays under contribution: The Quiet Man, with its feisty heroine, stranger with a murderous past, independent and amorous widow, horseracing on the sands, foregrounding of the word 'shift' and glorification of violence, is an optimistic restaging of The Playboy of the Western World. Ford's complex but ultimately affectionate irony at the expense of the images of Ireland produced by Yeats, Synge and de Valera is matched by self-irony: when Thornton first sees a barefoot, red-headed Mary Kate herding her implausibly clean flock through a sun-dappled green landscape, he asks, 'Is she real? She can't be'. His American perspective permits him to understand that this rural vision of Mary Kate is a postcard fantasy produced by his own emigrant nostalgia, and indeed she is never again seen in proximity to a sheep. Yet Ford wants it both ways: The Quiet Man continues to exploit stereotypes of the pastoral West of Ireland even as it acknowledges that Inisfree is far from being heaven. Sometimes kitsch is hard to tell from the real thing.

Such irony is not characteristic of later American appropriations of Yeats's work. For example, it is wholly absent from Francis Ford Coppola's underrated 1986 film, Peggy Sue Got Married, which uses Yeats's early love poem 'When You Are Old and Grey and Full of Sleep' as a guarantor of authenticity and value, as 'the real thing'. 'When You Are Old', itself an appropriation of Ronsard, is a poem about movement though time. In a circular trajectory, Yeats anticipates the old age of his beloved, and then imagines her returning in dreams to her youth (the present of his poem), in which she failed to take advantage of his devotion:

> When you are old and grey and full of sleep,
> And nodding by the fire, take down this book,
> And slowly read, and dream of the soft look
> Your eyes had once, and of their shadows deep. (*Poems* 41)

Peggy Sue Got Married, which employs literal time travel, reverses the direc-tional loop of Yeats's poem. The presently middle-aged Peggy Sue (Kathleen Turner) becomes a young girl again but retains her knowledge of the future she has already experienced. This return to her high-school days permits her to enjoy a brief affair with the poet Michael, a 'commie beatnik weirdo' whom she had vainly admired in her youth. Where Yeats's poem looks forward only in order to look back in regret ('Murmur, a little sadly, how love fled'), Peggy Sue goes back in order to find out what she missed, and to decide not to regret it. Michael is a handsome young man, but his poetry is terrible. When he recites his own lines as a prelude to seducing Peggy Sue, she is turned off by his disgusting imagery: 'Razor shreds of rat puke fall on my bare arms'. In *Glamour* magazine, a list of the 'Most overrated things about love' contains the item 'Him writing you poetry, unless he's Yeats',[16] and Michael swiftly gets the seduction back on track by recourse to a better love poet than himself. His hand unbuttons Peggy Sue's blouse as Yeats's lines roll off his tongue:

> How many loved your moments of glad grace,
> And loved your beauty with love false or true,
> But one man loved the pilgrim soul in you,
> And loved the sorrows of your changing face. (*Poems* 41)

Lest he be suspected of plagiarism, he adds hastily, 'I didn't write that. That's Yeats'. Peggy Sue is duly overcome by poetic emotion, but not too much to whisper, 'No more rat puke – try and write something beautiful'. In other words, something a bit more like the Master. Michael's hilarious response, 'I'll respect you for eternity', resonates at the end of the film, when Peggy Sue wakes up from her time travel to find at her bedside a volume of his poetry dedicated to her and called, in homage to Yeats's lines, *The Pilgrim Soul*. Unlike *The Bridges of Madison County*, which never engages more than superficially with 'The Song of Wandering Aengus', its facile marker for Irishness, *Peggy Sue Got Married* uses 'When You Are Old' to clever and subtle effect.

Michael takes good care to acknowledge his poetic debts: for him the Author is still alive and well and guarantees the authenticity of his work. Other cinematic Yeats quoters are not initially so scrupulous. A young flyer's deliber-ate plagiarism of 'An Irish Airman Foresees His Death' frames the action sequences of *Memphis Belle*, British producer David Puttnam's 1990 film about the last mission of the most famous American bomber of World War II. The film works hard to emphasize the distinctive ethnicity of this poetry-loving American airman. An army PR man, who is doing a feature on the crew for *Life* magazine in an attempt to 'sell' the war to less-than-enthusiastic folks back home, tells us in voice-over: 'This kid couldn't be more Irish if he tried. Danny Daly. "A" student, editor of the school paper, valedictorian, he volunteered the day after he graduated from college'. Danny's Irishness is emphasized throughout the movie: he has flaming red hair, he writes poems, he distributes shamrocks as good luck charms, and his theme song, which recurs at climactic moments, is the Irish classic 'Danny Boy'. 'An Irish Airman Foresees His Death' can hardly compete with 'Danny Boy' as a pop cultural artefact, but it gives the character his major dramatic moment and is used to define his hybrid cultural identity.

The scene in which the poem is spoken is loaded with symbolic visual detail. The mission is delayed by bad weather over the target, and the men climb out of their plane to await new orders for take-off. Although the opening titles identify the date as 13 May 1943, the *Memphis Belle* is parked at the edge of a cornfield being harvested by a man with a horse-drawn reaping machine. Since harvesting in England takes place in late August, the film risks an obvious seasonal absurdity in order to bond one member of the crew, the American farmer's son Clay, with the British rustic who can't make his reaper work. Clay, who has 'one just like it at home', offers to fix the picturesque machine. The shot of the lush, ripe cornfield also conveniently takes in the tower of an ancient English church; the national values being visually invoked here are Tradition, Land and Religion. But neither the land nor the religion belong to the Irish-American Danny, whose historical relationship to England is a good deal more conflicted than that of the aptly named Clay, and whose country of ancestral origin is neutral in the war against Germany.

Danny's link to his American 'home' is also more tenuous than that of his mates. Unlike the captain, for whose girlfriend the plane is named, Danny has no romantic interest waiting for him at the end of his tour of duty, and he cannot imagine what he will be doing after the war is over. He confides to a rookie airman that he is not particularly looking forward to leaving the base. The director's choice of Yeats's poem locates Danny in a political and emotional limbo, drained of affective ties except to his comrades and his vocation as airman. His situation is shared to a lesser extent by the whole crew, whose tension is palpable as they wait between life and death at the margin of the airfield, neither embarked upon nor relieved of their hazardous duty: the daylight bombing of the German city of Bremen. When they notice that Danny has been writing poetry in a notebook and ask him to recite some, an air of nervous jokiness pervades the scene. 'Poetry', elite culture, is too serious for most of them. But as Danny, after much hesitation, launches into 'An Irish Airman Foresees His Death', backed by a few quiet phrases from 'Danny Boy' played on the harmonica, the internal audience's resistance is overcome, and the silence at the end of the recitation is daringly stretched out. As in *Peggy Sue Got Married*, popular culture pays unconditional and non-ironical homage to high culture. Characters and audience understand that they are in the presence of 'the real thing':

I know that I shall meet my fate
Somewhere among the clouds above;
Those that I fight I do not hate,
Those that I guard I do not love;

. . .

Nor law, nor duty bade me fight,
Nor public men, nor cheering crowds,
A lonely impulse of delight
Drove to this tumult in the clouds;
I balanced all, brought all to mind,
The years to come seemed waste of breath,
A waste of breath the years behind
In balance with this life, this death. (*Poems* 135)

Unlike the other airmen, the audience is privileged to observe that Danny's notebook contains nothing but crossed-out lines of poetry: he speaks Yeats's words because he has none of his own. This plagiarism comes back to haunt him later, but his theft is rhetorically and performatively appropriate. The 'I' who voices Yeats's poem belongs to a ventriloquized dramatic speaker, whom Danny has been carefully constructed to resemble.

Yeats's historical Irish airman was Major Robert Gregory, the only son of his friend Lady Augusta Gregory, who was shot down over Italy in 1918. Yeats removes the hyphen from Gregory's ethnic identity, but he was an Anglo-Irish-man who volunteered to serve in the British Royal Air Force. Danny has a sim-ilarly hybrid cultural allegiance. The details of his character (Irish-American, volunteer, valedictorian, poet, editor, college graduate, radio operator, photog-rapher, apparently doomed youth) are drawn not only from 'An Irish Airman Foresees His Death', but also from Yeats's elegy 'In Memory of Major Robert Gregory', which laments the untimely loss of a multi-talented Renaissance man:

Soldier, scholar, horseman, he,
And all he did done perfectly
As though he had but that one trade alone. (*Poems* 134)

As Yeats's elegy also tells us, Gregory was a painter; the more modern but equally visual Danny may have trouble finishing a poem, but he is never with-out his camera. Although these subtle parallels will escape most audiences, and none of the American reviews that I have found mention Yeats at all, it is nevertheless clear that the British production team used his World War I poem not only to produce an intensely quiet moment before the 'tumult in the clouds' begins, but to devise an oblique way of suggesting the ethnic com-plexities of Irish-American involvement in World War II.

The poem is an appropriate vehicle with which to raise the question of tangled political loyalties, since they are the essence of its subject. During

World War I, conscription was never extended to Ireland, which since the Easter Rising of 1916 had been in open rebellion against the Empire. Gregory's decision to volunteer for a war in which he had no technical obligation to serve could be seen as a statement of his allegiance to Britain. As an Irish nationalist, and as elegist of the Irish rebels executed after the Rising, Yeats could not straightforwardly celebrate a death in the service of the Empire that had executed them, and was thus forced to justify Gregory's sacrifice in individualist, non-political terms. Hence the curious, rhetorically balanced evocation of political disinterestedness in the first verse: 'Those that I fight [the Germans] I do not hate / Those that I guard [the English] I do not love'. Because it names a specific Irish geographical location, Yeats's second quatrain about Kiltartan and its people is cut, and Danny resumes his recitation with lines that could describe any non-conscripted Irish-American: 'Nor law, nor duty bade me fight, / Nor public men, nor cheering crowds'. Many Irish-Americans were in fact opposed to America's entry into the war on the side of their old enemy, England. But, like Frank McGuinness's Jamie O'Brien, Danny has left behind ancient quarrels in order to throw his energies into the current fight.

Having jettisoned the conventional reasons for enlistment, Yeats offers a subjective explanation of Gregory's motivation: he is animated by 'A lonely impulse of delight' so intense that it renders both past and future 'A waste of breath'. Activating a paradox familiar to students of masculinity, he suggests that only a close encounter with death can make a man feel fully alive. I have always wondered whether poor Lady Gregory was much consoled by her friend's poem, which comes perilously close to saying that her son died because he got his kicks out of high-risk behaviour; but as a lead-in to an exciting battle sequence it works extremely well. Moreover, Yeats's intuition about flying is confirmed by an impeccable source: an article in the magazine *Airline Pilot* asserts that the poem 'enjoys almost cult status among fighter pilots, many of whom keep (or kept) it folded in their wallet or in a flightsuit pocket' (Hayhurst 28).[17]

The film's use of the poem will resonate differently for viewers depending on whether they know, as I originally did not, that the whole crew of the historical Memphis Belle survived. The war-movie formula requires that some of the characters get back alive, but in the interests of pathos it usually sacrifices several of them along the way. Yeats's lines mark the romantic Irish dreamer for death. When he is wounded and the film flashes back to the poem scene, the cliché appears to be closing in. Danny purges his Catholic conscience with a last confession of his plagiarism from a Protestant poet and falls back with the melodramatic gesture that usually signals cinematic demise. His heart has stopped; he is literally balanced between life and death. It takes his friend Val's successful administration of CPR to rescue the moment from sentimental predictability and cancel the misleading poetic omens. In attributing the poem correctly – 'Yeats. Yeats wrote that. W. B. Yeats. I couldn't . . .' – Danny transfers the death foreseen away from himself and back to the original Irish Airman. Plagiarism, it seems, can be fatal: better to cite your sources.

I have given a detailed modernist reading to what I consider *Memphis Belle's* modernist use of Yeats because, whether or not the audience recognizes them, the political resonances evoked by the poem in its cinematic context are as coherent and meaningful as those of the original. The allusion signifies in depth. When I consider contemporary appropriations of a better-known poem, 'The Second Coming', I am less certain that a modernist reading is appropriate. One line in particular, 'Things fall apart; the centre cannot hold', has entered the language so completely that it is normally used without attribution, especially by the headline writers and journalists of the *New York Times*, for whom it is a perennial resource. 'Will the Center Hold?' they enquire; or (more often) they lament that 'The Center Isn't Holding'. A recent book on the Supreme Court reassures us that *The Center Holds*. Still, for every writer who uses the phrase without knowing or caring where it comes from, there is another for whom, as the *New York Times's* 'Metropolitan Diary' asserts, 'Yeats *is* "The center cannot hold"'.[18]

Yet this is a curiously unpoetic line to have acquired such wide currency. There is nothing remarkable about the diction, except the degree of its abstraction. How can we explain its immense popularity? Perhaps, like Shakespeare's 'To be or not to be', lack of particularity is the secret of its success. 'Things fall apart' – but what things? 'The centre cannot hold' – but where is the centre? Centre is a relative term: one man's centre is another woman's periphery. Apart from the falcon image, which is seldom quoted, the opening section of 'The Second Coming' is the ultimate 'fill-in-the-blanks' poem. Lacking nouns, Yeats's superlative adjectives allow quoters to designate their own 'best' and 'worst', as Yeats himself was the first to do. Drafts of the poem reveal that his immediate inspiration was the political chaos in Europe after World War I. In 1919 when the poem was written, Yeats saw the Communist revolution in Russia as the major threat to world stability, but in 1938 he reinterpreted 'The Second Coming' as a prophecy of fascism.[19] He got away with this volte-face because in the process of revision he had obliterated all the specifics. Irish poems like 'September 1913' and 'Easter 1916' name names and mention places, but in 'The Second Coming' the loss of local reference allows for multiple readings. The twentieth-century record of genocide and mass death in two world wars, the Holocaust, the Gulags, Rwanda and Bosnia renders an image as generalized and yet as menacing as 'the blood-dimmed tide' endlessly applicable.

Although for some readers the poem's durability derives from its elegant restatement of the Second Law of Thermodynamics, for most American politicians and journalists 'the center' that either holds or falls apart is American democracy. As Al Gore graciously conceded the recent presidential election and George W. Bush responded in kind, John McCain proclaimed triumphantly, 'The center holds'.[20] An earlier NPR broadcast that highlighted the outbreak of Yeats-quoting among American politicians revealed that Democrats and Republicans, from Gore to his polar opposite Pat Buchanan, are equally fond of the Irish poet's resonant phraseology ('Politicians'). In November 1995, Bill Clinton told the Democratic Leadership Council, 'It is clear that the responsibility of the United States today is to lead the world away from division, to show the world that the center can hold; that a free and diverse people, through democratic means, can form a lasting union'. There is irony in Clinton's appropriation of Yeats, who was far from being a democrat himself and expected the Apocalypse rather than American hegemony. But the right-wing Republican Robert Dornan found Yeats adaptable to diametrically opposed purposes when he announced his 1996 run for the presidency by suggesting that, although Clinton was destroying the country, 'We're going to roll this decay back. We're going to restore the American dream. I am not going to watch as things fall apart. My favorite poet, William B. Yeats, wrote these words in 1939, the year Hitler began the world's most devastating war: "Things fall apart. The center cannot hold" '.[21] Dornan's mistake about the date of 'The Second Coming' demonstrates the compelling power of Yeats's reinterpretation of the poem as an augury of fascism, but his alignment of 'the center' with the Republican version of the American Dream is just as tendentious as Clinton's enrolment of Yeats as a Democrat.

The global, indeed the galactic applicability of 'The Second Coming' is demonstrated by the television science fiction series *Babylon 5*, which takes Yeats's apocalyptic poem more seriously than the politicians do. According to the opening voice-over, the Babylon 5 space station is 'our last best hope for peace. A self-contained world five miles long, located in neutral territory. A place of commerce and diplomacy for a quarter of a million humans and aliens. A shining beacon in space, all alone in the night'. Allegory is a staple of science fiction, and the use of Babylon 5 as an analogue for twentieth-century America is transparent. Babylon 5 is a melting pot in which 'aliens' like the Narns, the Minbari and the Centauri live in precarious amity with human beings, engaging in 'commerce and diplomacy' and clinging to their 'last best hope for peace'. The phrase 'our last best hope' comes from Lincoln's 1862 State of the Union speech, cited at length in the episode 'Points of Departure' (02/11/1994): 'The fiery trial through which we pass will light us down in honor or dishonor to the last generation. We shall nobly save or meanly lose our last best hope'. In the following episode of *Babylon 5*, which is called 'Revelations' (09/11/1994), 'The Second Coming' joins Lincoln's Civil War oratory as a warning about saving or losing the Union between humans and aliens in an apocalyptic galactic war.

'Revelations' demonstrates that even aliens appreciate Yeats. The title alludes to one of the poet's major sources, the biblical Book of Revelation, which describes the advent of the seven-headed beast, the Antichrist and the end of the world. In this episode, G'Kar, the Narn ambassador to Babylon 5, comes back from the outermost rim of known space with news of the return of 'an ancient race described in our Holy Books' who come from 'a dark and terrible place called Z'ha'dum', which has been 'dead for a thousand years'. These 'shadows', as they are called, are figures for the Satanic enemy in the perennial struggle between good and evil that animates so much fantasy and science fiction. As he describes them, G'Kar's language is saturated with Yeatsian echoes: he declares that 'something is moving, gathering its forces', and that 'after a thousand years the darkness has come again'. Unlike the journalists and politicians who borrow Yeats's most famous phrases without grappling with the complexity and obscurity of the poem from which they are taken, the writer John Michael Straczynski has read the difficult middle section of 'The Second Coming', although in deference to his mass audience he refrains from quoting it, sticking instead to the best known parts, the opening and the last two lines. G'Kar shows his fellow-Narn NaToth that he has been reading a human book. 'I've been studying their literature for a while, and I came across this. It would seem that they may be wiser than we had thought:

> Things fall apart; the centre cannot hold;
> Mere anarchy is loosed upon the world,
> The blood-dimmed tide is loosed, and everywhere
> The ceremony of innocence is drowned;
>   . . .
> And what rough beast, its hour come round at last,
> Slouches towards Bethlehem to be born?'

Even if the sight of a spotted green creature reciting Yeats makes you laugh, *Babylon 5* takes its poetry dead seriously, and television writer Straczynski mounts a defence of literary value that many English professors committed to postmodernist scepticism about hierarchies and absolutes would be embarrassed to offer:

> One aspect of the Yeats quote, and the Lincoln quote . . . is that I think a lot of folks at some point tuned out of, or aren't interested in, literature and poetry because they've never really been exposed to it. So just to be a little subversive, I work some of it into the show. I choose that which has meaning to the show, and the characters, in the hopes that . . . viewers will dig out the original material and be exposed to some *really* nifty writing. Granted that television must entertain at minimum; it should also elevate and ennoble and educate, and this is too good an opportunity to waste, provided one does not become didactic about it.[22]

You could hardly get less postmodern than that. Not only does Straczynski think of poetry and history, Yeats and Lincoln, as 'the real thing', but he also hopes that his viewers will return to the originals and be ennobled by them. Although Yeats is not named in the episode itself, Straczynski posted the complete text of the poem on the *Babylon 5 Lurker's Guide*. As theorists turn away from canonical works and great men towards the analysis of popular culture, some popular culture revalorizes the canon in a resoundingly old-fashioned way.

A now defunct series from the creator of *The X-Files*, Chris Carter's *Millennium*, offers a less reverent but no less canonical take on 'The Second Coming', which is juxtaposed with Nostradamus and the Book of Revelation to create a paranoid scenario that mirrors Yeats's own obsession with occultism, divination and apocalypse. In the pilot episode a serial killer mutters, 'I want to see you dance on the blood-dimmed tide . . . The ceremony of innocence is drowned', as he watches a stripper whom he will later hack to death with a kitchen knife. The killer, whose other targets are HIV-positive gay males, sees AIDS as one of the great plagues that will, according to Revelation, precede the end of the world. Like the speaker of Yeats's poem, the hero of the series, Frank, is blessed or cursed with the power to see into the heart of darkness: he experiences in his own mind the images of evil and destruction created by the mass murderer. The hip cinematic techniques of *Millennium* suggest a postmodern sensibility, in which Yeats's words might float free of their originating Author, and indeed, as Frank attempts to decipher them from a blurred videotape of the killer, they appear simply as disjointed fragments. These fragments, however, are meant to be reconstructed and interpreted correctly, and in a clunky realist scene Frank quotes and explicates the poem to the understandably baffled members of Seattle's police department, who look as if they have been abruptly returned to the horrors of Sophomore Lit. The poor quality of the series notwithstanding, Yeats finds an appropriate niche in the world of the paranoid and paranormal, and *Millennium* reflects the ominously blood-saturated tone of the poem more accurately than the comfortable platitudes of Clinton and Dornan.

Even soap opera, supposedly among the lowest of mass cultural genres and the least likely to be juxtaposed with high art, has got in on the Yeats act. In 1995 ABC's *One Life to Live* sent one of its heroines, Marty Saybrooke, to Inishcrag, an island off the west coast of Ireland. There she met Patrick Thornheart, an implausibly sexy professor of literature from Trinity College Dublin, who provides a textbook demonstration of what 'Irishness' means to the American media. To Aran sweaters, pubs and stories of magical islands where time stands still, Patrick adds the indispensable Irish ingredients of poetry and terror. Scattering lines of Yeats ('You're in Ireland now, and even the milkman quotes Yeats'), he flees the Men of 21, a shadowy paramilitary organization meant to evoke the IRA. Yeats becomes more than verbal decor when Patrick and Marty, after frustrations and delays worthy of those proto-soap-opera characters Tristan and Isolde (to whose expedient of the sword in the bed Patrick refers), finally make love.[23] The scene is orchestrated by two complete recitations of Yeats's not particularly famous love poem, 'Brown Penny'.

I whispered, 'I am too young',
And then, 'I am old enough';
Wherefore I threw a penny
To find out if I might love.
'Go and love, go and love, young man,
If the lady be young and fair'.
Ah, penny, brown penny, brown penny,
I am looped in the loops of her hair. (*Poems* 98)

The Manhattan Barnes and Noble sold out of Yeats's poems the day after this episode was broadcast, and Patrick Thornheart's home page on the Web (now discontinued) used to reproduce the full text of every poem he ever quoted – eight of them by Yeats. During the subsequent convolutions of the plot, the lines 'Ah penny, brown penny, brown penny / I am looped in the loops of her hair' acquired talismanic erotic status. In honour of Yeats's refrain and Thornheart's body, his enthusiastic Internet fan club members called themselves 'Loopers'.

The conclusion suggested by my examples is not a particularly fashionable one. It is that, at least in the case of Yeats, theorists of postmodern culture have somewhat exaggerated the demise of the Author, the dispersal of the canon and the abandonment of 'truth, meaning and history'. Unlike subversive 'zines and art house movies, which have a minority appeal, much mainstream popular culture maintains an 'awkward reverence' (Larkin's phrase) for a Norton Anthology version of the past. Although literacy levels in America are not especially high, most college graduates have taken required Sophomore Literature classes, in which 'The Second Coming' is a perennial standby. (Together with 'The Lake Isle of Innisfree' it frequently appears on the Web pages of those who are fond of launching 'My Favourite Poems' into cyberspace.) Even in a genre – soap opera – that embodies the essence of kitsch, nostalgia for the real thing survives. *One Life to Live* emphasizes the difference between itself and Yeats by granting the superior intensity of poetry; an intensity foreign to the redundant and repetitive aesthetic of soap opera, as the double rendition of 'Brown Penny' emphasizes. If we find the effect sentimental and melodramatic, we may still be intrigued by the way Yeats's poetry functions, and is appreciatively received, within a medium antithetical to his own lyric economy. Perhaps the high-cultural centre does not exactly hold; nevertheless, in Auden's powerful phrase, 'The words of a dead man / Are modified in the guts of the living' (*Poems* 197).

DISCREDITING DE VALERA
Tradition and Modernity

Discussions of politics and culture in Ireland often focus on the relation between tradition and modernity. The booming Irish economy and the concomitant explosion of cultural self-confidence, the retreat of institutionalized religion and the gradual solidification of the precarious peace in the North combine to suggest that Ireland's historical belatedness is itself a thing of the past. According to President Mary MacAleese, Ireland at the beginning of the third millennium is a modern, almost secular state that visibly demonstrates the benefits of EU membership and global capitalism.[1] This apparently uncritical enthusiasm for economic expansion and globalization dismays postcolonial scholars like David Lloyd and Kevin Whelan, who argue that we need to undo the hierarchical binaries that automatically place modernity above tradition, and be suspicious of any narrative of progress that represents history as an overcoming or discarding of the past. Such a narrative, they claim, camouflages a denial of England's responsibility for Ireland's painful history and casts the struggle in the North as an atavistic feud between rival Irish tribes rather than an anti-imperialist war of liberation. Lloyd suggests that the rejection of tradition amounts to complicity with the forces of colonialism, an assent to 'the displacement of indigenous forms of religion, labour, patriarchy and rule by those of colonial modernity' (*Ireland* 2).

Declan Kiberd has also suggested that the deep distrust of recent history displayed in so many contemporary Irish novels and memoirs (*Angela's Ashes*, for example) might be a source of cultural weakness, a refusal to work through the implications of a period too easily perceived as backward and enslaved to tradition. The biographical epic movie *Michael Collins*, Neil Jordan's attempt to do for de Valera what Frank McCourt did for Limerick, provides a concrete example of the modernizing instinct operating in a globally funded work of popular culture. Jordan's film both reflects and confirms a popular mood that rejects the recent past, a period that we may characterize as 'de Valera's Ireland', in favour of an earlier era, the War of Independence, and a hero who was not forced to stand the test of time and office, Michael Collins. Jordan's manoeuvre may be seen as a source of weakness or as proof that, as David Lloyd has suggested, 'the past remains a repertoire of possible developments that never took place.'[2] Within that repertoire of possible developments, Lloyd himself has in mind the Irish socialist worker's republic advocated by James Connolly; but the popularity of Jordan's film in Ireland suggests that quite different visions of 'what might have been' are more congenial to contemporary political taste.

The idea that cinema in Ireland can be used as an uncomplicated barometer of social and cultural change needs preliminary qualification. Even the term 'Irish film' is a contested one: cultural critics consider movies financed by American corporations and governed by Hollywood narrative conventions less authentically 'Irish' than the work of indigenous film-makers like, say, Cathal Black or Thaddeus O'Sullivan. The cinema going public, however, which is less fussy about such distinctions, embraced Jordan's populist Hollywood hybrid *Michael Collins* as the Irish equivalent of *The Birth of a Nation*. They turned out in thousands, not just to see it (its box office takings in Ireland have been surpassed only by *Jurassic Park*)[3] but also to participate in its making. Despite its graphic depiction of violence, the censor granted the film a General certificate, in recognition of what he called its national and pedagogical importance (O'Toole, 'Man').

When all the controversies about anachronistic car bombs, anti-British prejudice and covert support for the contemporary IRA had died away, it could fairly be said that *Michael Collins* had a lasting impact on the Irish self-image. In an *Irish Times* millennium poll conducted three years after the film's 1996 debut, Collins was voted Person of the Century. Such polls are not infallible cultural barometers any more than films are, but it is significant that 12.7 per cent of the respondents picked Collins, whose nearest rivals were Nelson Mandela, Gandhi, Hitler, Mother Teresa, Einstein, Martin Luther King and John F. Kennedy. Ninth in the poll, with a mere 2.82 per cent of the vote, was Eamon de Valera. Perhaps this reversal of accepted pieties reflects merely the political prejudices of readers of the *Irish Times*. Nevertheless it also suggests a public re-evaluation not only of Collins himself, but also of his rival, who dominated the social and political horizons of Ireland throughout the mid-century and beyond, and who assiduously kept the memory of his former comrade out of sight.

Like Tim Pat Coogan's 1990 biography of Collins, which was one of its main historical sources, Jordan's film closes with de Valera's prophecy, 'In the fullness of time history will record the greatness of Collins and it will be recorded at my expense'.[4] Jordan dedicates himself to fulfilling this prediction. Of course, the traditional narrative formula demands that the hero should have an antagonist, and, when the British withdraw from the South of Ireland, de Valera presents Jordan with a satisfying replacement.[5] The brilliantly neurotic and Machiavellian performance of the Englishman Alan Rickman strengthens our impression of de Valera's villainy. But more than structural aesthetics or the ethnic irony of casting is involved here. At stake in the discrediting of de Valera is no less than a redefinition of what it means to be Irish.

De Valera, the only surviving signatory of the Proclamation of the Republic, entered the Dáil in 1927, became Taoiseach in 1932, and held this position, with two brief intervals, until Seán Lemass took over in 1959. Between

1959 and 1973 he served as President. Ageing and blind, he functioned primarily as a figurehead, a symbol of the Republic. He lived on, however, not only in his party machine, Fianna Fáil, but in his Constitution of 1937, which enshrined the 'special position' of the Catholic Church in the Irish state, asserted the territorial claim of the Irish Republic upon the six counties of the North and attempted to keep women in their place within the home. If de Valera was, as the subtitle of Tim Pat Coogan's 1993 biography suggests, 'The Man Who Was Ireland', then Ireland was constitutionally Catholic, aspirationally united and devoted to traditional family life. We may laugh when we hear that whenever de Valera needed to ascertain the wishes of the Irish people he looked into his own heart; but perhaps this claim was not entirely ludicrous? Today his vision of a land of frugal comforts, cosy homesteads and comely maidens is guaranteed to produce a sophisticated sneer. Nevertheless, something in this rural, Gaelic, essentially asexual Utopia responded to the national desire to turn away from the cruelties committed by both sides in the Civil War by touching base with an identity perceived, however mistakenly, as originary and authentic. After all, if Ireland were to become culturally indistinguishable from England, where would be the justification for all that blood? Although de Valera had numerous political opponents and personal enemies, his narrative of Irish identity gradually became hegemonic: it was shared by Fianna Fáil and Fine Gael alike. He brought the rural pieties of Corkery's Hidden Ireland out of the closet in order to censor another Ireland, one that was less easy to contemplate with equanimity.

This other hidden Ireland was haunted not only by the unappeased ghost of Michael Collins, and other bitter legacies from the Civil War, but by sexual and physical abuse of women and children. It is ironic that the man who did most to ensure that these hidden things stayed below the threshold of consciousness was himself the product of secrecy, neglect and abandonment. Whether or not he was illegitimate,[6] and whatever the motives of his mother in sending her three-year-old son back from America to Ireland to live with her family, the early life of Eamon de Valera does not read like the rural idyll propounded in his notorious St Patrick's day speech. Thomas McCarthy's poem 'De Valera's Childhood' speaks of his 'sad youth', defined by poverty and the dutiful performance of rural labour (*Sorrow Garden* 15). His Constitution, designed to ensure that mothers 'shall not be obliged by economic necessity to engage in labour to the neglect of their duties in the home' (Article 41.2.2, *Bunreacht* 138), idealizes the nuclear family in reaction to his own dubious legitimacy and lack of a traditional two-parent household.[7]

As a symbol, then, 'de Valera' is both over-determined and contradictory. Politically, he represents the divisions of the Civil War, but in his continual if ineffective opposition to partition he also embodies the united Republic. Although opponents of contemporary Republicanism perceive him as a symbol of a cause they detest, his ruthless suppression of the IRA during the thirties complicates this identification. His insistence on preserving Irish neutrality during World War II, which occasioned his notorious visit of con-dolence to the German Embassy on Hitler's death, is sometimes blamed for the period of moral ambiguity known as 'the Emergency'. Economically, he repre-sents austerity: the austerity necessitated by his prosecution of the economic war against England in the thirties. His enthusiasm for the Irish language iden-tifies him with an experiment in linguistic engineering that many young people found oppressive or hypocritical, or both. Socially, he is the secular expression of the dominance of the Catholic Church in the life of the state, the 'lay Car-dinal', as Coogan calls him. Despite his marriage, his children and his long relationship with Kathleen Connell (dramatist Tom Mac Intyre suggests that during his visit to America he was 'devotedly fucking [his] devoted secretary' [187]), he is frequently represented as a priggish spiritual celibate, a spoiled priest, indifferent if not outright hostile to women and to sexuality in general. He is most often caricatured as a bespectacled, bony schoolmaster.

In *Good Evening, Mr. Collins*, which opened in October 1995 while *Michael Collins* was in production, Mac Intyre anticipated Jordan's critique of de Valera: 'Even as a young lad, I had an intuitive awareness of the cheerless tyrant in him, and, intimately linked, a perfervid feeling for the Cavalier in Collins'. Yet Mac Intyre allows de Valera's contradictions to express themselves through costume: he wears a mortarboard and academic gown for his lecture on Machiavelli and a clerical soutane for his last interview with the doomed Collins, but he also appears in a Chippewa head dress and the 'immaculate' evening clothes of a concert pianist (186, 219, 209, 216). While Collins was still alive, the play implies, a 'lubricious' de Valera was not averse to feeling the texture of 'comely' Kitty Kiernan's stockings, but, after his rival's death, 'De Valera slowly turned to stone, limestone, blue limestone' (210–11, 231).

Jordan's film focuses primarily on de Valera as a warmonger, the man who split his country in two, and it makes the case against him by distorting cer-tain crucial facts about his adversary Collins. The closing caption asserts that Collins died 'in an attempt to remove the gun from Irish politics'. Jordan can only make this Utopian and pacific claim by suppressing the information that, even as he fought to uphold the Treaty in the South, Collins was organizing gun-running to the North in an attempt to defend the beleaguered Catholic minority.[8] This oversimplified portrait of Collins as a reformed revolutionary appealed to a modern Irish nation weary of the Troubles, hopeful about the ongoing peace process and willing to make do with the truncated Republic that de Valera never accepted. But by choosing to depict the British in an uncompromisingly negative fashion, Jordan disguised the essentially moder-ate political agenda of his film. Both sides were fooled: British commentators were too indignant at being seen as murderous thugs to note that in con-demning de Valera's obstinacy over the Treaty *Michael Collins* aligns itself ide-ologically against the Republican tradition. *An Phoblacht*'s reviewer was too impressed by the representation of the British massacre at Croke Park to worry about the anti-Republican implications of the film as a whole.

In approaching the two thorniest questions about de Valera's behaviour – why did he go to America for a year during the war against the British, and why did he send Collins to negotiate with Lloyd George and Churchill instead of going himself – Jordan indulges his tendency to eroticize political choices. 'People rationalise their actions, but their deepest motivations are often secret and politics often masks other things', he has said.[9] Jordan represents de Valera's decisions as resulting not only from conscious political jealousy of Collins, but also from unconscious resentment of Collins's intense and intimate relationship with Harry Boland. Consequently the film suggests, without much historical sanction, that the Civil War was rooted in the dynamics of homo-eroticism. The primary love interest in Jordan's movies is frequently between men: *Michael Collins* takes up where *The Crying Game* and *Interview with the Vampire* leave off. Unproven rumours of homosexual promiscuity have long surrounded Collins, and Jordan omitted his well-documented heterosexual affair with Lady Hazel Lavery,[10] which had already been the central subject of the sentimental film *Beloved Enemy* (1936). His chaste involvement with Kitty Kiernan provides the sole love interest, but her importance pales beside Collins's emotional tie to Boland, which Jordan represents from the beginning in marital terms. Early in the film they bump into a bride who has nothing to contribute to the narrative but her symbolic importance. 'Maybe we should settle down?' says Collins, and Boland ripostes, 'Just the two of us?' Collins, Boland and even de Valera are shown in bed together, but always with their clothes on: like many contemporary artists Jordan flirts with homoeroticism as a fashionable shock tactic, rather than as a serious sexual choice.

For example, he gives a high camp account of de Valera's escape from Lincoln Jail, an episode solemnly celebrated in numerous school textbooks like Colm O'Loingsigh's 1983 *Pathways in History*, where it appears between the exploits of Florence Nightingale and Grace Darling. In less hagiographical contemporary newspaper accounts, Jordan discovered a cruel sexual metaphor for de Valera's character: 'The jail, apparently, was trawled by hookers so they [Collins and Boland] dressed de Valera in a fur coat and feathered hat and pretended to be two punters as they whisked him away' (*Michael Collins* 68–9). Running towards the getaway vehicle, de Valera exclaims, 'All I'm missing is the high heels'. As he sits in the hijacked taxi between Boland and Collins, de Valera the transvestite whore occupies a feminine position that symbolically parallels that of Kitty Kiernan, the woman they both love;[11] Collins even serenades his chief with the line 'I'll take you home again, Kathleen'. But unlike Kitty, who would like to keep both men happy, de Valera intends to come between Collins and Boland, and does so when he takes Boland with him to America. So Collins loses his best friend to the man his opponents liked to call 'the long hoor' or 'the cute hoor', and his prophetic joke in the taxi, 'Some died for Ireland, but Dev he whored for Ireland', becomes bitter reality. This is hardly the stuff of which school textbooks are made. Boland did indeed begin as Collins's ally and ended as de Valera's, but

Jordan creates a pathologically jealous rationale for de Valera's actions. When Collins objects to Boland's proposed trip to America on the grounds that 'I can't run a war without him', de Valera grimly replies, 'You could run it without me' (140).

On de Valera's return from America the rivalry between the two men escalates, and his sending Collins to London to negotiate the Treaty is represented as a Machiavellian set-up. In his Diary about the making of *Michael Collins*, Jordan calls this decision the 'mystery' of the story (*Michael Collins* 13), but there is no mystery about the film. De Valera condemns Collins to bring back the bad news that the Republic was never on the agenda; he must be tainted by the inevitable compromise while de Valera deliberately keeps himself above the fray: 'We need to keep a final arbiter in reserve . . . That will be the Irish people. And me as president of the Irish Republic' (176). Alan Rickman delivers this line with an unpleasantly self-satisfied little smirk.

Jordan, who was born in 1951, speaks as the representative of a generation for whom the elderly de Valera was the oppressive symbol of an Ireland that they wanted to escape. He is aware, however, that older people may see things differently. His short story, 'A Love', which opens in Dublin on the day of de Valera's funeral in August 1975, engages directly with this complex issue of double remembrance. His hero, Neil, encounters a former lover, a woman twenty-four years older than himself, and 'thought of how we would have two different memories of him. He was your father's generation, the best and worst you said. I remembered your father's civil war pistol, black and very real' (*Night* 103). Echoing Yeats's 'The Second Coming', Jordan leaves open the question of whether de Valera was the best or the worst, but his mention of the Civil War pistol leads the reader towards 'the worst / Are full of passionate intensity'. As the drums of the President's funeral cortège draw nearer, Neil observes, 'I knew I was out of step, it was all militarism now'. Ignoring the fact that de Valera outlawed the IRA in 1936, Jordan blames him, as the incarnation of the undivided Republic, for their current violence in the North of Ireland. It 'was swelling, the militarism I had just learned of before, in the school textbooks. Then I remembered something else about him, the man who had died, he had been the centre of the school textbooks, his angular face and his thirties collar and his fist raised in a gesture of defiance' (*Night* 105).

This visual image is recreated in *Michael Collins* when, before the Civil War begins, de Valera gives his notorious speech: 'The Volunteers may have to wade through Irish blood, through the blood of some members of the government, in order to get Irish freedom'. Alan Rickman's performance is, as Jordan notes (*Michael Collins* 58), uncannily accurate, and the words are taken almost verbatim from de Valera's speeches of March 1921, which were widely interpreted as incitements to civil war (Coogan, *De Valera* 310–11). Like *Michael Collins*, 'A Love' draws explicit parallels between the Civil War and the recent Troubles, and blames de Valera for both: 'Then I heard the band outside . . . playing the old nationalist tunes to a slow tempo. I felt I was watching an animal dying through the plate-glass window, an animal that was huge, murderous, contradictory' (*Night* 111). In contrast, the woman of an older generation remembers her successful indoctrination by her father: she was 'taught to idolise him, everyone was. I remember standing at meetings, holding my father's hand, waving a tricolour, shouting Up Dev' (113).

Although de Valera still retains many partisans from the era to which the woman in Jordan's story belongs, and even among the younger generation, Jordan's hostile analysis is far from unique. Southern Irish writers who distrust the contemporary IRA find de Valera a conveniently double-edged symbol: socially and economically he represents what is wrong with the South; politically he represents what is wrong with the North. Under both aspects he stands for tradition rather than modernity. Like 'A Love', Thomas McCarthy's poem 'State Funeral' contrasts the reactions of different generations to de Valera's funeral. McCarthy was born in 1954 and was therefore twenty-one years old when de Valera was buried in August 1975. As his family watches the funeral on television, his father's heroic memories of a great leader are countered by the resentful boredom of his son. We know from other autobiographical poems like 'The President's Men' that McCarthy's father was a Fianna Fáil activist and that campaigns and political meetings, on which the adult poet now looks back with an ironical eye, punctuated his youth. 'Party Shrine' remembers his father in the summer of 1966, the fiftieth anniversary of the Easter Rising, cleaning away the weeds and the pigeon droppings from a 1916 memorial:

> Weeds know nothing about the Party
> or how it emerged, genie-like,
> out of an abandoned shell case.
> The weeds and their friends the shitting
> pigeons want to bury this shrine
> in a single summer.
> I am holding the shovel for my father
> while he reads inscriptions on brass:
> sixteen golden names of the Party,
> the twenty six grammatical flaws. (*Non-Aligned Storyteller* 15)

With hindsight acquired after years of conflict in the North, the son chooses to emphasize the party's violent roots in 'an abandoned shell case' and the fact that, for de Valera and Fianna Fáil, as for the contemporary IRA, the twenty-six-county Republic was a betrayal, a grammatical flaw in the golden rhetoric of the Rising. McCarthy is evidently on the side of the shitting pigeons.

'State Funeral' takes for its epigraph the words of another party man faced with a memorial: in the Glasnevin episode of Joyce's *Ulysses* Joe Hynes, the loyal follower of Parnell, urges a quick visit to the chief's grave. Although his friend Mr Power repeats the myth that Parnell's coffin was filled with stones and that 'one day he will come again', Hynes regretfully concedes that 'Parnell will never come again. . . . He's there, all that was mortal of him. Peace to his ashes' (*Ulysses* 6.924.27, quoted in McCarthy, *First Convention* 10). In the context of de Valera's funeral, these lines have ambiguous implications: the comparison between Parnell and de Valera as authentic Irish heroes is established, but so is their joint irrelevance to the Irish future. Neither will enjoy a Second Coming. Moreover, the Civil War recollections of McCarthy's father in the second stanza of the poem remind us that both Parnell and de Valera split their respective political parties in two, and might be seen as symbols of disunity as well as of resistance.

In his title and epigraph, McCarthy does complex allusive work, mobilizing two literary giants against a political one. He traps de Valera between Joyce's *Ulysses*, a book of which he would never have approved, and a poem by his most determined cultural opponent, W. B. Yeats. McCarthy's title, 'State Funeral', together with the mention of Parnell in the line immediately below it, metonymically evoke Yeats's poem, 'Parnell's Funeral'. In the aftermath of the Blueshirt episode, Yeats attacked de Valera by scornfully asserting his inferiority to Parnell:

> Had de Valéra eaten Parnell's heart
> No loose-lipped demagogue had won the day,
> No civil rancour torn the land apart. (*Poems* 280)

Yeats's negative judgement on de Valera as a 'loose-lipped demagogue' and the author of 'civil rancour' shadows and questions the 'prayers of memory' reverently uttered by McCarthy's father.

The McCarthy family watches the funeral on television, enacting a secular 'boxed ritual' that both symbolizes the forces that were modernizing Ireland in ways of which de Valera was extremely suspicious[12] and provides an ersatz substitute for the religious ritual of interment that de Valera had made particularly his own. After watching so many political funerals at which de Valera had presided,

> There was a native *deja-vu*
> Of Funeral when we settled against the couch
> On our sunburnt knees. We gripped mugs of tea
> Tightly and soaked the television spectacle;
> The boxed ritual in our living room.

Although the family is still on its knees, the religious ritual is contained and turned to 'spectacle' by the modernity of the method by which it is transmitted. The 'prayers' at this funeral are the political and secular memories of a Fianna Fáil man:

> My father recited prayers of memory,
> Of monster meetings, blazing tar-barrels

> Planted outside Free-State homes, the Broy-
> Harriers pushing through a crowd, Blueshirts;
> And, after the war, De Valera's words
> Making Churchill's imperial palette blur.

Unlike his father, the young poet has no recollections of those monster meetings at which de Valera suggested that Irishmen might have to wade through each other's blood, nor of the subsequent Civil War in which 'blazing tar-barrels / [Were] Planted outside Free-State homes'. He did not experience the later clashes between de Valera's Broy Harriers and O'Duffy's Blueshirts, which might be seen as a reprise of the Civil War in a different guise. Born in 1954, he missed one of de Valera's finest moments, his dignified broadcast rebuttal of Churchill's splenetic attack on Irish neutrality just after the conclusion of World War II. For him, as for many people of his generation, de Valera embodies less the turbulent politics of the foundation of the Irish state than the stereotype of schoolmasterly austerity; the teacher of mathematics is a synonym for religiosity, frugal comfort and rural industry, the absolute antithesis of modernity:

> What I remember is one decade of darkness,
> A mind-stifling boredom; long summers
> For blackberry picking and churning cream,
> Winters for saving timber or setting lines
> And snares: none of the joys of here and now
> With its instant jam, instant heat and cream.

In a different memoir of childhood, the 'long summers for blackberry picking and churning cream' might be romanticized; here they are brusquely rejected in favour of the 'instant' pleasures of modern urban life: jam and cream off the supermarket shelves, central heating and of course the 'boxed' entertainment of the television. His father's 'prayers of memory' are reduced to a 'decade' (a decade of the rosary, perhaps) of 'darkness' and 'mind-stifling boredom'

> It was a landscape for old men. Today
> They lowered the tallest one, tidied him
> Away while his people watched quietly.
> In the end he had retreated to the first dream,
> Caning truth. I think of his austere grandeur;
> Taut sadness, like old heroes he had imagined. (First Convention 10)

Reversing the opening of Yeats's 'Sailing to Byzantium', which describes the Ireland of the mid-twenties as 'no country for old men', McCarthy designates the Ireland of de Valera 'a landscape for old men'. His funeral is no last apotheosis, no occasion for the fall of Parnell's blazing star or transformation into Yeats's exotic golden bird, but an affirmation of his fundamental irrelevance to a country that, McCarthy implies, has modernized itself since Seán Lemass took over as Taoiseach in 1959. In a deliberately trivial metaphor that resonates with the idea of frugal comfort and good housekeeping, he is not 'laid to rest' but 'tidied away'.

McCarthy concludes his poem on a dissonance. He suggests that in old age de Valera 'retreated to the first dream / Caning truth'. De Valera is often stereotyped as the eternal schoolmaster (a writer has only to make his protagonist a teacher of mathematics and his ghost is automatically evoked), but what does 'caning truth' imply? Repressing the desires of the young? Denying 'the joys of here and now'? Falsifying the historical record, especially with regard to his most bitter rival, Michael Collins? The poem juxtaposes this sour ambiguity with a final reluctant affirmation, as the speaker acknowledges that de Valera's 'austere grandeur' and 'Taut sadness' align him with the 'old heroes' of Irish myth.

McCarthy's attitude to de Valera allows room for unreconciled contradictions: the possibility that this supreme politician was also a great man, a genuine hero. The subsequent death of McCarthy's Fianna Fáil father, feelingly commemorated in the 1981 volume *The Sorrow Garden*, may be connected with the four poems about de Valera also contained in that collection. As we shall see when we turn to Jordan's novel *The Past*, the idea of fatherhood stands in metonymic relation to the idea of de Valera. 'De Valera's Childhood' is almost wholly positive in tone:

> Lloyd George was wary of his
> fox-like comings and goings:
>
> 'all that is truly dark
> and furtive and violent in
>
> the Irish mind' was what
> he thought. He should have
>
> known that such an animal
> existed only in colonial
>
> thought. Our home fox wanted
> to hunt in its own word-wood. (*Sorrow Garden* 15–16)

In rejecting the negative image of de Valera as 'furtive and violent', McCarthy politicizes Ted Hughes's 'The Thought-Fox'. Lloyd George's fox is a product of 'colonial / thought', which is incapable of understanding the influence of the 'folklore and folk-solitude' that the youthful de Valera absorbed on his dutiful morning milk rounds. But in 'Returning to de Valera's Cottage' ambiguity surfaces once more. The village where de Valera once lived is represented as 'brighter' without the weight of his intimidating legacy:

> not that he was held in awe,
> but the walking evidence of

> so intense a life frightened
> the whole village and kept them from serious thought.

Unlike many of de Valera's harsher critics, McCarthy speaks from within the culture of Fianna Fáil even as he interrogates it, and his evocation of de Valera's intensity of purpose as both admirable and alienating rings true. A pilgrimage to de Valera's rural roots is an acknowledgement of his constitutive effect upon the Irish psyche, both for good and ill:

> In finding his cottage we found a life that was
> inside ourselves. A small
> moment of sorrow. A tear
> riding down the glass of
> our eyes like blood fall-
> ing from a bullet wound.
> We kicked the heap of weeds
> with our heels and cursed the narrowness of the path.
> *(Sorrow Garden* 17)

The tear that turns into blood and the narrowness of the path symbolize the negative consequences of so intense a life: Civil War and social conservatism. But McCarthy adds a last, dialectical stanza about an 'old English / General' who dons 'a black tie for his / dead adversary' and invokes time as the solvent for historical wounds: 'After all, he was old, / he was a soldier. We both pulled through our wars' *(Sorrow Garden* 18). If the English can forgive de Valera, the implication is, the Irish should also be able to come to terms with what he embodied. McCarthy is too deeply engaged with de Valera's legacy to discount entirely the value of 'so intense a life'.

Paul Durcan takes a less nuanced view: for him de Valera's sexual 'narrowness' and his Republican politics are two sides of the same false coin. Some of the reasons for Durcan's political hostility to de Valera may be deduced from the title of his 1978 collection, *Sam's Cross.* Sam's Cross, a small village in West Cork, was the birthplace of Michael Collins. In 'Lament for Major General Emmet Dalton', which appears in the same volume, Durcan regrets that the Irish people have 'disowned' Dalton, who was a close friend and ally of Collins:

> Disremembering Michael Collins also
> Whom you held in your trembling arms
> As he lay dying at the Mouth of Flowers.
> *(Sam's Cross* 62; *Selected* 99; versions differ)

At the end of the poem Durcan rises to an unaccustomed pitch of rhetorical seriousness. Collins's body had to be brought back to Dublin from Cork by steamer, because the railway lines had been cut. Borrowing a phrase from Mr Casey's lament in *Portrait of the Artist as a Young Man*, 'Poor Parnell! . . . My dead king!' (*Portrait* 39), Durcan conjures up the image of Collins as the lost leader and Dalton as his faithful lieutenant:

> At dusk, on the River Lee, a steamer
> Steams out to sea with a dead King's coffin on board,
> And, beside it, keeping guard, the dead King's young friend;
> Whose habit was truth, and whose style was courage.
>   (*Sam's Cross* 62; *Selected* 100; versions differ)

Parnell is a flexible analogue, to be applied to de Valera or Collins according to political taste. Durcan admires Parnell and thus identifies Collins as a second 'dead king'.

Given his attitude to Collins, it is unlikely that Durcan would do de Valera justice. In 'Making Love outside Áras an Uachtaráin', also from *Sam's Cross*, Durcan yokes de Valera's 'green' politics to his illiberal social policies. Although it was his Cumann na nGaedheal opponents who introduced censorship in 1929, de Valera showed no desire to increase the freedoms of the press or of literature. Evoking the stereotype of an out-of-touch old man repressing the spontaneity of the boys and girls, Durcan constructs de Valera as 'censorious' in every meaning of the word:

> When I was a boy, myself and my girl
> Used to bicycle up to the Phoenix Park;
> Outside the gates we used lie in the grass
> Making love outside Áras an Uachtaráin.
>
> Often I wondered what de Valera would have thought
> Inside in his ivory tower
> If he knew that we were in his green, green grass
> Making love outside Áras an Uachtaráin.
>
> Because the odd thing was – oh how odd it was –
> We both revered Irish patriots
> And we dreamed our dreams of a green, green flag
> Making love outside Áras an Uachtaráin.
>   (*Sam's Cross* 47; *Selected* 85; versions differ slightly)

Durcan's speaker emphasizes that in his youth his opposition to de Valera was on sexual rather than political grounds: even as they lay in the 'green, green grass' with their minds on other things, both he and his lover shared a reverence for green flags and Irish patriots. As the parenthetical phrase 'oh how odd it was' demonstrates, Durcan has changed his mind since: his abhorrence of the IRA is well documented (in 'Margaret Thatcher Joins IRA', for example), and abhorrence of the IRA translates poetically into disdain for de Valera.

In the concluding stanzas of 'Making Love outside Áras an Uachtaráin', Durcan invokes the ancient Irish story of Diarmuid and Gráinne to expose the hypocrisy of censorship: de Valera promoted the Irish language and loved the old legends, but, according to Durcan, he would not have countenanced the remarkable erotic boldness of Gráinne, who abandons her suitor, Finn, 'a man that is older than my father' (Cross 373), to seduce and abduct the handsome young warrior Diarmuid. Like the original Diarmuid and Gráinne, who flee from the aged Finn's jealous pursuit through woods and mountains, the speaker and his girl pursue their illicit sexual union out of doors:

> But even had our names been Diarmaid and Gráinne
> We doubted de Valera's approval
> For a poet's son and a judge's daughter
> Making love outside Áras an Uachtaráin.
>
> I see him now in the heat-haze of the day
> Blindly stalking us down;
> And, levelling an ancient rifle, he says 'Stop
> Making love outside Áras an Uachtaráin'.
> (*Sam's Cross* 47; *Selected* 85; versions differ slightly)

The story that while he was interned in England de Valera memorized the whole of Merriman's bawdy Irish poem *The Midnight Court* suggests that Durcan is not being entirely fair, but the Ireland that in 1936 banned Kate O'Brien's *The Land of Spices* on account of its poignantly brief evocation of homo-eroticism, 'She saw her father and Etienne in the embrace of love', was unmistakably de Valera's Ireland. Durcan imagines the President as a modern Finn, using his 'ancient' rifle (a relic of the Civil War like the old pistol in Jordan's 'A Love') to 'stalk down' Diarmuid and Gráinne (the poet and his girl) as they make love on the grass outside his official residence. His political aggression is indistinguishable from his sexual intolerance. Inside his ivory tower he disapproves of 'the young / In one another's arms' (Yeats, *Poems* 193).

Not until the election of Mary Robinson in 1990 did Durcan return poetically to the Phoenix Park. In 'Making Love *inside* Áras an Uachtaráin' he interprets the President's symbolic decision to keep a light burning in the window of the Áras as an act of love towards the diaspora:

> At the left of the upper storey of its portico
> The light in the kitchen window
> Not only to the future of the unknown citizen
>
> But to the actuality of the unknown exile
> Whether he or she be a bus driver in Cleveland
> Or drilling for water in North-East Brazil. (*Greetings* 225)

The Áras is no longer de Valera's masculine ivory tower, but a modern Newgrange whose feminine 'solar orifice' symbolically proclaims 'Power is conditional on love'. Durcan's own 'love' for Mary Robinson, fully documented in the

last section of *Greetings to Our Friends in Brazil*, provides him with a poetic anti-
dote to de Valera/Finn's loveless wielding of 'power' over Diarmuid and Gráinne.

Julia O'Faolain's 1980 novel, *No Country for Young Men*, also founds itself
on the legend of Diarmuid and Gráinne, and contains a figure from the past,
the Republican politician Owen O'Malley, who is a portrait of de Valera.[13]
(The historical de Valera is invoked occasionally in the narrative, but all his
stereotypical attributes – frugality, hostility to women, readiness to wade
through Irish blood, ability to discern the people's wishes by looking into his
own heart – are given to O'Malley.) O'Faolain, whose father Sean O'Faolain
wrote a biography of de Valera, reacted against the romantic nationalism of
her parents, who themselves began as ardent supporters of the Republican
cause but subsequently became disillusioned.[14] She shares many of her
images of and judgements upon de Valera with McCarthy, Durcan and Jordan.
Like McCarthy, she turns Yeats's famous line 'That is no country for old men'
inside out. 'That country' is Ireland in the twenties and again in the seventies,
and both of these profoundly interconnected timescapes prove fatal to her
Irish-American 'young men', Sparky Driscoll and James Duffy. James Duffy,
the Diarmuid of the nineteen seventies, is seduced by Grania, the wife of
Michael O'Malley. Michael is the grandson of Owen O'Malley the patriot hero
and de Valera lookalike. Like Finn, this dead 'old man' frustrates the modern
love story through the violent actions of his political heirs, his nephew Owen
Roe (another Charlie Haughey figure who drives a Mercedes and was involved
in the 1970 Arms Trial) and Owen Roe's IRA sidekick, the sexless woman-
hater Patsy Flynn. Owen O'Malley also dominates the contemporary cultural
climate that O'Faolain evokes and critiques. 'How *did* you honour a grandfather who, having helped forge change through violence, ended his days
guarding the outcome from any further change?' wonders Michael (*No Country* 44), even as he plans to write a biography of 'the Grandda, Prime Mover
in his own and the country's life' (49).

O'Faolain's theological metaphor for de Valera is one that Neil Jordan will
take up and develop in his novel *The Past*, and, as we have seen, it has wide
cultural currency. Owen O'Malley has tried the Jesuit seminary before becoming a revolutionary: he is a 'spoilt priest' (*No Country* 121). De Valera did consider the priesthood, but was not encouraged by the three members of the
clergy to whom he confided his potential vocation (Coogan, *De Valera* 36–8).
Nevertheless the attribution has stuck, presumably because of its psychological and social explanatory power rather than its historical veracity. O'Faolain
develops the 'spoilt priest' idea as a way of indicting the subsequent development of Irish social policy. Explaining why Owen tried the seminary in the
first place, his sister-in-law Judith Clancy says, 'There was a great strike here
which became a lock-out and the people were starving. A lot of people started
singing the "Red Flag" and Owen turned his thoughts to heaven' (*No Country*
258). While the timing of Owen's vocation is not historically accurate (de
Valera dropped the idea of the priesthood in 1906, and the Dublin lock-out

was in 1913), the opposition that Judith posits between communism and the clergy is incontrovertible. In 1913 de Valera was a member of the St Vincent de Paul society, which was 'used during the lock-out as a strike-breaking weapon, being instructed by the Church authorities not to distribute aid to the families of strikers' (De Valera 51).

The 'spoilt priest' trope also works as shorthand for Owen O'Malley's attitude towards sexuality and as a way of explaining the conservative section on the family in de Valera's Constitution of 1937: 'The State recognises that by her life within the home, woman gives to the State a support without which the common good cannot be achieved' (Article 41.2.1, Bunreacht 136). As a young man Owen is engaged to Kathleen Clancy, but the American Sparky Driscoll thinks that he 'doesn't really like women at all', and speculates that he may be a closet homosexual (No Country 299). After Sparky's death, Owen marries Kathleen and has numerous children, but Judith, who intuits that her own femininity repels him, thinks he 'should have stayed in the monastery. . . . Now he was stuck with matrimony which he clearly suffered in a Pauline spirit' (192). The shadow of the Constitution hangs over Judith's observation that 'Women, for Owen, belonged in a domestic sphere' (190). If de Valera was not a supporter of socialism, he had even less sympathy with feminism. The novel is designed to bear out Judith's warning that, after independence, 'The men in this country would never let the women have a say' (213).

Judith herself, who links the time-worlds of the novel as a dedicated young Republican in the twenties and a dotty old nun in the seventies, provides the image that conveys this truth most forcefully. Although her buried memories contain the novel's central secret, and although she witnesses its climactic murder, Judith is a Cassandra whom no one believes, a Kathleen ni Houlihan who will never again walk the walk of a queen, a madwoman incarcerated in the attic of convent life by the brother-in-law, Owen O'Malley, about whom she knows too much.[15] Figuratively, Eamon de Valera is her most powerful oppressor: he forces her to remain in the convent, and she suspects that he ordered the electroshock treatment that has destroyed her dangerous memories and rendered her harmless to him. Judith's decline from intelligent and committed young woman to brain-damaged recluse is matched by that of her sister: the formerly lively political activist Kathleen is worn down by her 'life within the home', which consists of an absent husband who does not love her and seven children to look after. Together, Judith and Kathleen embody the cultural consequences of de Valera's strict political adherence to the social teachings of the Catholic Church. Their niece Grania O'Malley, who decides to indulge in a pleasurable illicit affair with James Duffy, defies powerful cultural sanctions. Irish women are either virgins or mothers; those who pursue an independent sexual life must be whores.

Although many Irish women played their part in the struggle for freedom, the promise of the Declaration of the Republic – to cherish all the children of the nation equally – was not fulfilled either in the Free State or the Republic that was declared in 1948. Gender fuses with class and political allegiance as Owen O'Malley tells Sparky Driscoll that the anti-Treaty diehards have a right to impose their will upon the will of the majority: 'The "people" are clay. You can do what you like in their name but, as Aristotle said of men and women, the formative idea comes from the male and the clay is female; passive, mere potentiality. . . . *We* are their virile soul' (*No Country* 314). The notorious passage from Aristotle that Owen quotes is included in O'Faolain's collection of writings on women, *Not in God's Image* (1973). She opens this book with a less well-known passage by a medieval French monk in which the female body is downgraded from clay to excrement:

> If her bowels and flesh were cut open, you would see what filth is covered by her white skin. If a fine crimson cloth covered a pile of foul dung, would anyone be foolish enough to love the dung because of it? . . . There is no plague which monks should dread more than woman: the soul's death. (*Not* xii)

In the novel, Grania O'Malley reflects that Irishmen's attitudes to sex have been formed by their clerical education. 'Monastic tradition described women as a bag of shit and it followed that sexual release into such a receptacle was a topic about as fit for sober discussion as a bowel movement' (*No Country* 155). Owen O'Malley's male descendants, Grania's husband Michael and her uncle Owen Roe, the first frigid and the second sexually voracious, are both products of the same anti-feminist tradition. Owen O'Malley himself, who thinks 'maidenly modesty was one of the ancestral virtues which he hoped would flourish in the new, free, and Gaelic Ireland' (317), is the epitome of Irish patriarchy.

Few historians would defend de Valera's conduct in repudiating the Treaty Collins had negotiated, and thus playing his part in precipitating the Civil War, but, as the writings of McCarthy, O'Faolain and Durcan demonstrate, in demonizing de Valera Jordan's *Michael Collins* took its place among a pre-existing group of texts that were concerned not only with his politics but with his social, religious and economic legacies. Like many successful creators of popular culture, Jordan was riding a wave that had been long gathering and that he did nothing to make; his skill (or his luck) was a function of good timing. Although his portrait of the Founding Father raised some eyebrows, apart from his granddaughter Síle de Valera surprisingly few members of Fianna Fáil objected publicly to Jordan's demolition job on the creator of their party. Historical revisionism, which set out to discredit the truth-claims of the de Valera narrative as established in such texts as Dorothy Macardle's *The Irish Republic*, had created a favourable climate for a political reassessment of 'the long fellow' himself. Although historians like Roy Foster, Paul Bew and Ruth Dudley Edwards objected strongly to aspects of *Michael Collins*, it was Jordan's negative depiction of the British, and glorification of his hero's anti-imperialist struggle, that drew their attention. On his hostile representation of de Valera, of which presumably they approved, most revisionists were silent. The same was true of English critics, who thought the film should have been re-entitled 'Brits Behaving Badly' but didn't object when de Valera was shown behaving badly too. De Valera was also unfortunate in his latest biographer, Tim Pat Coogan, who despite (or perhaps because of) his long tenure as the editor of de Valera's paper, the *Irish Press*, produced in 1993 an extremely unflattering assessment of his boss's effect on Irish political and social life.

Nevertheless, had Jordan's film been shot when he first proposed it, in 1982, it might have received a cooler welcome. Although the 'special position' of the Catholic Church had been removed from the Irish Constitution in 1972, in the eighties the time for a thorough social and religious reassessment of de Valera's legacy was not yet ripe. In 1983 the Republic voted by a two-thirds majority to insert in its Constitution a clause outlawing abortion. In 1984 the Ann Lovett and Kerry Babies cases lifted the veil of secrecy and silence that surrounded unwanted teenage pregnancy but produced no immediate change. (I discuss these incidents more fully in the next chapter.) In 1986 a proposal to permit divorce was defeated in a referendum. Nell McCafferty declared that the eighties were a terrible time for women in Ireland (*Goodnight* 1); inhabitants of the north-east corner were equally unhappy, although for different reasons.

In the nineties, however, things improved for both these constituencies. In retrospect, the election of Mary Robinson as Ireland's first female President looks like a symbolic turning point not only for women, but also for the whole country. In 1992 the revelation that Bishop Eamon Casey had fathered a son combined with the case of an Irish teenager denied the right to travel to England for an abortion to suggest the hypocrisy of clerical interference in private decisions involving marriage, sexuality and reproduction. In 1993, thanks to the efforts of Senator David Norris, Ireland found itself the possessor of Europe's most liberal legislation on homosexuality. And as Jordan notes in his Diary, the most important political development in the years between the creation of his first screenplay in 1982 and its realization in 1996 was the peace process, initiated by the IRA ceasefire of 1994 (*Michael Collins* 9).

In 1995, another referendum on divorce narrowly reversed the 'No' vote of the previous decade, and continuing revelations about priests living with their housekeepers and clerical abuse of children put the Irish Church on the defensive, where it has remained ever since.[16] In the Lincoln Jail sequence of *Michael Collins* Jordan shows us de Valera serving Mass in the flowing white robes of an altar boy. As he uses his special relationship with the unsuspecting Catholic chaplain to take an impression of the key of Lincoln Jail in the soft wax of a holy candle, he provides a striking visual image of clerical hypocrisy. Even as we admire his comic ingenuity and applaud the daring escape, we are reminded of his complicity with the Church.

Moreover, in the affluent mid-nineties, with the Irish economy enjoying the white heat of its own delayed technological revolution, frugal comfort was no longer a credible aspiration. Thus, the socio-religious aspects of de Valera's ideal Ireland were already disintegrating when Jordan stepped in to deliver the *coup de grâce*. According to Fintan O'Toole, who acknowledges Jordan's economic and aesthetic debts to Hollywood but accepts him as an 'Irish' film-maker:

> Jordan is, for modern Ireland, not just a famous movie director, but a peculiarly emblematic figure of cultural change. His work over the last two decades represents not just one man's pursuit of his ideas and ambitions, but a significant shift in a nation's culture. By starting out as a writer of literary fiction and re-inventing himself as a film director, he symbolises a much bigger change in the way the country sees itself. ('Man')

O'Toole follows Walter Benjamin in arguing that, by changing his 'means of production' from words to images, Jordan has altered the content as well as the form of Irish self-fashioning. O'Toole is sympathetic to the globalization of Irish culture, and Jordan himself sees film-making as a means of escape from the nightmare of Irish identity:

> The only identity, at a cultural level, that I could forge was one that came from the worlds of television, popular music and cinema which I was experiencing daily. Applied to literature this seemed strangely disembodied. It didn't have the surety of something handed down by tradition or my parents. . . . For me, to make films was to escape from these questions, these hankerings. In the world of cinema, none of these questions existed; there had never been an 'Irish' cinema. My mother and my sisters are painters. And I share with them the sense that the visual is free from the constraints and pressures of our literary tradition. The Irish question is – how to get rid of it. There are more interesting questions than the crippling one about 'Irish identity'. The encounter with other worlds – be it the world of cinema or painting which have no past for us – delivers a different sense of oneself. ('Imagining' 197)

Jordan claims that for his generation identity is media-driven and therefore a global rather than an insular construct, and his move from text to technology recapitulates the shift from tradition to modernity emblematized by his rejection of de Valera. The most striking metaphor for this shift occurs in 'A Love' when the spectators ignore the actual cortège passing behind them, focusing instead on its image refracted in shop window television sets. Reality itself is less convincing than its simulacrum on the small screen. Nevertheless, Jordan cannot 'get rid of it', especially in a film about the establishment of the state. Like many others, he aspires not to abolish Irish identity, but to remake it. 'Treat history as fiction in the making: a fiction that will create the future' (*Michael Collins* 41), he admonishes himself in his Diary. His project is the revision of genealogy: by telling a hitherto untold story about the birth of the nation, he wants to give Ireland a new imaginative paternity, to undo the textbooks' claim that de Valera is 'the father of us all'.

In an interview, Jordan mentioned Collins's death as a 'huge pathological drama' for Ireland. 'Like the death of a father, perhaps?' suggested the interviewer. 'No,' Jordan replied, 'it was the death of a son, really. De Valera was the father' (Billen). In his Diary he suggests that as de Valera writes to Collins from his prison cell near the beginning of the film, he 'becomes a father to the Republic and a father to Collins. A father who will betray him' (*Michael Collins* 60). If de Valera was the symbolic father and Collins the son, their encounter replicates a theme that has considerable resonance in Irish culture: Cuchulain's killing of his only son, Connla, and his subsequent battle with the waves. Yeats retold the story in his poem 'Cuchulain's Fight with the Sea', his play *On Baile's Strand* and his dance drama *Fighting the Waves*. More recently, in the 1985 film adaptation of *Lamb*, Bernard McLaverty's novel about a priest who tries to save a damaged boy from the cruelties of the Christian Brothers, Liam Neeson drowns his young charge to save him from life in an institution. In his subsequent attempt to drown himself he symbolically re-enacts Cuchulain's fight with the sea. The epic allusion recurs in Jim Sheridan's 1990 adaptation of J. B. Keane's *The Field*, when Bull McCabe's only surviving son is run over a cliff by cattle that his father has deliberately stampeded. At the end of the film another boy lies dead on the beach while another father wades out to do battle with the waves. The weight of this allusion is deeply pessimistic: in killing his only son the father destroys the potential dynamism of the as yet uncreated future and dooms the culture he represents to sterile repetition of the past, embodied in his own image. This story serves for Jordan as a parable about the relationship between Collins and de Valera and explains why, although he makes it plain in his Diary that 'the father' had no direct hand in the killing of 'the son', his treatment of this question in the film itself is so ambiguous.

Jordan admits in his Diary that de Valera, who had ceded power to IRA guerrilla fighters like Liam Lynch and Rory O'Connor, was not literally responsible for Collins's death. In what he calls 'A fiction, based on historical surmise' (*Michael Collins* 16), Jordan represents the ambush at Béal na mBláth as engineered by a remorseless young boy who represents the next generation of the IRA and, like the young Free State soldier who callously shoots Harry Boland in a previous scene, lacks emotional ties to former comrades. (His paired representation of the two young men as callous killers suggests Jordan's negative judgement both on contemporary Republican hardliners and on their counterparts, the over-zealous security forces.) The effect of the film is nevertheless extremely unclear: in an informal poll taken in the context of a talk to a non-specialist American audience, I discovered that more than two-thirds of those who had seen the film believed that de Valera had ordered Collins's assassination. Jordan's de Valera appears to have temporarily lost his mental grip, and when the boy arrives to tell him that Collins has come down to Cork in the hope of a meeting, he is indecisive. His historically accurate avowal of powerlessness, 'Doesn't he [Collins] know it's out of my hands?', appears in the screenplay but was cut from the film (*Michael Collins* 207). When de Valera later accompanies the boy to the pub where Collins is buying rounds, his physical presence, lurking behind the haystacks to hear Collins's passionate declaration of his former fealty, is visually sinister. His cry of grief and remorse is hard to understand, and his failure to reply to the boy's insistent request for a message might be interpreted as culpable negligence instead of evidence of an impending nervous breakdown. Historian Tom Garvin felt it necessary to defend de Valera against the perceived insinuation of complicity in Collins's assassination,[17] and even Garret FitzGerald, former leader of Fine Gael, protested that this episode was 'unfair to de Valera, then at the lowest point of his career'.[18]

Unfair, perhaps, but an essential part of Jordan's symbolic project. In his first novel, *The Past*, an exploration of the intersection of personal and national identity, the figure of de Valera haunts the narrative. Until the end he does not enter the plot but hovers on its periphery, his presence evoked by a photograph, an election poster, a Mass card. Jordan's story is driven by a single question, 'Who is my father?' His narrator's mother, Rene, has had simultaneous affairs with an older man, James Vance, and his teenage son, Luke.[19] With the help of Rene's childhood friend Lili, the narrator attempts to discover which of the two, father or son, was his 'true' progenitor.[20] The parallels between Rene and the Virgin Mary, pregnant by a Father who is consubstantial with his Son, are emphasized by one of the narrator's informants, Father Beausang, who after speculating on the circumstances of Rene's impregnation 'turned my mathematical inquiries to that exquisite system of triadic ambiguity that is Marian theology' (*Past* 166). When, some time later, the narrator asks 'if the Son fathered Himself, did He by that very act create His own Father?', Father Beausang replies, 'You are leaving out . . . the third corner of that exquisite triangle: the Holy Spirit' (182). In the context of the novel, the Holy Spirit appears to be de Valera himself. When the narrator retraces the footsteps of Rene, who toured the West with an acting company during her pregnancy, we discover that de Valera was also in Clare at the time, electioneering. As the pregnant Rene plays her final Rosalind on the stage at Lisdoonvarna, de Valera arrives: 'So he came in, said Lili, the father of us all. I didn't see him' (228). In the novel's closing moments, as Rene gives birth in a railway carriage that is blocking a level crossing, 'Dev patient as ever walks from the car through the field to the aqueous window' (232). The 'father of us all' is present, a bizarre godfather, at the narrator's birth.

If de Valera is the symbolic father of us all, Jordan's film reflects the sociological fact that in Ireland 'the fathers', both political and spiritual, have undergone a considerable diminution of prestige since the beginning of the nineties. Jordan's own father, like de Valera, was a teacher of mathematics: in an interview Jordan revealed that he censored his children's reading of comic books and was disturbed by the 'perverse' nature of his son's imagination. In his novel *Nightlines*, an obsessive attempt by a son to make peace with the shade of his dead parent, Jordan describes de Valera as a 'harsh deity' (41): fathers, gods and political leaders are conflated. *Michael Collins* is a transparently Oedipal attempt to rupture the tangled lines of personal and national filiation, to replace the prissy image of the bespectacled schoolmaster and the threatening image of the man with the raised fist with something much more sexy and up to date.[21] Yet Jordan chooses for this image of modernity a figure from the past, Michael Collins, who emerges out of the repertoire of possible developments that never took place to offer to Gerry Adams a model of that familiar decolonizing hero, the guerrilla who becomes a statesman when the armed struggle has made its point. Or, perhaps, the ideological journey of Gerry Adams inspired Jordan's construction of his movie. Despite the images of revolutionary violence that so disturbed the right-wing British press and the clichéed claim that Collins 'brought the British Empire to its knees', *Michael Collins* is a popular cultural text that both emerged from and contributes to the popular impulse towards peace. Jordan is on record as disdaining the revisionist critique of his film, but in discrediting all that de Valera stood for it shares the revisionist impulse towards modernity.

SEAMUS AND SINÉAD
From 'Limbo' to *Saturday Night Live* by Way of *Hush-a-Bye Baby*

Although they both write poetry, Seamus Heaney and Sinéad O'Connor do not, on the surface, have much in common. While Heaney's trademark is the personal reserve he characterized in 'Whatever You Say, Say Nothing' as 'the famous / Northern reticence, the tight gag of place / And times' (*North* 59), O'Connor uses the media to exhibit (her critics would say flaunt) the pain of her abused childhood and the complexities of her position as an Irish woman. What the poet and the singer do share is stardom. In their respective spheres of high and popular culture each is Number One; and being Number One imposes penalties. When on 3 October 1992 O'Connor tore up a picture of the Pope on NBC's *Saturday Night Live*, the ensuing public controversy was so fierce that she felt forced to leave America and her career took a nosedive. To this day, few articles about her in the popular press fail to mention this spectacular incident. When she bought a page of the *Irish Times* to explain in verse that she missed a Peace '93 concert because she needed privacy to experience her grief about her childhood, she was greeted by a torrent of vilification. Readers argued mockingly that they would gladly take on the pain of O'Connor's past if they could have the privileges of her present. She was a spoiled narcissist who needed to stop whingeing about her 'inner child' and acknowledge her advantages, which included the freedom to spend eleven thousand pounds on self-advertisement in the *Irish Times*.[1] Mockery redoubled when in 1999 she was ordained as a priest in an outlawed Tridentine sect that still celebrates the Latin Mass.

Because poetry is a less public art than popular song, Heaney has been less publicly castigated than O'Connor; but Desmond Fennell's hostile pamphlet, *Whatever You Say, Say Nothing: Why Seamus Heaney Is No. 1*, analyses the poetic–academic complex as a capitalist concern analogous to the rock music enterprise: 'Starting out, he did not know that the poetry business at the top in consumer capitalism is a verbal, emotional and intellectual circus; but having found out, he signed on and mastered all the acts – poetic, critical, professorial, oracular and mystical' (44). Fennell asserts that in Ireland 'Heaney is the only poet whom many people buy or give as a present', implying that what these deluded folk seek is not the verse but Heaney's celebrity. Similarly, Fennell writes, 'People who normally ignore rock or pop music will, when U2, Enya or Sinéad O'Connor make a noise in the media, purchase a record out of curiosity or to be with the crowd' (24–5). Fennell's main objection to 'Famous Seamus' is that he has bought his rock star popularity at the price of saying nothing meaningful about the conflict in the North of Ireland. He argues that the production of small, well-crafted and increasingly opaque lyrics has assured Heaney his massive contemporary reputation, his professorships at Harvard and Oxford, his high sales figures and his position as Number One, a position that was consolidated by the award of a Nobel Prize in 1995.

Despite his shrewd analysis of cultural institutions and his suggestive juxtaposition of poetry with rock music, Fennell's attack on Heaney smacks of begrudgery. Of course Heaney has said meaningful things, even if he has not provided the 'clear, quotable statements . . . about general matters' (14) that Fennell so simple-mindedly requires. Others have quarrelled with 'the extraordinary inflation of [Heaney's] current reputation' on more substantial grounds. David Lloyd argues that Heaney's poetic obscures the material determinants of Irish culture and politics. The bog poems, in particular, ignore 'the real basis of the present struggle in the economic and social conditions of a post-colonial state'. *North* refigures the current conflict in terms of sexual difference, 'which comes to provide for political, national and cultural difference a matrix of the most elementary, dualistic kind' (*Anomalous* 35, 19, 26).

Heaney's mythical deployment of sexual difference and iconic representation of femininity has also attracted the attention of female critics, including Edna Longley, Patricia Coughlan, Clair Wills and myself. Focusing primarily on *North* and the bog poems, these commentators critique Heaney's essentialist representation of the colonizer as seducer or rapist and the colonized as feminine victim in 'Act of Union' and 'Ocean's Love to Ireland' and challenge the quasi-pornographic voyeurism of 'Bog Queen' and 'Punishment.'[2] In 'Quicksand', a witty riposte to 'Punishment', Nuala Ní Dhomhnaill rejects the 'bogholes underground', where she fears she will find the subject of Heaney's poem, 'a drowned girl, / a noose around her neck', in favour of 'terra firma . . . hard sand' (*Poems* 85). Eavan Boland laments the objectification of Irish women in the male poetic tradition (without naming Heaney), but his persistent figuration of Ireland as a woman and the bogland itself as female (in 'Kinship' and 'The Tollund Man', for example) makes him an exemplar of the practice she deplores. Boland will not repeat the words 'Mise Éire' (I am Ireland); she 'won't go back' (*Journey* 10) to the emblematic subject position offered to Irish women in the poems of Irish men, where the feminine image becomes 'the passive projection of a national idea' (*Scar* 81). Although it has not reduced his popularity, then, the feminist case against certain aspects of Heaney's work has been clearly articulated.

I propose to recuperate both Heaney and O'Connor for feminist politics by juxtaposing canonical poet and popular singer through their joint participation in a third medium, Margo Harkin's television drama *Hush-a-Bye Baby*.[3] Heaney's poetry, Harkin's drama and O'Connor's transgressive appropriation of NBC's commercial format are not isolated exemplars of high, middlebrow and popular culture but events that exist on an Irish textual, cultural and political continuum. I do not, however, seek to impose unity and coherence upon the Heaney canon or O'Connor's various songs, texts and gestures. My juxtaposition and close reading of so-called 'literary' and 'popular' signifying practices is intended to contribute to the breakdown of the hierarchical opposition between mass and minority culture.

In Britain a product of contemporary 'high' culture is most likely to enter the popular consciousness through the syllabi for the 'O' and 'A' level examinations in English Literature: tests taken by schoolchildren at sixteen and eighteen years of age. Heaney's poems are frequently set for 'O' level (now called GCSE) in the six counties of the North of Ireland,[4] as they are throughout the United Kingdom, an institutional fact that may explain his sales figures better than Fennell's birthday present hypothesis. A Conservative member of the British parliament tacitly acknowledged the hegemonic power of the 'O' level English syllabus when he objected to the inclusion of Heaney's 'The Early Purges', a poem about the drowning of farm kittens, because it was 'sick' (Morrison 88–9).

The Irish feminist film-maker Margo Harkin has affirmed Heaney's dominating position in the literature curriculum. As a founder member of the Derry Film and Video Workshop, Harkin worked on the documentary *Mother Ireland*, which cogently presents the case both for and against representations of women as the Motherland. Although Heaney's poetry is not mentioned, some of it clearly falls within the terms of the film's critique. Yet in the Workshop's 1989 made-for-television drama *Hush-a-Bye Baby*, Harkin places Heaney at the centre of a feminist work through the generic frame of the 'poem in the classroom': a teacher reads Heaney's 'Limbo' to a group of fifteen-year-old girls studying for their 'O' level exams. The scene could easily have emphasized the pedagogical imposition of irrelevant high culture upon a reluctant teenage audience, but instead Harkin uses Heaney's lines as a crucial emotional focus for the film's concern with gender and reproduction. She has told me 'It was very much my desire to get that poem in'.[5]

The Derry collective believed that 'too often people are the passive recipients of a one-way flow of information from the dominant audio-visual institutions which do not reflect the values and aspirations of dissenting groups'.[6] Their project was to resist 'dominant audio-visual institutions', which would, ironically, include Channel Four, the British television company that funded them. Harkin is aware of the paradox involved in developing a culture of resistance within the mainstream media, but since 'the good ship Channel 4 professed a benign interest in the native culture' the natives were ready to take their money: 'If views were to be constructed of ourselves then we demanded a right to construct an indigenous perspective' ('No Plundering' 19). In *Hush-a-Bye Baby* Harkin creates a counter-hegemonic narrative about working-class Derry teenage girls coming to sexual maturity within a Catholic culture that represses and denies the facts of reproduction and contraception.

Though set primarily in the North, the film draws much of its emotional power from its reference to events in the South. As Sinéad O'Connor's friend Nell McCafferty has noted, 'The nineteen eighties will go down in history as a lousy decade for Irishwomen. During what have become known as "the amendment years", church and state fought for control of our bodies and our destiny. The Catholic Church won handily' (*Goodnight* 1). In 1983 the Republic voted by a two-thirds majority to insert in its Constitution a clause outlawing abortion. The pre-referendum debate was policed and controlled by the 'dominant audio-visual institution' of the state, RTE. According to Luke Gibbons,

> The kind of open-ended 'phone-ins', magazine programs, and talk shows (such as the controversial Late Late Show, the most successful show on Irish television) that had given women a voice, and had ventilated sexual issues frankly, were explicitly barred by the government-appointed broadcasting authorities from joining the debate. As a result, women's stories simply were not told. ('On the Beach' 13)

The next year, 1984, in what Gibbons has characterized as a return of the repressed, the fifteen-year-old Ann Lovett died giving birth to her illegitimate baby in a grotto dedicated to the Virgin Mary. Although the community of Granard had surmised that she was pregnant, no one had spoken about it to her or to her family. A few months later the body of a newborn that had been stabbed twenty-seven times was washed up on a beach in County Kerry. The young woman accused of this infanticide, Joanne Hayes, was cleared when her own illegitimate baby, dead at birth, was found in the field where she had buried it; but the police investigation spared no detail of her gynaecological or personal history. As women began to protest against the inquiry, and to contact phone-ins and talk shows with their own stories, the silence and secrecy that had surrounded Ann Lovett and Joanne Hayes, as they bore their stigmatized pregnancies to term in communities that refused to acknowledge their condition, was shattered.

The sleeve notes for *Hush-a-Bye Baby* refer to these incidents, as does the film itself, which presents a fictionalized narrative that has obvious connections with the Ann Lovett story, which also inspired Paula Meehan's poem, 'The Statue of the Virgin at Granard Speaks' (*Man* 40–2), Nuala Ní Dhomhnaill's *Thar mo Chionn*,[7] Leland Bardwell's short story, 'The Dove of Peace', and a song sung by Christy Moore and Sinéad O'Connor, 'Middle of the Island', on Moore's record *Voyage*. Harkin felt 'that the national consciousness of Ireland had been shocked by these events . . . and that it would be important to make some sort of contribution to or intervention in the subject'. To democratize the intervention as far as possible, the collective listened to the stories of numerous young Derry women who had experienced unmarried pregnancy (S. Mackay 29). Since the British Abortion Act of 1967 has never been extended to the North of Ireland, the position of pregnant women is similar on both sides of the border.[8] When the collective showed the script to Sinéad O'Connor and asked her to write the music, she had just finished reading *A Woman to Blame*, Nell McCafferty's book on Joanne Hayes (J. Brady 15). Although she had not paid much attention to the tragedies of Lovett and Hayes when they occurred in 1984, she was so moved and impressed by the script of *Hush-a-Bye Baby* that she requested a small part for herself. 'It was a film that really attracted me because it dealt with something I had first hand experience of – the horror of being young, single and pregnant in a country like Ireland with such backward views on femininity and sexuality' ('Interview'). Although O'Connor originally wanted to play a nun (she has said she would have liked to enter the religious life, but could not handle celibacy), she was eventually offered the part of the heroine's shy and prudish girlfriend, Sinéad.

The heroine, fifteen-year-old Goretti, is ironically rather than aptly named. Santa Maria Goretti was an Italian teenager beatified for preferring death to rape: she has been fetishized as an example to Catholic girls of the correct attitude towards sex. Unmindful of her namesake's example, Goretti gets pregnant by her boyfriend, Ciaran. Against the meticulously rendered Derry background of the supergrass trials and constant harassment by the army, the British lift Ciaran, who has Republican sympathies, before Goretti realizes her condition. She is left alone, unable to talk to a mother whose only concession to the female body is her monthly replacement of the significantly named 'Stay Free' sanitary towels hidden at the back of the laundry cupboard. At one point Goretti walks past the most famous of Northern murals, 'You are now entering Free Derry'. Harkin's point is that 'whatever she's going through was going on before the "troubles". One of the main reasons for doing the film is that, if we get what we want, if we get a united Ireland, if we get troops out, what kind of a country are we left with?' (Boatman 44). To underline this question, Harkin's setting shifts from the North to the Republic. Rendered completely *unfree* by lack of information, lack of choice, inability to communicate and sheer terror, Goretti mechanically adheres to her previous plan to spend the summer in the Donegal Gaeltacht with her friend Dinky, in order to learn Irish at the hearth of that quintessential image of Irish tradition, the *bean an tighe* in her whitewashed cottage.

Part of that rural faith-world is a wayside statue of the Virgin, ironically dedicated to the Immaculate Conception, which reminds Goretti of her own transgression and appears in her fevered dreams as a balefully watchful eye. Through swift intercutting, Harkin develops the familiar icon of the Virgin not as a loving mother, but as a frightening bogeywoman. (At the end of the film, when Goretti goes into labour, the statue appears to her again, with its swollen pregnant stomach pressing against the glass that encloses it. The image of her flattened knuckles is terrifying and grotesque.) The girls are nervous about passing the statue in the dark and Dinky tells it: 'Don't you fucking move!' In early 1985 statues of the Virgin in Kerry and elsewhere were reported to be moving, and attracted enormous crowds of believers. Conservative religious commentators argued that this phenomenon proved that Our Lady was grieved and angered by the terrible events of 1984, as well she might have been, but on what score?[9] On RTE Goretti hears a studio discussion of abortion in which the audience is reminded that it is almost a year since the referendum. Insisting that abortion is murder, one woman cites Bishop Joseph Cassidy's sensational pre-referendum claim that 'the most dangerous place for an infant to be is in the mother's womb'. She is challenged by another woman who asks what relevance these words have to the unfortunate Ann Lovett, and who claims that the vote has increased the 'fear and isolation' of desperate young women like Goretti.

To illustrate this fear and isolation, Harkin chooses an icon that is saturated with local meaning, although it would be lost on a non-Irish audience. Sitting alone and silent on a rocky beach, Goretti watches a discarded fertilizer bag wash in: a visual code for the Kerry babies case, in which the infant was washed ashore in just such a plastic bag. (See Fig. 8) This long, non-narrative scene is particularly important to Harkin, who writes that 'Evidence of infanticide by drowning seemed to me to crop up now and then in small newspaper articles since the time of the Joanne Hayes scandal. . . . It struck me that since we live on an island and the sea is such a feature of our lives it was obvious it would play a part in our most tragic, secret dramas' (Letter). Clearly, thoughts of abortion and infanticide, and possibly even suicide, are uppermost in Goretti's troubled mind. After leaving the Gaeltacht

Fig. 8. *Goretti Watches the Waves.*

she is further isolated by the imprisoned Ciaran's self-centred reaction to her news. Under the accusing gaze of another statue of the Virgin, this time iron-ically juxtaposed with a bottle of gin, she unsuccessfully attempts the alco-hol-and-hot-bath method of home abortion. When she returns to school, the options of marriage and abortion closed, and still hiding her pregnancy from everyone but the equally uninformed Dinky, an English lesson presents her with her last and most terrible choice.

Heaney's 'Limbo', a poem about a mother drowning her baby in the Done-gal fishing village of Ballyshannon, metaphorically takes her back to her vigil by the sea. The Heaney poem is the verbal complement of the visual image of the pregnant girl watching the waves. In the earlier scene Harkin had refer-enced the poem through a second iconic object, the fishing net in which the 'Ballyshannon baby' was recovered:

> I have referred to both the Caherciveen [Kerry] baby with the blue fertilizer bag, blue being the colour of the Virgin Mary, and to the Ballyshannon baby with the remnant of a fisherman's net, again blue. . . . I imagine those inanimate accessories trying to wash off their associated sins into infinity and I wish their inclusion to be an acknowledgement of the pain of these women. (Letter)

Harkin's obsession with blue leads her to alter the facts of the case: the fertil-izer bag that figured in the Kerry police inquiry was grey (McCafferty, *Woman* 56). The religious register of her language suggests the deep psychological hold that Catholic iconography and the Catholic sense of sin can exert in the unconscious minds even of those who rationally reject Catholic theology.

The 'poem in the classroom' scene is directly framed by a discussion (based upon a real incident) about a baby found abandoned in the grotto of Derry's Long Tower Church and promptly baptized by the local priest. 'How did they know it was a Catholic baby?' Goretti asks. 'Maybe the mother was just desperate'. Harkin cuts abruptly to the image of a baptism, which has a purely iconic, non-narrative function, since this infant plays no role in the plot. As the water pours over the unknown baby's head and a stained-glass window is mirrored in the ripples of the font, Goretti's woman teacher reads the opening stanza of 'Limbo', after which the image dissolves to the crucifix on the wall of the classroom. The icon of the baptized child coincides with the poem about the drowned, and presumably unbaptized, baby.

The doctrine of limbo, although it was always uncanonical and has now more or less disappeared as a theological concept (McCafferty *Goodnight*, 43), permeates Irish folk legend and belief. Limbo is a no man's land between Heaven and Hell reserved for, among others, the souls of unbaptized babies; they do not suffer, but neither are they permitted to see God. Abortion and infanticide are doubly heinous because the innocent victim is deprived of eter-nal happiness. Anne O'Connor argues that 'Child murderess and dead child traditions in Ireland are profoundly *religious* in character . . . the popular perception of the woman who takes the life [of her child] is that of a demonic and unrepentant murderer' (309). Folklore in this respect goes hand in hand with the rhetoric of militant anti-abortion groups like the Society for the Protection of the Unborn Child: since aborted babies cannot be baptized, they are candidates for limbo.

Heaney's poem, however, draws from this popular folk source only to revise sympathetically the traditional moral judgement contained within it. I can imagine two possible hostile readings of 'Limbo': as a mainstream male literary text appropriating a marginalized woman's pain; and as a re-inscription of Catholic male dominance over women like Goretti, who must not have an abortion or kill their babies because they will be exiled forever in limbo. Neither of these responses seems to me appropriate, however; and if we watch the *film* reading the poem, they become impossible. Limbo is indeed imagined, according to tradition, as a 'far briny zone' in which even Christ the fisher of men has no hope of a redemptive catch; and Harkin's striking use of sea and water imagery throughout the film underlines Heaney's metaphor. The child murderess, however, is not demonized: indeed, she is identified with Christ in her suffering. Harkin's shot of the crucifix graphically echoes Heaney's lines, 'She waded in under / The sign of her cross', while the camera's relentless focus on Goretti's face during the teacher's attempt to generate discussion of the poem emphasizes her own private Calvary

The poem's first simple declarative sentence depicts a shocking event in plain and unsensational language, as if the speaker were reading a newspaper account:

> Fishermen at Ballyshannon
> Netted an infant last night
> Along with the salmon.

These lines imply that catching an infant, while unusual, is within the parameters of an angler's experience; as indeed it may be in a culture that makes it hard for teenagers to obtain contraception. Angela Bourke has situated numerous Irish folk legends in which fishermen 'catch' newborns in their nets or on hooks in the contemporary context of the Kerry Babies case,[10] while Harkin speculates that infanticide has been and is common in Ireland, although 'the level of collusion and secrecy surrounding these incidents is so powerful in a country which denies abortion that the facts are hard to get at' (Letter).

Heaney's restrained style, his initial eschewing of descriptive or evaluative terms, nevertheless produces shock through the chilling contrast between the expected and the unexpected contents of the net: the salmon and the infant. His tight four-line stanza and terse diction reveal his debt to the Movement and the idea of the well-made poem, as does his organically unified angling metaphor: the baby is

> An illegitimate spawning,
>
> A small one thrown back
> To the waters. (*Wintering Out* 70)

The loaded adjective 'illegitimate' provides a major exception to the rhetoric of fishing. Totally inappropriate to the life cycle of the salmon, a symbol of untrammelled sexual energy (as in Yeats's 'the salmon-falls, the mackerel-crowded seas'), the obtrusive five-syllable word inserts the harshness of conventional human judgement into the amoral world of spawning. The temptation to judge is no sooner presented than resisted, however. The monosyllabic line 'A small one thrown back' evokes with understated pathos a fish/child too tiny to be worth the fisherman's keeping, too insignificant to deserve the ponderous stigma 'illegitimate'.

The fishing metaphor doubles as a birth metaphor, since the breaking of the 'waters' occurs early during delivery. The baby comes out of the waters of the womb and is returned to the waters of the sea. The mysterious and surreal opening shot of the film anticipates Heaney's lines by showing what at first sight appears to be a foetus floating in amniotic fluid against a rhythmic sound that suggests waves falling on the shore. On second viewing the connection with the Heaney poem becomes even stronger, as we make out a doll's hand amid a swirl of what might be hair or seaweed. Sinéad O'Connor devised the undersea sounds and produced the eerie wailing, a keen or lament for all the drowned babies and their anguished parents. Harkin has told me that she deliberately began the film with a visual and aural reference to the Ballyshannon baby 'thrown back to the waters'.

After this phrase the impersonal speaking voice of the poem changes:

> But I'm sure
> As she stood in the shallows
> Ducking him tenderly
>
> Till the frozen knobs of her wrists
> Were dead as the gravel,
> He was a minnow with hooks
> Tearing her open. (*Wintering Out* 70)

The word 'But' dramatically alters the trajectory of the poem, forestalling the reader's question, 'How could any mother drown her baby?' Adopting the first-person pronoun (which tempts readers to identify the speaker as Heaney himself), the poet interprets the mother's motives through a non-appropriative act of personal trust: 'But *I'm* sure'. He guarantees that her act was not lightly undertaken. He does not speak in her voice; he speaks on her behalf, with empathy. Harkin reinforces this empathy by giving us our first view of the female teacher's face on the phrase 'But I'm sure'. A woman – a teacher or a film-maker – can use Heaney's certainty for political and educational ends.

Any implications of maternal callousness derived from the metaphor of the unwanted catch tossed back into the sea are dispersed by the line 'ducking him tenderly'. Harkin's visual introduction to the poem, the watery, rippling shot of the baby at the font (a 'small one' who was *not* thrown back), reads the mother's action as an alternative, unconventional baptism: not drowning, but ducking. Through the surprising adverb 'tenderly' the violence one would normally associate with such an act is deflected from the baby back upon the mother herself.

The third stanza is entirely devoted to this reversal. The mother absorbs her child's death into her own body: her wrists 'Were *dead* as the gravel'. The infant is not a fish torn by the hook, he is that biological impossibility, a minnow with hooks, and she is the one torn open by the pains of his birth and his death. In birthing and killing her child she has murdered herself. Harkin has said that this part of the poem enabled her creative act:

> Heaney imagines himself with great compassion into her state of being . . . Heaney's gift here was that he helped me imagine a possible interpretation of [her state] and neither he nor I had experienced it. (I have no doubt also that a woman poet might have brought a lot more to it but that does not detract from the validity of Heaney's version and his right to do it. It's what we have demanded of men surely, that they imagine themselves into the female condition?) What is more important politically is that even if in the real case the person responsible for that act was full of rage and guilt he took her side and he collapsed into that poem the anguish and the loss and the love that may have clashed so violently in that destroying act and which we absolutely know is part of the desperate condition of so many women imprisoned in a religious culture so completely intolerant of a woman's right to choose. (Letter)

Harkin is certain, as I am, that although Heaney's imagination is steeped in the 'religious culture' of the Catholicism in which he was raised, his attitude towards it is equivocal and critical. The conclusion of the poem re-inflects the conventional images of crucifixion, limbo and Christ the fisherman:

> She waded in under
> The sign of her cross.
> He was hauled in with the fish.
> Now limbo will be
>
> A cold glitter of souls
> Through some far briny zone.
> Even Christ's palms, unhealed,
> Smart and cannot fish there. (*Wintering Out* 70)

The 'child murderess' endures a female Calvary that is compounded by her religious beliefs: the cross weighs heavily upon her because infanticide outrages both her feelings as a mother and her conscience, her sense of sin.

Ironically, the Church's refusal to countenance contraception or abortion, combined with its stigmatization of illegitimacy, forces her to the far more heinous act of killing a living child.

Although we might imagine that the limbo evoked at the conclusion is the destination of the baby, as it would be in popular superstition, Heaney's syntax is ambiguous. 'Now limbo will be / A cold glitter of souls' is open to the question 'For whom?' Harkin sees Heaney's reference to limbo not as

> a judgement of the mother of the Ballyshannon baby but if anything a judgement against the Church which has taken control from women and left them without a better choice in the circumstances of desperation. It has created a Limbo for women in the same way it so conveniently created one for unbaptized babies. No one can go in there, no one can talk about this experience, it is the loneliest place; it must be endured. It is a prison sentence without appeal.
> (Letter)

In these circumstances Christ cannot redeem the suffering of his daughter; nor can he judge her. Sharing limbo with her drowned baby she is beyond reach of his unhealed, smarting palms in 'some far briny zone'. He has failed her. For Harkin, Heaney's concluding images were 'powerful . . . and overwhelmingly sad and compassionate' (Letter). They permeate not only the scenes on the beach and in the classroom, and the symbolic opening underwater sequence, but the first naturalistic shot of the film: Goretti's niece, a little girl of about two or three, is shown 'drowning' her doll in the bath. Ann Lovett was fifteen, Goretti is fifteen; how old was the mother of the Ballyshannon baby? The child killer may have been a child herself.

Harkin's use of the Heaney poem as an objective correlative for the national trauma caused by the Lovett and Hayes cases climaxes when the teacher asks her inexperienced young class to comment on the lines that conflate the physical pain of birth with the woman's pain at the baby's death, 'He was a minnow with hooks / Tearing her open'. The camera stays focused on Goretti, for whom the lines clearly have a meaning far deeper than that available to the other girls; but in the background we hear Sinéad O'Connor offer a clumsy interpretation: 'Does it mean the baby was caught with the fisherman's hook, miss?' O'Connor's persona in the film is at odds with her reputation as the 'hairless hellraiser' ('Sinéad O'Connor' 34): she is sexually reserved, and shown fantasizing herself as the Virgin. Her slightly priggish devoutness impairs her ability to understand the poem. It is the pregnant Goretti, identifying with the mother, who offers an interpretation that would doubtless have earned her an 'A' in her 'O' level exam: 'She didn't want to kill her baby, miss. She must have been desperate. He imagines her ducking him tenderly. She was very unhappy'. The word 'desperate' brings Harkin's carefully structured sequence of words and images full circle: Goretti began by characterizing the mother of the baby abandoned in the grotto as 'desperate'.

Harkin says that the Workshop chose television as 'the most popular medium through which we could express our ideas' ('No Plundering' 20). She nevertheless understood the precariousness of an enterprise dependent upon support from Channel Four, which became 'nervous about its involvement with the workshop' after the banning of *Mother Ireland*. (The ban was incurred because the documentary featured IRA volunteer Mairead Farrell, murdered in Gibraltar by the SAS just before the programme was due to be aired).[11] Indeed, shortly after *Hush-a-Bye Baby*, Channel Four withdrew its funding for independent workshops and the Derry Film and Video collective went out of business. 'We . . . knew,' Harkin wrote, 'that they wouldn't let us do it for long, whatever it was that we were doing. Was it culture? Was it politics? Was it community activism? Was it art?' ('No Plundering' 19). Surely it was all of those things. In appropriating Heaney's art for cultural politics, *Hush-a-Bye Baby* inserts it into the sphere of community activism. By showing Goretti responding to the poem through her own pain, the film also proposes a populist literary politics: poetry is mimetic and expressive, response is affective and reading is a process of personal identification. Neither Heaney nor Harkin could stand up to the analysis of a Foucauldian constructionist feminist like Judith Butler, for whom the biological category 'sex' is as much a function of discourse as the social category 'gender', and even the category 'woman' is problematic (*Gender Trouble* 1–7). Nevertheless, as long as females have babies and males do not, an Irish 'woman' is someone whose womb (if she is fertile and Catholic) is susceptible to male clerical control. If any country requires a dose of strategic essentialism (a tactic Butler distrusts), it is surely Ireland

Harkin's feminist 'reading' of Heaney's text can be extended to two other poems with which it is linked by theme and proximity in *Wintering Out* (1972): 'Maighdean Mara' and 'Bye-Child'. In these poems, as in 'Limbo', which stands between them in the collection, the sexual conventions and prohibitions of Irish life that Heaney understands so well are shown as a deadly trap for both women and children: they lead to forced marriages, depression, suicide, infanticide and child abuse. What distinguishes them from the bog poems is that the female figures who inhabit them are not representatives of the land or of the national idea; nor are they icons of rural domesticity like the baking woman of 'Mossbawn'.

'Maighdean Mara' retells the folk legend of the mermaid who is compelled to marry the man who has stolen her magic garment: 'Follow / Was all that she could do'. Heaney comments, 'It is not an allegory for getting pregnant out of wedlock; but it carries that force all right'. He is exceptionally sensitive to the 'violated lives' of people 'who were trapped into a domestic life by mistake' (Interview 45):

> She suffered milk and birth –
> She had no choice – conjured

> Patterns of home and drained
> The tidesong from her voice. (*Wintering Out* 68–9)

It was all that she could do: she had no choice. Heaney has said that the poem was inspired by the suicide of a young married woman he knew who suffered from depression 'and had been inert on the bed in a kind of paralysis almost for months; and then one night left the house and drowned herself in Ballinderry river' (Interview 45). In the poem the mermaid who returns to the sea rather than remain in the prison of a marriage forced upon her by pregnancy is represented as corpse-like, 'her cold breasts / Dandled by undertow'. Although in some versions of the folk tale she returns at night to comb the hair of her human offspring, Heaney's mermaid suicidally divests herself of the domestic spell of 'her children's brush and combs'. They are completely abandoned. In 'Limbo', as we have seen, the baby is drowned. In 'Bye-Child', the most horrifying of the three poems, the woman imprisons her illegitimate child in a henhouse to avoid the shame his birth would bring upon her. He remains hidden there for years, a domestic 'feral child' who is incapable of speech:

> Your gaping wordless proof
> Of lunar distances
> Travelled beyond love. (*Wintering Out* 72)

Heaney does not attempt to imagine the state of mind of the mother who confines her child in a henhouse, a fate worse than being drowned at birth; but nor does he condemn her. The problem of child abuse is integrally related to the lack of reproductive choice in Ireland, as Heaney implicitly recognizes by situating 'Bye-Child' directly after 'Maighdean Mara' and 'Limbo'.

No one has been more vocal about the issue of child abuse than Sinéad O'Connor. The cover of *Success Has Made a Failure of Our Home*, for example, features a photograph of a beautiful little boy. The back reads, 'Nahaman Carmona Lopez. A street child who was attacked by police in Guatemala City, who later died from the injuries he received. 14 March 1990'.[12] The politics of the cover have nothing to do with the songs on the CD, a selection of golden oldies; but the singer's participation in *Hush-a-Bye Baby* merges artistic with political commitment. The shot that juxtaposes the image of O'Connor with the words of the Heaney poem also relates, through an audio-visual metonymy, the realms of high and popular art. O'Connor, who made the film just before she became famous in 1990 with 'Nothing Compares 2 U', also composed the score, sang her version of 'The Bells of the Angelus' and wrote the haunting 'Three Babies' that accompanies the closing credits.

'Three Babies' appears to respond directly to 'Limbo'. Read in the light both of the film and of O'Connor's biography (and O'Connor has often said that all her songs are personal [Hayes 68–70, 92]), this poem implies that the woman who sings has aborted her babies. As in 'Limbo', the mother's feelings for them are 'tender', but her assumptions about their ultimate fate are radically different. She asserts that she will hold on to them for ever:

> Each of these
> my three babies
> I will carry with me
>
> . . .
>
> In my soul
> my blood and my bones
> I have wrapped your cold bodies round me.
> The face on you
> The smell of you
> will always be with me.

Echoing and reversing the pessimistic conclusion of Heaney's poem, with its doctrine of limbo as a 'cold glitter of souls' who will be forever unreachable and unredeemable, she claims that she has 'wrapped your cold bodies round me'. Her own faith is defiantly optimistic:

> Each of these my three babies
> I was not willing to leave
> though I tried
> I blasphemed and denied
> I know they will be returned to me. (*I Do Not Want* 15)

Her religious terminology ('blasphemed and denied') reveals that, like Heaney and Harkin, she intuitively resorts to Catholic discourse even as she rejects it intellectually.

O'Connor's coded admission of abortion in 'Three Babies' changed to an outright political statement when in 1992 a fourteen-year-old Irish girl, pregnant as a result of rape, was prevented from travelling to England for a termination. The Attorney General cited as his justification the 1983 Constitutional amendment guaranteeing the right to life of the unborn. O'Connor took a spectacular role in the protests that erupted in Dublin, buttonholing the Taoiseach, addressing rallies, demanding a new referendum in which only women of childbearing age could vote and admitting to two abortions herself. Journalist Mary Holland wrote:

> In general, Irish women are extremely reluctant to talk of their experiences of abortion. Until rock star Sinéad O'Connor stormed the Dáil on Thursday, demanded to talk to Albert Reynolds and told the media she would face her Maker quite happy to explain why she had had two abortions, I know of just three women who had 'come out' since the start of the referendum campaign in 1983. ('Eire')

O'Connor, who used to wear T-shirts bearing the words 'Recovering Catholic', plausibly located the source of Irishwomen's reproductive dilemmas in the Vatican, which she called the primary source of evil in the world. Although she refused to call herself a feminist, many of her statements in the early nineties betray the influence of the activist intellectual Harkin and the experience of making *Hush-a-Bye Baby*. Like Harkin, she argues that 'The Catholic Church have controlled us . . . through their teachings on sexuality, marriage, birth control and abortion' ('Sinéad's Defense').

O'Connor was beaten by her mother, like many Irish housewives a Valium and alcohol addict (Hayes 12–17), and she claims that Ireland has the highest incidence of child abuse in Europe. Child abuse is linked with the denial of abortion, because, when women cannot control their own fertility and numerous offspring strain the resources of impoverished parents, mistreatment by both mothers and fathers is common. More shockingly, O'Connor asserted that 'in the schools, the priests have been beating the — out of the children for years and sexually abusing them' ('People' 78). Since the revelations that began to pour out after the case of the paedophile priest Brendan Smyth toppled the Irish government in late 1994, these accusations sound relatively uncontroversial, but O'Connor was making them in 1992 and earlier. She constructs a coherent if slightly broad-brush postcolonial theoretical trajectory from the Catholic Church through imperialism to child abuse, historicizing her antipathy to the Church by insisting on the intersection between religious and political colonization. In the twelfth century, Ireland was 'given' to Henry II of England by Popes Adrian and Alexander (Curtis 55–7), and O'Connor claims that 'the cause of my abuse is the history of my people, whose identity and culture were taken away from them by the British with full permission from The "Holy" Roman Empire' ('Sinéad's Defense').

O'Connor has a long history of confrontational political gestures that, unlike Madonna's ever-saleable masturbatory Catholicism, actually lessen her popularity. To protest the censorship of black rappers she refused to have the American national anthem played before one of her concerts, and she pulled out of an episode of *Saturday Night Live* because it was to be hosted by misogynist and homophobe Andrew Dice Clay. To their subsequent regret, the producers gave her another chance. On 3 October 1992 she rehearsed in the *Saturday Night Live* studio reggae singer Bob Marley's previously banned 'War'. The song, which itself challenged the anodyne formula of the show, is adapted from a speech made by Haile Selassie of Ethiopia, whom Rastafarians like Marley regarded as the only true God. (The speech was reproduced on Marley's original album cover.) O'Connor, who calls herself a Rastafarian (Hicklin), sang a cappella to ensure that every word was heard:

> Until the philosophy which holds one race superior and another inferior
> is finally and permanently discredited and abandoned
> Everywhere is war.

In choosing the Marley song O'Connor substantiated her frequent claims that hip-hop and rap were her biggest influences. She was going back to their source in reggae and to the religious philosophy that informed it. Rastafarians, the Jamaican descendants of slaves who developed a culture of resistance and sought an authentic racial identity in their African roots, accused Christian missionaries of concealing the fact that Adam and Jesus were black.[13] O'Connor's loathing of the Vatican is compounded by the fact that it 'blessed the bombs that went into Ethiopia'. She is referring, quite correctly, to Mussolini's infamous 1929 Concordat with Pope Pius the Twelfth, and his subsequent invasion of Haile Selassie's country in 1935. Her identification of Catholicism with fascism is strengthened by her conviction that Pius the Twelfth 'gave permission . . . for the Jewish people to be slaughtered' by not speaking out against the Nazi Holocaust ('People' 79). The unsuspecting producers failed to interpret the significance of the six-pointed star she was wearing round her neck or the Ethiopian flag that was wrapped around the microphone. But O'Connor also adapted the anti-racist lyrics of Marley's 'War' for her own purposes:

> Until the ignoble and unhappy regime which holds all of us
> through child abuse, yeah
> child abuse, yeah
> subhuman bondage
> has been toppled, utterly destroyed
> Everywhere is war.

That 'ignoble and unhappy regime', for her, is 'the Roman Empire, the people who invented child abuse' ('Sinéad Speaks' 53); but at the rehearsal she did not say so. At the end of the song she held up a picture of a young victim: she was priming the cameraman to compose the close-up shot. In the live broadcast, however, illustrating Marley's concluding words, 'We have confidence in the victory of good over evil', she replaced the picture of the child victim (good) by a picture of the Pope (evil). 'Fight the real enemy', she demanded, and then tore up the picture, stunning technicians, producers and audience into complete silence.

Unfortunately few people in America understood what she was doing, though a lot of people knew they hated it. Outside of the Irish context, the gesture seemed like gratuitous blasphemy. NBC received a torrent of protest calls, and O'Connor was subsequently booed at a Bob Dylan tribute in Madison Square Garden. In defiance, she again sang the Marley song instead of her scheduled Dylan number. The offending *Saturday Night Live* episode opened with a self-reflexive skit about NBC censoring the show because it had satirized General Electric, which owns the network. Ironically, when this episode was later rebroadcast NBC silently censored O'Connor by substituting the dress rehearsal footage for the Pope-ripping version, and they refused to supply me with a copy of the original tape. Lenny Pickett, a regular musician on the show, told me that she had 'violated its premises'. Direct political protest like O'Connor's ruptures the conventions of tame political satire, and Pickett suggests that, although the producers of Saturday Night Live (all white males) do not object to controversy, 'it wasn't *their* controversy.'[14] Indeed it was not, being a controversy peculiar to Irishwomen, racial minorities, and children everywhere. O'Connor has recorded a song called 'Jump in the River' with Jesse Helms's favourite target, the performance artist Karen Finley, and I read her attempt to make Saturday Night really Live as political performance art of a high order. Her subversive genre-bending produced a sensational shock effect, even on Madonna, who protested against 'ripping up an image that means a lot to other people'. Given her own use of the crucifix Madonna can hardly talk, but she did make one valid point: 'I think you have to do more than denigrate a symbol. I mean, burn a flag, but explain why' ('Sinéad's Outburst'). O'Connor, who said that her gesture was 'for Ireland' ('People' 79), spent many weeks explaining why. She had commandeered the most popular medium at her disposal to get an audience for the discursive clarification of the connection between the Pope, the history of Irish colonization and child abuse that she published in a widely circulated 'Open Letter' to the press.

Although her record sales dropped and her career faltered, subsequent events in Ireland demonstrated that O'Connor's crusade against child abuse was fully justified. In 1994 the Irish government fell over a controversy involving a paedophile Catholic priest. Father Brendan Smyth was convicted of sexually abusing children over a period of twenty years in Belfast, and was later charged with seventy-four such incidents in the Republic. His order had been aware of the problem, but did nothing about it. His case was only the most politically damaging of the many similar ones that then began to surface throughout Ireland. What looked to conservative critics like O'Connor's demented over-reaction to her own personal trauma proved instead to be a symbol of a far deeper social malaise.

Later in the decade, O'Connor accepted two cameo roles in Neil Jordan's The Butcher Boy (1997). The film, which demonstrates how life in small-town Monaghan turns a disturbed young boy into a psychopathic killer, is centrally concerned with the question of child abuse. Francie's alcoholic father batters his chronically depressed wife and thrashes his son, whose life with these sad parents moves from one occasion of psychological damage to another. When he is sent to a religious reformatory, Francie becomes the sexual target of the elderly priest Father Sullivan, who likes to dress him up in a girl's bonnet and cuddle him while masturbating. After their erotic assignations are discovered, the other priests cover for Father Sullivan, who is not exposed as a child abuser, but merely sent away for a rest: the Brendan Smyth parallel is explicit. It is therefore appropriate that Jordan asked child abuse crusader Sinéad O'Connor to play the Virgin Mary, who appears several times to the increasingly deranged Francie.

In *Michael Collins* Jordan had challenged the right of Eamon de Valera, the embodiment of traditional forms of religion and patriarchy, to be considered the father of his nation. *The Butcher Boy* continues the political project of *Michael Collins* in social and domestic terms: it critiques the traditional pieties of de Valera's ideal Ireland, which invested woman's 'life within the home' with a constitutionally approved aura of Marian sanctity. Jordan has said that, 'to film this novel would give me the chance to reinvent that extraordinary mixture of paranoia and paralysis, madness and mysticism that was the Ireland I grew up in in the 50s' ('Virgin'). Through his use of female iconic objects, Jordan suggests that de Valera's world has congealed into kitsch; nevertheless, his attitude towards these icons is creatively ambivalent.

Although newspapers speculated that his casting of the papal defacer as the Mother of God was deliberately calculated to give offence, Jordan demurred: 'I saw her in an early movie she made called Hushaby Baby, and thought she was wonderful. She reminds me of the statues I used to look at of the Virgin Mary, when I was younger. She has the same kind of profile' ('Virgin'). Jordan is referring to a scene in which Sinéad poses as the Virgin in front of her bedroom mirror, wimple on forehead and rosary in hand, while 'The Bells of the Angelus' plays on a tinkling music box. Immediately after 'trying on' the Virgin's outfit, Sinéad accompanies her girlfriends to a nightclub where she drools over a loutish lad nicknamed Clitoris Allsorts. Gratuitous in terms of the plot, this juxtaposition embodies the mixed messages sent to women in a culture hesitating between traditional symbols of chastity and the global world of American pop music in which, according to Cyndi Lauper, 'Girls Just Wanna Have Fun'. (See Fig. 9) Neil Jordan remembered the beauty of O'Connor's profile rather than Harkin's mocking collocation of the sacred with the resolutely secular. Yet in *The Butcher Boy* he recognizes that the values and the promises embodied in the statue of the Mother of God may be at once seductive and disappointing.

The image of the plaster Virgin also embodies the contradictions within the endlessly performative public persona of O'Connor herself, who frequently reminds interviewers that she was born on the feast of the Immaculate Conception (O'Hagan), and keeps her intense and paradoxical involvement with the Catholic Church in full public view. O'Connor has always demonstrated an offbeat identification with her own rebellious version of the Queen of Heaven. In reply to an interviewer who asked about her 'distinctly unvirginal line, "Ah, fer fuck's sake, Francie"', she replied, 'I tend to think if Mary was around now, she might say something like that. It's understandable, isn't it, given the state of things. I'd say she might even tear up the Pope's picture, too' (O'Hagan). Instead of rejecting the traditionally pure and submissive Virgin as an unrealistic and psychologically damaging ideal, O'Connor resituates her in opposition to the patriarchy.[15] This is not an original move (it is closely related to the 'goddess' feminism of the early eighties), but nor is it necessarily ineffective. It may be compared to the cult of the Virgin of Guadalupe among Chicana

Fig. 9.   *'Girls Just Wanna Have Fun': Goretti, Sinéad and Majella.*

women in Texas, who erect domestic shrines that are both monuments of kitsch and sources of power and consolation.

Rita Felski reminds us that 'the dividing line between a repressive stereotype and an empowering symbol of cultural identity is often a very narrow one' (37). The plaster Virgin is the essence of religious kitsch: it is the most familiar of the standardized, mass-produced and widely disseminated devotional objects that dominate both public and domestic spaces in Ireland. In 'The Recovery of Kitsch', David Lloyd has described the inevitable process by which religious and national icons, through their proliferation and their relative uniformity, devolve into kitsch, 'sentiment congealed into attitude'. But rather than deriding such vulgar and gaudy objects as evidence of cultural backwardness, he suggests that we should recognize that they occupy the 'alternative spaces of the non-modern' and appreciate the 'rich repertoire for resistance' that they offer to subaltern cultures (*Ireland* 90, 94, 96). Although it is hardly an example of political resistance, Jordan's investment in the image of the Virgin is far more positive than that of the feminists who made *Hush-a-Bye Baby*. In both *The Miracle* and *Michael Collins* he uses lighting to invest popular religious icons with a surreal clarity of colour and outline: the visual effect is at once comic, satiric and oddly reverent.

In Francie's dysfunctional home a sentimental, highly coloured portrait of the Virgin, unmistakably modelled on Sinéad O'Connor, hangs next to a cheap plate bearing a picture of John and Jackie Kennedy, the nearest Ireland ever came to a royal family. This juxtaposition of religious and diasporic kitsch is later replicated in the psychiatrist's office. The stand-off between Kennedy and Khrushchev produced by the abortive Bay of Pigs invasion and the ensuing Cuban missile crisis, which brought the world to the brink of nuclear war, provides a continuous political counterpoint to the story of Francie's descent into insanity. Though the words 'Bay of Pigs' are never spoken, they echo in the audience's mind as Francie acts out the English-identified Mrs Nugent's stereotypical ethnic slur 'Pigs'. Newsreels of American schoolchildren being taught how to 'duck and cover' and excerpts from Kennedy's speeches about Cuba fuel a paranoia about Communists that is shared by the whole town, which confidently expects the Virgin to appear and save them from the end of the world.

When Francie runs away to Dublin, he buys his mother a present that embodies the tourist stereotype of Irish identity. This plaster model of a white thatched 'Irish cottage', a 'cosy homestead' that mocks the reality of his own squalid house, declares that a mother's love is always a blessing. Both the cottage and the Virgin promise maternal consolation. But in Jordan's film, none of the promises embodied in kitsch are fulfilled. Francie returns with his pathetic present, but he comes too late: in his absence his desperate mother has committed suicide, and his father blames him for her death. The priest, however, leads him to the picture of the O'Connor Virgin and says that his mother has gone to be with Our Lady. Guilt-ridden, Francie defends the memory of his sad, inadequate parent by attacking the textbook mother Mrs Nugent, whose good housekeeping represents a kind of domestic colonialism: she has come back from England to take over the whole town.[16] Embracing her negative stereotype, Francie becomes a pig by defecating on her carpet. As a consequence, he is sent to the religious reformatory school, where we see an identical print of the O'Connor Virgin hanging on the wall. This standardized, commodified piece of kitsch circulates within the domestic, disciplinary and medical spaces through which the increasingly disoriented Francie is shuttled. It is not surprising, therefore, that when Our Lady appears to him she takes on the appearance of Sinéad O'Connor.

She materializes, wearing powder blue and gold garments, to reassure Francie about his goldfish problem. His only friend Joe Purcell has written to him that Philip Nugent, the perfect son of the ideal home, has given him a goldfish. Francie regards Joe's acceptance as a betrayal of their intimacy and determines to graduate from the reformatory in order to straighten things out. A vision of the Virgin is just the thing to impress the priests, and she obligingly materializes to comfort Francie by telling him, 'You shouldn't worry about those things. Joe's your friend, isn't he?' Our Lady's intentions are good but her information is out of date: Philip's goldfish does mark the beginning of the end, and Joe will not be his friend for much longer. The vision, moreover, leads directly to sexual abuse, since it attracts the attention of Father Sullivan (known to Francie as Father Tiddly), who masturbates while Francie is describing his divine experience. The juxtaposition of religious and sexual ecstasy is frankly hilarious: Jordan dares to make comedy out of paedophilia. The voice of Stephen Rea (the real star of the film) mediates between the horror of a priest abusing a child and the jaunty inflections of Francie's flippant response: 'This is amazing facts about Our Lady I'm telling you and you're jiggling away there. Man dear, what are you playing at?' Subsequently, Father Tiddly's attentions redouble: he gets Francie dressed up in a girl's bonnet and wants to know the worst thing he ever did. Since Francie thinks the worst thing he ever did was to kill his mother, he understandably refuses and attacks the priest with a paperknife, blowing their intimacy sky-high. No disciplinary action is taken against Father Tiddly, who is simply bundled off to recuperate with his sister. Father Bubble even tells Francie that he was a 'great man' and that 'not one of us is perfect'. The religious imperialism of Father Tiddly's service in the mission fields among the Belubas is implicitly paralleled with the sexual colonialism of his treatment of a child (albeit a very knowing child, who takes full advantage of his weakness). The priests cannot wait to get rid of Francie, whom they regard as 'fungus on the walls'. Although on his release from the reformatory Francie re-establishes a tentative relationship with Joe, he seals its demise when he tells his former friend what Father Tiddly did. Like the priests, Joe, who is increasingly identified with the conventional world of the Nugents, is nauseated and repulsed by the victim Francie, not by his clerical abuser.

In McCabe's book, Francie's visions of Our Lady end when he leaves the reform school. Jordan was so enamoured of moving plaster statues that he continued the motif all the way through his film. When Francie is forced to take responsibility for his incapacitated father he adopts the woman's role, putting on his mother's old apron to do the shopping, cleaning and cooking. His undelivered gift to her is joined on the sideboard by a goldfish, his undelivered gift to Joe Purcell: both are images of his lost emotional life. Outside the thatched cottage sits a plaster colleen playing the harp. The 'colleen' is one of de Valera's 'comely maidens' in her 'cosy homestead'; and the woman with the harp is an eighteenth-century figure for Ireland herself. Like the Virgin, the colleen, also played by Sinéad O'Connor, engages Francie on the subject of goldfish: she says that he gave Joe too many, but she adds, 'It's going to be all right, Francie. Joe's here'. On this, the police break in and we realize that Francie is sitting with his father's rotting corpse. Like Our Lady, the colleen is kind and motherly, but in Francie's bleak world her cheery optimism is completely misplaced.

O'Connor thus embodies the triple goddess of Irish national, domestic and religious femininity – the woman with the harp, the colleen in the cottage and the Virgin in the grotto – who has helped to drive Francie's hopeless mother first into lunatic parodies of homemaking (a deluge of butterfly buns) and then to her suicide in the river. Like the women in Heaney's poem 'Maighdean Mara', she has found herself unable to withstand the pressure of her domestic circumstances. The colleen's words to Francie are no less misleading than the

words she spoke as the Virgin, but Francie seems happy with whatever atten-
uated expressions of affection his miserable life affords him. When the portrait
of the Virgin pursues him into the mental hospital that is society's next attempt
to regulate a child who has just lost his whole family, his only friend and his
grip on reality, Francie is delighted to claim her acquaintance. In response to
the picture's broad wink, he tells the psychiatrist, 'Me and Our Lady go back a
long way. It's not every shitehawk she'll appear to, you know'. Nevertheless, the
direct result of Francie's claim to be on friendly terms with Our Lady is electroshock treatment.

When he returns to his wrecked home to catalogue his human losses, the
Mother of God appears on the broken television set, an ironic collocation of
a traditional image with the modern mass media. Francie is ready to accept
defeat and loss, but the Virgin is still peddling illusions: 'Ah, fer fuck's sake,
Francie . . . How could Joe be gone on you? Aren't you blood brothers?' Her
rendition of her party piece, 'Beautiful Bundoran', sends Francie off on the last
and most disillusioning of his travels. His parents had always kept alive the
image of their seaside honeymoon, which partook both of romance and Marian religion (they said the Rosary together on the rocks). In Bundoran Francie discovers that this image was a lie. Like their marriage, his parents'
honeymoon was a disaster, and his own life was contaminated at its source:
he never had a chance.

The Virgin's hint about Bundoran also sends him looking for Joe, who is
there at boarding school with Philip Nugent, and thus precipitates Joe's
humiliating public denial of their friendship. Our Lady's advice is consistently
lousy. She also fails to keep her appointment with the town, which lays on an
enormous festival of religious kitsch, 'The End of the World Show', to welcome her appearance and persuade her to avert the threat of nuclear disaster.
While everyone is distracted by fruitless hymn singing and prayer, Francie
takes advantage of the occasion to borrow the butcher's tools and slaughter
Mrs Nugent. The townspeople confuse the site of the gruesome murder with
the site of the promised apparition, but instead of the Mother of God they find
the blood of a murdered mother.

Many years later, as the adult Francie is finally being released from yet
another mental institution, the Virgin appears to him for the last time, and
she's still got goldfish on the brain. She tells him, 'God loves every one of us
Francie, but you know something? He has a very special place in his heart for
you'. If God has a special place in his heart for Francie he has a funny way of
showing it. This time the Virgin counsels resignation on the subject of Joe:
'Joe loves you too Francie, but the world goes one way and we go another. So
don't go bothering your head about goldfish any more, all right?' Though at
long last she seems willing to face facts, her mention of Joe and the goldfish
is hardly tactful and risks rekindling his homicidal paranoia. 'Tell me something, missus. Are all the beautiful things gone?' he asks her sadly. No, she
answers, they're still there. And she throws him a snowdrop, which is still in

his hand when he returns to his doctor on the bench. The snowdrop suggests that, despite the Virgin's poor track record as a guide to practical action, she may remain a source of beauty and maternal consolation. Jordan's concentration on her image is funny and loving, and O'Connor's gentle performance establishes that, while all mothers are fallible, even the Mother of God, they are vastly preferable to the fathers, lay or clerical. While I doubt if this amounts to a recovery of local kitsch as resistance, at least not the kind of resistance that David Lloyd would prefer, both Jordan and O'Connor keep the religious image in creative play rather than consigning it to the wastebasket of outdated traditions.

O'Connor's 1999 ordination as a priest in the Tridentine Order of Mater Dei (Mother of God) has intensified her public engagement with religion at the same time as it continues her struggle against 'official' male Catholicism. Mater Dei, she told *The Times*, is 'a relatively enlightened order which ordains not only women but married and gay priests' and is not recognized by the Catholic Church. She knows that 'they are anti-abortion, and I have to respect that's how they feel although I'm pro-choice. But they're not locked in old ways of thinking. They are prepared to move and change'. Since she came out as a lesbian (she later modified her description of her orientation to 'bisexual') just after being promoted to Archdeacon, Mater Dei is obviously a fairly flexible organization. 'I always knew that God was there despite religion, and I've always been interested in rescuing God from religion', says Sinéad Mother Bernadette Maria O'Connor, as she is now called (Williamson).

Although her new album *Faith and Courage* contains a song, 'The Book of the Lamb', in which she appears to apologize for the pain that her Pope-ripping exploit may have caused, in several recent newspaper interviews O'Connor asserts that she offers no apologies for the incident itself (Williamson; Hicklin; M. Edwards). Meanwhile, the Pope has issued a millennial apology to just about everybody, including women and ethnic minorities. The hysterical derision that regularly greets O'Connor's actions, especially from Irish journalists (one of whom described her as 'a few wafers short of a Mass' [quoted in Mulholland]), seems out of proportion to her offences and suggests that she unfailingly hits a raw nerve. Like Princess Diana, she has been written off as unstable, self-destructive, egotistical, manipulative and spoiled. She may well be all of those things, but, also like Princess Diana, she has used her power as a pop culture icon to enact performances that raise serious social and political issues. Diana's embraces of AIDS patients, lepers, sick children and landmine victims were scenarios played directly to the camera in search of empathy from her global audience. O'Connor's angrier gestures were staged in pursuit of similar, although more local, ends. Her current public 'performance' of the Catholic priesthood (she regularly appears in 'ecclesiastical drag', complete with dog collar and crucifix) serves a precise political purpose. Women will one day be ordained as Catholic priests, if only because the profession is already being abandoned by men and will therefore soon cease to be worth defending as a male preserve. Celibacy is similarly doomed. Twenty years from now, O'Connor, despite her personal fragility and career-threatening displays of idealism, will look more like a pioneer than an eccentric. Re-applying to her transgressive performances Margo Harkin's question about *Hush-a-Bye Baby* – 'Was it culture? Was it politics? Was it community activism? Was it art?' – I answer: Yes.

Heaney, Harkin, O'Connor and Jordan all make extensive use of Catholic imagery, which is so fundamental to their imaginative processes that they would be unable to create without it. Even Harkin, the most self-consciously critical of the four artists, shows Goretti holding her sister's baby and lighting a candle in front of a statue of Our Lady while O'Connor sings a powerful and non-satirical version of 'The Bells of the Angelus'. Like the image of Mother Ireland, the image of the Virgin Mary is Janus-faced: a source of power, peace and consolation for some, a repressive nightmare for others.[17] A political as well as a religious icon, she is also a highly visible representation of the theological difference between Irish Catholics and English Protestants. The work of Jordan and O'Connor suggests that Our Lady is too profoundly embedded in Irish culture to be discarded. She may be critiqued and revised, but not forgotten. The term 'critical nationalism' has been coined to describe a politics that, while it acknowledges the absence of Ireland's Others from the national narrative, sees this gap as a function of imperial intervention rather than of limitations inherent in the nationalist position itself, and continues to draw on traditional images and political energies as a source of strength for the future. The Irish artists that I have been considering here are practising a form of 'critical Catholicism': without losing sight of the negative effects of religious orthodoxy on women and gays, or of the appalling reality of clerical child abuse, they retain their connection to a religious tradition that, for better and worse, has helped to define the Irish experience. Like critical nationalists, they do not want to throw the baby out with the bathwater.

NOTES

Introduction

1 For an anthology of this debate, see C. Brady. For a polemical analysis from a revisionist perspective, see Howe. For a literary application of the postcolonialist thesis, see Kiberd, *Inventing*. For an example of the debate as it concerns the *Field Day Anthology* and nationalism, see Gibbons, 'Constructing'; Mulhern; Gibbons, 'Dialogue'.

2 For 'Dublin 4', see J. Waters 103–10.

3 See the pamphlets by Eagleton, Jameson, and Said collected as *Nationalism, Colonialism and Literature*.

4 See Deane, *Strange Country*, and Lloyd, *Ireland*.

5 For a summary of these positions, see *Ireland* 101–8.

6 Cullingford, 'Thinking of Her'.

7 'Gender and Colonialism' conference, Galway 1992.

8 For the best and most careful presentation of both sides of this question, see *Mother Ireland*.

9 For a brief discussion of Pearse's poem, see E. Walshe, 'Introduction' 4–5.

10 See Gibbons, 'Dialogue' 30; Coulter 101–4.

11 Thanks to Declan Kiberd for first suggesting this point to me.

The Stage Englishman of the Irish Drama

1 For analysis of the construction of the nation, see Colley; Colls and Dodd; Langford.

2 Following the exemplary models of Curtis's *Apes and Angels*, Deane's 'Civilians and Barbarians' and Leerssen's *Mere Irish*, numerous critics have dissected the negative stereotypes of Irishness.

3 In *Inventing Ireland* Kiberd posits a process of mutual misrepresentation (9–63).

4 Quoted in Meisel, *Shaw* 18.

5 From 1695 to 1829 the Penal Laws forbade native Catholics to bear arms, attend university, practise law, take state office, serve in the army, own land on a long lease, or vote.

6 I borrow this formulation from A. Murphy, *But the Irish Sea* 6–7.

7 For the stage Irishman, see Duggan, *The Stage Irishman*; Graves, 'The Stage Irishman among the Irish'; Kiberd, 'The Fall of the Stage Irishman'; Kosok, 'John Bull's Other Ego'; Nelson, 'From Rory and Paddy to Boucicault's Myles, Shaun and Conn'; M. Waters, *The Comic Irishman*.

8 The commentaries on Boucicault to which I am most profoundly indebted are by Cave; Gibbons, 'Romanticism'; Krause, 'The Theatre of Dion Boucicault'; Pine, *Dion Boucicault*; Watt 1–88. Harrington's *Irish Play*, which appeared simultaneously with the first version of this chapter, shares its emphasis on reconciliation, as does Grene's recent *Politics of Irish Drama*.

9   Harrington, *Irish Play* 25.

10   The exception is Kosok, who concludes his discussion of the stage Irishman with a brief survey of the stage Englishman that mentions Shadwell, O'Casey, Behan, Shaw and Friel ('John Bull' 29–33).

11   Harrington argues for Boucicault's 'politics of reconciliation' (*Irish Play* 9–33).

12   On gender and colonialism, see Cairns and Richards, *Writing Ireland* 49–50; Cairns and Richards, 'Tropes and Traps'; Cullingford, *Gender and History* 55–72; Howes 16–43; Kearney, 'Myth and Motherland'; Leerssen, *Mere Irish* 246–50; Loftus; *Mother Ireland*; MacCana; Nandy 7–10.

13   Quoted in Hogan, *Dion Boucicault* 81. For a defence of Boucicault, see Krause, 'The Theatre of Dion Boucicault' 38–42; for a defence of Synge, see Kiberd, 'The Fall' 46–9.

14   An exception is Anna Maria Hall's *The Groves of Blarney*, whose heroine is an English widow (Cave 90–2).

15   On Irish villains, see Watt 66, 69–70, 84.

16   See Herr.

17   See Nelson for the excision of references to 'the wicked landlords' from an 1885 play (80).

18   Cave argues that Boucicault, because he could not take his audience's politics for granted, wrote more complex plays (116).

19   Herr 11, 15–17. The wartime Defence of the Realm Act (DORA) drastically restricted freedom of speech.

20   His Irish plays influenced Shaw, Synge, O'Casey, Behan and Friel. For Boucicault's influence on the cinema, see Gibbons, 'Romanticism' 210–21.

21   For information on Parker and Patterson, see Richtarik, 'Stewart Parker'.

22   See McCormick 5.

23   Fawkes 125–6.

24   Gibbons, 'Romanticism' 210–4 and Deane, 'Dion Boucicault' 2: 234.

25   For both versions see Walsh 193–6.

26   See Duggan 242–60. Before Boucicault, two familiar stage Irishmen were the wily servant and the boastful soldier, descendants of the parasite slave and the miles gloriosus of Plautine comedy. Watt cautions that they do not exhaust the variety of Irish characters on the London and Dublin stages (5–6).

27   For English opinion of the Fenians, see McCord 40–55.

28   Fawkes 154–8, 170.

29   Krause, 'The Theatre of Dion Boucicault' 33. For the political energy of the Irish street ballad, see Lloyd, *Anomalous* 89–100.

30   Fawkes 170.

31   Hall 228. Watt notes the aptness of Hall's analysis to Boucicault, Whitbread and O'Grady (51).

32   See Newsinger 29, 40, 50–5, 61–4; and Lyons 111–28.

33   For Arnold and Ireland, see Cairns and Richards, *Writing Ireland* 42–57.

34   For an excellent account of Molineux, see Cave 107–12.

35   Newsinger 76.

36   See Duggan 271–8; and M. Waters 45.

37   For a discussion of this motif in the novel, see Corbett 51–70. For its origins in Swift, see Trumpener 133–7.

38   See Harrington, *Irish Play* 27.

39   For the model of homosocial desire, see Sedgwick 1–27. For the exogamous
     transfer of women between male kinship groups, see Rubin 157–210.
40   See Fawkes 196; Molin and Goodefellowe 136.
41   For the numerous Emmet plays, see Hawkins. For Emmet's rebellion, see Elliott
     282–322.
42   Cave 127n.
43   Watt calls Sirr a 'reprehensible British soldier' (84); but according to Finegan he
     was born and died in Dublin Castle (34, 75, 81).
44   See Landreth 350n and Hawkins 133.

Decent Chaps

1   See J. Mackay and Thane, 191–3.
2   On Shaw and national stereotypes, see Kiberd, *Inventing* 51–63. Though I dif-
    fer with him occasionally, this chapter is deeply indebted to Kiberd's work.
3   Kiberd 57.
4   Harrington, *Irish Play* 41.
5   For 'reconciliation', see Watt 64–76.
6   Sedgwick 1.
7   Kiberd 63.
8   Rubin *passim*.
9   See Sedgwick 21.
10 For an excellent close reading of this episode, see Cheng 151–62.
11 For Engels on the Irish, see Corbett 102–5.
12 Grene makes this suggestion, but he pulls back from it (*Politics of Irish Drama*
    149).
13 See Seamus Shields's comment in *Shadow of a Gunman* (O'Casey, *Three Plays*
    122).
14 For a perceptive discussion of the way Bessie's death inverts the nationalist logic
    of patriotic sacrifice, see S. Harris, *Bodies and Blood* 279–81.
15 Gibbons' critique of Lean's pastoralism ('Romanticism' 196–200, 228–31) does
    not mention Major Doryan.
16 Curtis, *Apes* 42–3.
17 Andrews calls *Translations* 'a play about late twentieth-century Ireland' (120).
    Longley concurs: 'Poetry and Politics' 28–9. See also Richtarik, *Acting* 28–64.
18 The connection between Yolland and Broadbent has been noted in Roche 249.

'There's Many a Good Heart Beats Under a Khaki Tunic'

1   Bennett attacks Jordan's film for its stereotyped representations of 'terrorists';
    Lloyd catalogues its historical improbabilities (*Ireland* 64–76). The central act of
    hostage taking, which Lloyd censures as anachronistic, derives from literary tra-
    dition rather than contemporary events.
2   Jordan, Interview 20.
3   Lance Pettitt argues that, despite attacks on the film's representations of trans-
    sexuals, women and blacks, it 'retains positive aspects for gay viewers' ('Pigs,
    Provos and Prostitutes' 269).

4   See McIlroy 59 for a similar interpretation.
5   See Allen 27–51.
6   For a feminist critique of *The Crying Game*, see Edge; on Dil and race, see hooks 55–7.
7   See Rose 34–59.
8   McGuinness, 'All about My Mother'.
9   For the ports and the war, see Lee 242–70; Coogan, *De Valera* 507–619.
10   Lee 244–5.
11   For an impressive reading of Rosie Redmond, see S. Harris, *Bodies and Blood* 266–70.

'Brits Behaving Badly'

1   I am indebted to Herr's long introduction to these plays (3–64). I differ with her on their aesthetic merits but not on their historical interest and importance.
2   In poems like Ó Rathaille's 'The Redeemer's Son' (*An Duanaire* 156–61).
3   Furlong 116, 127–35.
4   P. J. Bourke's account is roughly accurate (Kinsella 190–1).
5   For an account of 'Croppy Biddy', see O'Donnell.
6   Kiberd assumes he is an Englishman (*Inventing* 219).
7   See the chapter on Sean O'Casey in S. Harris, *Bodies and Blood*.
8   For the shoot-to-kill policy (1982), see Bell 652–6.
9   For Sheridan on the aesthetics of the three-act structure, see Byrne 124–33.
10   For a highly critical view of *Hidden Agenda*, see McIlroy 93–6.
11   *Daily Mail*, 11 November 1996. Online. Lexis-Nexis.
12   Here I diverge from Gibbons, who thinks that Jordan cleanses *The Godfather* stereotype of its sinister associations. I think they resist such sanitizing. 'Framing History' 51.
13   Gibbons, 'Framing History' 50.

Romans and Carthaginians

1   Schneider discusses the analogy briefly (88–90).
2   A fourteenth died later. On Bloody Sunday, see McCann 15–22, 91–129.
3   For Field Day see Richtarik, *Acting*; Richards; McCormack, *Battle* 53–60.
4   See Andrew; MacDougall 7–27.
5   I am grateful to Stan Walker for clarifying my ideas on this point.
6   In formulating these ideas I am indebted throughout to Said, *Orientalism*, as well as to Deane and to Cairns and Richards, who have adapted its theoretical model to Ireland.
7   Some Greek scholars thought they were the world's oldest race (Rice 19), and Herodotus reports that the Scythians made this claim themselves (280–1).
8   See Canny and Carpenter, who cite Olaus Magnus as a representative example (182n).
9   The old English poem *Andreas* recounts how St Andrew rescued St Matthew from the anthropophagous Mermedonians, whom the editor identifies as Scythians (xvii–xxx).

10   For Strabo, see Leerssen, *Mere Irish* 32–3.

11   See Brown.

12   See Coughlan, 'Some Secret Scourge' 52, 63–5; Jones and Stallybrass 158–61.

13   See Leerssen, 'On the Edge of Europe' 101, 111n.

14   McCormack discusses Herodotus, but not Edgeworth's alteration of the story ('Introduction' xix–xxi).

15   'Grace Nugent' was the name of a popular tune by the Irish composer Carolan; McCormack demonstrates the Jacobite connections of many of the historical Nugents ('Introduction' xxii–xxiv).

16   On the characterization of Orientals as feminine, see Said, *Orientalism* 206–8. For the supposed effeminacy of the Jews, see Gilman 40–3. Lew notes the relevance of Bernal's work to Irish Orientalism (62–5).

17   Also see Canny, on whose work most later commentators draw.

18   See Lew 51–3, 59.

19   On *aisling* poetry see Leerssen, *Mere Irish* 246–50. For the long tradition of feminizing the land, see Dalton; MacCana; Kearney, 'Myth and Motherland' 74–8; Loftus 44–86; *Mother Ireland*; Cairns and Richards, 'Tropes' 128–32; Innes, *Woman* 9–25.

20   See also Cairns and Richards, 'Writing Ireland' 43–50.

21   Conyngham; Ferguson.

22   See *Preoccupations* 56–60. For commentary, see Corcoran 118–20 and Cullingford, 'Thinking' 2–3.

23   For a critique of Heaney's use of gendered myths to elide social and historical conditions, see Lloyd, *Anomalous* 26–7.

24   Longley thinks it is ('North' 78–9), while Morrison argues that 'Kinship' affirms the idea of 'slaughter for the common good' (67–8). Like Corcoran (118–20) and Coughlan ('Bog Queens' 105), I read the phrase as ironic.

25   Morrison 67–8.

26   For feminist critiques, see Wills 69–70; Coughlan, 'Bog Queens' 99–108; Cullingford, 'Thinking' 2–3. In *Scar*, Boland challenges the Irish practice of gendering the nation as female without mentioning Heaney by name.

27   See Corcoran (114) and Hart (90) for readings of the poem that ignore the Phoenicians.

28   See Cullingford, *Gender* 55–92.

29   On the psychodynamics of colonialism see Nandy 7–10. On the weakness of the Irish patriarchy, see Kiberd, 'The War' 44–9.

30   The OED gives 1547 as the first use of 'pale' in the Irish context.

31   Bartolini argues that the Phoenicians got their name from the colour (81).

32   Parker writes as if the metaphor referred only to the Church (145–6). Longley dismisses the poem as coarse ('North' 70).

33   See Pine, *Brian Friel* 154; Peacock 127.

34   See Deane, 'Civilians and Barbarians'.

35   In 1798 the French under General Humbert landed at Killala Bay, near Sligo, to assist the Irish rebels. Yeats, whose spiritual home was Sligo, set his play about 1798 near Killala.

36   See also Kearney, 'Language Plays' 142; McGrath, 'Brian Friel' 247–8; McGrath, *Brian Friel* 181–95.

37   For the ahistoricity of this threat, see Andrews, 'A Paper Landscape' 120–2.

38   McGuinness confirms the importance of his allusion to St Malachy (telephone conversation). For the Roman liturgical and administrative take-over, see Condren 136–8.

39   Buttrey advances this thesis, but E. T. Harris finds it improbable (17–33).

40   Zwicker 190. I am grateful to James D. Garrison for this point.

41   Unless otherwise indicated, all references will be to this version.

42   For gender as performance, see Butler 134–9. For a defence of drag, see Tyler.

43   See Koestenbaum 207, 229–30n.

44   Letter to the author.

45   In *By the Bog of Cats* Marina Carr goes even further than McGuinness in undoing the traditional meaning of the Carthage analogy: her character Carthage Kilbride is a deserter and a destroyer, who betrays his lover Hester and drives her to murder their child and kill herself.

46   I am grateful to Ed Madden for drawing my attention to the Cranberries' song, and to their hit 'Zombie', which deals with the violent deaths of children on the streets of Belfast. O'Connor has also demonstrated that she is versed in the anti-colonial tradition (see my chapter, 'Seamus and Sinéad').

47   A. Murphy 93–6.

Phoenician Genealogies and Oriental Geographies

1   See Kiberd, *passim*. The groundbreaking work on this topic was done by Innes, *Devil's Own Mirror*.

2   See A. Murphy 11–12; O'Toole, *Black Hole* 55; Bornstein 171–2.

3   For this debate, see C. Brady and Howe.

4   For Joyce and Triestine politics, see Manganiello, Chapter 2.

5   Joyce, *Dubliners* 254n. See Mullin for an extended discussion of the sexual meaning of Buenos Aires.

6   For a feminist reading of 'The Dead' that does not focus on Molly Ivors, see Norris.

7   'I have reproduced (in *Dubliners* at least) none of the attraction of the city . . . I have not reproduced its ingenuous insularity and its hospitality' (*Letters* 166).

8   For a revised and more pessimistic account of the ending of 'The Dead' by Deane, see 'Dead Ends' 33–6.

9   *Ulysses* 5.75, 8.184, 8.958–76, 15.450–1, 15.590–1, 15.758–60, 15.2011–12, 15.2724, 15.2854, 15.4298–9, 15.4951–6. See Nadel 211 and Davidson 54–7.

10   Costello 217–19.

11   See O'Toole, *Black Hole* 55–69.

12   Historians cite Geoffrey Keating's 1633 *History of Ireland* as the originator of this tale; Keating's own source was the *Lebor Gabála*.

13   Curtis, *Apes*.

14   See Bornstein for a discussion of Afro–Celtic connections.

15   Cheng notes their symbolic connection, but not the physical description of Freddy Malins (140).

16   Personal communication.

17   See Morrison 64–6; Corcoran 120–1; Parker 142.

18   Thanks to Kevin Whelan for help with this passage.

19   For an account of the Munster rebellion and Ralegh's role, see Curtis 190–200.
20   Harbison contests this theory: in his view the excavations at Lough Boora in County Offaly 'make it clear that we can no longer afford to envisage Ireland's earliest Mesolithic families as having come only to northeastern Ireland' (24).
21   See Bornstein 171–2; O'Toole, *Black Hole* 55.

'John Wayne Fan or *Dances With Wolves* Revisionist?'

1   In writing on this topic the term 'cowboys and Indians' is hard to avoid, because most artists retain the derogatory name 'Indian' rather than 'Native American'.
2   The Irish Seminar, International Graduate Programme in Irish Studies, Dublin, 1999.
3   The Irish Seminar, International Graduate Programme in Irish Studies, Dublin, 1999.
4   'Cowboy Poetry Gathering To Start', Associated Press 23 January 1998. Online.
5   Vardac 25–31.
6   The most complete account of Ford's career is by Gallagher.
7   For Quincannon in the trilogy, see Morgan.
8   For another version, see McMahon, *Irish Ballads* 30.
9   See Thomas 83.
10   For a thorough critique of the Western from a feminist viewpoint, see Tompkins.
11   McGlynn analyses the reasons for this popularity.
12   Stanfield argues that the Western style was appropriated by 'hillbilly' musicians anxious to transcend their Appalachian roots (22–5).
13   J. Waters evokes this milieu throughout *Jiving*.
14   For a reading of the play's ideology, see O'Toole, *Politics* 130–42.
15   See Bell 157–61.
16   The groundbreaking work on this issue was done by Canny.
17   For an extremely astute reading of this poem, see Osborn.
18   Flier posted to me by Reality Tours.
19   For an account, see Kane.
20   Boucicault's sources for *The Story of Ireland* demonstrate his familiarity with colonial discourse. For comparisons between the Irish, the Native Americans and the Africans, see Allen 27–51, Gibbons, *Transformations* 150–3.
21   Bogdanovich 34. Ford quoted in Bogdanovich 86.
22   The film is loosely based on Sandoz.
23   Sinclair 198.
24   For an excellent discussion of Ford and the Native Americans, see Maltby.
25   Ford also anticipates Costner's climactic image of the buffalo slaughtered 'not for food but for their hides' by white hunters.
26   Thanks to Declan Kiberd and Bill Rolston for this information.

Reading Yeats in Popular Culture

1   Thanks to Pat Sheeran for giving me this magazine.
2   For Yeats's occult obsessions, see R. Foster, *W. B. Yeats* 46–52 and *passim*. For New Age theosophy, see Goldstein 1–19.

3   For Yeats and literary tourism in Ireland, see Thompson, 'The Romance of Simulation'.

4   See Thompson, 'James Joyce and Tourism'.

5   For critiques of 'heritage' in England, see Higson and Corner.

6   For an extremely positive assessment of Strokestown as an 'emancipatory' experience, see Brett 139–53. I share his view of the museum.

7   An excellent exhibition at the Musée de la Publicité in Paris (2000) questioned these theoretical objections through the richness and humour of the examples it presented. See Carrière-Chardon.

8   'Politicians and Their Quoting of William Butler Yeats'.

9   The posters appeared in 1992. Thanks to George Bornstein for this information.

10   The site has now been taken down.

11   Thanks to George Bornstein for this information.

12   Yeats documentary Cast a Cold Eye by Sean O Mordha.

13   See website: trailblazer.ie/regions/galway/visitor/017.html

14   Things have not changed a great deal since Ford's time, if the brochure of the photographic company 'Images of Ireland' is anything to go by.

15   For the national icon of the woman with the harp, see Mother Ireland.

16   Thanks to Juli White for this information.

17   I am grateful to Eric Friedman for sending me the magazine.

18   For a representative example, see Friedman. I cannot cite all my sources here without inflating my bibliography to unmanageable size. Readers can play 'Spot "The Second Coming"' for themselves.

19   Cullingford, Yeats, Ireland and Fascism 116–7, 222.

20   Interviewed on 'Larry King Live', CNN, 13 December 2000.

21   I found Clinton's and Dornan's remarks on websites which have subsequently been removed.

22   See Babylon 5 Lurker's Guide at http://www.midwinter.com/lurk/guide/024.html

23   See http://abc.go.com/daytime/soaps/onelifetolive/history/yearly/oltl_1995f.html

Discrediting de Valera

1   'Opening Remarks', Ireland: Culture, Politics and Identity, Kennedy Center, Washington, May 2000.

2   'Response to Seamus Deane', Ireland: Culture, Politics and Identity, Kennedy Center, Washington, May 2000.

3   See Burns for the box office figures.

4   For Jordan's approbation of Coogan, see Michael Collins 24. For the quotation, see Coogan, Michael Collins 432.

5   See Jordan's 'Diary' for the necessity of a villain and Jordan's interest in having an Irish rather than an English one (Michael Collins 7).

6   Kevin Myers and Proinsias MacAonghusa recently debated the question yet again in the columns of the Irish Times (Myers).

7   See Myers for a discussion of de Valera's childhood.

8   As Jordan well knew: see Michael Collins 66.

9   Quoted in Haslam.

10   See Sinead McCoole, Hazel 63–106.

11   See Sedgwick.
12   Information from Robert Savage.
13   Cahalan says that Owen Roe O'Malley, Grania's uncle, is 'a clone of de Valera' (151), and that Owen O'Malley himself is a partisan of the Free State (153). Owen Roe O'Malley, a worldly and womanizing driver of expensive cars, may resemble Charles Haughey, but he is nothing like de Valera, and Owen O'Malley is identified as a Republican throughout.
14   For Sean O'Faolain's disillusionment, see *Vive Moi* 212–18. For readings of *No Country for Young Men*, see Weeks 179–90; St. Peter 82–8.
15   St. Peter 84–5.
16   Margo Harkin's pessimistic *Hush-a-Bye Baby* (1990) and Orla Walshe's more upbeat *The Visit* (1996) reflect different attitudes towards out-of-wedlock pregnancy.
17   For the first reactions of Garvin and other Irish historians, see C. Byrne.
18   G. FitzGerald was otherwise highly enthusiastic ('Collins Film').
19   Haslam, 'Stories to Do with Love Are Mathematical'.
20   Rene is also the name of the female protagonist in Jordan's *The Miracle*, a film which exactly replicates this relational structure, as does Jordan's short story 'A Love' and his later novel *Sunrise with Sea Monster* (published in America as *Nightlines*.)
21   No one has ever accused the founders of the Free State, the Cumann na nGaedheal party led by Cosgrove, of being either sexy or up to date, but they, not the contemporary IRA, were the direct heirs of Michael Collins.

Seamus and Sinéad

1   The poem appeared on 10 June 1993. For a representative selection of responses (a few pro as well as con), see *Irish Times*, 16 June 1993. Online Lexis-Nexis.
2   See Wills, 'Women Poets' 254–5; Coughlan, 'Bog Queens' 99–108; Cullingford, 'Thinking' 1–3; Longley, 'North' 65–95.
3   Thanks to Luke Gibbons for first alerting me to the importance of *Hush-a-Bye Baby* in a paper at the 'Gender and Colonialism' conference in Galway, 1992.
4   Information from Thornhill College, Derry, courtesy of Margo Harkin.
5   Telephone conversation. My heartfelt thanks are due to Margo Harkin, who answered my questions with illuminating fullness, sent me a large file of materials and cuttings and generously spent her time supporting the project of someone she had never met.
6   Quoted in sleeve notes for *Hush-a-Bye Baby*.
7   For a translation, see A. Bourke.
8   See Northern Ireland Abortion Law Reform Association, 'Abortion' *passim*. For a full discussion of the issue, see Smyth, *Abortion Papers passim*.
9   Tóibín has collected various testimonies and commentaries on these events.
10   Unpublished lecture given at the Yeats International Summer School, 1988.
11   For an account of this censorship, see Goldson, 'Allegories' 8.
12   See also her poem 'What Happens to a Child' on *Am I Not Your Girl?*
13   For Rastafarianism, reggae and British popular culture, see Hebdige 30–45.

14   Telephone conversation.
15   For the classic account of the history and ideology of the figure of the Virgin, see Warner.
16   In McCabe's book, Mrs Nugent is a less monstrous and less political figure; Francie attacks her at least partly because he would like to belong to her family and guiltily rejects this desire as a betrayal of his own mother (P. McCabe 60). Thanks to Stephen Rea for clarifying my thinking on this point.
17   For an account of the conflation of Mother Ireland, the Virgin Mary and Mother Church, see Innes, *Woman and Nation* 35–42.

BIBLIOGRAPHY

Mc is treated as Mac.

Allen, Theodore W. *The Invention of the White Race*. Vol. 1. London: Verso, 1994.

The Alliterative Morte Arthure. Ed. Valerie Krishna. New York: Franklin, 1976.

Amistad. Dir. Steven Spielberg. DreamWorks, 1997.

Andreas. Ed. Kenneth R. Brooks. Oxford: Clarendon Press, 1961.

Andrew, Malcolm. 'The Fall of Troy in *Sir Gawain and the Green Knight* and *Troilus and Criseyde*'. In *The European Tragedy of Troilus*. Ed. Pietro Boitano. Oxford: Clarendon Press, 1989. 75–93.

Andrews, John, Brian Friel and Kevin Barry. '*Translations* and *A Paper Landscape*'. *Crane Bag* 7.2 (1983): 118–24.

Arkins, Brian. 'The Role of Greek and Latin in Friel's *Translations*'. *Colby Library Quarterly* 27.4 (1991): 202–9.

Arnold, Matthew. *Lectures and Essays in Criticism*. Ed. R. H. Super. Ann Arbor: University of Michigan Press, 1982.

Atlantean: An Irishman's Search for North African Roots. Dir. Bob Quinn. Cinegael, 1983.

Attridge, Derek, and Marjorie Howes, eds. *Semicolonial Joyce*. Cambridge: Cambridge University Press, 2000.

Auden, W. H. *Collected Poems*. Ed. Edward Mendelson. New York: Random House, 1976.

Babylon 5. Television series, Warner Brothers and PTEN, 1994–98.

Back to the Future 3. Dir. Robert Zemekis. Universal Pictures, 1990.

Backus, Margot. 'Revising Resistance: *In the Name of the Father* as Postcolonial Paternal Melodrama'. In McKillop 54–70.

Bardwell, Leland. 'The Dove of Peace'. In *Territories of the Voice*. Eds. Louise DeSalvo et al. Boston: Beacon, 1989. 244–56.

Barrow, R. H. *The Romans*. Chicago: Aldine, 1964.

Bartlett, Thomas. 'Bearing Witness: Female Evidences in Courts Martial Convened to Suppress the 1798 Rebellion'. In D. Keogh and Furlong 64–86.

Bartolini, Piero. 'Commerce and Industry'. In *The Phoenicians*. 78–85.

Bateman, Colin. *Divorcing Jack*. New York: Arcade, 1995.

Beautiful People. Dir. Jasmin Dizdar. Trimark Pictures, 1999.

Behan, Brendan. *An Giall/The Hostage*. Trans and ed. Richard Wall. Washington: Catholic University of America Press, 1987.

Beloved Enemy. Dir. H. C. Potter. United Artists, 1936.

Bell, J. Bowyer. *The Irish Troubles: A Generation of Violence 1967–1992*. New York: St. Martins Press, 1993.

Bennett, Ronan. 'The Bomber Next Door'. *Guardian,* 23 November 1992. Online. Lexis-Nexis.

Bérard, Victor. *Les Phéniciens et l'Odyssée*. Paris: Armand Colin, 1927.

Bernal, Martin. *Black Athena: The Afroasiatic Roots of Classical Civilization*. 2 vols. New Brunswick: Rutgers University Press, 1987.

Bew, Paul. 'History it Ain't'. *Daily Telegraph*, 14 October 1996. Online. Lexis-Nexis.

Billen, Andrew. 'The Observer Interview: Forgive Me, Father'. *Observer*, 8 September 1996. Online. Lexis-Nexis.

The Birth of a Nation. Dir. D. W. Griffith. Epoch Corporation, 1915.

Boatman, Joe. 'Look Who's Not Talking'. (Review of *Hush-a-Bye Baby*.) *Living Marxism* (June 1990): 44–5.

Bogdanovich, Peter. *John Ford*. Berkeley: University of California Press, 1968.

Boland, Eavan. *A Kind of Scar: The Woman Poet in a National Tradition*. In *A Dozen Lips*. 72–92.

——. *The Journey and Other Poems*. Manchester: Carcanet Press, 1987.

Bono, Barbara. *Literary Transvaluation: From Vergilian Epic to Shakespearean Tragicomedy*. Berkeley: University of California Press, 1984.

Booth, Michael R. *English Melodrama*. London: Jenkins, 1965.

Bornstein, George. 'Afro-Celtic Connections'. In *Literary Influence and African-American Writers*. Ed. Tracy Mishkin. New York: Garland, 1996. 171–88.

Boucicault, Dion. *Arrah-na-Pogue*. In *The Dolmen Boucicault*. Ed. David Krause. Dublin: Dolmen Press, 1964.

——. 'Leaves from a Dramatist's Diary'. *North American Review* 149 (1889): 228–36.

——. *Selected Plays*. Ed. Andrew Parkin. Gerrards Cross: Colin Smythe, 1987.

——. *The Story of Ireland*. Boston: Osgood, 1881.

Bourke, Angela. 'Silence in Two Languages: Nuala Ní Dhomhnaill and the Unspeakable'. Unpublished Essay.

Bourke, P. J. *For the Land She Loved*. In Herr 310–59.

——. *When Wexford Rose*. In Herr 259–360.

The Boxer. Dir. Jim Sheridan. Written by Jim Sheridan and Terry George. Universal Pictures, 1997.

Bradley, Anthony. *Requiem for a Spy*. Cork: Mercier Press, 1993.

Brady, Ciaran, ed. *Interpreting Irish History*. Dublin: Irish Academic Press, 1994.

Brady, Joan. 'It's Not about Sinéad with Her Hair on'. *Evening Herald*, 3 October 1989.

Brenton, Howard. *The Romans in Britain*. London: Methuen, 1980.

Brett, David. *The Construction of Heritage*. Cork: Cork University Press, 1996.

The Bridges of Madison County. Dir. Clint Eastwood. Warner Brothers, 1995.

Brooks, Peter. *The Melodramatic Imagination*. New Haven: Yale University Press, 1976.

Brown, Paul. 'This Thing of Darkness I Acknowledge Mine: *The Tempest* and the Discourse of Colonialism'. In *Political Shakespeare*. Eds. Jonathan Dollimore and Alan Sinfield. Manchester: Manchester University Press, 1985. 48–71.

Browne, Henry. *Handbook of Homeric Study*. Dublin: Browne and Nolan, 1905.

Bunreacht na hÉireann. Dundalk: Dundalgan Press, n.d.

Burns, John, and Eamon Lynch. 'Oscar Victory Is Last Hope as *Michael Collins* Flops in US'. *Sunday Times*, 15 December 1996. Online. Lexis-Nexis.

Butch Cassidy and the Sundance Kid. Dir. George Roy Hill. Twentieth Century Fox, 1969.

The Butcher Boy. Dir. Neil Jordan. Warner Brothers, 1997. Based on Pat McCabe's *The Butcher Boy*.

Butler, Judith. *Gender Trouble: Feminism and the Subversion of Identity*. New York: Routledge, 1990.

Buttrey, John. 'A Cautionary Tale'. In *Dido and Aeneas: An Opera*. Ed. Curtis Price. New York: Norton, 1986. 228–35.

Byrne, Ciaran, and Olga Craig. 'Hollywood's Rewrite of Irish History Clouds Peace Process'. *Sunday Times*, 14 January 1996. Online. Lexis-Nexis.

Byrne, Terry. *Power in the Eye: An Introduction to Contemporary Irish Film*. London: Scarecrow Press, 1997.

Byron, George Gordon, Lord. *Don Juan*. Eds. T. G. Steffan, E. Steffan and W. W. Pratt. New Haven: Yale University Press, 1982.

Cahalan, James M. *Double Visions: Women and Men in Contemporary Irish Fiction*. Syracuse: Syracuse University Press, 1999.

Cairns, David. *Writing Ireland: Colonialism, Nationalism and Culture*. Manchester: Manchester University Press, 1988.

———. and Toni O'Brien Johnson, eds. In *Gender in Irish Writing*. Milton Keynes: Open University Press, 1991.

———. and Shaun Richards. 'Tropes and Traps: Aspects of "Woman" and Nationality in Twentieth-Century Irish Drama'. In Cairns, *Gender in Irish Writing*. 128–37.

Cameron, Ian, and Douglas Pye, eds. *The Book of Westerns*. New York: Continuum, 1996.

Canny, Nicholas. *Kingdom and Colony: Ireland in the Atlantic World, 1560–1800*. Baltimore: Johns Hopkins University Press, 1988.

Canny, Nicholas, and Andrew Carpenter, eds. 'The Early Planters: Spenser and his Contemporaries'. In Deane, *Field Day Anthology* 1: 171–4.

Carr, Marina. *By the Bog of Cats*. Loughcrew, County Meath: Gallery, 1998.

Carrière-Chardon, Sarah. *L'Art dans la Pub*. Paris: Musée de la Publicité, 2000.

Cave, Richard. 'Staging the Irishman'. In *Acts of Supremacy: The British Empire and the Stage, 1790–1930*. Eds. J. S. Bratton et al. Manchester: Manchester University Press, 1991. 62–128.

Chambers, John. 'Nobel Prize Winner Predicted Alien/Human Hybrids'. *UFO Universe* 7.1 (1997): 54–8.

Chaucer, Geoffrey. *The Works*. Ed. F. N. Robinson. 2nd ed. Boston: Houghton, 1957.

Cheng, Vincent J. *Joyce, Race, and Empire*. Cambridge: Cambridge University Press, 1995.

Cheyenne Autumn. Dir. John Ford. Warner Brothers, 1964.

Clinton, William Jefferson. *Between Hope and History: Meeting America's Challenges for the Twenty-first Century*. New York: Random House, 1966.

Colley, Linda. *Britons: Forging the Nation, 1707–1837*. New Haven: Yale University Press, 1992.

Colls, Robert, and Philip Dodd, eds. *Englishness: Politics and Culture 1880–1920*. London: Croom Helm, 1986.

The Commitments. Dir. Alan Parker. First Film Company/Dirty Hands, 1991.

Condren, Mary. *The Serpent and the Goddess*. San Francisco: Harper, 1989.

Conrad, Joseph. *The Heart of Darkness*. Ed. Robert Kimbrough. 3rd ed. New York: Norton, 1988.

Conlon, Gerry. *In the Name of the Father*. New York: Plume, 1993.

Conyngham, David Power. *Ireland Past and Present*. New York: Sheehy, 1884.

Coogan, Tim Pat. *Eamon de Valera: The Man Who Was Ireland*. 3rd ed. New York: Harper, 1996.

——. *The Man Who Made Ireland: The Life and Death of Michael Collins*. Colorado: Roberts Rinehart, 1992.

Corbett, Mary Jean. *Allegories of Union in Irish and English Writing, 1790–1870*. Cambridge: Cambridge University Press, 2000.

Corcoran, Neil. *Seamus Heaney*. London: Faber, 1986.

Corner, John, and Sylvia Harvey. 'Mediating Tradition and Modernity: The Heritage/Enterprise Couplet'. In *Enterprise and Heritage: Crosscurrents of National Culture*. Ed. John Corner and Sylvia Harvey. London: Routledge, 1991. 45–75.

Costello, Peter. *James Joyce*. Schull, West Cork: Roberts Rinehart, 1992.

Coughlan, Patricia. '"Bog Queens": The Representation of Women in the Poetry of John Montague and Seamus Heaney'. In Cairns, *Gender in Irish Writing*. 88–111.

——. '"Some Secret Scourge Which Shall by Her Come Unto England"': Ireland and Incivility in Spenser'. Coughlan, *Spenser* 46–74.

——, ed. *Spenser and Ireland*. Cork: Cork University Press, 1989.

Coulter, Carol. *Ireland between the First and Third Worlds*. In *A Dozen Lips* 93–116.

The Cranberries. 'Yeats's Grave'. *No Need to Argue*. Island Records. 314-524050-2. 1994.

Cross, Tom Peete, and Clark Harris Slover, eds. *Ancient Irish Tales*. Rev. ed. New Jersey: Barnes and Noble, 1969.

The Crying Game. Dir. Neil Jordan. Miramax, 1992.

Cullingford, Elizabeth Butler. *Gender and History in Yeats's Love Poetry*. Cambridge: Cambridge University Press, 1993.

——. 'Thinking of Her . . . as . . . Ireland': Yeats, Pearse and Heaney'. *Textual Practice* 4.1 (1990): 1–21.

——. *Yeats, Ireland and Fascism*. London: Macmillan, 1981.

Curtis, Edmund. *A History of Ireland*. London: Methuen, 1961

Curtis, L. P. *Anglo-Saxons and Celts*. Bridgeport, CT: University of Bridgeport Conference on British Studies, 1968.

———. *Apes and Angels: The Irishman in Victorian Caricature*. Washington DC: Smithsonian Institution, 1971.

D'Alton, E. A. *History of Ireland from the Earliest Times to the Present Day*. London: Gresham Publishing Company, 1913.

Dalton, G. F. 'The Tradition of Blood Sacrifice to the Goddess Eire'. *Studies* 63.252 (1974): 343–54.

Dances with Wolves. Dir. Kevin Costner. Orion Pictures, 1990.

Davidson, Neil. *James Joyce, Ulysses, and the Construction of Jewish Identity*. Cambridge: Cambridge University Press, 1996.

De Valera, Eamon. *Speeches and Statements: 1917–73*. Ed. Maurice Moynihan. Dublin: Gill, 1980.

Deane, Seamus. 'Dion Boucicault'. In Deane, *Field Day Anthology* 2: 234.

———. 'Civilians and Barbarians'. In *Ireland's Field Day* 33–42.

———. 'Dead Ends: Joyce's Finest Moments'. In Attridge and Howes 21–36.

———, ed. *The Field Day Anthology of Irish Writing*. 3 vols. Derry: Field Day Publications: 1991.

———. 'Heroic Styles: The Tradition of an Idea'. In *Ireland's Field Day* 45–58.

———. 'Irish National Character: 1790–1900'. In *The Writer as Witness: Literature as Historical Evidence*. Ed. Tom Dunne. Cork: Cork University Press, 1987. 90–113.

———. *Strange Country*. Oxford: Clarendon Press, 1997.

Desmond, Marilynn. *Reading Dido: Gender, Textuality, and the Medieval Aeneid*. Minneapolis: University of Minnesota Press, 1994.

Destry Rides Again. Dir. George Marshall. Universal Pictures, 1939.

Devlin, Anne. *After Easter*. London: Faber, 1994.

———. *Ourselves Alone*. London: Faber, 1986.

Dillon, Martin. *The Dirty War*. London: Arrow, 1991.

Dixon of Dock Green. Television series. BBC, London. 1955–78.

Dorgan, Theo. 'Right from the Heart'. *Irish Times*, 31 December 1999. Online. Lexis-Nexis.

Doyle, Roddy. *The Commitments*. London: Minerva, 1988.

———. *Paddy Clarke Ha Ha Ha*. London: Secker and Warburg, 1993.

A Dozen Lips. Dublin: Attic Press, 1994.

Duffy, Enda. *The Subaltern Ulysses*. Minneapolis: University of Minnesota Press, 1994.

Duggan, George. *The Stage Irishman*. New York: Blom, 1937.

Dunlop, Robert. *Ireland from the Earliest Times to the Present Day*. Oxford: Oxford University Press, 1922.

Durcan, Paul. 'Foreword'. In Evans viii–ix.

———. *Greetings to Our Friends in Brazil*. London: Harvill, 1999.

———. *O Westport in the Light of Asia Minor*. London: Harvill, 1995.

———. *Sam's Cross*. Portmarnock, County Dublin: Profile Poetry, 1978.

———. *The Selected Paul Durcan*. Ed. Edna Longley. Belfast: Blackstaff, 1982.

———. *Teresa's Bar*. Dublin: Gallery, 1986.

Eagleton, Terry. *Against the Grain: Essays 1975–85*. London: Verso, 1986.

——. *Saint Oscar*. Derry: Field Day, 1989.

——, Fredric Jameson and Edward W. Said. *Nationalism, Colonialism, and Literature*. Minneapolis: University of Minnesota Press, 1990.

East is East. Dir. Damien O'Donnell. Miramax Films, 1999.

Eat the Peach. Dir. Peter Ormrod. Skouras Pictures, 1986.

Easthope, Antony. *Literary into Cultural Studies*. London: Routledge, 1991.

Edge, Sarah. 'Women Are Trouble, Did You Know That, Fergus?' *Feminist Review* 50 (1995): 173–86.

Edgeworth, Maria. *The Absentee*. Eds. W. J. McCormack and Kim Walker. Oxford: Oxford University Press, 1988.

Edwards, Mark. 'Nothing Compares 2 Her'. *Sunday Times*, 29 October 2000. Online. Lexis-Nexis.

Edwards, Ruth Dudley. Letter. *Daily Telegraph*, 15 October 1996. Online. Lexis-Nexis.

Eliot, T. S. *Collected Poems 1909–1962*. London: Faber, 1963.

Elliott, Marianne. *Partners in Revolution*. New Haven: Yale University Press, 1982.

Ellmann, Richard. *James Joyce*. Oxford: Oxford University Press, 1965.

Eogan, George. *Knowth and the Passage Tombs of Ireland*. London: Thames and Hudson, 1986.

ET. Dir. Steven Spielberg. Universal Pictures, 1982.

Evans, E. Estyn. *The Personality of Ireland: Habitat, Heritage and History*. Dublin: Lilliput Press, 1992.

Farrell, Michael. 'Long March to Freedom'. In *Twenty Years On*. Ed. Michael Farrell. Dingle: Brandon, 1988. 54–74.

Fawkes, Richard. *Dion Boucicault*. London: Quartet, 1979.

Fay, W. G., and Catherine Carswell. *The Fays of the Abbey Theatre*. New York: Harcourt, 1935.

Felski, Rita. *Beyond Feminist Aesthetics: Feminist Literature and Social Change*. Cambridge, MA: Harvard University Press, 1989.

Fennell, Desmond. *Whatever You Say, Say Nothing: Why Seamus Heaney Is No. 1*. Dublin: ELO, 1991.

Ferguson, M. C. *The Story of the Irish before the Conquest*. London: Bell, 1868.

The Field. Dir. Jim Sheridan. Avenue Pictures, 1990.

Finegan, John. *Anne Devlin: Patriot and Heroine*. 2nd ed. Dublin: ELO, 1992.

Finlay, Fergus. *Mary Robinson: A President with a Purpose*. Dublin: O'Brien Press, 1990.

FitzGerald, Garret. 'Collins Film a Triumphant, Deeply Moving Experience'. *Irish Times*, 14 September 1996. Online. Lexis-Nexis.

Fitzgerald, Jennifer. 'The Arts and Ideology'. *Crane Bag* 9.2 (1985): 60–9.

Fitz-Simon, Christopher. *The Irish Theatre*. London: Thames and Hudson, 1983.

Fort Apache. Dir. John Ford. RKO, 1948.

Forster, E. M. *A Passage to India*. New York: Harcourt, 1984.

Foster, John Wilson. *Fictions of the Irish Literary Revival*. Syracuse: Syracuse University Press, 1987.

Foster, Roy. *Modern Ireland*. London: Allen Lane, 1988.

———. *W. B. Yeats: A Life. 1: The Apprentice Mage: 1865–1914*. Oxford: Oxford University Press, 1997.

Friedman, Thomas. 'Will the Center Hold?' *New York Times*, 30 June 1996. Week in Review: 15.

Friel, Brian. *Dancing at Lughnasa*. London: Faber, 1990.

———. *Making History*. London: Faber, 1989.

———. *Translations*. London: Faber, 1981.

Friel, Brian, John Andrews and Kevin Barry. '*Translations* and *A Paper Landscape*: Between Fiction and History'. *Crane Bag* 7.2 (1983): 118–24.

Furlong, Nicholas. *Fr. John Murphy of Boolavogue: 1753–1798*. Dublin: Geography Publications, 1991.

Gallagher, Tag. *John Ford, The Man and his Films*. Berkeley: University of California Press, 1986.

Gandhi. Dir. Richard Attenborough. Columbia Pictures, 1982.

Geoffrey of Monmouth. *Histories of the Kings of Britain*. Trans. Sebastian Evans. London: Dent, 1912.

Gerould, Daniel. 'Melodrama and Revolution'. In *Melodrama: Stage Picture Screen* Eds. Jacky Bratton, Jim Cook and Christine Gledhill. London: British Film Institute, 1994. 185–98.

Gibbons, Luke. 'Constructing the Canon: Versions of National Identity'. In Deane, *Field Day Anthology* 2: 950–5.

———. 'Dialogue Without the Other'. *Radical Philosophy* 67 (1994): 28–31

———. 'Framing History: Neil Jordan's *Michael Collins*'. *History Ireland* 5.1 (1997): 47–51.

———. 'On the Beach'. *Artforum*, October 1992: 13.

———. 'Romanticism, Realism and Irish Cinema'. In *Cinema and Ireland*. Eds. Kevin Rockett, Luke Gibbons and John Hill. London: Routledge, 1988. 194–257.

———. *Transformations in Irish Culture*. Cork: Cork University Press, 1996.

Gilbert, Stuart. *James Joyce's Ulysses*. New York: Knopf, 1952.

Giraldus Cambrensis. *Expugnatio Hibernica*. In *Historical Works*. London: Bohn, 1863.

———. *The History and Topography of Ireland*. Trans. John O'Meara. Portlaoise, Ireland: Dolmen Press, 1982.

Glob, P. V. *The Bog People*. Trans. Rupert Bruce Mitford. London: Faber, 1969.

The Godfather. Dir. Francis Ford Coppola. Paramount Pictures, 1972.

Goldson, Annie. 'Allegories of Resistance'. *Afterimage*, May 1989: 8–9.

Goldstein, Matthew. *Theosophy, Culture, and Empire*. Dissertation, University of Texas at Austin, 2000.

Gone With the Wind. Dir. Victor Fleming. MGM, 1939.

Graves, Robert. 'The Stage Irishman among the Irish'. *Theatre History Studies* 1 (1981): 29–39.

Grene, Nicholas. *The Politics of Irish Drama*. Cambridge: Cambridge University Press, 1999.

Hackett, Francis. *Ireland: A Study in Nationalism*. New York: Huebsch, 1918.

Hall, Stuart. 'Notes on Deconstructing "The Popular"'. In *People's History and Socialist Theory*. Ed. Raphael Samuel. London: Routledge, 1981. 227–40.

Harbison, Peter. *Pilgrimage in Ireland: The Monuments and the People*. New York: Syracuse University Press, 1992.

Harford, Barbara, and Sarah Hopkins, eds. *Greenham Common: Women at the Wire*. London: Women's Press, 1984.

Harkin, Margo. Letter to the author, 28 June 1993.

——. 'No Plundering at This Port: Derry Film and Video Workshop'. *Irish Reporter* 6 (1992): 18–21.

Harnden, Toby. 'Collins Film "Is Insult to Murdered RUC Officers"'. *Daily Telegraph*, 22 October 1996. Online. Lexis-Nexis.

Harrington, John P., ed. *The English Traveller in Ireland*. Dublin: Wolfhound Press, 1991.

——. *The Irish Play on the New York Stage, 1874–1966*. Lexington: University Press of Kentucky, 1997.

Harris, Ellen T. *Henry Purcell's Dido and Aeneas*. Oxford: Clarendon Press, 1987.

Harris, Eoghan. '*Michael Collins*: A Tale of Bad History and Art'. *Sunday Times*, 10 November 1996. Online. Lexis-Nexis.

Harris, Susan Cannon. *Bodies and Blood: Gender and Sacrifice in Modern Irish Drama*. Ann Arbor: UMI, 1998. AAT 9837975.

——. '"Watch Yourself": Performance, Sexual Difference, and National Identity in the Irish Plays of Frank McGuinness'. *Genders* 28 (1998). (http://www.genders.org/g28/g28_watchyourself.html).

Hart, Henry. *Seamus Heaney: Poet of Contrary Progressions*. Syracuse: Syracuse University Press, 1992.

Haslam, Richard. 'Stories to Do with Love Are Mathematical: Neil Jordan and the ABC of Narratology'. Unpublished paper.

Hawkins, Maureen S. G. 'The Dramatic Treatment of Robert Emmet and Sarah Curran'. In *Woman in Irish Legend, Life and Literature*. Ed S. F. Gallagher. Gerrards Cross: Colin Smythe, 1983. 125–37.

Hayes, Dermott. *Sinéad O'Connor: So Different*. London: Omnibus, 1991.

Hayhurst, James L. 'The Fighter Pilot's Poem'. *Airline Pilot* 67.6 (1998): 28–32.

Heaney, Seamus. *The Cure at Troy*. London: Faber, 1990.

——. *The Government of the Tongue*. London: Faber, 1988.

——. Interview. Bo Almqvist, 'Of Mermaids and Marriages'. *Béaloideas* 58 (1990): 43–50.

——. 'Mother Ireland'. *The Listener*, 7 December 1972. 790.

——. *North*. London: Faber, 1975.

——. 'An Open Letter'. *Ireland's Field Day* 23–9.

——. *Preoccupations*. London: Faber, 1984.

——. 'Unhappy and at Home'. *Crane Bag* 1.1 (1977): 61–7.

——. *Wintering Out*. London: Faber, 1972.

Hebdige, Dick. *Subculture: The Meaning of Style*. London: Routledge, 1988.

Herodotus. *The History*. Trans. David Grene. Chicago: University of Chicago Press, 1987.

Herr, Cheryl, ed. *For the Land They Loved: Irish Political Melodramas 1890–1925*. Syracuse: Syracuse University Press, 1991.

Herring, Phillip F. 'Joyce's Politics'. In *New Light on Joyce*. Ed. Fritz Senn. Bloomington: Indiana University Press, 1972. 3–14.

Hewson, Paul (Bono). 'The White Nigger'. In *Across the Frontiers: Ireland in the 1990s*. Ed. Richard Kearney. Dublin: Wolfhound Press, 1988. 188–91.

Hicklin, Aaron. 'Angelic Upstart'. *Sunday Herald*, 25 June 2000. Online. Lexis-Nexis.

Hidden Agenda. Dir. Ken Loach. Hemdale Films, 1990.

High Noon. Dir. Fred Zinnemann. United Artists, 1952.

Higson, Andrew. 'Re-presenting the National Past: Nostalgia and Pastiche in the Heritage Film'. In *Fires Were Started: British Cinema and Thatcherism*. Ed. Lester Friedman. Minneapolis: University of Minnesota Press, 1993. 109–29.

Hogan, Robert. *Dion Boucicault*. New York: Twayne, 1969.

Holland, Mary. 'Eire: Girl on a Nation's Conscience'. *Observer*, 23 February 1992. Online. Lexis-Nexis.

——. 'Tongues of Fire As Hope and History Rhyme'. *Irish Times*, 12 October 1995. Online. Lexis-Nexis.

hooks, bell. *Outlaw Culture*. New York: Routledge, 1994.

Howe, Stephen. *Ireland and Empire: Colonial Legacies in Irish History and Culture*. Oxford: Oxford University Press, 2000.

Howes, Marjorie. *Yeats's Nations: Gender, Class, and Irishness*. Cambridge: Cambridge University Press, 1996.

Hugill, Barry, and Dean Nelson. 'Peace for One Year – but the War Is Still Not Over'. *Observer*, 27 August 1995. Online. Lexis-Nexis.

Hush-a-Bye Baby. Dir. Margo Harkin. Derry Film and Video, 1988.

Ignatiev, Noel. *How the Irish Became White*. New York: Routledge, 1995.

The Informer. Dir. John Ford. RKO, 1935.

Innes, Lyn. *The Devil's Own Mirror: The Irishman and the African in Modern Literature*. Washington, DC: Three Continents Press, 1990.

——. *Woman and Nation in Irish Literature and Society*. New York: Harvester, 1993.

In the Name of the Father. Dir. Jim Sheridan. Universal Pictures, 1993.

Interview with the Vampire. Dir. Neil Jordan. Warner Brothers, 1994.

Into the West. Dir. Mike Newell. Miramax Films, 1992.

Ireland's Field Day. Notre Dame: University of Notre Dame Press, 1986.

Ishiguro, Kazuo. *The Remains of the Day*. New York: Vintage, 1993.

Jackson, Kevin. 'A Hero Too Good to Be True'. *Independent*, 10 November 1996. Online. Lexis-Nexis.

Jenkins, Simon. 'Stories That Get in the Way of Facts'. *Times*, 12 March 1994. Online. Lexis-Nexis.

Johnston, Jennifer. *Three Monologues: Twinkletoes; Musn't Forget High Noon; Christine*. Belfast: Lagan Press, 1995.

Johnson, Paul. 'The *Guardian*, Mr. Jordan and a Simple Case of Mass Murder'. *Spectator*, 2 November 1996: 30.

Jones, Ann Rosalind, and Peter Stallybrass. 'Dismantling Irena: The Sexualizing of Ireland in Early Modern England'. In *Nationalisms and Sexualities*. Eds. Andrew Parker et al. New York: Routledge, 1992. 157–71.

Jordan, Neil. *The Crying Game*. London: Vintage, 1993.

——. 'Imagining Otherwise'. In Kearney, *Across the Frontiers*. 196–9.

——. Interview. *Film Ireland* 32 (April/May 1993): 20.

——. *Michael Collins*. New York: Plume, 1996.

——. *A Neil Jordan Reader*. New York: Vintage, 1993.

——. *Night in Tunisia*. London: Vintage, 1993.

——. *Nightlines* (first published as *Sunrise with Sea Monster*). New York: Random House, 1994.

——. *The Past*. London: Vintage, 1993.

Joyce, James. *The Critical Writings of James Joyce*. Ed. Ellsworth Mason and Richard Ellmann. New York: Viking, 1964.

——. *Dubliners*. Ed. Terence Brown. Harmondsworth: Penguin, 1992.

——. *Letters*. Vol. 2. Ed. Richard Ellmann. New York: Viking, 1966.

——. *A Portrait of the Artist as a Young Man*. Ed. Seamus Deane. Harmondsworth: Penguin, 1992.

——. *Stephen Hero*. London: Cape, 1969.

——. *Ulysses*. Ed. Hans Walter Gabler. New York: Vintage, 1986.

Joyce, Stanislaus. *The Complete Dublin Diary*. Ed. George H. Healey. Ithaca: Cornell University Press, 1971.

Jurassic Park. Dir. Steven Spielberg. Universal Pictures, 1993.

Kane, Kathleen Mary. *To Hell or Pine Ridge: Legislation, Literature, and the Trans-Atlantic Development of the Reservation*. Ann Arbor: UMI, 1997. AAT 9822628.

Kearney, Richard, ed. *Across the Frontiers: Ireland in the 1990s*. Dublin: Wolfhound Press, 1988.

——. 'The Language Plays of Brian Friel'. In Kearney, *Transitions*. Dublin: Wolfhound Press, 1988. 123–60.

——. 'Myth and Motherland'. *Ireland's Field Day*. 59–80.

——. *Postnationalist Ireland: Politics, Culture, Philosophy*. London: Routledge, 1997.

——. *Transitions: Narratives in Modern Irish Culture*. Dublin: Wolfhound Press, 1988.

Keating, Geoffrey. *The History of Ireland*. Vol. 1. Trans. David Comyn. London: Irish Texts Society, 1902.

Keenan, Brian. *An Evil Cradling*. London: Hutchinson, 1992.

Keogh, Daire, and Nicholas Furlong, eds. *The Women of 1798*. Dublin: Four Courts Press, 1998.

Keogh, Dermot. *Jews in Twentieth-Century Ireland: Refugees, Anti-Semitism and the Holocaust*. Cork: Cork University Press, 1998.

Kiberd, Declan. 'The Fall of the Stage Irishman'. In *The Genres of the Irish Literary Revival*. Ed. Ronald Schliefer. Norman: Pilgrim, 1980. 39–60.

——. *Inventing Ireland*. London: Cape, 1995.

——. 'The War against the Past'. In *The Uses of the Past: Essays on Irish Culture*. Eds. Audrey S. Eyler and Robert Garratt. Newark: Delaware University Press, 1988. 24–54.

Kingsley, Francis, ed. *Charles Kingsley, His Letters and Memories of His Life*. Vol. 3. London: Macmillan, 1901.

Kinsella, Ann. 'Nineteenth-Century Perspectives: The Women of 1798 in Folk Memory and Ballads'. In D. Keogh and Furlong 187–99.

Kinsella, Thomas. *Fifteen Dead*. Dublin: Dolmen Press, 1979.

Koestenbaum, Wayne. 'The Queen's Throat: (Homo)sexuality and the Art of Singing'. In *Inside/Out: Lesbian Theories, Gay Theories*. Ed. Diana Fuss. New York: Routledge, 1991. 205–34.

Kosok, Heinz. 'John Bull's Other Ego: Reactions to the Stage Irishman in Anglo-Irish Drama'. In *Medieval and Modern Ireland*. Ed. Richard Wall. Gerrards Cross: Smythe, 1988. 19–33.

Krause, David. 'The Theatre of Dion Boucicault'. In *The Dolmen Boucicault*. Ed. David Krause. Dublin: Dolmen Press, 1964. 9–47.

Lamb. Dir. Colin Gregg. Channel Four Films, 1985.

Landreth, Helen. *The Pursuit of Robert Emmet*. New York: McGraw Hill, 1948.

Langford, Paul. *Englishness Identified: Manners and Character 1650–1850*. Oxford: Oxford University Press, 2000.

Larkin, Philip. *The Whitsun Weddings*. London: Faber, 1977.

Lawrence of Arabia. Dir. David Lean. Columbia Pictures, 1962.

Lebor Gabála Erenn. Ed. and trans. R. A. MacAlister. 5 vols. Dublin: Irish Texts Society, 1938–56.

Lee, J. J. *Ireland 1912–1985: Politics and Society*. Cambridge: Cambridge University Press, 1991.

Leerssen, Joep. *Mere Irish and Fíor-Ghael*. Cork: Cork University Press, 1996.

——. 'On the Edge of Europe: Ireland in Search of Oriental Roots, 1650–1850'. *Comparative Criticism* 8 (1986): 91–112.

——. *Remembrance and Imagination*. Cork: Cork University Press, 1996.

Lew, Joseph W. 'Sidney Owenson and the Fate of Empire'. *Keats-Shelley Journal* 39 (1990): 39–65.

Little Big Man. Dir. Arthur Penn. National General Pictures, 1970.

Lloyd, David. *Anomalous States: Irish Writing and the Post-Colonial Moment*. Durham, NC: Duke University Press, 1993.

——. *Ireland After History*. Cork: Cork University Press, 1999.

———. Response to Seamus Deane. *Ireland: Culture, Politics and Identity*, Kennedy Center, Washington, May 2000.

Loftus, Belinda. *Mirrors: William III and Mother Ireland*. Dundrum, County Down: Picture Press, 1990.

Longley, Edna. '*North*: "Inner Emigre" or "Artful Voyeur"?' In *The Art of Seamus Heaney*. Ed. Tony Curtis. Bridgend: Poetry Wales, 1982. 65–95.

———. 'Poetry and Politics in Northern Ireland'. *Crane Bag* 9.1 (1985): 26–40.

Lowe, Lisa. *Critical Terrains*. Ithaca: Cornell University Press, 1991.

Lyons, F. S. L. *Ireland Since the Famine*. London: Weidenfeld, 1971.

MacAleese, Mary. Opening Remarks. *Ireland: Culture, Politics and Identity*. Kennedy Center, Washington, May 2000.

McAliskey, Bernadette. 'Playboy Interview: Bernadette Devlin'. *Playboy*, September 1972: 67–91.

Macardle, Dorothy. *The Irish Republic*. London: Corgi, 1968.

McCabe, Colin. *James Joyce and the Revolution of the Word*. London: Macmillan, 1978.

McCabe, Patrick. *The Butcher Boy*. London: Picador, 1993.

McCafferty, Nell. *The Best of Nell*. Dublin: Attic Press, 1984.

———. *Goodnight Sisters*. Dublin: Attic Press, 1987.

———. *A Woman to Blame: The Kerry Babies Case*. Dublin: Attic Press, 1985.

McCain, John. Interview. *Larry King Live*, CNN, 13 December 2000.

MacCana, Proinsias. 'Women in Irish Mythology'. *Crane Bag* 4.1 (1980): 7–11.

McCann, Eamonn. *Bloody Sunday in Derry*. Dingle: Brandon, 1992.

McCarthy, Thomas. *The First Convention*. Dublin: Dolmen Press, 1978.

———. *The Non-Aligned Storyteller*. London: Anvil Press, 1984.

———. *Seven Winters in Paris*. London: Anvil Press, 1989.

———. *The Sorrow Garden*. London: Anvil Press, 1981.

McCoole, Sinead. *Hazel: A Life of Lady Lavery 1880–1935*. Dublin: Lilliput Press, 1996.

McCord, Norman. 'The Fenians and Public Opinion in Great Britain'. In *Fenians and Fenianism*. Ed. Maurice Harmon. Dublin: Scepter, 1970. 40–55.

McCormack, W. J. *The Battle of the Books: Two Decades of Irish Cultural Debate*. Mullingar: Lilliput Press, 1986.

———. 'Introduction'. In *The Absentee*. Ed. W. J. McCormack and Kim Walker. Oxford: Oxford University Press, 1988. ix–xlii.

McCormick, John. 'Origins of Melodrama'. In Pine, *Dion Boucicault* 5–12.

McCourt, Frank. *Angela's Ashes: A Memoir*. New York: Scribner, 1996.

MacDougall, Hugh A. *Racial Myth in English History: Trojans, Teutons, and Anglo-Saxons*. Montreal: Harvest, 1982.

MacDubhghaill, Uinsionn. 'People of Derry Urged to Seek "Further Shore" of Lasting Peace'. *Irish Times*, 1 December 1995.

McGlynn, Mary. 'Play That Country Music Whiteboys: Or, Garth Brooks in Ireland'. Unpublished paper, ACIS National Conference, 1999.

McGrath, F. C. 'Brian Friel and the Politics of the Anglo-Irish Language'. *Colby Quarterly* 26.4 (1990): 241–8.

——. *Brian Friel's (Post)Colonial Drama: Language, Illusion, and Politics*. Syracuse: Syracuse University Press, 1999.

McGuinness, Frank. 'All about My Mother'. Interview with Fiachra Gibbons. *Guardian*, 17 May 2000. Online. Lexis-Nexis.

——. *Carthaginians and* Baglady. London: Faber, 1988.

——. *Dolly West's Kitchen*. London: Faber, 1992.

——. 'A Dramatist Deep-Rooted in Ireland'. Interview with Sue Summers. *Daily Telegraph*, 7 July 1992. Online. Lexis-Nexis.

——. *Mary and Lizzie*. London: Faber, 1989.

——. *Mutabilitie*. London: Faber, 1997.

——. *Observe the Sons of Ulster Marching towards the Somme*. London: Faber, 1986.

——. Programme. *Carthaginians*. Dir. Frank McGuinness. Galway: Druid Theatre, 1992.

——. *Someone Who'll Watch over Me*. London: Faber, 1992.

——. Telephone interview. 16 August 1994.

McIlroy, Brian. *Shooting to Kill: Filmmaking and the 'Troubles' in Northern Ireland*. Trowbridge: Flicks, 1998.

Mac Intyre, Tom. *Good Evening, Mr. Collins*. In *The Dazzling Dark: New Irish Plays*. Ed. Frank McGuinness. London: Faber, 1996. 173–233.

Mackay, Jane, and Pat Thane. 'The Englishwoman'. In Colls and Dodd 191–229.

Mackay, Susan. '(Unwilling) Mother Ireland'. *Fortnight*, January 1990: 29.

McKillop, James, ed. *Contemporary Irish Cinema*. Syracuse: Syracuse University Press, 1999.

McLaverty, Bernard. *Lamb*. London: Cape, 1980.

McMahon, Sean. 'The Wearing of the Green: The Irish Plays of Dion Boucicault'. *Eire/Ireland* 2 (Summer 1967): 98–111.

——, ed. *The Poolbeg Book of Irish Ballads*. Dublin: Poolbeg Press, 1991.

McMillan, Joyce. 'What Did You Do In The War, Dolly?' *Scotsman*, 12 October 1999. Online. Lexis-Nexis.

MacNeice, Louis. *Collected Poems*. Ed. E. R. Dodds. New York: Oxford University Press, 1967.

Madonna. 'Sinéad's Outburst'. *Irish Times*, 17 October 1992. Online. Lexis-Nexis.

Mahoney, Rosemary. *Whoredom in Kimmage*. Boston: Houghton, 1993.

Maltby, Richard. 'A Better Sense of History: John Ford and the Indians'. In Cameron and Pye 34–49.

Manganiello, Dominic. *Joyce's Politics*. London: Routledge, 1980.

Margolick, David. *Strange Fruit: Billie Holiday, Café Society, and an Early Cry for Civil Rights*. Philadelphia: Running Press, 2000.

Mattingly, H. 'Introduction'. *Tacitus on Britain and Germany*. Harmondsworth: Penguin, 1948.

Mazza, Federico. 'The Phoenicians as Seen by the Ancient World'. *The Phoenicians*. 548–67.

Meehan, Paula. *The Man Who Was Marked by Winter*. Oldcastle, County Meath: Gallery, 1991.

Meisel, Martin. *Shaw and the Nineteenth-Century Theater*. Princeton: Princeton University Press, 1963.

Memphis Belle. Dir. Michael Caton-Jones. Prod. David Puttnam. Warner Brothers, 1990.

The Miracle. Dir. Neil Jordan. Miramax Films, 1991.

Mitchell, G. F. 'Prehistoric Ireland'. In *The Course of Irish History*. Eds. T. F. Moody and F. X. Martin. Rev. ed. Cork: Mercier Press, 1987. 30–42.

Molin, Sven Eric, and Robin Goodefellowe. 'Nationalism on the Dublin Stage'. *Eire/Ireland* 21 (Spring 1986): 135–8.

Monette, Paul. *Becoming a Man*. New York: Harper, 1992.

Montague, John. *An Occasion of Sin*. Eds. Barry Callaghan and David Lampe. Toronto: Exile Editions, 1992.

Montaigne, Michel de. 'On Cannibals'. In *Essays*. Trans. J. M. Cohen. Penguin: Harmondsworth, 1958. 105–19.

Moore, Christy. 'Middle of the Island'. *Voyage*. WEA Records. 82034-2. 1989.

Morgan, Jack. 'The Irish in John Ford's Seventh Cavalry Trilogy: Victor McLaglen's Stooge-Irish Caricature'. *Melus* 22.2 (1997): 33–44.

Morrison, Blake. *Seamus Heaney*. London: Methuen, 1982.

Mother Ireland. Dir. Anne Crilly. Derry Film and Video, 1988.

Muldoon, Paul. *Madoc: A Mystery*. London: Faber, 1990.

——. *Meeting the British*. Winston-Salem: Wake Forest University Press, 1987.

——. *Quoof*. Winston-Salem: Wake Forest University Press, 1983.

Mulhern, Francis. 'A Nation, Yet Again: *The Field Day Anthology*'. *Radical Philosophy* 65 (Autumn 1993): 23–9.

Mulholland, John. 'Irreverent Mother'. *Observer*, 9 May 1999. Online. Lexis-Nexis.

Mulvey, Laura. 'Visual Pleasure and Narrative Cinema'. *Screen* 16.3 (1975): 6–18.

Mullin, Katherine. 'Don't Cry for Me, Argentina: "Eveline" and the Seductions of Emigration Propaganda'. In Attridge and Howes 172–200.

Murphy, Andrew. *But the Irish Sea betwixt Us: Ireland, Colonialism, and Renaissance Literature*. Lexington: University Press of Kentucky, 1999.

Murphy, Tom. *Plays: Two*. Introduction by Fintan O'Toole. London: Methuen, 1993.

Myers, Kevin. 'An Irishman's Diary'. *Irish Times*, 3 June 1999. Online. Lexis-Nexis.

Nadel, Ira. *Joyce and the Jews*. London: Macmillan, 1989.

Nandy, Ashis. *The Intimate Enemy: Loss and Recovery of Self under Colonialism*. Oxford: Oxford University Press, 1983.

Nelson, James Malcolm. 'From Rory and Paddy to Boucicault's Myles, Shaun and Conn'. *Eire/Ireland* 13 (1978): 79–105.

Newsinger, John. *Fenianism in Mid-Victorian Britain*. London: Pluto, 1994.

Ní Dhomhnaill, Nuala. *Selected Poems*. Trans. Michael Hartnett. Dublin: Raven Arts Press, 1991.

Nolan, Emer. *James Joyce and Nationalism*. London: Routledge, 1995.

Norris, Margot. 'Stifled Back Answers: The Gender Politics of Art in Joyce's "The Dead"'. *Modern Fiction Studies* 35.3 (1989): 479–503.

Northern Ireland Abortion Law Reform Association. 'Abortion: The Case for Legal Reform in Northern Ireland'. *The Abortion Papers: Ireland*. Ed. Ailbhe Smyth. Dublin: Attic Press, 1992. 40–6.

Nowlan David. 'Ambitious Play With a Logical Fallacy: *Dolly West's Kitchen*'. *Irish Times*, 8 October 1999. Online. Lexis-Nexis.

——. 'President Calls for Hope and History to Rhyme in Somalia'. *Irish Times*, 8 October 1992. Online. Lexis-Nexis.

O'Brien, Conor Cruise. 'An Unhealthy Intersection'. *New Review* 2.16 (1975): 3–8.

O'Brien, Flann. *At Swim-Two-Birds*. New York: Plume, 1976.

O'Casey, Sean. *Autobiography (Book 4): Inisfallen Fare Thee Well*. London: Pan Books, 1972.

——. *Three Plays*. London: Macmillan, 1966.

O'Clery, Conor. 'In the Name of the Irish'. *Irish Times*, 10 March 1994. Online. Lexis-Nexis.

O'Connor, Anne. 'Women in Irish Folklore: The Testimony Regarding Illegitimacy, Abortion and Infanticide'. In *Women in Early Modern Ireland*. Eds. Margaret MacCurtain and Mary O'Dowd. Dublin: Wolfhound Press, 1991. 304–17.

O'Connor, Frank. *Guests of the Nation*. Dublin: Poolbeg Press, 1987.

O'Connor, Sinéad. *Am I Not Your Girl?* Ensign Records. F2-21952. 1992.

——. Interview. *Hot Press*, February 1990.

——. *I Do Not Want What I Haven't Got*. Woodford Green: International Music Publications, 1991.

——. 'My Name is Sinéad O'Connor'. *Irish Times*, 10 June 1993. Online. Lexis-Nexis.

——. 'People Need a Short, Sharp Shock'. *Time*, 9 November 1992: 78–9.

——. 'Sinéad O'Connor: Artist of the Year'. *Rolling Stone*, 7 March 1991: 32–7.

——. 'Sinéad Speaks'. *Rolling Stone*, 29 October 1992: 52.

——. 'Sinéad's Defense'. *Los Angeles Times*, 24 October 1992. Online. Lexis-Nexis.

——. *Success has Made a Failure of Our Home*. Ensign Records. F2-24803. 1992.

——. 'Troy'. *The Lion and the Cobra*. Chrysalis Records. F2-21612. 1987.

Odd Man Out. Dir. Carol Reed. Two Cities Films, 1947.

O'Donnell, Ruan. 'Bridget "Croppy Biddy" Dolan: Wicklow's Anti-Heroine of 1798'. In D. Keogh and Furlong 87–112.

O'Faolain, Julia. *No Country for Young Men*. Harmondsworth: Penguin, 1980.

——, and Lauro Martines, eds. *Not in God's Image: Women in History from the Greeks to the Victorians*. New York: Harper, 1973.

O'Faolain, Sean. *Vive Moi*. Boston: Atlantic Monthly, 1964.

O'Hagan, Sean. 'Virgin Territory: Sinéad, the New Madonna'. *Observer*, 15 February, 1998. Online. Lexis-Nexis.

O'Loingsigh, Colm. *Pathways in History*. Dublin: Educational Company, 1983.

O'Regan, Michael, and Dermot Kelly. 'Clinton Renews Pledge'. *Irish Times*, 2 December 1995. Online. Lexis-Nexis.

Osborn, Andrew. 'Skirmishes on the Border: The Evolution and Function of Paul Muldoon's Fuzzy Rhyme'. *Contemporary Literature*. 41.2 (Summer 2000): 323–58.

O'Toole, Fintan. *Black Hole, Green Card: The Disappearance of Ireland*. Dublin: New Island Books, 1994.

——. *The Ex-Isle of Erin*. Dublin: New Island Books, 1997.

——. 'The Man Who Shot Michael Collins'. *Independent*, 3 November 1996. Online. Lexis-Nexis.

——. *A Mass for Jesse James: A Journey Through 1980s Ireland*. Dublin: Raven Arts Press, 1990.

——. *The Politics of Magic: The Work and Times of Tom Murphy*. Dublin: Raven Arts Press, 1987.

O'Tuama, Sean, and Thomas Kinsella, eds. *An Duanaire 1600–1900: Poems of the Dispossessed*. Trans. Thomas Kinsella. Saint Paul: Irish Books, 1985.

Owen, Wilfred. *The Collected Poems of Wilfred Owen*. London: Chatto, 1964.

Owenson, Sydney (Lady Morgan). *The Wild Irish Girl: A National Tale*. 3 vols. London: Richard Phillips, 1806.

Parker, Michael. *Seamus Heaney: The Making of the Poet*. Dublin: Gill & Macmillan, 1993.

Parker, Stewart. *Three Plays for Ireland*. London: Oberon, 1989.

Parsons, Tony. 'Biggest Casualty in *Collins* is Truth'. *Daily Mirror*, 7 November 1996. Online. Lexis-Nexis.

Paulin, Tom. *A State of Justice*. London: Faber, 1977.

Peacock, Alan. 'Translating the Past: Friel, Greece and Rome'. In *The Achievement of Brian Friel*. Ed. Alan Peacock. Gerrards Cross: Smythe, 1993. 113–33.

Peggy Sue Got Married. Dir. Francis Ford Coppola. TriStar Pictures, 1986.

Petley, Julian. Sleeve notes. *Hush-a-Bye Baby*. Derry Film and Video Workshop, 1989.

Pettitt, Lance. 'Pigs, Provos and Prostitutes: Gay Representation in Recent Irish Film'. Walshe 252–84.

——. *Screening Ireland: Film and Television Representation*. Manchester: Manchester University Press, 2000.

The Phoenicians. Eds Moscati Sabatini. Milan: Bompiani, 1988.

Pine, Richard. *Brian Friel and Ireland's Drama*. London: Routledge, 1990.

——, ed. *Dion Boucicault and the Irish Melodrama Tradition*. Special Issue of *Prompts: Bulletin of the Irish Theatre Archive* 6 (1983).

——. 'Frank McGuinness: A Profile'. *Irish Literary Supplement* 10.1 (1991): 29–30.

Plato. *The Symposium*. Trans. Walter Hamilton. Harmondsworth: Penguin, 1983.

The Plough and the Stars. Dir. John Ford. RKO, 1936.

'Politicians and Their Quoting of William Butler Yeats'. *All Things Considered*. National Public Radio, 15 March 1996.

Pound, Ezra. *Personae: The Shorter Poems of Ezra Pound*. Eds. Lea Beechler and A. Walton Litz. New York: New Directions, 1990.

Pownall, Thomas. 'A Description of the Sepulchral Monument at Newgrange'. *Archaeologia* 2 (1773): 236–75.

Purcell, Henry. *Dido and Aeneas: An Opera*. Ed. Curtis Price. New York: Norton, 1986.

The Quiet Man. Dir. John Ford. Republic Pictures, 1952.

Quinn, Bob. *Atlantean: Ireland's North African and Maritime Heritage*. London: Quartet, 1986.

Rea, Stephen. 'Actor Stephen Rea Relishes the Ambiguity of Irish Life'. *Los Angeles Times*, 4 January 1993. Online. Lexis-Nexis.

Red River. Dir. Howard Hawks. United Artists, 1948.

'Rhyming Hope and History'. Editorial. *Irish Times*, 2 December 1995: 15.

Rice, Tamara Talbot. *The Scythians*. London: Thames, 1957.

Richards, Shaun. 'Field Day's Fifth Province: Avenue or Impasse?' In *Culture and Politics in Northern Ireland 1960–1990*. Ed. Eamonn Hughes. Milton Keynes: Open University Press, 1991. 139–50.

Richtarik, Marylnn. *Acting Between the Lines: The Field Day Theatre Company and Irish Cultural Politics 1980–1984*. Oxford: Clarendon Press, 1994.

———. 'Stewart Parker's Heavenly Bodies: Dion Boucicault, Show Business, and Ireland'. Forthcoming in *Modern Drama*.

Rio Grande. Dir. John Ford. Republic Pictures, 1950.

Roche, Anthony. *Contemporary Irish Drama*. New York: St. Martin's, 1995.

Rockett, Kevin. *Irish Filmography: Fiction Films 1896–1996*. Dublin: Red Mountain Media, 1996.

———. 'An Irish Film Studio'. *Cinema and Ireland*. Eds. Kevin Rockett, Luke Gibbons and John Hill. London: Routledge, 1988. 95–126.

Rolston, Bill. *Drawing Support: Murals in the North of Ireland*. Belfast: Beyond the Pale, 1992.

Rose, Kieran. *Diverse Communities*. Cork: Cork University Press, 1994.

Roustabout. Dir. John Rich. Paramount Pictures, 1964.

Ruane, Medb. 'The Dev Collectors'. *Irish Times*, 30 July 1997. Online. Lexis-Nexis.

Rubin, Gayle. 'The Traffic in Women'. In *Toward an Anthropology of Women*. Ed. Rayna R. Reiter. New York and London: Monthly Review, 1975. 157–210.

Rudkin, David. *The Saxon Shore*. London: Methuen, 1986.

Ryan's Daughter. Dir. David Lean. MGM, 1970.

Said, Edward. *Culture and Imperialism*. London: Vintage, 1994.

———. *Orientalism*. New York: Vintage, 1979.

Sammy and Rosie Get Laid. Dir. Stephen Frears. Written by Hanif Kureishi. Cinecom Pictures, 1987.

Sandoz, Mari. *Cheyenne Autumn*. New York: McGraw, 1953.

Savage, Robert. 'The Tear and the Smile'. *Ireland: Culture, Politics and Identity*, Kennedy Center, Washington, May 2000.

Schindler's List. Dir. Steven Spielberg. Universal Pictures, 1993.

Schneider, Ulrich. 'Staging History in Contemporary Anglo-Irish Drama: Brian Friel and Frank McGuinness'. In *The Crows Behind the Plough: History and Violence in Anglo-Irish Poetry and Drama*. Amsterdam: Rodopi, 1991. 79–98.

Sedgwick, Eve Kosofsky. *Between Men: English Literature and Male Homosocial Desire*. New York: Columbia University Press, 1985.

Seidel, Michael. *Epic Geography: James Joyce's Ulysses*. Princeton: Princeton University Press, 1976.

Shakespeare, William. *The Complete Works*. Ed. David Bevington. 4th ed. New York: HarperCollins, 1992.

Shaw, George Bernard. *Collected Plays with Their Prefaces*. Vol. 2. London: Bodley, 1970–74.

She Wore a Yellow Ribbon. Dir. John Ford. RKO, 1949.

Sheridan, Richard Brinsley. *Six Plays*. Ed. Louis Kronenburger. New York: Hill, 1957.

Sinclair, Andrew. *John Ford*. New York: Dial, 1979.

Sir Gawain and the Green Knight. Eds. J. R. R. Tolkein and E. V. Gordon. 2nd ed. Rev. by Norman Davis. Oxford: Clarendon Press, 1967.

Smyth, Ailbhe, ed. *The Abortion Papers: Ireland*. Dublin: Attic Press, 1992.

The Snapper. Dir. Stephen Frears. Written by Roddy Doyle. Miramax, 1993.

Some Mother's Son. Dir. Terry George. Written by Terry George and Jim Sheridan. Columbia Pictures, 1996.

Sophocles. *Philoctetes*. In *Electra and Other Plays*. Trans. E. F. Watling. Harmondsworth: Penguin, 1953.

Spenser, Edmund. 'A Veue of the Present State of Ireland'. In *The Complete Works in Verse and Prose of Edmund Spenser*. Ed. Alexander B. Grosart. Vol. 9. London: Spenser Society, 1882–84.

Spivak, Gayatri. 'Can the Subaltern Speak'. In *Marxism and the Interpretation of Culture*. Ed. Cary Nelson and Lawrence Grossberg. Urbana: University of Illinois Press, 1988. 271–313.

Stagecoach. Dir. John Ford. United Artists, 1939.

Stanfield, Peter. 'Country Music and the 1939 Western'. In Cameron and Pye 22–33.

St. Peter, Christine. *Changing Ireland: Strategies in Contemporary Women's Fiction*. London: Macmillan, 2000.

Synge, J. M. *The Playboy of the Western World*. Dublin: Dolmen Press, 1971.

Tacitus, P. Cornelius. *Tacitus on Britain and Germany: A Translation of the Agricola and the Germania*. Trans. H. Mattingly. Harmondsworth: Penguin, 1948.

Taylor, Paul. 'A Hit and a Myth'. *Independent*, 8 April 1991. Online. Lexis-Nexis.

Thomas, Deborah. 'John Wayne's Body'. In Cameron and Pye 75–87.

Thompson, Spurgeon. 'James Joyce and Tourism in Dublin: Quotation and the Mass Commodification of Irish Culture'. *New Hibernia Review* 1.1 (1997): 136–55.

———. 'The Romance of Simulation: W. B. Yeats and the Theme-Parking of Ireland'. *Eire-Ireland* 30.1 (1995): 17–34.

Tóibín, Colm. *Seeing is Believing: Moving Statues in Ireland*. Mountrath, County Laois: Pilgrim, 1985.

Tompkins, Jane P. *West of Everything: The Inner Life of Westerns*. New York: Oxford University Press, 1992.

Tookey, Christopher. 'A Powerful Case of Distortion'. *Daily Mail*, 11 February 1994. Online. Lexis-Nexis.

Toolan, Michael. 'Language and Affective Communication in Some Contemporary Irish Writers'. In *Cultural Contexts and Literary Idioms in Contemporary Irish Literature*. Ed. Michael Kenneally. Gerrards Cross: Smythe, 1988. 138–53.

Trumpener, Katie. *Bardic Nationalism: The Romantic Novel and the British Empire*. Princeton: Princeton University Press, 1997.

Tyler, Carol-Anne. 'Boys Will Be Girls: The Politics of Gay Drag'. In *Inside/Out: Lesbian Theories, Gay Theories*. Ed. Diana Fuss. New York: Routledge, 1991. 32–70.

Tymoczko, Maria. *The Irish Ulysses* Berkeley: University of California Press, 1994.

Vallancey, Charles. *An Essay on the Antiquity of the Irish Language*. Dublin: Powell, 1772.

Vance, Norman. 'Celts, Carthaginians and Constitutions: Anglo-Irish Literary Relations, 1780–1820'. *Irish Historical Studies* 22.87 (1981): 216–38.

Vardac, A. Nicholas. *Stage to Screen: Theatrical Method from Garrick to Griffith*. New York: Blom, 1968.

Virgil. *The Aeneid*. Trans. W. F. Jackson Knight. Harmondsworth: Penguin, 1958.

'Virgin On The Ridiculous?' *Belfast News Letter*, 19 February 1998. Online. Lexis-Nexis.

The Visit. Dir. Orla Walsh. Róisín Rua Films, 1992.

Walsh, Townsend. *The Career of Dion Boucicault*. New York: The Dunlap Society, 1915.

Walshe, Éibhear. ed. *Sex, Nation and Dissent in Irish Writing*. Cork: Cork University Press, 1997.

———, 'Introduction'. *Sex, Nation and Dissent* 1–15.

Warmington, B. H. *Carthage*. New York: Praeger, 1960.

Warner, Marina. *Alone of All Her Sex: The Myth and the Cult of the Virgin Mary*. New York: Knopf, 1976.

'Warner's Profit, Ulster's Loss'. Editorial. *Daily Telegraph*, 15 October 1996: 23.

Waters, John. *Jiving at the Crossroads*. Belfast: Blackstaff, 1991.

Waters, Maureen. *The Comic Irishman*. Albany: SUNY Press, 1984.

Watt, Stephen. *Joyce, O'Casey, and the Irish Popular Theater*. Syracuse: Syracuse University Press, 1991.

Waugh, Evelyn. *The Loved One*. New York: Back Bay, 1977.

W. B. Yeats: Cast a Cold Eye. Dir. Sean O'Mordha. Araby Productions, 1989.

Weekes, Ann Owen. *Irish Women Writers: An Uncharted Tradition*. Lexington: University of Kentucky Press, 1990.

Whelan, Kevin. 'Settlement Patterns in the West of Ireland in the Pre-Famine Period'. In *Decoding the Landscape*. Ed. Timothy Collins. Centre for Landscape Studies: Galway, 1994.

The Wild Bunch. Dir. Sam Peckinpah. Warner Brothers, 1969.

Williamson, Nigel. 'Cross to Bear'. *The Times*, 1 July 2000. Online. Lexis-Nexis.

Wills, Clair. *Improprieties: Politics and Sexuality in Northern Irish Poetry*. Oxford: Clarendon Press, 1993.

Wills, Gary. *John Wayne's America*. New York: Touchstone, 1997.

Woodworth, Paddy. 'Sheridan's Stories'. *Irish Times*, 19 March 1994. Online. Lexis-Nexis.

Woolf, Virginia. *Three Guineas*. New York: Harbinger, 1966.

Wordsworth, William. *Peter Bell*. Ed. John E. Jordan. Ithaca: Cornell University Press, 1985.

Yeats, W. B. *Autobiographies*. London: Macmillan, 1966.

——. *Collected Plays*. 2nd ed. London: Macmillan, 1952.

——. *Collected Poems*. Ed. Richard Finneran. London: Macmillan, 1989.

——. *A Critical Edition of Yeats's* A Vision. Eds. George Mills Harper and Walter Kelly Hood. London: Macmillan, 1978.

——. *The Variorum Edition of the Poems of W. B. Yeats*. Eds. Peter Allt and Russell Alspach. New York: Macmillan, 1940.

Zwicker, Steven N. *Politics and Language in Dryden's Poetry*. Princeton: Princeton University Press, 1984.

INDEX